# TOM MERTON

## A PERSONAL BIOGRAPHY

# TOM MERTON

## A PERSONAL BIOGRAPHY

by

## JOAN C. MCDONALD

MARQUETTE
UNIVERSITY
PRESS

# ≠ 72871210

**Library of Congress Cataloging-in-Publication Data**
McDonald, Joan C., 1933-
  Tom Merton : a personal biography / by Joan C. McDonald.
    p. cm.
  Includes bibliographical references and index.
  ISBN-13: 978-0-87462-016-0 (hardcover : alk. paper)
  ISBN-10: 0-87462-016-3 (hardcover : alk. paper)
  1. Merton, Thomas, 1915-1968. 2. Trappists—United States—Biography. I. Title.
  BX4705.M542M35 2006
  271'.12502—dc22
  [B]

                                                                    2006032860

Queries regarding rights and permissions should be addressed to:
Marquette University Press
P.O. Box 3141
Milwaukee WI 53201-3141

Milwaukee, Wisconsin 53201-3141
All rights reserved.
www.marquette.edu/mupress/

COVER
*Kanchenjunga, India's highest mountain (28,169 feet) and third highest in the world (Everest
and K2 being the highest of the Himalaya mountain range). Merton dreamed of this mountain
when he viewed it in 1968 from Darjeeling, and concluded that the significance was that
there was "another side to the mountain." He concluded that whatever he had come to Asia
to find seemed hidden from view, but was the only part worth seeing.*
*Webshots.com photo by Siddhesh Bhadkamkar*

♾The paper used in this publication meets the minimum requirements of the
American National Standard for Information Sciences—
Permanence of Paper for Printed Library Materials, ANSI Z39.48-1992.

MARQUETTE UNIVERSITY PRESS
MILWAUKEE

The Association of Jesuit University Presses

*Photograph of Thomas Merton by John Lyons. Used with permission of the Merton Legacy Trust and the Thomas Merton Center at Bellarmine University.*

# Illustrations

# Table of Contents

# Dedication

This book is dedicated to all who have worked to develop the monastic tradition. Like Father Timothy (Laurence Vander Vennet), O.C.S.O., they collectively built and maintained an infrastructure which consistently survived the upheavals and cultural changes in the Church. Through centuries of effort, groups including the Cistercian Order have inspired writers like Thomas Merton to share their values with readers throughout the world.

Particular thanks go to the monks and staff of The Abbey of Our Lady of Gethsemani, the director and staff of the Thomas Merton Center at Bellarmine University, and the members of the International Thomas Merton Society and of the Thomas Merton Society of Great Britain and Ireland. They contributed significantly to my knowledge and understanding of the monastic tradition which prepared me to undertake this book.

# To the Reader

If you are familiar with the work of Thomas Merton, you probably know that many good biographies have been published about him and his work. I do not attempt to replace any of them. My representation is of Tom Merton, the very human, very devout, very understandable seeker we want to know better.

This is the first biography of Merton that combines the details of his diaries with other circumstances of his life that have been published in a number of different places. I have chosen to title the book with his original name, Tom, to emphasize the personal approach I have taken to present him to you.

Merton did not choose to keep his most personal writing secret. He provided for it to be released 25 years after his death. He undoubtedly chose to be remembered as a monk who was only too human, determined that his most human faults should be revealed. He wanted his readers to believe that the principles he espoused are in fact practicable for anyone, not just those who live like a saint. He proved he had flaws by carefully recording them. It was a most generous gift.

To highlight this point, I have extrapolated the events of Merton's life at certain key times by insertion of dialogue and self-analysis in italicized passages, which is purely the result of my imagination. The factual material is accurate and based on virtually all of the previously published material by and about Merton I could pull together. I combined this material to reach the reader in the same spirit used by Merton in his autobiographical material. Additionally, I have added some explanatory historical and liturgical information not commonly known to put the events in context.

You might ask how I qualify to represent Merton so personally? My own life experience echoes some of Merton's: teaching college English, as he did, living through three major wars, the turmoil of the 1960s, and the effects of the Second Vatican Council, and travel to most of the same countries.

At the outset, I wish to acknowledge my use of the resources of the Merton Center at Bellarmine University, Louisville, KY, the International Thomas Merton Society, and the Thomas Merton Society of Great Britain and Ireland. I appreciated the courtesy extended to me at the Abbey of Gethsemani and at Oakham School. In addition, I was assisted in my research at the Library of Congress, Georgetown University Library, and the Catholic University of America Library, Washington, DC, as well as the Broward County Library in Fort Lauderdale, FL.

The staff of the Marquette University Press made an invaluable contribution to the completion of this work. Dr. Andrew Tallon, the Director, is to be commended for his technical advice and assistance, which made the final project a reality.

Personal thanks go to my four children who contributed generously to see me through the project: Allan, who accompanied me to Louisville, Washington, Toronto, and dozens of bookstores; Carter, who taught me to use a computer; Mary, who accompanied me to Cluny and other French churches and museums and located hard-to-find books for me; and Sarah, who furnished me with the seclusion required to write the first draft, translated French texts for me, and accompanied me to Cistercian abbeys in France, to Buddhist temples in Japan and China, and monasteries and churches in England, France, Germany, and Italy.

Dr. Glen M. Tucker, my husband, has been invaluable in providing technical information and personal assistance in the final stages of the book's publication. I could not express my appreciation and gratitude for his help.

A special word of gratitude goes to my sister Connie, and her husband, Jack, who prayed for me through the entire process.

Finally, my greatest acknowledgement is to Tom Merton himself. When I was lost in the liturgical and philosophical changes being considered in the Church, he found me. I will be eternally in his debt.

Joan C. McDonald
January 31, 2006

# Introduction

The 21st century seems to be unfolding faster than we could ever have imagined. World events remind us every day that reality, even as it is rapidly changing, differs with every viewer. What we see as progress or even as right and wrong depends on who we are.

Thomas Merton grappled with this difficulty, and his life bore witness to the truth he found. His reliance on social structures evaporated like the morning dew as his lifetime unfolded. In the whirlwind of events during the 1960s, Merton resorted to the philosophy of depending on the Almighty God while standing on his own two feet. He concluded that the answer to mankind's global survival, both physical and spiritual, lay in bolting together the remnants of one's beliefs and forming a unified body of very different individuals.

Thomas Merton's life is one of prisms: he reveals himself to his readers through his experiences that resonate in each individual. We see our own image in Merton's actions and assertions, identifying those things about our reality that we choose to see.

Some say Merton should be recognized as a saint. Others question whether his drift into an interest in Eastern beliefs might have weakened his Christian faith. Others contend he was ahead of his time in seeking to identify the unifying aspects of every person's search without regard to their traditional beliefs. All would agree that Merton's life brought him down a most unorthodox path.

For readers who have not yet met Thomas Merton, a few facts will introduce you. His nationality: French, British, and American. By adoption he was a son of Rome. By choice, he was an American, with a British passport most of his life. His occupation: by training, a writer and philosopher. By choice, additionally, he was a teacher, linguist, artist, photographer, and bongo player. By calling, he was a monk. His life was a sequence of paradoxes. He traveled as a youth more than probably any other boy of his day, and in his adult years less than most people. He crossed the Atlantic by ocean liner nine times before he was nineteen. He visited other countries six times as a youth, then lived in one secluded place for the next 27 years. His death was unexpected and premature. Many consider it a mystery.

America in the 1960s tested his patience and drove him to take actions that were radical and challenging. He believed he was called to a leadership role in the Church through these controversial times.

By coincidence or deliberate action, Merton was silenced. Merton wrote about a black leader in the Civil Rights movement who had been assassinated in 1965. The statement was prophetic of his own death just a year later.

> Malcolm X first outgrew the ghetto underworld of prostitution, dope, and crime. He then outgrew the religious underworld, the spiritual power structure that thrives on a ghetto mystique. He was finally attaining to the freedom and fullness of understanding that gives some (still rare) American Negroes the sense of belonging to a world movement that makes them independent, to some extent, of purely American limitations and pressures. Malcolm grew too fast. He was too articulate. He was made to pay for it. The impact of his message to others that may follow him has only been made harder and more emphatic by his death .... His autobiography reveals a person whose struggles are understandable, whose errors we can condone. He was a fighter whose sincerity and courage we cannot help admiring, and who might have become a genuine revolutionary leader—with portentous effect in American society. (*Continuum* magazine, vol. 5, no. 2, Summer 1967)

Merton made a prophecy about his own life that appeared at the conclusion of his autobiography, *The Seven Storey Mountain*. In the prophecy, God spoke to him in a mystical tone: everything that touches him would burn him, and he would draw away his hand in pain, dying to all joy and being left alone. Finally, he would learn to know the Christ of the burnt men.

Merton never explained this prophecy or its origin. He leaves us to divine any explanation we can discern by examining the known events of his life.

*Moderns ... miss the lessons of the past, and especially the chief lesson, which is that the developments of society follow no mechanical process; that their way is not the way of an arrow, but of a serpent. Ignorant of this, men fall into the simple error of taking the tangent to the curve, of prolonging the actions of causes immediately before their eyes, and of conceiving the future in terms of the present, as children do.*

Hilaire Belloc, *The Cruise of The "Nona"*

# BOOK ONE

*Photograph of Thomas Merton. "Tom drawing an aeroplane, 1918" by Ruth Merton. Used with permission of the Merton Legacy Trust and the Thomas Merton Center at Bellarmine University.*

# Chapter 1

*I did not know very much when I was six years old.*

*I knew my name was Tom Merton. I was a skinny little tow-head, at least that's what my grandfather called me.*

*I knew I had a good mother and father, and a baby brother, John Paul, who was not so good sometimes. Mother's name was Ruth, and Father's name was Owen. Mother was always busy around the house taking care of John Paul and me. Father was always working, either in the neighbors' yards or playing the piano at the movies. John Paul was two and into everything since he could move around, and he was always smiling.*

*I knew we lived in a small town in New York. We had a very, very small house, two rooms upstairs and two rooms downstairs, that were sometimes too hot or too cold. My parents always seemed worried and sad.*

*I also knew I was almost old enough to go to school. Mother gave me a little schoolroom of my own in the corner of our living room, with a desk and blackboard my size. She taught me to read books and the names of a lot of birds.*

*I knew I had a grandfather and grandmother nearby. I called them Pop and Bonnemaman. But we mostly saw them when they came to our house on Sundays. We didn't go to their house much because it was too far to walk. We didn't have a car.*

*I had another grandmother who lived really far away. She only came to see us when John Paul was born. Her name was Gertrude, but I called her Granny.*

*One day Mother told me we were moving to Pop and Bonnemaman's house. It was o.k. with me, because they had a big house with lots of things to do. The rooms were full of beautiful things. There were some little trees I could climb in the back yard. And everybody was pretty happy.*

*One day Father told me that Mother was really sick and he had to take her to the hospital. Now John Paul and I were pretty much alone with our grandparents. Father was at the hospital most of the day.*

*I missed my talks with Mother and our little school. I missed our house even if it wasn't as big and pretty as my grandparents' house. Now I didn't have a home. Now I slept in the same room with Father and John Paul.*

*Days and weeks passed by, and Father kept going to the hospital to visit Mother. One afternoon he came home with a paper in his hands that was for me.*

*I ran to the back yard and sat under the maple tree I liked to climb. It was the place I would go to practice reading my books that Mother was teaching me before she got sick. I held my breath as I opened the letter. It was the first one I had ever received. It was my first message from Mother since the day she kissed me good-bye when Father took her to the hospital.*

*I opened it slowly and carefully because the paper was as soft as I could remember my mother's hands.*

*Dear Tom,*

*You will not see me again because I am very ill and cannot live much longer. I don't want you to see me because I want you to remember me as I was. So this is good-bye. Be a good boy and do as your father tells you.*

    *Love always,*
    *Mother*

*The next thing I remember was a very rainy day soon after, sitting in a rented car with a hired driver outside the hospital. Father went in with Pop and Bonnemaman to see Mother. A couple of days later I was back in the rented car with the hired driver. It was raining again. We waited outside a red brick building in Queens. Nobody explained anything to me about what was going on, and I didn't ask any questions. But I figured out that Mother was going up in thick gray smoke out of the chimney of this building.*

*When we got back to my grandparents' house, Father went into our bedroom and shut the door. I went in to be with him, and he was crying.*

*Bonnemaman went to her room and shut the door, too. I went to her to talk about Mother. She was crying really hard. She told me she would always remember the way Mother laughed. I could not ever remember Mother laughing, but I didn't say anything.*

*John Paul was sad, too, but couldn't understand what happened to Mother. John Paul did not get a letter from her like I did. I guess she figured he didn't need one because he couldn't read yet. He was so young I couldn't explain anything to him that was going on.*

*Father tried to make a life for John Paul and me. He came back to the house from work every day tired and sad. I knew things had to change soon. The summer was over now and I was supposed to be starting real school.*

My earliest childhood memories have always stayed with me, even though I didn't know much about what it all meant at the time. Later, as a man, I understood the picture much better.

My parents were two starry-eyed artists studying in Paris, with high hopes for success and self-fulfillment. And they were sophisticated world travelers, especially in their time, just after the turn of the century, when most people didn't even have a car.

World War I intervened at the beginning of their life together in the south of France. Nobody was buying art, and Father could not make a living there. Mother was as delicate as the china she painted, and, like Father, could speak French. She could even dance like a professional dancer. When they had to come to America to escape the fighting in Europe, Mother held on to the one last shred of her time in France, teaching me to call my grandmother "Bonnemaman," or Grandmother, in French.

Father was only thirty-three years old when Mother died. By that time the war was over, people had money to buy paintings, and were free to travel between America and Europe. Father did not have to work in odd jobs to pay for our family anymore, because Pop and Bonnemaman offered to help with us children. He was free again to restart his career.

For me, the journey was only beginning, and without home or country.

*Building of the former Tudor-Hart art school, attended by Merton's parents, Ruth and Owen, before they married. The address is 1911 rue d'Assas, Paris, VI.*

# Chapter 2

Tom Merton's parents, Ruth and Owen, were young artists who found each other in Paris in 1911, both studying at the same school. It was the academy of Percyval Tudor-Hart, a Canadian artist and teacher who was known for teaching painting in connection with the other arts, particularly music. Both Ruth and Owen may have chosen this school because they were musically inclined and appreciated the fine arts.

Merton's mother, Ruth Calvert Jenkins, came to Paris from New York. Her family had become comparatively upper class through the enterprising efforts of her father. She made the long trans-Atlantic voyage to Europe that only those of the most privileged American families could afford at that time. It was probably not her first trans-Atlantic crossing. Her father loved to take his family on vacations around Europe, so they may have been to Paris together before Ruth enrolled in school there.

Ruth grew up in Douglaston, Queens, New York, and carried a Welsh name. She was a thin, serious and reserved, reddish haired woman of strict upbringing. She graduated from a college-level private school called at that time Bradford Academy and was considered a bright student. Ruth enjoyed writing for her school journal. She once won a monetary prize for an essay. She acquired a serious interest in the arts from her mother. The family had a kiln for molding and painting china housed in a cottage in their back yard. After her graduation she persuaded her parents to let her study the decorative arts and interior decoration in Paris.

Ruth's father provided her with her own apartment in Paris, but not near the art school. She lived across Paris at 9, rue Scribe, in the fashionable ninth district. Even now this is an elegant, six story duplex apartment complex adorned with decorative French wrought-iron grillwork and six large ceiling to floor windows across the front on each level above the fashionable shops on the street level. The top floor is the garret level where maids normally were housed for occupants who chose to have a live-in maid. The building is across the street and to the rear of the massive Paris Opera (now called the Opera Garnier). Some architects consider the opera house to be the finest building constructed in the 19ᵗʰ century worldwide. Inside the entrance of the apartment house, there is a large courtyard. On each side of the passage, identical entrances face each other with matching floors of pink and white marble squares that lead the way to an elegant curved white marble carpeted stairway with an iron grillwork banister. A small elevator, like a wooden cabinet, is behind the stairway's base, considered a luxury item in French architecture at this time. Across the street is the fashionable Café de la Paix.

A young single woman living alone in Paris studying art had to be very careful to protect her reputation, and Ruth could certainly maintain her decorum in the place her father provided. It was directly across the street from the subway entrance, the Paris Metro, to go from the Right Bank to the Left Bank Metro stop, Notre Dame des Champs. Two blocks from this station was the art studio.

The school was situated on the Left Bank, strategically located at 78, rue d'Assas, across the street from one of the entrances to the elegant park known as the Gardens of Luxembourg, in the sixth district of Paris. Its view from the upper floors provided the ambience for art students in what was otherwise a very drab area. It is located in Montparnasse, the preferred meeting place for the artistic and literary figures of that time. Large, affordable studios were also available in this area, which was conveniently located to the bohemian Latin Quarter where many artists lived.

Tudor-Hart's art school was located in a building that lacked much of the decorative French architectural style of the time. What it lacked in appearance it more than made up for in size: a five story stone structure on a corner of a busy street. (It still stands today.) The ground floor contains a garage and several small businesses. Above the street level on the front of the building there are seven rather plain ceiling to floor windows with shutters and a small wrought-iron railing to enclose the opening on each floor above the street. There are two additional windows of equal height on each floor above the street level on the side around the corner, for a total of thirty-six windows, which would provide an unusual amount of natural light for a building in Paris.

Owen Heathcote Grierson Merton, Tom's father, was advanced in his art training and experience when he met Ruth, although they were the same age, both born in 1887. Owen had worked with Tudor-Hart for several years and was using the school as a means of self-support while trying to sell his paintings. He performed janitorial duties and found models for the school who would pose in the nude for the classes. Tudor-Hart maintained a separate department for his male and female students, probably because he employed nude models. Therefore, ironically, Merton's parents did not meet until they went on a school outing to Rome to study the city's classical art.

Owen was handsome, sandy haired and quite personable, with a shy, self-conscious personality, but well spoken and polite, which made him attractive to Ruth. He had come to Paris from New Zealand to further his career, which had already showed promise in local exhibits.

Owen's mother, Gertrude Grierson Merton, was born in 1855 in Wales, her father a Scotsman and mother Welsh. Gertrude's mother was from the Bird family, descended from the Celts. She was the pride of the family, with good reason. She distinguished herself as one of the first women to attend University College, Canterbury, where she won a senior scholarship in English and German. Having a strong constitution, she lived to the age of 102. She also had pronounced facial characteristics, which Tom noted were evident in his father, Aunt Kit, and himself. These features were primarily in the brow, the look in their eyes, and a rather sheepish grin.

The Mertons were originally from Suffolk, England, and emigrated to New Zealand in 1856. Owen's parents were musicians and teachers at Christ College in Christchurch, New Zealand, which Owen attended. He also studied at the Canterbury College School of Art and was a protégé of Alfred Stieglitz. In 1909 Owen was elected a member of the Royal Society of British Artists in London. He produced oil and watercolor paintings, as well as pen drawings and sketches. He studied under the accomplished New Zealand painter, Frances Hodgkins, and accompanied her on visits to Paris and the south of France to work with her before he relocated to Paris. Aunt Maud supplemented his income to make all this possible.

Owen had experienced limited success as a painter of impressionistic landscapes in the style of Cézanne before his marriage, although his work did not sustain him financially. Tudor-Hart believed Owen had a great deal of potential and tried to help him get showings to sell his paintings. Ruth was impressed that he had earlier had some success in New Zealand, England, and France, and was optimistic about his eventual success financially as an artist.

Ruth and Owen had a romance-novel courtship in Paris. She returned home in December 1913 to announce she was going to marry Owen.

*Apartment house where Ruth Jenkins lived in Paris before she married Merton's father, Owen. This is located in an exclusive area at 9, rue Scribe, near the Paris Opera.*

*Entrance stairway at 9, rue Scribe.*

She brought with her a collection of fifteen of Owen's paintings and organized an informal showing in the family home for their friends. To her disappointment, none were sold, but she attributed this to the adverse weather. The family naturally had misgivings about the uncertainty of an artistic career as the basis for supporting a family. Ruth and Owen were both 27 years of age, so they accepted Ruth's decision. At that time Tudor-Hart was just closing his school in Paris and relocating to London. Owen's friend, Dr. Tom Bennett, from New Zealand now lived in London, so Ruth and Owen decided to be married there. The wedding took place in the spring of 1914 in St. Anne's Church, an Anglican church in Soho. It was known as the artists' church as well as a headquarters for activity in promoting social causes. This choice was consistent with their parents' religious backgrounds. Ruth's family was Episcopalian, although very definitely free thinkers, and Owen's family belonged to the Church of England.

They began married life in southern France, in the small town of Prades. This is in the Eastern Pyrenees, a scenic mountainous area in the Catalan lands bordering Spain that attracted tourists and artists. The town is at the foot of Mount Canigou, a 2785-meter mountain. Below Canigou there was an old monastery, St. Martin-du-Canigou. The setting was picture-perfect. It was a dramatic setting for two young artists beginning their lives together. Six of their artist friends from Paris visited them during the brief time they lived there.

But world events were not in sync with the young artists' plans. World War I was just beginning in Europe. By French law, Owen was subject to conscription into the French army, even though he was not a French citizen. Without vacationers, Owen found himself unable to support his wife by selling paintings there. Fortunately he was able to do some local landscaping work, and in fact liked to work barefoot in the rich soil and share fellowship with the other workers. He also played the piano in a local movie house to earn enough money to support the family.

The couple rented a two-story house in Prades on Rue du 4 Septembre. It had a large upstairs room they used as a studio. There was also a wine cellar below that was not part of their quarters. This house stood partly on the ruins of the monastery of St. Michel de Cuxa, built in the ninth century, and in an area of many former monasteries. The newlyweds preferred the romantic and scenic outdoors for their work. Ruth and Owen often camped out in a tent that their art teacher, Percyval

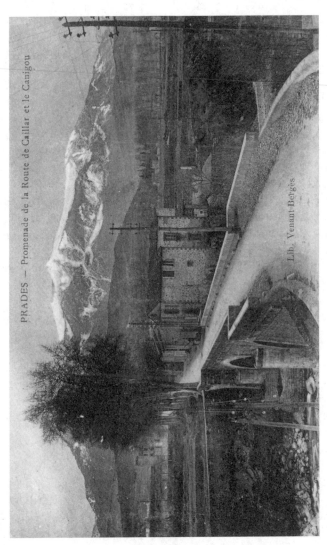

PRADES — Promenade de la Route de Caillar et le Canigou

Lib. Venant-Bergès

*Prades, France, Merton's birthplace. From undated old French postcard.*

Tudor-Hart, gave them for a wedding present. Tom was conceived at this time.

Tom was born on the cold snowy night of January 31, 1915, a Sunday, at just after 9:00 p.m., in the tenth month of their marriage. His birth was a little premature, indicated by a 4.4 pound birth weight. He was registered as a French national. Ruth chose his name, and insisted that it would be Tom, not Thomas. However, Tom's school records later showed his full name as Thomas Feverel Merton. Owen took Tom to the French town hall, or Mairie, after he was born to establish his birth record.

He was named after Dr. Tom Izod Bennett, Owen's old friend and his physician. After Tom's birth Dr. Bennett visited the family in Prades and performed Tom's circumcision. Ruth and Owen asked him to be Tom's godfather, and Owen also designated the Doctor to be Tom's guardian in the event of Owen's death. The choice of the name "Feverel" is unknown. It could have been from the popular 19th century novel, *The Ordeal of Richard Feverel*, although this seems a bit unlikely.

Tom believed he was baptized in Prades probably due to his father's background in the Church of England, but the records, if any, were lost. Ruth had become interested in the Quaker faith as she observed world events leading up to World War I, so may not have been involved in the baptism, if it occurred. She did not record it in Tom's baby book.

The war forced Ruth and Owen to give up their dream. Owen had been willing to enter military service in France so they could stay there, but Ruth's parents opposed this and persuaded them to come to New York to escape the danger in Europe. The young family traveled west across France, away from the combat, and sailed from Bordeaux, France, to New York City in July 1916. Tom was eighteen months old. It was a smooth voyage, although the ship was outfitted with artillery for defense purposes in case it was attacked. America had not yet agreed to enter the war, and Ruth's family hoped the U.S. could avoid it.

First the little family lived in an experimental farming community in Maryland. This was soon found to be unsatisfactory. By November they had moved to a community near Ruth's parents. They rented a four-room cottage at 57 Hillside, Flushing, Long Island. It was only a few miles from Ruth's family home in Douglaston. However, Owen's attempts to sell paintings in New York did not prove any more successful than in Prades. Owen again resorted to other employment as a landscape gardener, a piano player in a silent movie house, and later an organist in

289 — St-MARTIN-du-CANIGOU, près VERNET-les-BAINS
Vue d'ensemble de l'Abbaye

*St. Martin du Canigou abbey overlooks the Catalan countryside in the eastern Pyrenees.
From undated old French postcard.*

the Episcopalian church where Ruth's family were members. Ruth spent her leisure time writing articles for the local newspapers. She published an article in *The Ladies Home Journal* magazine about life in France as an American housewife. According to Tom, she also published articles about how to be a "scientific" housewife and how to bring up children according to all the latest methods in 1915. She enjoyed decorating their modest home, as well as caring for Tom. Owen planted a vegetable garden to help with the food bill. Once Owen caught their landlord, a local tavern keeper, stealing rhubarb from the garden. Owen stopped him, but Tom, though a young child, expressed concern about whether his father had the right to interfere since it was not their property.

Owen once painted a portrait of Ruth that has been described as "strangely ethereal," with a cold, classical pose, painted with impressionistic brushwork and conveying warmth only in her hair color. It is unknown where this painting was originally placed, but it ultimately fell into the possession of Elsie, who later married Ruth's brother, Harold.

The family's meager subsistence only satisfied Owen's pride. He would not accept money from Ruth's parents. He worked long hours to avoid taking their charity, even if it meant not having time for his painting. He actually loved gardening and gained some local recognition for his landscaping. He worked barefoot just as he did in France. He also enjoyed socializing with the local black and Latin workers who lived in nearby cabins where he tended the gardens, just as he had in Prades.

Owen's choice of employment was not acceptable to Ruth's parents, who had educated their daughter for a much more comfortable and satisfying lifestyle than Owen provided. As they lived in the shadow of the dynamic growth that was underway in New York City, they were amazed that Owen chose to work as a gardener in the country in part-time jobs. Ruth's father enjoyed commuting to the city by train every day. He was proud of their family home that had been built by Ruth's brother, Harold. Ruth's parents thought their daughter's home was a rented shack. For two and a half years the young family persevered living in a hand-to-mouth lifestyle. Actually, Ruth did not mind the poverty and preferred having few possessions. She spent her time painting her china and also painted landscapes and designed houses she might someday want to live in.

Ruth's interests centered on her training of Tom, a handsome child with large, soulful, pale bluish-gray eyes, much like his mother's. He had his father's thin blond hair and a very fair complexion. With the added feature of dimples, he could have posed as a child in a Norman Rockwell painting of a typical American family of that time.

Ruth recorded her first-born's every accomplishment in a scrapbook she called Tom's Book. By two years of age, she noted, Tom had a vocabulary of five hundred English words. Ruth also taught Tom the names of birds they saw, and added these to his reading lists of words to learn. Ruth also recorded the names of Tom's best friends, Jack and Doolittle, his imaginary playmate and dog, in his book. She was a bit displeased that Tom resorted to imaginary companions to entertain himself, but there were no other children nearby. She probably was unaware of the fact that it is a fairly common occurrence for children to create playmates when they are without diversion. Ruth said that Tom loved to imitate the chiming of the church bells he had heard in Prades, and would sing a chanting type of sound. He was preoccupied from his earliest days with his books. Ruth said he would look at a book, turning each page as though reading it, and look with pleasure at the pictures. She tried to interest him in such learning activities as putting a cork in a bottle, but he was not interested because he was not manually inclined.

When John Paul was born on November 2, 1918, Tom was almost four years old. Tom had been an only child just long enough to have become used to it. He did not adjust well to sharing, especially the attention of his mother, so he threw temper tantrums to get her attention. This brought forth a stern reaction from Ruth. She was determined to raise Tom "by the book." She saw his behavior as jealousy, a character defect to be corrected. She had high expectations for Tom.

She ordered a book by mail on how to teach children at an early age. Included with the instructions were a small desk and blackboard for his work. Tom later called it her "little University." As a result, Tom was reading books before he started school. This was the beginning of his life-long habit, burying himself in his books without regard to his surroundings.

Six months after John Paul was born, Owen's mother, Gertrude, came from New Zealand to visit them for the first time. She brought her daughter, Kit, whose name was Agnes Gertrude Stonehewer Merton, a single woman now of 30 years. Now that World War I had ended, she wanted to see Owen and meet his family, as well as visit her daughter, Gwyn, whose name was actually Gwynedd, and her sister, Maud Pearce, in London. She had financed Owen's education as well as some of his exhibitions in New Zealand and England before his marriage. Now a widow of 64 years, she could not have been happy to see him struggling to support a family at the expense of his art, although seeing her grandchildren for the first time and meeting Ruth were certainly a pleasure for her. She had been corresponding with Ruth since the beginning of the marriage, and Ruth had sent her a current photograph of Owen.

Gertrude was not content with the training Tom had been receiving from Ruth, however. She found that Tom had not been taught to pray, so she taught him The Lord's Prayer. She liked to look at the stars and taught Tom the names of some of the stars and constellations. She told him to look up at them whenever he was lonely at night and to think of her. Up to this time, Tom's interests centered around books about geography and Greek myths. His love of looking for star formations now developed into a lifelong interest in astronomy.

Ruth was confirmed in her pacifism as the war spread virtually worldwide. The huge losses during World War I put an end to her dream of ever being able to return to the south of France to pursue the artistic lifestyle she and Owen had planned.

Soon Ruth's discouragement was eclipsed by her physical condition. The doctor had diagnosed it as cancer of the stomach. It was a terrible surprise.

Owen could no longer ignore the invitation to move the family in with Ruth's parents. He also needed their help to bear the costs of supporting a wife who required major medical treatment and two children.

Ruth's parents had been pressuring the Mertons to move in with them so that their daughter and grandchildren could enjoy a more comfortable life. Their home was in the quiet suburban community of Douglaston, New York, five miles away, at 50 Virginia Road, now called Rushmore Avenue. It was a two-story proper New England white Colonial home with shuttered windows and three dormer windows topping the roof. It was a mansion compared with the cottage where Ruth and her family had been living. In the back yard there was a small white cottage that echoed the appearance of the house which served as the artist's studio for Martha's pottery work. Occupants of the property included Ruth's parents, her brother Harold, three dogs, several cats, more than a few chickens, and a parrot on the back porch. Ruth's father drove the family Buick. There were two employees, a laundress and a cook.

Ruth's parents were Samuel Adams Jenkins and his wife Martha. Tom called them Pop and Bonnemaman. Martha was a devoted and dutiful wife, mother, and grandmother, quietly but efficiently managing

Main Street, Flushing, N.Y.

*Scene of Main Street, downtown Flushing, New York, as it looked during Merton's youth when he lived in nearby Douglaston. From an old undated post card.*

the household. She had a preoccupation with her appearance, careful
to maintain her thin figure. She loved clothes that suited her artistic
taste, which Tom later described as somewhat outlandish. Tom once
said she sat endlessly at her dressing table applying lotion to her face
to maintain her looks. Ruth described Martha to Owen's mother,
Gertrude, in one of her letters, as "one of those happy, generous people
who make friends everywhere," with "a house full of guests" and "never
the least bit of formality or ceremony." Sometimes as many as three or
four people drop in during a meal and "Mother is always pleased to
have them." She mentioned to Gertrude ownership of a property on
the Riviera so "Owen will never have to tie himself to earn our living by
his painting." It is unknown whether this was an exaggeration to ease
Gertrude's concern about the couple's welfare, or, if true, what might
have been the disposition of this property.

Pop was a larger-than-life dominant figure, mostly bald, with a prominent bulbous nose and steady gaze in his eyes. Tom described Pop as
a real "livewire." He was the typical American entrepreneur. First he
had been a newsboy, then worked as a traveling salesman of books and
sheet music. Eventually he advanced by the mid-1890's to the position
of Publicity Manager at Grosset and Dunlap, a major publisher of a
wide variety of fiction and non-fiction. It was located in the Chelsea
section of Manhattan at 26th Street and Broadway, not beyond walking distance from Penn Station. This area was known for the historic
Chelsea Hotel where famed writers stayed, including Mark Twain and
Thomas Wolfe.

In 1923 Sam Jenkins created a picture book about film stars that
was so successful, it soon led to his considerable advancement. He was
instrumental in getting some of the novels published by Grosset and
Dunlap made into motion pictures. When he arrived at home each night
after commuting by train, he would roll up his newspaper and slap the
stair banister with it, calling with all the power of his portly chest cavity
for the family and his supper. He and Martha both liked to play their
piano. Pop prided himself particularly on his ability to whistle entire
classical music compositions, including arias from operas. He probably
perfected this skill when he was selling sheet music. He was outspoken
on any subject he felt strongly about. He had little patience with social
conventions, particularly the procedures followed in other countries.
He often embarrassed Tom and Owen with his remarks when they
traveled together on vacations around Europe.

Pop frequently brought books home from the office for Bonnemaman and Harold as well as Tom. Then Pop would secretly throw them away after they had been around for a while. Sometimes he would give the

*Original Douglaston train station for commuters to New York City, the station that Merton and his grandfather would have used.*
*From the Douglaston/Little Neck Historical Society web site.*

books he was carrying to cab drivers. For Pop, new books were give-aways and an endless resource.

Occasionally Pop brought Tom to his office to read books. They both enjoyed these outings from the beginning in Douglaston. Tom undoubtedly enjoyed seeing the activity at the nearby train station. The Douglaston Depot at this time was a large two story dark-shingled structure in the elegant Queen Anne style, with wide sloping roof. The second floor apparently served as the stationmaster's residence, according to Joseph B. Hellman, historian for the Douglaston Little Neck Historical Society. Landscaping around the structure included an intricate flower garden. The depot was as imposing in appearance as its purpose, embodying what now includes all commercial and personal shipping, mail delivery, and telegraphic dispatches, as well as all individual travel. Its functions preceded the construction of U.S. highways and airports. The Depot was the center of community activity. Originally local residents went to the depot for their mail, having seen in the daily paper that mail had arrived for their pickup. In addition, telegrams were dispatched here. The stationmaster also served as freight agent for all commercial shipments.

Tom was excited about the train ride into the city, too. Penn Station was the biggest place Tom had ever seen. Tall buildings were everywhere, and more were being constructed in every direction. Pop worked on an upper floor of one of these grand buildings. Pop had picture books of all kinds scattered around his office. Tom also liked to go down to the company's showroom to look at the new books on display. Grosset and Dunlap published the Rover Boys series, which particularly fascinated Tom. He also liked the Bobbsey Twins and Tom Swift. Tom learned to love books under Pop's influence as well as his mother's instruction.

Pop had access to the Bayside Studios at nearby Alley Pond on Long Island, where motion pictures were sometimes produced. He often took Tom and John Paul with him to watch the action when they were filming. They saw top stars like Gloria Swanson and W. C. Fields, with the added advantage of seeing the action behind the scenes. Pop also took the boys to the movie theater in Bayside where Owen played the piano as background music, one of his part-time jobs. Pop's love for films was contagious. Both Tom and John Paul grew up as avid moviegoers.

Mrs. Jenkins, or Bonnemaman, loved nothing better than taking care of Pop, working in her studio, firing pottery and painting the dishes she made. Ruth was her student and probably got the idea of going abroad from her mother, to perfect her own artistic skills in painting porcelain and learning more about interior design. Ruth also had originally had a serious interest in dancing as a career, but abandoned the idea when she decided to study art in Paris. Tom later described her in this way: " … she danced those dances people do on the stage, with pierouettes and so on."

Ruth's brother, Harold Brewster Jenkins, was also a good student. He was a graduate engineer, a reticent young man devoted to his parents. Pop persuaded Harold to design and supervise the construction of their family home. When it was finished, he moved in with them. He worked professionally as an engineer and lived with his parents until their deaths. He participated in the construction of Radio City in New York.

Bonnemaman engaged a live-in companion, Elsie Hauck Holahan, from nearby Great Neck. Elsie was a widow with two children, Peter and Patricia. She became a friend to Martha and later helped to care for Tom and John Paul. Pop was vocal in the home about being pro-Protestant and anti-Catholic. Elsie was a devout Catholic and did not hesitate to tone down Pop's anti-Catholic remarks, if not his bias. There was no religious activity in the Jenkins household. They contributed financially to the Zion Episcopal Church and other religious organizations without being active in any of them. Pop belonged to an organization called the Knights Templar, but it was apparently only a social connection for him. Martha read books on Christian Science but did not practice it. Harold attended an Episcopalian secondary school, St. John the Divine, but it was chosen for its scholastic value more than religious affiliation and apparently awarded him a scholarship.

Owen eventually gave up hope of supporting his family by selling his paintings in New York. When his mother came to visit after John Paul's birth, he left Tom and John Paul with their grandparents and followed his mother to England, probably with her encouragement as well as financial assistance. In July 1921 he was teaching art classes outside London. He must have returned to New York when Ruth discovered the severity of her illness. Soon Owen accompanied Ruth to Bellevue Hospital in Manhattan. Owen visited her regularly, but did not take the children to see her because of hospital prohibitions against it.

During Ruth's illness, Owen took Tom to the Quaker meeting house that Ruth had recently been attending. He also took Tom to the Zion Church where Ruth's parents were inactive members when Owen played the organ to make a few extra dollars. Tom was impressed with the tall white frame church building with its grand steeple. He loved the beautiful stained glass window above the altar with its picture of a large anchor on it. It reminded him of some of the high adventure stories his father read to him. It did not occur to Tom to attribute a sacred meaning to the anchor, even though it was the centerpiece of the church's decoration.

In a few months' time, Ruth died. It was October 3, 1921. The adjustment was not quick or easy for the family. Tom continued to pore over his books as he had since he was four, when his mother's attention had turned primarily to caring for her new baby. He was now six and just starting to school. Ruth had prepared him so well for school that he was almost immediately advanced to the second grade. This required a second adjustment to a new group of classmates, and this was an older group. Meanwhile, John Paul was left at home without mother or big brother for most of the day.

Soon Owen began to travel again, sailing from one continent to another with little plan or preparation. Initially Owen tried to include Tom in his travels. After one brief trip, he returned to Douglaston to take Tom with him to Cape Cod. Owen painted while Tom drew pictures, with no thought of enrolling him in a school. Not surprisingly, this attempt to start a new life with Tom did not work out, and in short order Owen brought him back to his grandparents' care.

The following summer, Owen's sister, Tom's Aunt Ka, Beatrice Katharine Merton, came from New Zealand to help her brother with his two motherless boys. Owen rented a small cottage in Provincetown, Massachusetts, hoping to paint there. Tom came down with the mumps. Owen read to him regularly, especially the adventure stories they both loved. After the summer vacation, Owen returned the boys to Douglaston and continued traveling, seeking places where he wanted to paint and friends with mutual interests. Tom was re-enrolled in public school to resume his education.

The family changes had their effect on those left behind. One day when John Paul was about five, he set a match to the fifteen or so magazines that Pop and Bonnemaman always kept on the coffee table. It was like a small bonfire. Fortunately the family extinguished it without much damage. Tom related this incident to a class he was teaching at Gethsemani many years later. John Paul and Tom were probably both seeking attention from the family under their adverse circumstances of this time.

Tom usually played with his Douglaston friends, Russ and Bill, and largely ignored John Paul. Once they built a fort from scrap wood that they had gathered in the neighborhood. John Paul wanted to help, but Tom and his friends threw stones at John Paul to chase him away. John Paul was not as concerned about the stones as he was of being left behind by the older boys. Tom took John Paul's affection for granted until one day when the tables were turned. Some bullies from across town came to frighten Tom and his friends. Only John Paul stood up to them. Tom was amazed at this gesture which seemed to him to be so courageous. Neither Tom nor John Paul realized that the bullies wouldn't hurt him because he was so much smaller than all of the other boys.

Tom's return to school lasted only a few weeks. In the fall of 1922, when he was eight, Owen took him to Bermuda. Sailing out of New York harbor, two days later they arrived in Somerset, a village at the west end of the island at the furthest point from the more developed towns. At that time Bermuda was not the trendy, sophisticated British resort it became. Featuring a Nature Reserve and harbor, it probably reminded Owen of his youth in New Zealand. Again John Paul had been left behind.

Owen and Tom moved in with Owen's old friend, Evelyn Scott, a novelist, and her common-law husband, Cyril, who was also a friend of Owen's. They had a son, Creighton, around the same age as Tom, but the two boys had little else in common. Creighton complained that Tom kept him awake at night grinding his teeth, probably in frustration. The Scotts were sophisticated world travelers and active on the artistic circuit. Owen left Tom at the Scott home while he returned to New York for a brief period to sell some paintings. This created a problem for the Scotts as well as for Tom.

It became obvious that the arrangement of Tom living with the Scotts was impossible. Tom's presence in Owen's life at this time was equally unworkable. Tom and Evelyn Scott were unable to get along with each other. Tom was jealous of an evolving romantic relationship of his father with Evelyn and the closeness of his father with both Evelyn and Cyril. To make matters worse, Owen left the disciplining of Tom to Evelyn. She considered the child to be self-centered, disobedient, and an unhappy reminder of Owen's domestic ties. Tom did not believe she should have authority over him and disregarded her instructions whenever he could. Owen enrolled him in a private school on the island, but after several weeks Tom simply dropped out. His father ignored it. Tom would interrupt his play and hide behind some bushes whenever he saw his former teacher coming down the road on her bicycle.

For a while Tom's father put him in a boarding house while he went off with his friends to paint. The other boarders used foul language, and Tom, having no other companions, copied their attitudes and speech. Owen soon discovered it was obviously no place for a child alone, so he took Tom with him to live with the group.

In the spring of 1923, Owen took Tom to stay with the Garland family in Buzzards Bay, Massachusetts, while he and the Scots traveled to Europe and North Africa. The Garlands were also artists, but they were affluent. Tom noticed that they used a checkbook to buy things, and apparently assumed that checks were merely a method for drawing funds from some outside source. He decided to use their checks in the same way. When packages started to arrive for Tom, the Garlands were furious. With Owen out of touch, they contacted the boy's grandfather. Pop came up to bring Tom to a conventional home life and back to school at Douglaston. Tom was actually relieved to be back with his grandparents after what must have been a traumatic experience.

*Scenes of St. Antonin, where Merton and his father built a home in the Tarn-and-Garonne area of central France. From old undated French postcards.*

Meanwhile Owen traveled abroad, trying to deal with his conflict between his love for Evelyn and his responsibilities to his two sons. The feelings between Evelyn and Tom were obviously strained and probably irreparable. After a tortured period, Owen decided to drop the illicit relationship and concentrate on his work, which was not particularly successful. He then went to France and Algeria to paint, but soon came down with an undetermined illness. In desperation, he went to London to consult his close friend, Dr. Tom Bennett. He had not seen his doctor since his visit to the south of France after Tom was born.

When Tom was nine, his grandparents received a letter from one of Owen's friends, warning them that he was seriously ill and might die quite soon. Pop and Bonnemaman felt it appropriate to break the news to Tom. After they spoke with him, he went outside to be alone. He felt numb. His fear and loneliness were so internalized he could not express himself. However, Owen soon recovered. He returned to Douglaston and his sons in June of 1925.

Tom did not remember Owen as he now looked, and he did not like what he saw. Owen was wearing a beard. He usually had worn a small, neat moustache. He appeared to be ill, and it was obvious that living on the meager earnings from the sale of his paintings had not been good for him. Owen's fortunes had recently changed, however. His work had been accepted by three commercial galleries between 1918 and 1925 and was beginning to be recognized for the luminescent quality of his water color landscapes. He had just had a successful exhibition at Leicester Galleries in London, which probably provided the funds for his passage back to New York. His success encouraged him to come back to visit the boys and make a new proposal to Pop.

Owen's relationship with Evelyn Scott was more than just an amorous one. Both she and Cyril, her live-in companion, assisted Owen in promoting and showing his paintings. Owen knew that marketing his work was critically important to his success. He had to get textual material published that praised his work and adequately described his style. He collaborated with his friend, Cyril, who wrote text for his exhibitions, including the two shows at the Daniel Gallery in Manhattan in 1923 and 1925. Owen visited dealers and museums and joined artists' societies to keep his name and work before the public. From his early experience in New Zealand with self-organized exhibitions, he had learned that his showings had to be more structured to meet the competition in

London and New York. He was exhibited at least 24 times in the U.S. between 1916 and 1925, including twice in Flushing.

Owen offered to take Tom with him to France if Pop would finance the trip. It is believed that Owen still wanted to marry Evelyn Scott and take the boys to start a new life with her. Sam Jenkins firmly opposed this idea, and refused to contribute funds for this purpose. Pop took the family to a summer home that Pop had recently purchased in Ashuelot, New Hampshire. Reportedly Owen contemplated suicide there. The incident resolved itself by Pop's agreement that he would assist Owen financially to move to France with Tom if Owen broke off his relationship with Evelyn Scott. John Paul would stay with his grandparents for the present, but could follow later after Owen established a home there. Owen accepted Pop's proposal.

Tom was relieved that his father had recovered from his near-fatal illness, but he was not eager to be uprooted again from his comfortable life in Douglaston during the past two years. He did not relish going to a new and strange place with his father after his experiences in Bermuda and in Massachusetts. Tom cried when he realized that his father would not change his mind.

The family arguments were now silenced, but Tom could not have overlooked the attitude of his grandparents towards Owen. The boys, now seven and ten years old, had begun to enjoy playing together. They both liked to devise pranks. Tom would miss John Paul and wondered when they would live together again. Eventually his sense of adventure took over, though, and he looked forward to starting a new life with his father all to himself in a new and exciting place. Tom and Owen left on August 25. It was the feast of St. Louis, he was to learn later, a date that would become significant to him.

Two years later, in 1927, Owen's mother, Gertrude Merton, helped Owen to finance the cost of designing and building a home for her son and grandsons. With both Pop and Gertrude to help him, Owen was able to manage financially for the time being until he could paint and sell some more of his work.

*Note: The descriptions of the Tudor-Hart art school and the apartment house where Ruth lived in Paris were obtained by this author by personal visits to the sites.*

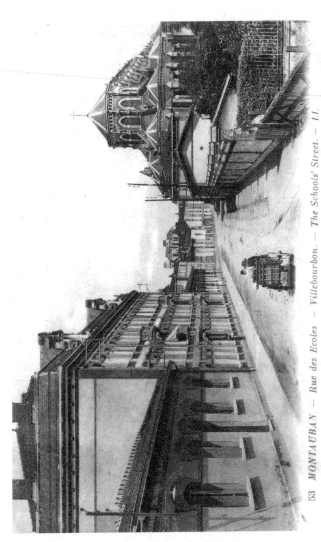

53 *MONTAUBAN — Rue des Ecoles — Villebourbon. — The Schools' Street. — I.I.*

*Scene of Montauban, France, where Merton attended a boarding school. From undated old French postcards.*

*Merton would have attended this church. From a 1918 postcard.*

# Chapter 3

Surprisingly, Owen did not choose to return to the Midi town at Prades where he and Ruth had begun their life together. Instead, he selected St. Antonin- Noble-Val, a village near the south of France in South-East Midi. This was a rural area, far from the beaten track of tourists, but close to a scenic terrain that Owen believed would be ideal for his painting.

Owen purchased a lot of 1400 square meters just outside of town on the Aveyron River in January 1926 for 800 French francs. It overlooked the Calvaire, a small mountain outside the village, and there was a beach nearby on the Bonnette River for swimming. He and Tom moved into an apartment on the edge of town where they stayed until Owen could create the home he had in mind. He enrolled Tom in the local school in St. Antonin, primarily to learn French, so that he could prepare for a more sophisticated educational program.

Tom was only ten years old when he was thrown into this challenging experience of adapting to a new school in a different culture, while living in a construction site rather than a home and far from everyone he knew except his father. To make it even more difficult, it was all occurring in a foreign language that he was only gradually learning to speak and understand.

Since Tom could not speak or understand any French, he was placed with much younger children. With sheer determination he quickly learned to speak the language fluently. He even excelled in his studies in the French language to the point that he soon outgrew the local school's curriculum. Tom hated to leave his new home, but there was no other school in St. Antonin. Owen had consulted Dr. Bennett's wife, Iris, who was a French native. She recommended a boarding school, The Lycée Ingres, a public school dating back to the seventeenth century in Montauban, a nearby larger town west of St. Antonin. She actually had no first-hand knowledge of this school, but had heard of its reputation. Montauban was a much more industrial town than St. Antonin and much less picturesque, although it was situated on the Tarn and the Garonne Rivers and dated back to the eighth century. Tom was impressed by the church of Saint Jacques by the bridge in his walks around the town, still referencing its influence on him in his diary in 1961.

Merton perfected his fluency in French at the Lycée. He won prizes in English, gymnastics, and fencing for the school year 1926-27, his first year. During the second year, 1927-28, he received recognition in French, history, geography, and art.

The school schedule comprised a five-and-a-half-day week. Tom had to take an antiquated commuter train back to St. Antonin just to spend the partial weekend time he had with Owen. Tom's extended separation during the week brought about lonely and disconnected feelings at the Lycée that he could not conceal. As a result, the other boys at Montauban were aggressive and cruel to him in every imaginable way, probably because he was from a different background and obviously detached from their world. Tom called them bullies. To make matters worse, he began to have health problems, and he was frequently ill with a fever. He did form a friendship with a small group of boys who liked to write stories and share them with each other. He discovered that he enjoyed writing simple romantic stories too, although his friends did not seem to care much for his work.

Owen began to speak to Tom about spiritual matters, although he did not express an interest in any organized religion. He and Tom attended a church in St. Antonin only once, apparently. Owen asked Tom to pray for him and for the success of his painting. The life-threatening illness that Owen had experienced before this venture probably created a need for more than the financial help he had been receiving from his mother and the Jenkins family.

Owen was fascinated with French medieval towns and the ruins of their ancient churches and monasteries. He also liked the company of the spirited French peasants. Owen undertook the building of a two-story stone house that he designed with the help of local workmen at the foot of The Calvaire. Owen and Tom gathered stones together during their weekend visits. Owen purchased a window from a 13th or 14th century monastery ruin to build into the house. Owen also purchased two old houses nearby, merely for the stone in them, for approximately four British pounds each. Owen built the bedrooms on the second floor, which overlooked the town and the monastery ruins that Tom loved to play in. A winding stone staircase led down to the large room below with the chapel window. There was a fireplace, and to the right, Tom carved his initials, "TM."

Owen called their house his hermitage. He expected to spend considerable time there in a self-imposed solitude away from Evelyn and his other artist friends. With an eye to permanence, he planted two small poplar trees in the names of his two sons in the front yard. He laid out a large garden that he prided himself in cultivating. He also purchased a second lot in 1928 for 500 French francs which was already under cultivation, probably to be used for additional gardening as well.

On school breaks Owen took Tom on trips to nearby historical sites. They could get to Paris in about four hours from Montauban, and to London by ferry from the Normandy coast. Owen had a favorite place he liked to stay in Paris, the Hotel Rocamadour, on the Bois de Boulogne. This small hotel overlooked the city's largest park, where Tom could run freely. It probably reminded Owen of the park across the street from Tudor-Hart's Paris studio. This hotel was named after a French shrine in southern France near St. Antonin that Owen and Tom had visited in the summer of 1926.

Owen planned to bring John Paul over to St. Antonin when he got settled so that he could raise the two boys together. The plan was that Pop and Bonnemaman would bring John Paul over to Europe every other year, in even numbered years, to visit his father and Tom and to enjoy joint sightseeing trips during the summer vacation period. In the odd numbered years, Tom and Owen would travel to Douglaston until John Paul could be relocated to France. But this was not to be. As it turned out, Tom would never again live with his brother. They were only together in summers and on holidays. In effect, Pop and Bonnemaman acted as John Paul's parents. They sent him to boarding school at St. John the Divine, the Anglican secondary school Uncle Harold had attended. He later graduated from a military academy in Gettysburg, Pennsylvania. He was a student at Cornell University before the two brothers' paths crossed again in a significant way.

During the summer vacation of 1927, Tom was suspected of having contracted tuberculosis. For the entire summer his father arranged for him to live at the home of the Privats at Murat, a small village in the Auvergne, a short distance south of Montauban. The Privats were typical of the people in this mountainous central region of France, settled primarily by people of Celtic origin and devoutly Catholic. Owen had met the couple once when he was painting in that area, and he had taken Tom there to spend the previous Christmas vacation. Tom was only twelve when he moved in with the Privats. He enjoyed living in their traditional rural home, although he missed his father terribly. By the beginning of the fall term, Tom had recovered, so he could return to Montauban. Owen was told it might have been fatal if not treated. Tom later attributed his restored health as well as his Christian faith to the prayers of this couple.

Soon Owen tired of the French setting and of being confined to one place. He felt obliged to stay with the present arrangement, although he was working on the house more than painting. He took short trips to paint in other areas between Tom's weekend visits. Tom had been at the Lycée for most of two years altogether when suddenly, with no notice, Owen appeared at the school and withdrew him.

They were leaving the Gallic side of the Channel and moving to London, Owen announced with great spirit. Tom was so miserable at Montauban that he did not even ask his father why they were leaving France and all their plans for the family home. The dream of living with his father in the house they were building together was over. In fact, Owen could no longer afford to live without financial assistance. His sister, Maud Grierson Pearce, living in England, had offered to house them and pay for Tom's education. Owen believed this would be better for both of them. Owen could not afford to continue painting unless he accepted her invitation.

They left directly from school. Tom felt as though he was being released from chains of imprisonment. He immediately began to dismiss from his thoughts all the French he had learned. Amazingly, he shed his adopted French culture like a coat. With eagerness he was ready, like his father, to begin again in another environment. Tom probably unduly minimized the adjustment this move would involve, since now he would be speaking his native language. He soon found, though, that there were many differences between American and British schools and culture. He had an entirely new syntax of English expressions to learn in order to communicate with his classmates, and a distinctly new way to pronounce almost everything.

In May of 1928, Tom and Owen moved in with Aunt Maud and her husband, Ben Pearce, near London. Ben was the retired headmaster of Durston House School. Tom was now fourteen, and soon became comfortable living with the Pearces. They anticipated the adjustment Tom had to make and enrolled him in the Ripley Court School, where Aunt Maud's sister-in-law was headmistress, in the well-to-do area of Surrey south of London. Unfortunately, Tom had not studied any Latin before, so was assigned to a much lower grade level with younger boys. It was another humiliating experience for Tom, especially since he was now older and therefore felt the embarrassment of being different from the other boys even more acutely than before. Tom had no one to confide in much of the time. Owen was largely unavailable to Tom in any way. He often came and went from his sister's home in order to sell his paintings.

Tom became attached to his Aunt Maud, who brought a great deal of stability to his life. He described her once as "so like an angel." She counseled him about his future, and brought a degree of realism into his life that he hadn't experienced before. She took him shopping for school clothes so that he would be appropriately dressed to look like the English boys. He relied on her at this time when everything around him was new and different, and he was away from all of his family.

Tom was excited about living in London. This was nothing like France and the quiet village-towns he and Owen knew there. It was not the city of tall buildings like Manhattan, but it was big and stately and he knew he would love it, especially after those grim days at Montauban. Tom loved to ride the double decker buses downtown with Aunt Maud. Tom noted that the city shops on Oxford Street and Regent Street were as sophisticated as his Aunt was simple, although he loved both extremes, he discovered. Soon Tom was caught up in the refinements of British style. He quickly absorbed the culture, mannerisms, and speaking patterns of his new family as though he were a native. Tom was determined to disappear into the local group so as not to call attention to his differences.

By the next term in the fall of 1929, Tom had mastered enough Latin to progress to a school at his grade level. Dr. Pearce arranged for Tom's enrollment at a prestigious public school at Oakham in Rutland, England, in the East Midlands. This was 104 miles north of London, a two-hour train ride from Kings Cross Station.

By this time, Owen was finally enjoying some success in selling his paintings, although it became necessary for him to accept financial assistance once more from Sam Jenkins to cover Tom's not inconsiderable educational expenses. Mr. Jenkins contributed reluctantly. He had a running feud with Owen about educating Tom abroad. He would have preferred that Tom be educated in American schools like John Paul. To his advantage, Owen had the support and assistance of his sister as well as his best friend, Dr. Bennett. He therefore would not even consider sending Tom back to the U.S. for his education.

*Scenes of Oakham and the boarding school Merton attended in Rutland in central Britain. The three-scene presentation is a contemporary postcard from Rutland. The school scene was photographed by the author in winter 2002.*

# Chapter 4

Oakham was a small school in the center of a simple country town. Its reputation for academic excellence dates back to 1587. Dr. Pearce knew personally of the quality of its faculty and thought that Tom could meet the high standard expected in spite of his unconventional academic background. Tom later made light of his attendance at Oakham, probably because he knew that the average American would not have heard of its reputation in the UK, through four centuries.

Oakham was built on the grounds of a former monastery. Adjacent to the campus is a fourteenth century church with a majestic gray spire. It made such an impression on Tom that he referenced its tower in his diary in a reminiscence in 1961. The school had its own chapel as well as sturdy red-brick dormitories and classroom buildings. Tom loved the grounds and often took long walks around the school property to enjoy the natural setting. It overlooked Brooke Hill, which added to the beauty of the landscape. The town developed around the school, with one main street of small shops within minutes of the campus.

After a short settling-in period, Tom became active in a variety of school programs. He was captain of the boxing team, played rugby, acted in a school play, and belonged to the debating team. His main interest was the school magazine, "The Oakhamian," for which he wrote amusing articles and poems, drew humorous pictures, and eventually became its editor. Sometimes he would bicycle over to nearby Uppingham, a scenic, historic town south of Oakham that offered more in the way of view and shops. Tom's portable phonograph made him popular with his classmates, who would go on outings with him to listen to popular records. He still loved movies, and now with sound, he could not resist occasionally sneaking away from the campus on a Saturday afternoon to the movie theater that was just around the corner in town. In his dormitory room he pinned up pictures of stars he thought beautiful or exciting. Pop sent American books and magazines to Tom regularly, especially about the film industry. Tom also took part in school pranks, even though he foresaw that he would probably suffer physical punishment from his superiors when he was caught. At the top of the stairs in the dormitory, the initials "TM" remain visible, along with other students' designations.

One of Tom's fellow students, John Barber, said that Tom loved to read serious books well beyond what was expected at his level. In fact, he had a reputation for doing just about everything to excess at the school. When Mahatma Gandhi introduced a non-violent protest of British control of his native India, Tom was strongly impressed by the power of his approach. Tom's British classmates were totally in disagreement with Ghandi's movement, but it left an indelible impression on Tom. His respect for Gandhi became the basis for his lifelong belief in nonviolence as an alternative to war as well as an effective technique for social change. In his youth, social issues were much more important to Tom than religious matters. Tom attended religious services at Oakham only when it was required. In an adolescent protest, he bragged in his diary that he kept his lips firmly closed when the students recited group prayers because he could not relate to them.

In the summer of 1928, Tom and his father traveled around England as well as to St. Malo, an ancient walled town on the northern coast of Brittany. It was not a resort town at that time. Originally it was a twelfth century pirate base. Owen obviously chose places where he would find the setting interesting for his painting, as well as for Tom's education and enjoyment.

Tom's first creative writing probably began in the fall of 1928 when Tom was at The Lycée Ingres in Montauban. His first story was called "The Five Emeralds." It shocked Tom's French classmates because the hero got into financial problems. Tom, a 13-year-old at the time, allowed the character to solve his problem by borrowing money from the heroine. He had completed eighteen pages and carefully illustrated it when he showed it to his friends. They laughed at Tom and told him the hero's action was unacceptable in a traditional romance, so Tom decided not to finish writing it. The similarity of Tom's hero to his father had obviously not been evident to him, and he had probably not realized the typical social reaction to one who borrows funds to manage his affairs.

He resumed his writing in England with his second story, "The Haunted Castle," in 1929. He wrote it for his younger cousins, Frank and Richard, Aunt Gwyn's sons. He also illustrated the fifteen pages of this story. Tom usually spent school holidays with Aunt Maud and Uncle Ben in Ealing, or at Aunt Gwyn Trier's home in West Horsley, suburbs of London. Gwyn Trier was Owen's younger sister. Tom enjoyed making up plays and acting them out with Aunt Gwyn's sons, Frank Merton and Richard Trier. Tom liked to play the part of narrator. He devised a fake beard on an elastic thread that he enjoyed wearing as he directed the plays.

In April 1929 Tom wrote a story he called "Ravenswell." It comprises 158 pages with illustrations. He wrote it on an Easter vacation trip to Canterbury with his father while Owen was painting a picture of the Cathedral there. It is an adventure of a family who found a treasure their ancestors had acquired during the Spanish conquests in the New World. Tom may have been inspired by a book called 'Ravenshoe' by Henry Kingsley. He had been awarded a copy of this book in 1928 by the headmistress of Ripley Court, Tom's first British school.

One other story has been found from Tom's early writing attempts. It was titled "The Black Sheep" and was written when he was a student at Oakham. This story seems to be semi-autobiographical, with a description of a boy who does not let the reality of corporal punishment stop him from misbehaving. Tom added an Appendix to the little story, informing the reader that the person he described lusts for fame, enjoys flattery, and is "rather sensitive." He adds that this person is a "decent fellow" but does not have the will to keep himself "in the straight + narrow path." Finally he states he often "hates the sight of his face in the looking glass."

In the following summer of 1929, Tom and his father traveled to Scotland and were guests of Owen's friends, the Haughton family. Owen had been ill and thought the summer in Scotland would help him to recuperate. But soon after their arrival Owen collapsed. He immediately returned to London to see Dr. Bennett, leaving Tom with the Haughton family. This was a difficult circumstance for Tom again, placed in a living arrangement with people who did not share his interests or temperament. He was coerced into tending the family's horses in spite of his obvious distaste for the job. Tom's relationship with the Haughton siblings deteriorated rapidly. He resorted to sequestering himself to read and escape the family's activities. A few weeks later Tom received a telegram from his father. Sent from a London hospital, it said, "Entering New York harbor. All well." Tom knew his father was in serious condition—mentally as well as physically. And he feared the worst was yet to come.

The remainder of the summer vacation was more miserable than before. When Tom returned to London, his Uncle Ben informed him that

Owen had a brain tumor and that Dr. Bennett would perform surgery at Middlesex Hospital in an attempt to remove it. Several surgeries were attempted, but failed. Owen asked his son to pray for him, but Tom could not relate to his father's request at that time.

When he became ill, Owen had been negotiating to sell his property to pay bills and raise cash for his expenses. In September 1929, Owen gave power of attorney to Dr. Bennett so that the property at St. Antonin could finally be sold. The sale was completed in March 1930 for 15,000 French francs. There was a heavy spring storm at that time that flooded the house, which was still officially termed a "house under construction." After paying various debts, Dr. Bennett had to report that Owen had little money left in his last days.

Pop, Bonnemaman, and John Paul came in the summer of 1930 on their regularly scheduled visit in spite of the Depression. It was obvious that Owen was beyond cure, and it was apparent that it would be their last opportunity to visit him. He was now unable to speak. Pop gave Tom a pipe on this visit, probably as a symbol of his recognition of Tom's maturity. To relieve Tom's concern, Pop explained his financial arrangement to provide for the support of the two boys through their school years. Tom had not even thought of the problem, let alone the solution. Pop's gesture comforted Tom, as always, with this expression of care for him.

On one visit Owen was drawing pictures of bearded old men who looked like Byzantine saints. Tom wondered if this was his father's memory of his romantic trip to Rome when he fell in love with Ruth and his later trip with Tom on vacation. Owen's bed was covered with little blue slips of paper, each with one of these drawings. They were totally different from anything he had ever drawn before. He apparently had never sketched human figures.

Tom spent the summer visiting Owen and talking to him, even though his father could not respond. He kept his emotions in check when he was with Owen to the extent that he could. The large malignant brain tumor protruded from Owen's forehead. Tom was visibly shaken as he saw the deterioration sap the very life from his father. The experience was almost unbearable, but he had to return to school.

# Chapter 5

For the fall term in 1930, Tom spent his holidays in London with his godfather, Dr. Bennett, who continued as Owen's attending physician. Tom could then visit Owen often and be knowledgeable of his father's current condition. Owen had designated Dr. Bennett to be Tom's legal guardian when Owen died. These holiday stays marked the beginning of the transition.

Dr. and Mrs. Bennett gave Tom a great deal of attention, exposing him to a life he could have only read about. He adopted the Bennetts' lifestyle of a successful intellectual in London at that time. Dr. Bennett was prominent in the city's social circles and his wife, Iris, had come from a privileged French family, which further enhanced Dr. Bennett's image. The Bennetts had a home at 29 Hill Street, Berkeley Square, in the exclusive "W1" area of London, with its rows of elegant Georgian houses. The area was also noted for the fact that several prominent figures of the past had lived in that neighborhood, including Elizabeth Barrett Browning, Samuel Taylor Coleridge, Benjamin Disraeli, George Frederick Handel, and Isaac Newton.

Tom's day typically started with breakfast in bed served by the Bennetts' French maid, and ended with formal meals served on expensive china by the kitchen staff. Tom adapted as readily to this new regimen as he had in all the previous changes to his situation. He studied the art of conversation that they displayed at the dinner table, revealing their refined tastes in literature and the fine arts. A new and different world was opening up for Tom—a contrast to the homes of his father's two sisters. Tom returned to Oakham after the holidays with a new sophistication and altered view of his world.

It was just before his sixteenth birthday. On January 18, 1931, the Headmaster at Oakham called Tom into his office and handed him a telegram. Owen was dead. Tom fell into the numbness he had experienced at his grandparents' home when he was nine, when a letter had come from London, informing the family that Owen may be dying.

It was like the end of a painfully sad story.

All the good times Father and I had had seemed strung out in my memory as one long trip. I always seemed to be living out of my luggage when I was with him. Either we were travelling together or I was with him on a school break. Our life together was really many short interludes. I always hoped that his feelings for me were not like that, yet his comings and goings seemed to reflect no continuity of concern for me.

I felt guilty about our relationship. I owed him my allegiance, but wondered had he always wanted it? Did he want to be freer of John Paul and me? I accepted his need to go alone on trips to do his painting. But I did not tell him so.

However, I could not accept Evelyn and Cyril Scott. I wondered if Father held it against me that I so detested their affection for him that I made life unbearable for all of us in Bermuda. Father let Evelyn discipline me, just as he had left it to Mother. I could not bear Evelyn's harshness or the power he gave her over me. It was hard enough to take it from Mother.

He wanted to be a good father to John Paul and me, but I don't think that he knew how. He had to accept money from Pop, but he could not win the family's acceptance. Father could never accept Pop's values, and thought his lifestyle was ordinary. Father simply could not pick himself up after Mother's death. The woman he chose to replace her was undoubtedly unacceptable to Pop as well as to me. Should I have held back my feelings and let him make a new life with them in Bermuda? No, I wasn't wrong. But did he forgive me for my interference?

He could only show me by his actions that we must all follow our dream, doing what we must to be true to ourselves without regard to the opinions of others, and believing in ourselves and our ability to express our inmost feelings. If this meant to live as outsiders from society, it was to have chosen the better part. He believed that art was the highest form of self-expression and should never be abandoned, even for life's necessities.

I wondered if I was the reason Father never really made a name for himself in the art world. Or did he blame me for his lack of success, whether or not I was the cause of it?

It was like Mother's departure from my life. Owen never told me he was dying. I had to see his deterioration and ask Dr. Bennett what it meant. The telegram was another piece of paper given to me stating the fact of death of a parent.

I cried bitterly, knowing we never spoke of these things. And now we never could.

*After the telegram, I didn't hear anything further from Father's family or Dr. Bennett about a funeral, so I am not sure there was one. I don't know what they did with his remains. I never had the heart to ask, and I was too ashamed to bring the matter up with anyone. I tried to pretend it was a relationship that was finished, so that it didn't matter afterwards how it was all handled. No one spoke of the disposition of Owen's paintings, which were obviously his most important possessions, or offered me anything for a keepsake. I was left with no tangible remembrance of him. At the time it didn't seem important. It would be years before I recognized the reality of my father's influence on the rest of my life, the real value of his life to me."*

Tom was apparently not told of the disposition of his father's paintings. It was reported that Owen left forty paintings to Cyril Kay Scott, a number of them to the Bennetts, and about 150 in Tudor-Hart's possession that were later moved to Canada and then to the U.S. Several paintings survived in New Zealand, probably early works painted before he moved to Europe. Aunt Gwyn had two or three paintings, but apparently did not tell Tom about this.

During Owen's illness the financial world was also in chaos. The New York Stock Exchange collapsed in 1929, and the U. S. was in a depression of major consequence. Sam Jenkins had to be one of the most perceptive businessmen in New York, because he averted the catastrophe that occurred in most people's lives. The inheritance from Tom's grandfather was in stark contrast to his father's failure to provide for Tom in the disposition of his possessions. In 1930 Pop quickly set up a trust fund for his two grandsons, including stock in his employer, Grosset and Dunlap. He also bought and sold real estate as an investment, including lots on Long Island, an island in Maine, and building lots in Coral Gables, Florida. Sam arranged for Dr. Bennett to administer this trust fund until Tom's 21st birthday. As a result, Tom could travel extensively on school breaks, following his father's vagabond lifestyle without much thought or plan.

For the Easter vacation of 1931 following Owen's death, Tom traveled south through France to Rome and Florence, retracing some of the steps he and his father had taken together much earlier. It was a lonely trip. Tom tried to make sense of the Byzantine figures his father had made on the little papers before he died, but couldn't come up with an answer that satisfied him.

He visited a number of old Catholic churches looking at the art his father had so much enjoyed. He felt self-conscious in these churches because he felt he was an intruder. Not being a member, he felt it was not really proper to be there just to look at the art. He hoped he wouldn't embarrass himself by doing or failing to do something that would reveal that he had no business being there.

One day when Tom was hiking along a road just outside Rome enjoying the Italian scenery, a group of rowdy Nazi soldiers in a passing car startled him. They drove so close to him that he was forced into a ditch in panic. Tom wondered if this was a sign of more trouble in Europe, repeating the agony of what was later known as the First World War. This was Tom's first experience of a somewhat sinister nature. Although in later years he tried to pass it off as a bit amusing, he nevertheless recorded it as an incident that for him foretold significant events of a horrendous nature.

For the summer break in 1931, Tom went back to New York, for the first time without his father on the ocean liner. After a year at an all-male school, Tom was ready to have a real life adventure with the opposite sex, instead of just fantasizing about it from pin-up pictures of movie stars. He met a girl named Norma Wakefield, twice his sixteen years, he hated to admit, and also married, but traveling with two aunts. She was obviously trying to look younger than her age, and Tom was trying to look older. Norma and Tom had a brief infatuation on the trip that apparently neither tried to stop. On the last night of the trip, Tom kissed Norma, and declared his love for her. She gently but firmly told him to forget it. Tom was more despondent than he could ever imagine a girl could cause him to be.

The next day in the New York newspapers there was the report of a man who committed suicide on another ship in the harbor on the same night Tom was turned down by Norma. He stayed in the depths of an adolescent depression for the rest of the summer. He returned to England on the same ship, which he described as a glorified cargo boat, for his final year at Oakham. On this second solo sailing, Tom forgot about girls and looked forward to the school year ahead. He was going to be house prefect as well as editor of the school magazine. He believed he had achieved real status. Now with a private dorm room, he decorated it with copies of Impressionist painters, a picture of Venus, and a collection of contemporary political pamphlets and novels to create a scholastic image that would impress his classmates.

During the Easter vacation of 1932 Tom went on a hiking trip to Germany, but soon had to return due to an infection in his foot. Then he developed a severe toothache. The school dentist performed an extraction without a sedative and Tom developed an infection. He then developed gangrene in his toe. Tom became so ill, probably from blood poisoning, he thought he might die. He was moved to the school sanatorium, where his recuperation lasted a month. During his stay, he composed an essay on the modern novel written from several different cultural viewpoints. He was awarded the Bailey English Prize, a collection of specially bound books, and his first literary award. More significant to Tom later, the Headmaster loaned him a book that introduced him to the poet, Gerard Manly Hopkins.

The summer vacation of 1932 reflected the effect of the hard financial times. Instead of "doing" Europe, Pop, Bonnemaman, and John Paul came to England to visit Tom. They stayed two months at a seaside resort, Bournemouth. Tom met a girl at the beach by the name of Diane, but they soon had a falling out. He gave her the name of a nearby post office where she could write to him, if she wanted to, when she returned home. Tom became so depressed that he went camping by himself in the nearby New Forest. Soon he got sick on his own cooking or from the water he was drinking from a stream—he wasn't sure which. He moved to a nearby inn at Beaulieu, still close enough to receive Diane's letters. What he found there instead was a Cistercian abbey in ruins. He admired the broken arches, still beautiful to him in their simplicity. It reminded him of the ruins in France that he had visited with Owen. He decided to get on with his life and forget this romance. He burned Diane's letters in his campfire. When the fire was completely out, he returned to school.

School had not yet resumed, so Tom got in touch with his friend, Andrew Winser. Andrew invited Tom to come visit him and his family on the Isle of Wight. Tom and Andrew were on the Oakham debating team together, and loved to hold late night discussions about issues of concern to them. Tom attended church services with the Winser family, led by Mr. Winser, who was rector of Brooke. At one of the services, Mr. Winser asked Tom to read a Biblical parable to the congregation. He put so much emotion into the story that Andrew said later that Tom had embarrassed him. He said Tom was un-English because he often failed to demonstrate the self-control in social situations that Andrew believed was expected. Andrew said that Tom never adopted conventional attitudes and had a tendency to mock the spurious and contentious, with a love for having fun on any occasion. Once Tom threw himself down on a hillside at Oakham, arms outstretched, and said, "I love the earth."

Tom returned in the fall to Oakham and sat for exams. He wanted to receive the higher certificate, in French, German, and Latin. He passed successfully, without much effort. He was proud and eager to tell the Bennetts. In December of 1932, Tom competed for a scholarship to Clare College of Cambridge University, called the Johnson Exhibition. During the Christmas break he received notice that he had won it. He was to read modern languages at Clare College. He was thrilled at his accomplishment and knew it would please all the family. Andrew also competed in the exam and won a scholarship to St. Catherine's College. They both felt on top of their world.

Tom was now free until the next term, to begin in October 1933, ten months away. His eighteenth birthday occurred just after the news of his success, and the Bennetts rewarded Tom with a birthday party. They presented him with a very expensive wallet, purchased from Finlay's, an exclusive shop in Bond Street. Inside, there was sufficient money for him to travel during the extended break he would have before entering Cambridge. Soon he set out for another trip to Italy.

By this time Tom spoke with a British accent like a native Brit. Tom dressed in high fashion for young men of the time, in three-piece tweed suits custom fitted. He put behind him all the unpleasant experiences of his childhood in the U.S. and France. At this point Tom was cocky and self-assured. From his diverse education and travels, he capitalized on his facility with languages and eventually found himself speaking French, Italian, Spanish, some Portuguese and German, and was comfortable reading Greek and Latin classics.

At maturity Tom was a good looking young man with deep-set piercing eyes, a high forehead, straight thin blond hair, high cheekbones, and to complete the picture, dimples in his cheeks and in the middle of his chin. He was of average height, 5 feet, 8 ½ inches, and had developed his slight build of 155 pounds particularly in the neck and shoulders in school sports. He had small hands and feet and rather short legs. His voice was of medium pitch and quite resonant, and he used it with maximum effect in conversation and debate.

Spending time visiting in the London home of the Bennetts, Tom had become acquainted with urban nightlife. He further developed a love for jazz that he had first enjoyed with his father. He built a record collection, primarily of jazz and current hits, and a book collection of the top writers of the time in addition to the classics. He smoked Craven A cigarettes, and also took up smoking the pipe his grandfather had given him. He continued to enjoy American films, stimulated by Pop's enthusiasm, particularly comedies of Charlie Chaplin and the Marx Brothers. In fact, Tom thoroughly participated in and enjoyed just about any recreation available to a young man of his time in London.

Tom was ready for an extended vacation to the warmth of Italy after his exams. He enjoyed visiting ancient churches and ruins again, as he had with his father. One night in his hotel room in Rome, he began to read the New Testament furnished by the hotel. He could not put it down. Suddenly Tom had the eerie feeling that he saw a vision of his deceased father. He was stunned.

Even though the vision was only like a flash, it was like a thunder-bolt. Suddenly he became aware of the shallow and worthless reality of his lifestyle. He broke down and cried about the meaningless life he had been living. He believed he had not even been trying to meet his father's expectations. He promised himself that he would improve his lifestyle.

The next morning he returned to one of the churches he had visited earlier, Santa Sabina. He took holy water for the first time, approached the altar rail, kneeling for the first time in a church, and prayed the Lord's Prayer. It was the only prayer he knew. This time he did not feel self-conscious. With difficulty, he asked for Divine assistance.

*Oh God, please show me the way.*

Scenes from
Cambridge University.
From undated postcards.

Cambridge, Clare College & Bridge.

# Chapter 6

In Santa Sabina Church, Tom felt a deep religious longing for faith, but did not know what to do about it or what it meant in his life. He believed his Creator was in touch with him. The "Our Father" that his grandmother, Gertrude Merton, had taught him, seemed inadequate to him to express his feelings, but he did not know any other way to act on this experience.

He felt he was being cleansed of his sins and suddenly freed from his past. He then went outside Rome to the sixteenth century Trappist monastery of Tre Fontane, or Three Fountains. The site is considered sacred, particularly the grotto and nearby marshes where it is believed that Jesus' disciple, Paul, was beheaded. Some visitors have claimed they have seen apparitions of Mary there. The thought then came to Tom that he would like to be a Trappist monk, although he knew little about it. He was beginning to find Jesus Christ but did not understand it.

When he returned from Italy, he was ready to go back to the U.S. again. It was the summer of 1933. Tom was visibly unhappy during his stay in Douglaston that year. He was involved in analyzing different religions other than the Catholic Church, and discarded each of them as he explored their teachings. He continued reading the Bible, although he did it in private, not wanting to risk the possibility of any sarcastic comments from family members. He decided to revisit the family church, the Zion Episcopal Church, where Owen had played the organ. It was a relatively new church building now, rebuilt since the fire there in 1924. The anchor in the stained glass window that Tom had admired as a child was gone now, and in fact the whole experience left him feeling empty. He knew he would have to look further.

Tom also explored the Quaker faith at the Meeting House of the Society of Friends in Flushing, NY, that his mother had attended. He was immediately impressed with the silence of the proceeding, but found that any persons who wanted to speak could break the silence with their comments. Surprisingly, one lady broke the group's long silence stating that she had a picture of the Lion of Lucerne statue she had taken on a European trip that she wanted to show them. Her remark had no relevance to any religious subject that Tom could imagine. He walked away feeling that this group was as disappointing as all the other religions he had explored. He thought, the minister is usually the one saying commonplace things, and in this group anyone can say such things.

Tom's restlessness persisted, as he awaited the start of his new life at Cambridge. He decided to amuse himself by going to Chicago to see the 1933 World's Fair. One of the shows there claimed to recreate Paris burlesque. It was called "The Streets of Paris." Tom thought it was a joke rather than any realistic representation, but he succeeded in getting himself employed as a barker for this concession just for the fun of it. After a few days Tom was disgusted and quit. He commented later to his friends that he never got paid for his work because he supposedly had not increased revenues. Tom concluded he was therefore another person who was fleeced by the second-rate concession.

When he returned to New York, he got in touch with his father's old friend, Reg Marsh. Reg now had a studio in Greenwich Village. He invited Tom to spend the rest of the summer with him. Reg and Tom went to burlesque shows, prizefights, amusement parks at Coney Island and Jones Beach, and to movies of all kinds. Tom said Reg looked like a retired prizefighter. Tom and Reg drank and talked about their opinions on everything. Tom was beginning to question whether he was really cut out for the British diplomatic service as a career. Dr. Bennett had high expectations for him as a diplomat, but he was not so sure it interested him sufficiently. He thought now that he would prefer to live the life of what he thought was a bohemian. He believed he might prefer to be a journalist and political cartoonist so that he could analyze and comment on social problems. Reg was working as a cartoonist and eventually became one of the first cartoonists for *The New Yorker* magazine as well as a noteworthy painter of scenes of New York City. Reg later married Betty, the daughter of Bryson Burroughs, who was curator of paintings at the Metropolitan Museum of Art in New York. The Marsh and Burroughs families were all neighbors in Douglaston and friends of Owen's.

It was hard for Tom to leave the lifestyle he was enjoying with Reg in the Village, sail the ten days back to England alone, and return to school life. Now that he had advanced to the college level, he saw himself as accomplished and self-sufficient. He did not realize that he was not mentally prepared to accept his new status with any degree of seriousness.

Tom soon discovered that his Cambridge experience would be a disaster.

Before he could get organized, his Aunt Maud died in November—another loss for Tom that connected him to the father he missed so much. Her funeral was very upsetting to him. In fact, it was his first funeral. Her passing was unexpected for him because he had not kept in touch with Owen's family. He wondered why he hadn't realized her importance to him-- he had become so disconnected from the family.

He felt his childhood was being buried with her. It closed the door to his connection with Owen's family in England, who no longer represented to him what he thought English life was all about. Now he was a ward of Dr. Bennett, who was in a different social class, and Tom was a University student with a sophisticated worldview. He saw no reason to visit the other Merton family members again after Aunt Maud's funeral.

Tom found himself arriving with many students at Clare College, one of a composite of 31 separate colleges in a "town and gown" city. He found a room at 71 Bridge Street, a quaint old building that offered a few rooms for students above a small shop. The campus extends down an embankment to the River Cam, where the students enjoy boating in narrow, flat-bottomed boats, called punts, with square ends and propelled by poles. Punting on the Cam was a popular recreation. Lower down the river, the "bumps," rowing competitions in conventional boats, take place annually between colleges. Tom was on the Clare team. He also took an active part in track events and boxing. Tom found it easy to assimilate at Clare because it was another all-male school. Initially he bicycled around town, limiting himself to visiting his old friends from Oakham. Soon he was enjoying the camaraderie of his new classmates. He could not concentrate on his studies with so many interesting diversions and new experiences.

Religious thoughts were not really divorced from his consciousness, however, as his diary reflects. He undoubtedly reacted to all the significant religious symbols that he encountered, including the famed Kings College Chapel, with its world class medieval stained glass windows and gothic fan vaulting that credit it as one of the most perfect buildings in the world. In 1961 he references the effect on him of the bell chiming in the cloister tower of St. John's at night, easily heard in his room in Bridge Street. During an Easter holiday trip to Germany in 1932, Tom wrote to Reg Marsh about his reaction to the Cologne Cathedral as " ... the most magnificent gothic building I have ever seen ... above Notre Dame and Strasbourg, but I think there is no Cathedral I like better than Canterbury: I do not like Cologne Cathedral: it rather frightens and awes me … ."

Tom said years later that the only good that came out of his time at Clare College was his introduction to the poetry of Dante. Professor Bullough introduced Tom to Dante's "Divine Comedy" with its description of the seven circles of Purgatory and fires of Divine Love. Tom was so impressed with this concept that it later became the theme of his autobiography, *The Seven Storey Mountain.*

Merton had developed a theory by this time that he could tackle the problems in his life by personal research and applying what he read to his life. He knew he was dissatisfied with his lifestyle, but did not think he knew how to improve it. He decided to research the field of psychology. He began a self-designed study of Freud and other behaviorists to analyze what he could do to be happier. He reached the incredible conclusion that the cause of his unhappiness was sex repression and living like an introvert.

He therefore went about remedying this situation with a series of girlfriends. He dated the local girls frequently, one named Joan and one more seriously by the name of Sylvia. He brought girls up to his room, which was usually tolerated provided his door was unlocked. He was soon threatened with eviction, but then became bolder and more devious about concealing his romantic activities. Tom was known to climb in and out of windows and helped girls do the same.

To avoid getting caught in his room with a girl, he would sometimes go with her to a secluded place in the college's Boat House that belonged to his punting team. He admitted later that he frequently attended parties where drinking and sex sometimes got out of control. He enjoyed himself thoroughly at parties, especially when he could play the piano.

One time he was arrested for riding on the running board of a car, and on another occasion he threw a rock through a shop window. He was known to cut more classes than he could afford to miss, and was often more interested in creating the poetry and cartoons he contributed to the undergraduate magazine, "Granta," than on attending lectures. Tom liked to frequent "The Red Cow" to drink beer with his companions, as well as to participate in private parties. He once entered an amateur competition for playing the drums, just for the fun of it. He frequently went to London for weekends and college breaks, and often took his friends from school with him. Iris Bennett sometimes refused to house them because of their raucous conduct, so Tom would take them to a London hotel and pay the bill out of his trust fund.

At one group get-together they decided to hold a mock crucifixion for their amusement. One student was to pretend to be nailed to a cross. It is said that Tom admitted to being that volunteer. The event got out of hand, probably due to their drinking, and apparently Tom's right hand was injured. Tom wrote about this incident in a fictional work he called *My Argument with the Gestapo*, but apparently never told anyone about the actual occurrence, other than that he was at a party where a mock crucifixion occurred.

Tom's lack of concern for his financial status grew steadily critical. He spent money recklessly on his social life, his travel, and purchases, especially books, records, and tailor-made clothes. One friend later reported that Tom had bought a velvet-lined cape. Dr. Bennett warned him about the need to take more care with spending his inheritance, but Tom was indifferent and irresponsible. Eventually he resorted to pawning his leather luggage and the Zeiss camera he had bought in Germany just to meet his current expenses. In April 1934, nearing the end of the academic year, his godfather called him to London to discuss his extravagant lifestyle.

*"My memories from attendance at Clare's are a lesson in how ecstasy and pain can be so intertwined that one cannot distinguish where one stops and the other begins.*

*I thought I was redefining sophistication by becoming a mainstay at student parties that I now only remember as orgies and occasions of drunkenness. My ability to do quick study served me well to fake my way along academically. School for me was an interlude to social activity. Beautiful girls paid attention to me and fed my insatiable appetite for their affections and admiration. Life was a song and I danced happily to its tune without regard to consequences.*

*Dr. Bennett summoned me to his office to speak with him, or rather to hear what he had to say to me. This was not the first occasion for his reprimands. His remarks were a total rejection of all that I had done that year. I could think of nothing whatever to explain my behavior, other than that I had made mistakes and did not want to hurt anyone. I thought this would put matters to rest in the English manner of practical solutions and social delicacy. I didn't know what the consequences would be for me.*

*I soon realized that he had washed his hands of my life and career. I hoped he would believe that his stern remarks would serve to correct my behavior.*

As it turned out, I lost more than I realized. I lost my guardian's respect. As a consequence, I was deprived of all that he could give me in the world, including the promising diplomatic career he had planned for me after I would have graduated from Cambridge.

While I was in Douglaston on summer vacation, he wrote to me suggesting I remain there under the supervision of my grandparents. It was another shocking, life-transforming letter I was to receive. He said my scholarship would probably not be renewed because of my grades, and my trust fund could probably not bear the cost of continuing at University there without it. It was therefore the end of my attendance at Cambridge or residence in England.

I tried to forget it, but I never could. How could Dr. Bennett expect me to forget the loss of my guardian, as well as my godfather. I had thought he would understand I was just trying to live the sophisticated life he seemed to admire so much in writers like Hemingway and D. H. Lawrence. I did not think he would apply such a strict code of behavior to me. I did not think he would stop caring about me after I made mistakes. Maybe he never cared for me.

I made a very sober return visit to England to apply for a resident alien's status to pursue further studies in the U.S. since I was not a U.S. citizen. I had been traveling on a British passport since Father put me on his passport when we lived in France. I did not feel like a Brit or an American. I felt more inclined to relate to the Catalan land in France. I had wanted to live a life free of bondage from the cultural norms that were suffocating me and had only succeeded in creating a greater imprisonment in my own weakness. My very identity was now a question mark.

# Chapter 7

Tom had even selected his room for the coming year at Cambridge before he left at the end of the term. He had passed his tripos in modern languages, French and Italian, with a Second. He thought that would be good enough to get him by. He never dreamed that Dr. Bennett would abandon him. His scholarship to Cambridge might have been withdrawn due to his failure to receive a First, but Tom did not wait to find out because he could not continue at Cambridge without additional funds.

Since he had only a visitor's visa to be in the U.S., he had to return to England to apply for a resident alien's status to stay in the U.S. indefinitely. In the process of gaining this status, he was amused that he was required to swear he was not a Communist or active homosexual and had no plans for the violent overthrow of the U.S. Government. Nothing could be further from the case. Tom maintained his British passport until he became a U.S. citizen in 1954.

When Tom arrived back in Cambridge, he went to see his old friend, Andrew Winser. He packed his books, most of his clothing, and his portable phonograph. Later he was shocked to learn from a fellow student that a friend had committed suicide by hanging himself. Tom was grateful that he would be spared from such an outcome himself. He closed out his affairs at Cambridge and returned to New York, scrapping his original plans for a life in England and determined to make a new start.

Now with the advice of Pop and probably financial assistance as well, he enrolled in Columbia University in New York City. Tom decided to pursue a career as a journalist. He was attracted by its renowned Journalism School which had been founded by Joseph Pulitzer. He could commute from Douglaston and study on the Long Island Rail Road commuter train, with a transfer at Penn Station to the New York subway to Columbia. He had not returned from England until December, so waited until the January 1935 term to enroll.

Life for Tom took on a new air at Columbia. He was in America now—the land of infinite possibilities. New York City was at its most dynamic, with construction crews all over the downtown area erecting skyscrapers. Tom thought this growth could be a metaphor for what was happening in his life—to grow and progress like the city he passed through every day on his way to Columbia. Only the few most pros-perous who survived the Depression could attend college, especially a private university with a reputation like Columbia's, and Tom knew and appreciated how fortunate he was to be there.

Tom soon began to feel comfortable. His curiosity was boundless. He investigated every aspect of student life that even remotely appealed to him. When some of his new acquaintances teased him about his British accent and colloquial expressions, he quickly eliminated them. He ran on the track team. He joined a social fraternity, Alpha Delta Phi, in 1935. He joined the National Students' League and the Young Communist League, which were popular with the students. Both the social and political organizations failed to hold his interest for long, so he soon dropped out of them.

For purposes of the Young Communist League, Tom chose the alias of Frank Swift, thinking how apt for an expression of his social views towards reform. He agreed with the Communist idea of social justice as an end in itself, but after a brief acquaintance with the organization he dropped out because it did not live up to the ideals he thought they had put forward. He only attended one meeting and saw it was not remotely what he had expected. At that time cynicism about the capitalistic system was a popular subject, especially among students, and Communism was thought to be a solution. He concluded that Communism adequately identified the evils of society, but did not offer the correct solution. He particularly agreed with their "No More War" slogan.

Like Clare College, Columbia at this time was an all-male school for upper middle class gentlemen. Tom typically wore one of his three-piece suits with a dress shirt to class every day. He hung a gold watch chain from his vest pocket, even though he had no watch. A businessman's brimmed felt hat completed the outfit. It was the look of the privileged set in New York, which Tom wanted to imitate, and he wanted to be accepted by the other students who actually were part of that group.

Tom's personality showed even in the way he walked. It was a distinc-tive walk, like fireworks every time his heel hit the ground, one friend said, and he actually bounced with joy. He walked rather rapidly, his feet pointing outward. There was something of Tom's mother's training there. When she taught him to walk, she probably also showed him how to dance a bit, too.

He often liked to do gangster imitations, and his broad, slightly pug nose helped the image. Tom was popular with his fellow students. They gave him the nickname, "Mertie." He briefly grew a thin moustache and a small fringe of blond beard when some of his friends were experimenting with a bohemian look, but it obviously did not suit him.

Tom began to produce cartoons that he submitted to school publications. The journalism students worked primarily on the fourth floor of John Jay Hall, where their newspaper, *Spectator*, and the *Jester*, their humor magazine, were produced. This hall was also the site of the undergraduate student center. By the end of the 1936 school year, Tom had succeeded his new friend, Robert Lax, as editor of the *Jester*. Almost every issue contained stories and cartoons of Tom's. In the same year he was elected yearbook editor and was a regular contributor to the newspaper and magazine. He was coeditor of the *Columbia Review* with Robert Giroux, who would soon play a prominent role in Tom's life. Only one year later Tom was named editor of the University yearbook. He now wrote for nearly every campus publication. He was voted the "Best Writer" at Columbia in 1937. Tom's work on the Jester paid many of his bills at this point. *Jester* staff wore a golden jester's crown to distinguish them, and Tom displayed his crown on his watch chain across his vest, even though he still had no watch.

Academically, the highlight of Tom's years at Columbia was his association with Mark Van Doren, his English professor and a well-known writer of the time. Van Doren became his mentor as well as a lifelong friend. Tom had not revealed his admiration to Van Doren at the time, however. Van Doren said in his autobiography that he first learned of his influence on Tom when he read his *Seven Storey Mountain* several years later. He said that Tom had hidden his thoughts "behind the twinkle in his eyes." From the beginning of their relationship, Van Doren had read and critiqued Tom's poetry and advised him about various publishers that he thought might be interested in his work.

The one major depressing experience Tom had at Columbia was a class visit to Bellevue Hospital in New York. It was a field trip for a course he was required to take, called Contemporary Civilization. To Tom's horror, the class was escorted down to the hospital morgue. There they viewed the cadavers that had been found around the city and were unclaimed. They had died of contemporary civilization, Tom reflected. His mother, Ruth, had died at this hospital and would have been temporarily in this morgue. Tom would probably have known this, but apparently did not record the incident as a horrible coincidence.

Tom found himself for the first time really enjoying his school life. He adopted a breezy, witty persona that attracted his fellow students to him. Some of his friends called him "Murtog." He soon became part of a very close-knit group, including Ed Rice, Seymour (Sy) Freedgood, John Slate, Ad Reinhardt, Bob Gibney, Bob Gerdy, and Jim Knight, whom Tom called "the red-headed Southerner." They were almost like a mini-fraternity who spent all of their free time together in various combinations, or all together on outings and holidays. They could invariably be found at the Lion's Den, a below street-level tap room on the campus that was a popular place for student discussions.

They called each other "old boy," a term Tom obviously had brought with him from his English background. The American students found it amusing, but Tom soon removed from his vocabulary all the British expressions he had so carefully learned in order to fit in at Oakham. He did not want to be different from his new American friends. Tom's British accent disappeared except for a trace while he was at Columbia. There was one exception. Tom and Bob Gibney were walking in Manhattan one day and met some English sailors. Tom immediately fell into a perfect Cockney accent. Gibney could not believe what he heard. He told their friends later that Tom had made a complete transformation during the conversation. Tom must have been embarrassed at the attention this incident drew from the group.

Tom wanted to be attractive to the female students as much as his new-found male classmates. Girls in the group included Lilly Reilly, Jinny Burton, Peggy Wells, and Donna Eaton. They attended Barnard College, the women's counterpart school and a corporate college of Columbia.

Gibney and Tom often went together to the Center Theater to pick up the girls they knew who were in the show. Sometimes they went out, or they would just escort them to the Rehearsal House where many of the girls in the shows lived. Peggy Wells had a bit part in one of the shows. Gibney and Tom also went a number of times to the World's Fair, particularly to visit the Cuban Pavilion. They especially liked the flamenco dancers. Bob Gibney's family had a home in Port Washington where he invited the group to join him on weekends. Gibney had a studio in the basement for his drawing and wood sculpture. The group loved to go to Gibney's home, but Tom would grow restless after a day and want to return to the city before the others were ready.

Tom also visited at the home of the Freedgoods on Long Beach, along with other members of the group. They often went on outings in the area on their school breaks. The Freedgood family made the students feel comfortable doing what they pleased on their own schedule when they were there.

Tom spent weekends and holidays at nearby homes of several of his friends, but never apparently had any of them out to Douglaston to his grandparents' home. He often hosted his friends later when he had his own apartment.

Tom's friends came from a variety of backgrounds and beliefs. Many of his male companions became lifelong friends. The girls dropped out of his life soon after he left Columbia. Lax, Seymour, and Gerdy were Jewish. Ed Rice and Robert Giroux were Catholic. Tom had found a group of friends with whom he could successfully combine his intellectual pursuits with good times, so he was not tempted to sacrifice one for the other. They enjoyed studying and arguing philosophical principles as well as partying, all with the same degree of enthusiasm.

Robert Lax became one of Tom's closest friends both in and out of school. Lax was tall and very thin, with thick dark hair and sharp features. Tom once said he had a long face like a horse. He also had a wit to match Tom's. Once Lax was up against a deadline to finish a short novel for a novel-writing course he was taking. In the typical reaction of this close-knit group, several of his friends volunteered to each take a section and write it for him simultaneously. It was decided that Tom and Donna Eaton would take on parts of it, with Lax, to finish it overnight. Tom said they were all satisfied to receive a B-minus on their product; Lax's professor was obviously never the wiser.

Ed Rice became another lifelong friend. He and Tom shared many of the same feelings about writing and about the search for truth in their lives. Ed was the typical Ivy League intellectual as a student, in dress as well as in his actions, serious about his work, but devoted to the friendship and camaraderie of the group.

Tom was able to capture the essence of what interested his collegial readers in his cartoons. He transformed the sadness from his past into his humor. Tom and Ad Reinhardt shared an interest in cartoon art of a satirical nature. They both continued to pursue this medium of expression into later life. Reinhardt's "A Portend of the Artist as a Yhung

Mandala, Joke by Ad Reinhardt" in 1956 satirized the museum and its portrayal of the history of art. It is unknown whether Tom ever saw this work, although the Museum of Modern Art later recognized it as a major product of Reinhardt's legacy. Tom's equivalent work may have been the cartoon art published anonymously in *Jubilee* magazine issues during 1967 and 1968 called "The Adventures of Tyng." It mimicked the history of philosophy, including *The Seven Storey Mountain*. Although no one has published an attribution of these drawings to Merton, there is a resemblance to Merton's earlier cartoon work.

*Tyng's Lives of Eminent Religious Thinkers," a series of 20 cartoons portraying eminent figures. They were published anonymously, but the author believes they are probably a Merton product. The submission on Bernard, pictured here, references Merton's autobiography,* **Seven Storey Mountain Jubilee,** *Vol. 15, No. 4, October 1967. This magazine went out of business the following year.*

Tom had first written stories at Montauban and illustrated articles with some cartoons at Oakham and at Clare, but not of the quality that he produced at Columbia. Some said his cartoons much resembled the style in *The New Yorker*, one of his favorite magazines. It seemed so sophisticated and urbane—just like him. Even without the celebrated top hat of their icon, Tom was as worldly and self-consumed as the magazine's Regency dandy, Eustace Tilley. Actually, *The New Yorker* was such an important publication for Tom and his fellow journalist friends that several of them later obtained positions on that magazine (Gerdy, Lax, and Charles Saxon).

Bob Gerdy was particularly interested in reading and discussing philosophy with his friends. He had a baby face and thick curly hair, which was incongruous with his very serious view of life. He was from a Jewish family. He converted later to the Catholic religion. Gibney also shared an interest in Catholic principles, but did not convert to Catholicism. He thought he should receive some kind of a sign in order to take this step, and he never believed he had been so directed.

Tom and his friends liked playing word games, in imitation of the writings of James Joyce. They devised words, names, and even sounds and sometimes amused themselves by making jokes with invented language in public. Tom's interest in this went back to his school days at Oakham. Once when Robert Lax and John Slate were traveling on school vacation, they carried on a conversation entirely in dog barks on a French train, to the absolute amazement of their fellow passengers. Tom's friends said he once kept the group awake one night at the Lax family's cottage talking aloud in an unintelligible language and laughing uncontrollably. Tom did not even remember the dream.

Tom apparently taught himself to play the piano. He often practiced in an empty room used by the school's glee club. He loved to play "The St. Louis Blues," which he had also played at Clare College for his friends. He said he might have ruined the pianos he banged on. Some said his style sounded like several people playing pianos together.

On summer vacations Tom got jobs through Miss Wegener, who ran Columbia's placement service. In the summer of 1936, Tom worked as a tour guide at Rockefeller Center, for which his Uncle Harold was a consulting engineer. He conducted tours of Radio City on the 86th floor, with an admission fee of $1.00. Tom was enthusiastic about making the tour worthwhile. Among his friends he enjoyed mimicking the tourists he met. He was paid $27.50 a week for a full eight-hour schedule, and he was happy to get it. For additional funds he worked as a free lance writer for an advertising firm for paper products. The company was also located in the RCA Building, but Tom did most of the work at home. Later, when he moved into the city, he also tutored children in Latin at his landlord's school in the apartment house.

In the fall, October of 1936, another loss occurred in Tom's short life: Pop, his beloved grandfather, died suddenly and unexpectedly. Bonnemaman gave Tom the news when he arrived home from school. Tom found Pop's body in his bed where he had died just hours earlier. Tom fell on his knees and prayed for him at his bedside. He hurriedly got up before Bonnemaman came into the room, because he was not comfortable with his feelings, even in front of his grandmother.

Before Tom could learn to live without his grandfather, Bonnemaman became seriously ill, although she had suffered from diabetes and had poor health for a number of years. She died less than a year after her husband, in August 1937. Tom could never forget his happy days with Pop and Bonnemaman. He particularly remembered sitting in Pop's big, soft, leather easy chair in his office reading picture books, one beautiful book after another. Tom prayed for Bonnemaman at her bedside during the last months of her life. Both of Tom's grandparents were cremated and placed with Tom's mother at the Fresh Pond Crematory. Tom fell into another state of depression. He felt himself to be more of an orphan than when Owen died.

Tom's uncle, Ruth's brother, became John Paul and Tom's guardian. In October 1938 Harold married Elsie Holahan, Aunt Martha's companion until her death. They continued to live in the family home. Harold Jenkins was as inflexible and one-dimensional as Tom was diverse. He had been living in the home witnessing all the events in his nephews' childhood and adolescence and was less than impressed with their track record. Tom and John Paul kept their distance from Uncle Harold. When he took over the management of their inheritance from Pop and Bonnemaman, they grew even more reticent about their lives, especially trying to avoid his critical eye. Harold may have been resentful of sharing the estate left by Pop and Bonnemaman with his sister's *avant-garde* sons, although there is no specific reference to this sentiment in Merton's work. John Paul remained friendly with Elsie's daughter, Patricia, from her first marriage. They were close to the same age and had occasion to get acquainted after Tom and Owen moved to France.

Soon after Pop's death, Tom became ill while he was running on the cross-country team. He was depressed and preoccupied with his responsibilities on the school publications. He had tried to run without having first gone into training. He threw himself face down on the ground at the end of the run, out of sheer exhaustion. He never went back to the track.

Then he was struck with an illness he did not understand while he was on the commuter train going to school one day in November of 1936. Terrified, he got off the train and went across the street from Penn Station to the Pennsylvania Hotel and checked in. He called room service for a physician. It was thought to be an attack of gastritis, combined with stress and lack of rest. The doctor gave him a sedative, but it did not help much. His attempt at sleep was futile, so he returned to Douglaston. He was relieved that Elsie was there to take care of him. Tom thought he was having a nervous breakdown. He had experienced an intense fear of the height of the hotel room when he looked out of the large picture window.

The immensity and dynamic growth of Manhattan that had so excited Tom when he came to Columbia and so stimulated him now seemed paradoxically to be working against him. Size and space now brought forth a terror in him that was becoming unmanageable. He had always admired the immensity of Penn Station, covering no less than nine acres stretching across two city blocks, and its majestic waiting room with its clerestory windows, the latest steel-frame technology making possible the extensive use of glass in the train shed. The three-ton golden eagles hovering over the place, once appearing majestic to him, now seemed ominous. The Empire State Building was just down the street, and he feared that even taller buildings would follow. He had now lost his models of American spirit and entrepreneurial achievement, Pop and Bonnemaman, and he now felt adrift.

Elsie's doctor told Tom that this attack would probably lead to ulcers and suggested he eat a lot of ice cream. He decided to follow the doctor's advice about his diet, but wondered if he might be losing his mind. He continued to suffer from chronic digestive problems. On several occasions he reexperienced a milder version of the panic he felt when this attack occurred. He began to realize he could not take his health for granted, and that he, too, was mortal.

# Chapter 8

The Douglaston house was not the same without his grandparents, and Tom could not bear living there any longer. In June 1937 Tom moved into the city, to a small room on the top floor of a seven-story apartment house. It was in the Morningside Heights section of the Upper West Side of the city, at 584 West 114th Street. He paid $7.50 a week, which he believed was a bargain because it was directly behind the University's Butler Library. He kept this room for the next year and a half.

Tom graduated with his Bachelors' degree in February 1938. He received his diploma at the registrar's office. Tom said he didn't mind that there was no mid-year commencement ceremony because he was enrolling in the graduate school program for the following semester. When the June graduation occurred, Tom could not resist participating in the ceremony at the last minute. He had not ordered a cap and gown, but nevertheless managed to borrow one from a girl who had one from her Barnard College graduation. He even went through the receiving line. He wanted to shake hands with the University's President and Dean, Dr. Nicholas Murray Butler. He had been President of Columbia since 1912, was a Nobel Prize recipient, was a confidante of several U.S. Presidents, and had been decorated by fifteen governments. Tom would not miss the opportunity to meet such an accomplished person.

Tom's original plan was to obtain a college degree as soon as possible to get an early start in his career, so chose to study modern languages. Since he already had a great deal of proficiency in several languages, he reasoned that he could move through the curriculum faster, then seek an internship on a newspaper. Now he began thinking more of a teaching career, along with writing at the same time. He decided to major in English for his Masters' Degree with a specialty in eighteenth century English literature.

By this time Tom was searching for some significant meaning in his life. He eagerly pursued the books recommended by Mark Van Doren and his friends. He purchased a copy of Etienne Gilson's book, *The Spirit of Medieval Philosophy*, which was recommended highly by several of his friends. When he opened it on the train going home, he discovered it carried an "Imprimatur" and "Nihil Obstat." He knew that this meant it had been reviewed by Catholic hierarchy, who had found it contained no material in disagreement with Catholic teachings. Tom was so angry about this that he said he felt like throwing it out of the train window. Although his knowledge of Catholic procedure in publishing works by Catholic authors was limited, he firmly believed this to be censorship of the worst kind. He couldn't resist reading it anyway. To his surprise, he found Gilson's concept of the existence of God provided a clarity of understanding he had not found before in his studies. It was the beginning of Tom's respect for the Catholic faith. Soon he began to have a desire to go to church for the first time in his life.

Lax urged Tom to read Huxley's *Ends and Means*, because it presented a great deal of information about monastic orders as well as major world religions. Tom had thought that Huxley was a religious skeptic. He found, again to his surprise, that Huxley offered a defense of mysticism and a world of nonviolence, and urged a life of discipline in order to achieve one's highest end. Tom was struck by this idea, but had difficulty understanding how Huxley could find Christianity to be a less pure religion than the Eastern mystical beliefs such as Buddhism. Tom began an exploration of Buddhism and a further study of Gandhi's nonviolent philosophy, within the context of Huxley's idea of a transcendence running through all religious systems.

Through Lax and other friends, Tom met a Hindu monk who called himself Mahanambrata Bramachari. The Indian term, *Brahmachari*, means a celibate, although Tom probably remembered reading in Gandhi's writing about the principle of *brahmacharya*, meaning complete control over all the senses. Bramachari's monastery, near Calcutta, had received an invitation to send a speaker to an international congress of the religions in Chicago. The monastery selected Bramachari to represent them, since he spoke English and was fairly young for such a long journey. Not being familiar with material matters, the monastery provided him with a mere $100 for the trip. Fortunately for Bramachari, he eventually made it from Calcutta to Chicago, but only by his wits and a rather unique presence that attracted people to him.

By the time he arrived in Chicago, the congress had long since disbanded, and Bramachari had no funds to return to Calcutta. Somehow he managed to stay on as a student and even to earn a Ph.D. degree at the University of Chicago. During this time he met Helen Freedgood, Sy Freedgood's sister and also a student there. She was impressed by Bramachari's unique persona and persuaded him to go to New York, where she arranged for him to be met by Sy and his friends. By coincidence, this soon included Tom.

Helen bought Bramachari a pair of blue sneakers for his trip. He was happy for Helen's assistance, and Sy and his friends looked forward to meeting the monk, based on Helen's recommendation. When he arrived at Grand Central Station, the group was amused by his ludicrous appearance: he was wearing the blue sneakers with his yellow turban with red Hindu lettering and a white cloak. Soon he had fascinated the entire group. Sy and Bob Lax housed him secretly in their dormitory room in Furnald Hall. Push button elevators were now installed in many of the school's buildings, but this dorm still used the old manually operated crank mechanism, which required an operator. The elevator operator was astonished at his first sight of Bramachari. He was never deterred by the public's reaction to his appearance, which was in no way representative of the impression he made when speaking of his beliefs. Remarkably, the most sophisticated school officials he met would invite Bramachari to lecture at the prestigious schools they represented, including Smith College. Frequently Bramachari would simply go to Grand Central Station to meet people casually, and they would frequently give him contributions. Eventually he raised enough money to return to his monastery.

Based on reports from Sy and his other friends, Tom really anticipated meeting Bramachari, and commented that he wondered if he would receive an electric shock when he shook hands with him. Tom was not disappointed. He asked Bramachari for advice about what to read to pursue answers to his questions about the meaning of life. He was particularly impressed with his approach to spirituality. Bramachari advised him to read St. Augustine's *Confessions* and Thomas a Kempis' *Imitation of Christ*. Tom was amazed that Bramachari would refer him to Catholic writers, but nevertheless followed his advice. This was a turning point for Tom. Bramachari told Tom that Catholic churches were the only American churches he had visited where people looked like they were actually praying.

In a short time Bramachari had virtually become one of Tom's group in their entertainment as well as their serious discussions. On New Year's Eve, 1938, the group was partying at the Freedgoods' home, and John Slate decorated Tom with the red and yellow strip of cloth that Bramachari wore as a turban.

During the summer of 1938, Tom worked on his study of William Blake for his Masters thesis and enjoyed visiting the major museums in Manhattan, in particular the Cloisters, the Metropolitan's Museum of Medieval Art at Fort Tryon, New York. Part of the cloister of Saint Michel de Cuxa had now been brought there and reassembled. This had originally been housed in the monastery above Prades where Tom was born. It was a reminder of his childhood days in France when his father allowed him to play in the ruins of cloisters that were similar to this one.

Now when he visited Douglaston, Tom began to attend the Zion Episcopal Church and found himself actually enjoying the sermons. He also began walking the seven blocks from his Manhattan apartment house to the nearest Catholic Church, Corpus Christi, to attend Mass. He did not take Communion since he was not a member, but nevertheless enjoyed this church's American colonial simplicity, historic stained glass windows, and paintings, as well as its traditional liturgical music.

Tom seemed to make the decision to join an organized religion, the Roman Catholic Church, quite suddenly. It happened when he was sitting in his room on 114th Street reading the biography of Gerard Manley Hopkins, an English cleric and poet of the nineteenth century. Hopkins had written to John Henry Newman, an English convert to Catholicism and later a Cardinal, for advice about converting to Catholicism. At the time Hopkins was a student at Oxford University, and he had thought perhaps he should not make this decision until he graduated. Newman told Hopkins to come from Oxford to see him in Birmingham to be received into the Church. It was a rainy, cold October afternoon in 1866, just as it now was in Manhattan in 1938. Suddenly Tom heard an inner voice asking him what *he* was waiting for. He first tried to ignore this experience as an overactive imagination and continued reading the Hopkins biography. But it was persistent. Tom told himself that he didn't know what he was waiting for.

He put on his coat and walked over to Corpus Christi Church. He had been happy just attending services there as a spectator, although he was self-conscious about not being a member of the Church. Now he asked to see the pastor, Father George Ford, about becoming a Catholic. Corpus Christi Church was the official parish church for Columbia students, located on 121st Street, just behind Teachers College, and Father Ford was the appointed counselor. So Tom confidently approached him to ask for information about joining the Catholic faith.

Tom began to discover peace of mind for the first time in his life. At Father Ford's suggestion, he enrolled in a six-week catechism class that was just beginning. He never missed a class. The only thing that disturbed him was a talk on Hell during a retreat he attended after he completed the classes. His reaction was that he could hardly wait for his Baptism so that he could elude eternal damnation. He was convinced that his past transgressions would surely have doomed him otherwise.

He was baptized by Father Moore at Corpus Christi Church on November 16, 1938. This was a provisional Baptism because Tom was unsure about the possibility of his Baptism at Prades. He chose Ed Rice as his sponsor and godfather, and Father Moore himself served as the second sponsor. Witnesses were Robert Lax, Robert Gerdy, and Seymour (Sy) Freedgood. During the ceremony, at the point of exorcism, Tom said later, he had the feeling of losing a frightened legion of spirits that had been living inside him for the past 23 years. He said it was more than seven years, for sure.

Tom had not consulted any of his friends about his decision to become a Catholic. When Tom announced his conversion to Lax, Tom threw his new brown felt hat at Lax like a Frisbee. He was so enthusiastic that some of the group wondered if this was only a passing interest for Tom rather than a permanent change in his life.

About six months after his Baptism, Tom received the sacrament of Confirmation, administered by Bishop Donohue, on May 29, 1939. He took the name of James as his new middle name, for reasons unexplained. This solemn occasion further deepened Tom's faith and devotion to the Church that he had finally chosen as his spiritual anchor.

Tom's days at Columbia were a combination of social and intellectual activity in a great deal of inner restlessness. He saw quickly that his father's attempt at dealing with the same feelings could not be solved through friendships and extensive travel. Tom hoped that joining the Catholic Church would give the meaning to his life he so intensely missed. He was convinced that writing was to be his life's work, but had not yet begun to market any of his material.

Tom received his Master of Arts degree in English in February 1939. His Master's thesis was on "Nature and Art in William Blake: An Essay in Interpretation." His father had read Blake's poetry to him as a boy. Blake's work influenced Tom for most of his life.

Blake is considered in some literary circles as an eccentric poet and painter of the post-eighteenth century. Essentially self-taught, he portrayed a visionary world in reaction to the rational thought that produced the Industrial Revolution. His work is frequently considered an acquired taste. His apocalyptic view of the cosmos is definitely outside the British tradition of artists and is thought by some to be a bit otherworldly. His mythical men and women, gnomes, and serpents excited Tom's imagination. Tom related to Blake's desire to restore the world to its lost spirituality.

Blake was a window for Tom to the world of the spiritual. Like Tom, Blake was strongly influenced by Dante's *Divine Comedy* and the importance of the concept of good and evil. Blake married the visual medium with the written word. Up to this point, Tom had only employed the two media of expression in satire. He would soon experiment with sketches of a spiritual nature, though not in Blake's style of graphic pictorial scenes of the afterlife.

After completing his Master's degree, Tom decided to revisit Bermuda for a few days' vacation. Surprisingly, he found Bermuda to be a more beautiful place than he remembered. Memories of his stay there with Owen were undoubtedly repressed. He arranged to get back to Manhattan in time to say goodbye to Bramachari, who was leaving for India.

Tom took an apartment in Greenwich Village, at 35 Perry Street, on the second floor. He described it as consisting of a pleasant living room ten feet wide, with a dark bedroom facing the rear of the building. It had a small balcony with a wooden floor that was partly rotting. He liked to sit on the good boards and hang his feet through the rotten ones when he was reading.

Tom's apartment allowed him the space to entertain his friends, and with his new telephone, he could call and set up their get-togethers. He often invited them to spend the night, even though he had to sleep on the floor or a chair to encourage their stay for late night discussions, especially if they had had too much to drink.

Tom continued at Columbia, beginning a doctorate program paid for by a grant-in-aid from the school. His subject of concentration was Gerard Manley Hopkins, the Anglican priest who eventually became a Roman Catholic and a Jesuit priest. It was a transition that inspired Tom in his own spiritual search.

Tom finally succeeded in getting a few poems published and sold some book and movie reviews to the *New York Herald Tribune* and *The New York Times*. This gave him quite a bit of encouragement, but the limited success only whetted his appetite for a greater degree of acceptance of his work. The reputation he had gained on campus through college publications only intensified his pursuit of a serious writing career. Joining the Church had the same kind of effect. Religion seemed to stimulate an intense pursuit of spirituality rather than satisfy his needs for a moral compass.

# Chapter 9

Manhattan was a distraction to Tom's writing, and living in a small apartment intensified the lonely experience. Tom and his friends found a solution to their need for companionship by leaving the city together on school breaks. Lax's family had a hotel and summer home in Olean, in western New York state, in the Allegheny Mountains. For Tom it was a substitute for his lost connection to Douglaston and his family.

Lax's mother was a student at St. Bonaventure College, a Franciscan school outside Olean. Lax often used the cottage there that belonged to his sister, Gladys, and her husband, Benji Marcus. Tom began to join Lax and a number of their other Columbia friends for school breaks there. They would take the Erie Lackawanna Railroad train to and from the city if they could not get a ride with someone who had a car.

The Marcus cottage was a dark brown shingled one-story frame house with white trim and a peaked roof. It was anything but imposing. It had a large stone fireplace and enough of the comforts of home to appeal to the students. There was also a garage the group used for overflow company in the summer. Located in the hills above the town, the property overlooked Olean as well as the nearby countryside. Tom loved the natural setting as well as the fellowship with his friends, especially in contrast to the congested environment of New York City. The group usually included some combination of Sy and his wife-to-be, Helen, Gerdy, Gibney, Reinhardt, Rice, Lax, Knight, and Tom, as well as Peggy Wells, Nancy Flagg, and Norma Prince.

Tom and his friends found the atmosphere there conducive to pursuing their creative interests. They brought their portable typewriters with them. Tom spent most of his time working on a novel, taking breaks for conversations. Often the discussions centered on philosophy, especially after meeting Bramachari.

Tom went with Lax over to the Bonaventure College library to check out books about Catholic theology and mysticism. Although he was Jewish, Lax had an intense interest in Catholicism. Initially Tom had a negative impression of the campus because of the number of crosses and statues. After his Baptism, Tom changed his attitude and eventually was also checking out books. They were both pursuing a search for the meaning of religion in their lives. One day Lax told Tom he should try to become a saint. Tom was struck by the suggestion, which seemed to him at that time an unattainable objective for almost anyone.

Merton was experiencing a disconnect in his spiritual life, attending Mass on Sunday, and following a secular academic life for the rest of the week. Eventually he determined he could only integrate his life into a unified meaningful whole by joining a religious order. He decided that living a spiritual life must take precedence over everything—even earning a living or writing.

Lax and Gerdy had been attending lectures given by Dan Walsh, who was on the faculty of Sacred Heart College at Manhattanville, and at that time came to Columbia twice a week to lecture on St. Thomas and Duns Scotus. The following year he offered a philosophy course at Columbia on Thomas Aquinas. Lax and Gerdy were impressed with his clarity of thought and believed Tom should meet him.

Dan was the stereotype of an Irishman, with a round face, robust laugh, and quick wit, expressed out of the side of his mouth. He was also a man of strong principle and deep faith with a broad knowledge of theology. Some of the top theologians were friends of his. He knew Gilson and Maritain personally.

Tom was happy to know Walsh and to be introduced to a new set of ideas and associations. Dan introduced Tom to Maritain in the spring of 1939. Tom was surprised to find him to be a stoop-shouldered and gentle man at their first meeting, possessing a brilliant understanding of Thomistic philosophy. It was the beginning of a relationship of great importance to Tom.

After attending Dan Walsh's talks for a time, Tom decided to consult him about his confusion over a potential religious vocation. It was September of 1939, and Dan had recently made a retreat at the Abbey of Gethsemani near Louisville, Kentucky. Dan recommended Tom also make a retreat there to see if he might want to consider joining the Trappists. Officially called the Order of Cistercians of the Strict Observance, the Trappists formed under the Benedictine Order. From his research, Tom thought the Trappists to be a sort of Marine Corps of the Benedictines, with a lifestyle too arduous for him.

Dan also recommended that Tom investigate the Franciscans, which had much more appeal for him. The Franciscans at St. Bonaventure College had just given Dan an honorary degree that spring, and Tom knew that Lax's family thought highly of the order. Walsh gave Tom a note to present to Father Edmund at the Franciscan monastery on Thirty-first Street in Manhattan. After several long talks, Tom thought the academic lifestyle would best suit him, and requested that Father Edmund recommend him to be accepted by the Order. Father Edmund told Tom he was welcome to enter the Order. The next class would be ten months away, in August 1940. Tom was disappointed at the delay. He asked to be accelerated on the basis of his philosophy studies with Dan Walsh, but Father Edmund was not encouraging about an exception to the policy.

To apply for admission, Tom had to obtain the necessary documents from his former pastor, Father Ford, at Corpus Christi Church where he was baptized. When Tom visited Father Ford, he advised Tom not to join a religious order, but instead to become a secular priest. This would give him a better opportunity for an assignment in a large city and more freedom than a priest in an order. But Tom was not looking for a big city life or the opportunity to be his own boss within a religious lifestyle.

Now that he lived on Perry Street, he was in St. Joseph's parish, so he asked Father Cassery at the rectory to bypass the paperwork with Father Ford. To obtain the baptismal certificate from Corpus Christi, Tom made another trip uptown. He felt fortunate that Father Ford was away so that he could get the document without further discussion. Tom did not want another discussion with Father Ford about his choice of religious groups. In fact, Father Ford had told Tom he might be happier remaining free in the world, living his religious vocation as the author of spiritual books. Tom knew that while waiting for the Franciscans he might be vulnerable to Father Ford's well-meaning advice, and he did not want to consider any alternative to the path he had chosen.

Tom noticed that his emotions had become increasingly fragile. He seemed easily knocked off balance by many only slightly unexpected circumstances that occurred. One day Tom found himself in a situation that clearly illustrated his current emotional state. He was in his apartment in the middle of a meditation about the concept of giving one's possessions to the poor. A man came to his door saying he had read Tom's review in *The New York Times* of a book written by one of Tom's former Columbia professors. Tom was frightened that anyone could get his address. The instant notoriety was unsettling. On top of that, the man seemed to be somewhat confused about his purpose for visiting Tom, and said he had no money to return home. Tom cheerfully gave him a dollar and the change in his pocket to get him out of his apartment and on his way as quickly as possible. After the man left, Tom found an additional dollar in his pocket that he had overlooked in his anxiety, and wondered if he should chase after the man to give it to him. He thought that would probably be in the Franciscan tradition, but decided his conscience did not require him to pursue his visitor.

Tom knew he had to be exposed to the public if his writing was to be effective, though he certainly did not relish the prospect. He decided to volunteer to speak to groups to get accustomed to some public exposure. Tom gave his first public lecture in May of 1939, on the subject of poetry, to the Columbia Writers Club. He was nervous and self-conscious, but he knew he needed the experience to prepare himself for his future. He would need employment to tide him over until his admission to the Franciscans. He decided to seek a teaching position to give him more experience before the public.

Later that summer Tom was excited about the arrival of the 1939 New York World's Fair, the Number One attraction of the year drawing visitors from everywhere. It was held out in Flushing Meadows, Queens, for two consecutive years. It became known by its symbolic trademark, the Trylon and Perisphere, a white obelisk and sphere. Gibney and Tom went together a number of times, only a ten-minute trip from midtown Manhattan. The Trylon was the height of an 18-story building. The Perisphere was twice the size of Radio City Music Hall. Television was introduced to America there. Women were buying nylon stockings—a new industry.

Tom particularly enjoyed the French pavilion, especially after his reaction to the one staged earlier in Chicago. For this fair there was an elegant glass-fronted hall with a curving flight of stairs overlooking a lagoon and a movie theater showing French travel pictures. Every country was represented at the 3½ mile long, mile-wide fair with the exception of Germany and China, Tom noted, who were excluded because of the war. The Fair stimulated Tom's imagination, especially the General Motors' Futurama exhibit forecasting how America would live in 1960, "The World of Tomorrow."

He met a nurse working at the fair by the name of Wilma Reardon, and they enjoyed long talks at the Fair's outdoor cafes on several occasions. Tom was particularly impressed by the Cuban Pavilion. He especially appreciated the ability of the flamenco dancers, based on his appreciation of dancing, obviously acquired from his mother. Following his father's example, Tom had the urge to travel when he was restless. He decided to visit Cuba the following year.

The first publication of Tom's work was on June 18, 1939, with a poem in *The New York Times*, "Fable for a War," along with an article announcing he had won the Mariana Griswold Van Rensselaer Award of $50. Recognition of any kind only whetted Tom's appetite for more success in publishing his work. He decided to discard his first attempt at a novel, "Straits of Dover," except for four pages. He would begin a second novel as his summer project.

For the summer of 1939 Tom sub-let his apartment to Sy Freedgood's wife and went to the Olean cottage to write with Rice, Lax, and Lax's brother-in-law, Marcus. It provided a place of rest and recuperation from the fast, competitive pace of the city so that he could recover the energy required to function in Manhattan. In Tom's imagination he saw the cottage as a sort of hermitage or ashram to the Hindus. He wrote his novel, *The Labyrinth*, that summer. Again he was unsuccessful in selling it to a publisher.

At this time Tom dropped "Feverel" as his middle name for reasons unexplained, and submitted his manuscripts to publishers in the name, Thomas James Merton, using his Confirmation name. Names and nicknames were a preoccupation for Tom at various key points in his life, but he never commented on his personal use of them.

Tom and his friends would sometimes take serious breaks from their creative effort. One night the Olean group went over to Bradford, to a travelling carnival. Tom played the slot machines and the group generally had too much to drink. They all lost money playing a game of chance that was rigged, but they had had too much to drink to realize it. On the way home, the police stopped them and gave them oversight protection from the possibility of a worse fate on the trip home.

Tom liked to drink what he called "good Scotch." Once when they were cooking out, Tom decided to marinate some hamburger meat with his Scotch, expecting this would enhance the burgers. The group immediately told him they tasted so bad they couldn't eat them. He then threw every one of them over the roof of the house like baseballs. The group had fun no matter what they were doing.

Tom often took walks in the woods near the cottage. He liked to climb the tree where Gibney had built a tree house to get away to read. Sometimes they would hitchhike to nearby cities for an outing, but most of the time they would sit around the cottage, have discussions about literary or philosophical subjects, or sing and dance to records. Tom sometimes played some African bongo drums that Benji had left at the cottage. Helen Freedgood danced.

While they all enjoyed the holiday getaway, they were also ready to return at the end of their break to the city in all its complexity and intellectual challenge.

They all loved the New York lifestyle. New York City was the world capital of publishing. By this time, the city had 350 publishers, 70 literary agents, 40 book clubs, 8 daily newspapers in English, and hundreds of weeklies, monthlies, and quarterlies. 7 ½ million New Yorkers supported this industry. Greenwich Village, "the Village," attracted writers and artists, political activists, nonconformists, and provided all-night bookstores. Radio City Music Hall was the biggest theatre in the world. Aspiring actors came to New York from everywhere to seek a role on Broadway. Times Square, the great white way, was termed "the world's epitome of splash." There were some 200 dance orchestras by 1940. People commonly took formal instruction to master the waltz, fox trot, rumba, samba, and jitterbug. Benny Goodman played regularly at the Penn Hotel.

Nightclubbing in Manhattan was routine for Tom and his friends on the weekends and school vacations when they were in the city. The Stork Club and other "smart" places were well known to the group, especially clubs with live bands and dance floors. Hollywood and Broadway stars frequented these clubs when they were in New York. Humphrey Bogart was a "regular" at the Stork Club.

In Harlem, a number of popular black musicians performed in the dance halls and nightclubs such as the Zebra Room of the Lenox Lounge. Regular performers included Louis Armstrong, Duke Ellington, Count Basie, Billie Holliday, and Ella Fitzgerald. Tom and his friends were attracted like magnets to the excitement of the creative music.

Tom was energized by the experience. His friends said he could have been a professional jazz pianist or a professional dancer. One of his favorite clubs was the circular bar at Nick's, with their three-piano jazz concerts. Tom played piano himself after hours when they went to El Chico's, a Latin club in Manhattan. Jazz has been called an envelope that the musician puts himself into. Tom seemed to find in jazz a place he could go to, to escape the world he coped with. His musical ability was extemporaneous. Once he entered a drum competition at one of the clubs he frequented, just for the fun of it. Apparently he never formally studied any type of music.

He liked to go dancing at El Chico's with Jinny Burton, who was an equal match for Tom on the dance floor. They would often swap partners with the two exhibition dancers there. This was the era of the exhibition ballroom dancer, highlighted in movies with stars such as Fred Astaire and his glamorous female partners as well as in live floor shows in nightclubs. In the 1940s many actresses were professional tap and ballroom dancers. Tom's proficiency on the piano and bongo drums and his ability to dance were remarkable, since he never apparently had formal training in any of them.

During this period Tom particularly enjoyed his friendship with Jinny Burton, a very attractive and highly animated girl with brown curly hair and brown eyes. The group considered her to be very cute as well as amusing. She became a close friend to Tom as well as a companion, and he respected her opinions. She urged him to plan his writing career above anything else. He once accompanied her to her home in Urbanna, Virginia, for a Labor Day weekend party in 1939. On this occasion, he developed a serious toothache from an impacted wisdom tooth that almost disabled him. Nevertheless, he participated in the Regatta on the Rappahannock River. By evening, "Mertie," as he was often called by his friends, was entertaining the group with his humor in the style of the old Alpha Delta Phi parties he attended in his first year at Columbia. His friends said he had the ability to make an audience laugh like a professional entertainer. He was quite impressed there with a girl called Missy. Nevertheless, Tom at this time was still serious about his life and was trying to find his way in a path that would be right for him. During this party, news reports announced that Britain was now in the war. Tom feared for his British relatives and friends, but tried to evade the thoughts that kept surfacing of the impending disaster that he knew would be inevitable.

On some of the frequent occasions when he was out with Jinny, Tom confided in her that he had a serious interest in a religious life. He appreciated her encouragement. Tom told some of his friends later that he had considered marriage as a vocation but thought it would be an impediment to his writing. Tom apparently never indicated an interest in marriage to any girl he dated. His closest friends were not sure whether he had ever been seriously in love, since he never discussed the depth of his feelings. He recorded in his journal, June 23, 1965, more than twenty years later, that Jinny was the kind of girl he thought he should have fallen in love with but didn't, and that she was one he loved with a love of companionship, not of passion.

Living in the city for Tom was confining, and he often went out for long walks, just as he did out at Olean. From his Greenwich Village apartment, he liked to walk over to the Chicken Dock and watch the ships load and unload their cargo. After so many trans-Atlantic trips, Tom was comfortable around large ships. He enjoyed just staring out across the water.

Once he was walking with Peggy Wells after a group get-together, and they ended up at the Chicken Dock before he walked her to the subway. He told Peggy he had been trying to formulate a plan for the future and thought he was going to be a priest and enter a monastery. She did not react to his statement, probably because they did not know each other very well. But Tom startled himself with this admission. This was the second time he found himself saying that he was planning to enter a monastery without knowing in advance that he was going to say it or even that he had in fact made such a decision. He felt it was almost like someone was speaking for him. It had happened exactly the same way a few years earlier in Italy after Tom visited the old Trappist monastery ruins.

Tom walked around the neighborhood aimlessly until dusk. He passed St. Francis Xavier Church, a Jesuit church on Sixteenth Street. He decided to enter the lower church in the basement when he saw the door was open. There he saw the round, white sacred host exhibited in a golden container on the altar, called a monstrance. The service was just concluding. The priest blessed the congregation with the sacred object he knew to be Jesus, his Lord. As Tom was blessed, he found himself praying, "make me a priest."

He was attending Mass every day, but did not restrict himself to his parish church. He enjoyed visiting a number of different churches, including Our Lady of Guadalupe Church, St. Patrick's Cathedral, Our Lady of Lourdes, Corpus Christi, and St. Francis of Assisi near Penn Station. At the same time he still enjoyed nightlife in Manhattan, along with his writing and studies.

Tom fortunately found an entrance level teaching position to tide him over financially until he could enter the monastery. Beginning in September 1939 he would be an Instructor at Columbia University's Extension Division of the School of Business Administration, teaching

English composition three nights a week. The same semester he would be able to continue with his regular course schedule toward a doctorate degree in English.

Tom was making the rounds trying to find a publisher for his two novels, *The Labyrinth* and a second novel he had now completed, *The Man in the Sycamore Tree*. The results of his efforts were consistent: he was rejected by Farrar and Rinehart, then Macmillan, Viking, Knopf, and Harcourt Brace. Not deterred, he tried Curtis Brown and there met Naomi Burton. She was the first to be interested in Tom's writing. She offered to represent him as his agent.

Naomi Burton was a young career woman, just four years older than Tom, who had just moved to New York from London to advance her career in the publishing business. She was an attractive girl with beautiful green-blue eyes much like Tom's, and short, curled brown hair. When Tom visited her office, he noticed she wore a plain and modest dress, and was serious to a fault. She presented herself to Tom as a person who could efficiently get the job done for him. He was ready to trust her with his work.

Tom thought this would be a step in the right direction, since he was not having any results representing himself directly to publishers. He believed he had perhaps been overconfident about his knowledge of how the New York publishing business worked, given his grandfather's position at Grosset and Dunlap, a major publisher of the time. Naomi was encouraging, but success continued to elude him.

Tom suffered continually from bad teeth. He had several of the worst ones pulled in December 1939. Tom's dental problems were a lifelong burden. He apparently never saw a dentist except in an emergency. Eventually he lost many of his teeth without replacing any of them.

After one semester he resigned his instructor position. In the coming term he would have to teach English grammar, which he disliked as a subject in itself. It was too rigid and unimaginative for him. On the other hand, he loved literature because it was storytelling and could be dramatic or amusing. It stimulated his imagination. He still had some credit remaining from his grant-in-aid, so he stayed on at Columbia as a student. He signed up for two classes, one a philosophy course with Dan Walsh.

The following April Tom had an emergency appendectomy. While he was confined to bed recuperating, he became restless again. He decided to plan another trip, this time as a sort of pilgrimage, to Cuba.

The following month, May 1940, he went by train south, sailing out of Miami to Havana.

Tom was surprised to find Havana an exciting experience, both culturally and spiritually. He wasn't prepared for the charm of the people. Their way of life resonated with him in a sort of linkage to his childhood experiences that he had lost touch with in recent years. The atmosphere was eclectic: luxury hotels, the docks and bay with its historic fort, children jumping around begging for tourists' dollars on the waterfront boulevard, exotic food and drinks, and sophisticated nightlife featuring professional Cuban dancers and bands. Mainline Hollywood stars like Fred Astaire and Buster Keaton performed in nightclubs. This was a devout Catholic city where large numbers of Cubans of all ages went to weekday Mass, and formal religious processions were common on feast days.

He wanted to visit the renowned Cuban shrine dedicated to Our Lady of Cobre. On the eastern end of Cuba, near Santiago, The Virgin of Charity, called in Cuba, *Virgen de la Caridad del Cobre*, was crowned by the Archbishop of Santiago in 1936. The stately Basilica del Cobre houses an elegant shrine of the mulatta virgin, Cuba's patroness. The statue is carved in wood, 18 inches tall, wearing a long cape and gown of golden fabric and golden crown. The statue is encased in glass on an ornate white marble pedestal above the altar. Behind the statue there is a small room with mementos donated by believers whose prayers were answered. Tom was impressed by the displayed baby clothes, crutches, handcuffs, photographs, and letters describing the favors received.

Tom said later that he had made promises to Our Lady there concerning his future devotion to her if she would help him to realize his vocation. He wrote a poem in her honor, believing it was the first real poem he had ever written. In Canaguey he visited a shrine dedicated to Our Lady of Solitude, another favorite devotion of his.

At the Church of St. Francis in Havana, Tom believed he had a religious experience. Like a flash of lightning, he felt as though he was lifted off his feet, into the presence of God and thousands of saints, with Heaven right in front of him. Tom was so amazed at this experience, he did not dare tell anyone about it. He only recorded it in his journal.

Tom did not know why Mary seemed to take on different identities, or different names at least, in the various locations where she appeared. Nevertheless, people seemed to get prayers answered and all sorts of favors granted when Mary was approached with faith under these names, Tom noted.

Later in his room at the Andino Hotel in Havana, he noticed that the Church of Our Lady of Carmel reflected in the mirror. This also seemed like an event of spiritual significance, but he could not understand what either of these occurrences meant. Thinking about it further, he remembered at Cambridge he had seen a painting of Mary appearing to Saint Simon Stock in 1251, giving him the small brown cloth square called the scapular, to be worn as a devotion to Our Lady of Mount Carmel.

Maybe he could bring something good out of his life, beginning from its lowest point at Cambridge. He left Cuba eagerly anticipating his life as a Franciscan, which was to begin very soon. Father Edmund had told him he would probably be assigned to a teaching position at St. Bonaventure College, with time for independent study and writing. He eagerly awaited the day he would enter the novitiate to prepare for his new life.

Tom decided to spend the summer at Olean until August when he would report to the Franciscans. En route to Olean in June, Tom routed his train trip through Ithaca to say good-bye to John Paul at Cornell before he would enter the monastery. He was happy to see John Paul again. His brother was as handsome as ever, with the same basic looks as Tom, but taller now than Tom and with thicker blonde hair and bluer eyes than Tom. John Paul had upsetting news for him, though. He would not be graduating after all. John Paul had secretly purchased a second-hand Buick and was taking flying lessons. He had not informed Uncle Harold of any of his activities since he knew that Harold would have never consented to any of his expenditures. John Paul was living the good life in the footsteps of his brother, and it was painful for Tom to witness it. Before Tom left, they attended a Mass together. John Paul expressed a general interest in the Catholic faith, but Tom did not assume there was any depth to his brother's sentiments.

Tom left his brother at Ithaca wondering when he would see him next and what would happen to his brother now that he had lost interest in his education. When Tom arrived at Olean, he found there was a larger number of guests than usual at the cottage. He went over to St. Bonaventure's and asked to stay there for a couple of weeks during the summer vacation to get the feel of the place as well as to get acquainted with the staff since he had been told he might well be teaching there eventually. He was to report to St. Anthony's novitiate in Paterson, New Jersey, for his orientation in August. He received an orientation packet in the mail from the Franciscan Order listing the articles he was to bring with him. To Tom's amazement, the list included an umbrella. This struck him as an unusually worldly concern, but nevertheless proceeded to get his possessions organized and to plan for disposition of the things he would discard before he left.

He enjoyed the quiet campus atmosphere and friendliness of the monks who had stayed there during the summer, but he was also happy to return after a few weeks to the Olean cottage to spend his remaining time. Daydreaming about his forthcoming life, he decided to choose a name in advance for himself. At St. Bonaventure's library he discovered that all the names that really appealed to him were already taken and that duplications were not allowed. He decided to choose the name, Frater John Spaniard, a name that he thought had a certain dash about it. He tried the name out on Sy for his reaction, which was positive. Later he reflected back on this experience as a foolish exercise on his part.

One evening at dusk Tom was out on the cottage grounds reading the Bible when he was struck by a passage from the Book of Job, ninth chapter. The stars were just coming out, and he felt as if he were receiving a message from the story. He was reading the passage about the ability of God to shut off the stars and about the wrath of God that is visited on sinners who try to justify themselves. Tom believed these words had a dark fire in them that made him feel burned and seared. He fell into a depression that he could not understand. A premonition of some adverse event would not leave him.

# Chapter 10

Tom's moods were a mirror of the times, melancholy and foreboding. World War II had intensified throughout much of Europe. He learned that his old friend, Bill Hemmings from Oakham days, had joined the Royal Air Force. He wondered if Bill would be killed in action. He dreaded seeing the headlines in *The New York Times* every morning, but could not resist checking to see what had been destroyed in the past day.

The summer of 1940 was a quiet one for Tom as well as his friends. Everyone was watching the advancement of the Nazis in Europe, wondering which country would be next. France fell in June. Tom wanted to spend his last days before entering the monastery at the Lax family cottage in Olean. He was hoping he could produce a manuscript that would finally appeal to a publisher before he left. To relax, he liked to lie in the hammock in the yard which overlooked a scenic valley. One day he had a surreal experience. He imagined that "enemy" troops were coming up and attacking him with guns or bayonets. He knew he was suffering from depression and hoped it would leave him when he entered the novitiate. He knew instinctively that he had no hope of shaking it before then.

Tom remembered his experience with the Nazis running him off the road in Italy when he was hiking there on a school break. The news from Europe grew steadily worse. Places where he and his family had lived and traveled, and cities where his friends and relatives currently lived, were being bombed and invaded, and there was no way he could learn what was happening to any of them. He feared the war would spread to the U.S. He could not even imagine the effect such a prospect would have on his life and that of his family.

Tom accurately foresaw the reality of what was to come. Some fifteen million people died in the five years of World War II before the Nazi surrender in Rheims, France. More people were killed than anyone even imagined at the time. The total destruction of Western Europe hung in the balance. Eventually Tom later learned that some of his friends from school days had indeed failed to survive the war in Europe.

Tom thought about his mother's love of pacifism and her devotion to the Quakers' philosophy. While Tom couldn't accept the organization, he nevertheless wholeheartedly agreed with the Quaker point of view. Tom had taken "the Oxford Pledge" in November 1934 while he was a student at Cambridge, promising he would never participate in any war.

After he became a Catholic, he researched the "just war theory," which goes back to the time of St. Augustine. The just-war doctrine is a reluctant moral justification for wars that become necessary under certain circumstances. The principle applies to both the initiation of war and the way war is conducted. To be considered "just," all other means for restoring peace must be impractical and ineffective and be seen as having a high degree of success in restoring a peaceful state. In addition, the arms used may not be expected to cause worse damage than the evils that would be eliminated. The target is never to be innocent people, but only those responsible for the war and their means to conduct war.

Tom was convinced that his pacifism was consistent with the tradition of his new-found faith. He would not oppose a war that was fought for a just cause, but Tom did not believe any of the wars in his lifetime had been justified. He recognized that technological advances required a new moral evaluation of the conduct of war. Traditionally, wars had always been fought between armies, with a secondary effect on civilian populations. The introduction of aerial warfare in World War I brought the issue of the morality of warfare under heated discussion because innocent people were killed *en masse* without their participation in the conflict. Before the 20th century, noncombatant immunity was not considered a significant issue.

It was only weeks before Tom was to enter the novitiate in New Jersey. He began to feel a growing torment about his past faults and mistakes. He thought he had experienced a false humility. He told himself that his repentance was a hell of pride and self-love. He began to think that he had presented an inaccurate picture of himself to Father Edmund and to Dan Walsh. If they had known what he was like before his conversion, he thought, they would probably have a much lower opinion of him.

*"I thought I would have been happily anticipating my coming life as a Franciscan. Instead, I began to have nagging doubts about the degree of my candor to them. I had presented myself as a job applicant, stressing the qualifications I had to offer the Order, especially my ability to write. I began*

*to have misgivings about my honesty and whether I should have painted a more realistic picture of my past life. Better to have it out in the open from the beginning, and not become a bad discovery later.*

*I decided to go back and make a full disclosure to Father Edmund of my indiscretions and weaknesses, and ensure that I was being accepted with eyes wide open. I made an appointment to see Father Edmund again. I still remember how the large amiable man changed his demeanor when I told him what I was there for.*

*I laid out my story trying to convey all the humility I could credibly express. I didn't eliminate the drinking, the parties, the girls, or the foolish handling of my trust fund.*

*For a minute there was a silence so intense it was quieter than in church. Then he asked me a few questions. He told me he would look into it and that I should come back tomorrow to see him.*

*I walked the streets in the neighborhood in the hot August sun for hours, not caring how miserable I felt. I wondered what Father Edmund would say and how he would treat me with this revelation. I thought maybe my lack of being forthcoming initially may seem a sign of basic dishonesty, and I would have to prepare myself to counter the argument. I thought I could handle the explanation and move toward a clearer understanding of my vocation and need for the penitential life I had selected. I hoped above all that the decision would ultimately be in Father Edmund's hands, and that I would not be turned down by someone I could not personally discuss it with.*

*The next day finally came, after a sleepless night, trying to read my favorite passages in the Bible to bolster my courage. Back in Father Edmund's office, I nervously awaited his answer. He coldly advised me to seek another vocation, that I was unsuitable for the priesthood. He asked me to withdraw my application for admission by a letter to the Provincial.*

*I felt I had turned to stone. My lips started agreeing with him, and I asked him to withdraw my name for the novitiate. Before I knew it, I was back out in the blistering sun walking nowhere, not sure what it all meant.*

*I wanted to go to Church and ask God for help. The nearest Church was Franciscan, so I kept walking. Finally, blocks later, I found the Church of the Capuchins across Seventh Avenue. It was open and I went in. I sat down and cried bitterly.*

*There was a priest hearing Confessions. I stood in line waiting what seemed like an endless time. Finally, I poured out my story to the priest in the confessional. Despite the small screened opening with the sliding wooden door that was my only view, the light was such that I could see he was a stern looking, bearded, thin priest with dark hair and sharp features. I couldn't help breaking down from the shock and sorrow I felt, like I had experienced the sudden death of a loved one. He sounded like a recording of Father Edmund, saying that as a recent convert, I was experiencing an emotional reaction to having been fired from the novitiate, and probably for good reason. He undoubtedly thought I was out of control and therefore emotionally unsuitable for a monastery or the priesthood. Furthermore, he told me I was insulting the sacrament of penance by going to confession over this matter and was wasting his time.*

*I walked the noisy streets of Manhattan until my legs ached. The Church that had so welcomed me, that had lured me into a false sense of security, offering me the home I could never have, now shut the door on me. It was too cruel. All my confidence about my new-found place in doing God's work was gone. I was cut loose and I was adrift again.*

*The rosary beads John Paul had given me for Christmas started to fall apart. I suppose I pressed them too tightly in my anxiety. I had to switch to a rosary I already had. It was made of small wooden beads painted black. I had bought it for 25 cents at a church sale.*

*I wanted to give God everything—all my energy and love—for the rest of my life. I could not understand why He didn't accept me."*

Shortly after Tom's rejection by the Franciscans, he accepted an invitation from Jinny Burton and her girlfriends, Lilly Reilly and Marge Walker, to help them fix up a cottage on a bluff above the Rappahannock River in Virginia. On the train ride down, Tom looked forward to being with Jinny, a friend who would not question why his plans for the priesthood had changed. In fact, Jinny assumed that Tom's desire to be a writer had overtaken his attraction to the religious life, and Tom did not otherwise enlighten her. In July, after about a week, Tom took the train back to New York, first to Douglaston, then to Olean for an extended stay, he hoped.

Walking down the main street in Olean a few days later, Tom unexpectedly ran into John Paul coming out of the Post Office recruiting station. Tom thought he was still in school in Ithaca. To Tom's amazement, he said he was investigating the possibility of joining the Naval Reserve. He was more relaxed than the last time Tom had seen him at Cornell, but he was obviously still as compulsive in his behavior.

John Paul had been under the financial supervision of Uncle Harold after his grandparents' death just as Tom had been, but with more direct control since he was younger and still a full-time student. He had recently been studying photography and thought he might pursue it as a career. Earlier he had been learning Russian, but had lost interest in it. He seemed to be living a carefree life while the good times still lasted. Since he was an American citizen, unlike Tom, he feared he would soon be drafted if the U.S. entered the war. He was hoping to avoid the infantry and to find an alternate military assignment. He really wanted to fly, but had already been turned down by the Army for flight school. Unlike Tom, John Paul had a car and loved to drive. He suggested the two of them drive over to Douglaston to visit the family. He and Tom talked it over as they drove.

In the fall John Paul appeared again in Olean. He had just parted company with the Naval Reserve after failing their test. He had been on a cruise to the West Indies and was released when the ship returned to the States. He had bought a new Buick convertible roadster with his pay and was on his way to Mexico and to Yucatan to photograph the Mayan temples. John Paul at this time was more at loose ends than Tom. He invited Tom to meet him in Mexico. Tom was noncommittal and even considered it, inasmuch as his future was only a question mark at this point. Later he decided not to make the trip.

Now that he had been rejected by the Franciscans, Tom realized that he had been happier in Olean than in any other place. He decided to apply to St. Bonaventure College to teach English literature in the fall term. He had heard that one of the faculty was being transferred. Tom hitchhiked over to the interview from the cottage instead of walking, as he and Lax usually did, since he was wearing his best blue suit.

The college's president, Father Thomas Plassman, was a large man with a very warm and kind manner. He was a long-time member of the Order of Friars Minor and had been President of St. Bonaventure since 1920. He and Tom both admired Columbia and Dan Walsh, and Tom was impressed to learn that Father Plassman was a noted Biblical scholar and authority on dogmatic theology. Father Plassman found Tom to be a suitable candidate for the teaching position and offered Tom a salary of $45. a month plus room and board. Tom believed he was fortunate to be so well employed. The Depression had recently limited the professional opportunities for young college graduates. Now a war would greatly reduce the number of students who could attend college as well as the number of positions needed to teach them.

Tom already had one friend on the faculty. Father Irenaeus had helped Tom to become familiar with the school library and had helped him to learn how to pray the Canonical Office. Father Irenaeus was a French native, a scholar, and known authority on Franciscan bibliography and history. Tom's friendship with Father Irenaeus lasted through his life. He familiarized Tom with the life of St. Therese and introduced him to the concept of a hermitage for leading a solitary life. Tom felt reassured that he would now be employed and housed at a place he liked and be near the Lax cottage as well.

Tom quickly gave up his apartment on Perry Street and moved into the dormitory room assigned to him in Devereux Hall. Luckily he had not yet given away his books, typewriter, and portable phonograph. He was still preoccupied with pursuing a religious vocation and decided to begin by experimenting with cutting back on habits he would have to forego in a religious life. He began with whiskey and cigarettes. Then he eliminated meat from his diet. So far, so good. He stopped going to movies, which he had always loved, and rid himself of some books and music he considered no longer appropriate for him. He was curious to see if he could live permanently without these habits. He found it surprisingly easy to discipline himself in their use. He began to read a number of daily prayers and religious devotions. Still, he felt incomplete. He was unsure what his life should really consist of, other than his writing.

Tom taught three sections of Sophomore level English literature. His students appreciated him, even those who were not in the least interested in literature. They came from backgrounds covering a wide spectrum and included seminarians, athletes, and boys from the nearby coal fields. In his night class, Tom also had women students, who were only admitted as part-time students since St. Bonaventure had been established as an all-male school. Years later Tom's students remembered his reading in Old English dialect and his ability to explain the levels of meaning in the works they studied. They also recalled that he often wore a tweed coat that didn't fit properly, chino pants, and saddleback shoes. He hitchhiked into town along with the students and always seemed to be carrying a notebook. At night in the dorm, he played his bongo drums and jazz records. The students used to call out to him from their rooms, "Professor Merton, cut out the bongo drums!"

He went to the library every day after class to check *The New York Times* for news about the war. He read carefully about the bombing of London and other English cities he loved. The news was progressively worse. One day there was an announcement that all students and secular staff had to register for the draft. A man in civilian clothing came to the campus to obtain their names. He gave a small white card to each man to carry as proof that he was registered for military service. Tom had no choice but to register.

Tom decided to become a member of the Franciscan Third Order, with the concurrence of Father Plassman. Tom thought a spiritual organization for people outside the religious life would be a good intermediate step for him, away from a secular life toward the religious way of life he still believed was meant for him. He now wore the scapular, a small brown cloth on a thin cord, under his shirt as a devotion. He also had purchased a breviary of four prayer books and was reading the same prayers that priests were required to read every day.

He decided to speak to Dan Walsh again about the Trappist Order to get more information. Now that he had been living a life of limited deprivation, he thought it might be possible for him to pursue a life devoid of modern comforts and pleasures. He hoped that Dan might dispel some of the bizarre stories he had heard about Trappists sleeping in coffins and praying for their death as something to be desired. He wanted to know if it were true that they were commonly former criminals or others of sordid background, because he could not imagine living the rest of his life among such an unsavory group of men. Dan persuaded Tom to apply for an Easter retreat at Gethsemani to see the Trappists for himself in their rural Kentucky facility.

Tom still thought he had a vocation to the priesthood in spite of his rejection by the Franciscans as well as the Capuchin priest he had spoken to in the confessional. He thought Dan Walsh's idea about the Trappists might have merit.

Tom wrote to the Abbot requesting a retreat at Gethsemani during his Holy Week break at school. After he mailed it, he did not completely look forward to the experience, thinking he could still back out at the last minute. On the other hand, travel adventures always offered hopes of solutions for Tom. He was ready for both at this point. A few days later, in the same mail, he received a note of acceptance for the retreat and a notice from the Draft Board to report for a physical exam.

Tom quickly composed a reply to the Board requesting the status of a partial Conscientious Objector asking for non-combatant service. He showed his letter to two priests at the college, Father Plassman and Father Gerald, then hitchhiked into Olean and had it notarized and mailed it. Not able to wait for a reply, Tom telephoned the local draft board for more information. He wanted to be able to get the Draft Board's decision regarding Conscientious Objector status before he made the trip to Gethsemani. It was explained that his request would only be dealt with after he completed the physical exam, which was not yet scheduled. After two long weeks of suspense, the Draft Board scheduled the exam. Several days later Tom received a notice that he was classified 1-B, not currently eligible for the draft due to lack of teeth. During the examination the doctor had told Tom this was probably going to be the Board's decision, but this was too important an outcome for Tom to take for granted.

On the Saturday before Easter weekend, Tom left by train for his retreat in a Spring downpour that did not stop until he reached Ohio. It was a long trip from Olean to Louisville, so he took a hotel room in Cincinnati for the weekend and crossed over the river to downtown Louisville on Monday morning. Then he took a local train for the 25-odd mile trip to Bardstown, the nearest town to Gethsemani. Tom once described it as "the old L & N," (Louisville and Nashville Railroad), "the modest train (that) could only be persuaded to crawl out of town under cover of darkness."

At that time Bardstown was a rural stop on the train route south of Louisville, and twelve miles from Gethsemani. Bardstown was a town that did not develop as planned. In anticipation of its future growth, the Church visualized Bardstown as a future center of Catholicism and built a cathedral as well as two other churches there. It was the first Catholic cathedral built west of the Allegheny Mountains. Gethsemani was located nearby, originally built by the Sisters of Loretto. It included a Catholic school, which the monastery later discontinued after a fire destroyed the classroom building. Bardstown, although small, retained its early charm as well as a considerable Protestant presence.

The monastery sent a local man to meet Tom's train and drive him to Gethsemani. He noted the landscape was poor and forlorn with sparse trees and few lights. His first view of the monastery was of the church steeple brightly reflecting the light of the full moon. At last he was at Notre Dame de Gethsemani, the Cistercians' tribute to the Mother of

God. When he arrived, Brother Matthew, the monk who opened the gate for him, asked Tom if he had come there to stay. Tom replied he could not stay because he had a job he had to return to. Brother Matthew said no more, so Tom thought the monk had accepted his response as a reasonable explanation.

ABBEY OF GETHSEMANE, NELSON COUNTY, NEAR BARDSTOWN, KY.

577-29

*View of the Abbey of Gethsemani as it looked when Merton first visited there. From an old postcard.*

# Chapter 11

The intensity of the monks' devotion stimulated Tom as nothing before had. The monks as a group performed deep body bows, worshipping the God they all believed was contained in the white wafer on the altar. They chanted medieval music Tom had never before heard. Like a tidal wave, it drowned him with its impact, he said later.

Tom threw himself into the daily schedule of the monastery, getting up at 1:30 a.m. for the first prayers of the day. At night he spent much of his sleeping time in maintaining a diary of his impressions of the day to take home with him. Before he realized it, he had pushed himself to near physical exhaustion.

He knew he liked the Trappist lifestyle, but he also began to think about the Carthusians. From what he had read about them, they seemed to offer more solitude than the Trappists. He knew, though, that it was impossible for him now. Carthusians had not yet come to the U.S. and the Carthusian groups in Europe were inaccessible to him because of the war.

By the fifth day of the retreat, Tom began to experience a reverse reaction to the monastery program. He had planned to observe all the physical restrictions practiced by the monks, even though retreatants were free to come and go as they pleased. The confinement began to make him feel frustrated and rebellious. He decided to go for a walk outside of the enclosure. He wondered why he found himself trying to justify his need to be free, and only to himself.

Soon Tom had to face the reality of returning to his own life. Before he left, he decided to visit the church and pray the Stations of the Cross, the fourteen stages of Christ's crucifixion. Tom had learned during the retreat that some believe that when praying the Stations, God might grant anything requested at the last station, when Christ is taken down from the cross to be buried. At the last station, impulsively Tom asked God to make him a Trappist.

The day after Easter he returned to St. Bonaventure's. He was out of the Court of the Queen of Heaven now, as he later described Gethsemani, and again in the world. He could not bear to think about trying to join the Trappists because the Franciscans and the priest in the Confessional had already told him that he was unsuitable for the priesthood. His rebellious reaction to the enclosure during the retreat reinforced his fear in asking the Trappists for a more liberal interpretation of his fitness for the religious life there.

He decided to sketch a picture that had come into his mind while he was at Gethsemani. It was an image of Christ standing in the background removing a veil from the face of a beautiful but sad young woman, who is staring off to the right of the picture. He titled the sketch, "Christ Unveils the Meaning of the Old Testament." The woman's face was haunting. He did not know where he got the idea for the picture—it just came to him suddenly, as if in a dream. He was pleased with his sketch when he finished it and decided to save it. If he had nothing else to remind him of Gethsemani, he would have this picture that had come to him when he was there.

In May of 1941 John Paul stopped by to see Tom on his way back from Mexico and Yucatan. He drove Tom in his now dusty Buick to the cottage at Olean, as they shared their recent experiences. John Paul asked about Tom's conversion to the Church. Tom told him how his new-found faith had brought genuine happiness into his life. John Paul expressed an interest in knowing more about the faith and thought maybe he would explore it for himself. Tom wondered if this would be another of John Paul's passing interests.

Tom then began writing his novel, *The Journal of My Escape from the Nazis*. His idea was to combine some of his experiences with a fictional overlay to disguise the connection. He believed this would be the novel that would sell.

During the summer session at St. Bonaventure's, Tom happened to attend a talk on campus given by Catherine de Hueck, a former Russian Baroness noted for her charity work in Harlem. Forced to leave Communist Russia, she first settled in Canada and founded an organization in 1930 to aid the deprived and to bring about social justice. Then she moved to New York and expanded her program. She established a place called Friendship House in New York City where people could come for help with basic needs. Later she expanded the program into other US cities. In Manhattan it was located on 135th Street and Lenox Avenue in two four-story buildings on both sides of the street, including apartments, a library, recreation room, and a clothing room. In her talk, she expressed her belief that white people practiced economic injustice to the Negroes, and that this had encouraged the spread of Communism. She said she believed that Catholics were hypocrites in social practice. Tom was impressed by her straightforward presentation. He spoke with her after her talk and again the following day before she left. He found himself volunteering to work for her on his next school break.

On August 15, 1941, Tom went to Friendship House for the first time. He dressed up for the event, even though there was a hard rain underway. He brought a bouquet of flowers for the Baroness, a habit he obviously had acquired in Europe. When he was asked by one of the Baroness' staff why he brought them, he said he thought the place would probably be drab and the people might appreciate something beautiful to look at, a remark that quickly embarrassed him. The Baroness was a large woman in every sense of the word. She took an immediate liking to Tom.

The Baroness accepted Tom's offer of voluntary service, so he re-rented his old room on West 114th Street for the two-to-three week vacation period. Now living at St. Bonaventure's, Tom could not possibly commute to Manhattan on a daily basis. He worked primarily in the Clothing Center and mopped floors. In the recreation room he supervised Ping-Pong games and played the piano for the group, who were mostly teens. He drew pictures for the children, one of the Blessed Mother. It was a pleasure to cheer these homeless visitors, but he soon found himself looking forward to the end of his time there.

For the Labor Day weekend in September, he planned to visit a second Trappist monastery. He wanted to see if his spiritual experience at Gethsemani was more than a single experience. He chose a Trappist monastery near by, Our Lady of the Valley near Providence, Rhode Island. He concluded at the end that this was not a second Gethsemani experience. He prayed for guidance, because he did not know what to do. He said later that the main thing he got out of this visit was a bad cold.

Tom corresponded with the Baroness after he returned to St. Bonaventure's for the fall term. She recommended he write in some medium for the poor. In fact, he thought it appropriate to consider some type of social action as a vocation. The Baroness invited him to join her on a permanent basis at Friendship House rather than continuing his teaching. Under the pressure he felt she put on him, he accepted her offer. He told her he promised to come to work for her at the end of the fall term.

Tom believed that this decision would end his uncertainty about his future. He was tired of researching the various religious orders in the library's *Catholic Encyclopedia* to find a religious group that would seem to be a fit for him. Still, he felt preoccupied about his future. He decided to pray over it during a retreat in November at the college during the Thanksgiving break.

# Chapter 12

Tom could not stand the uncertainty any longer. In desperation he decided to try something he had heard of but never dreamed he would resort to. He would ask God directly what to do by opening his Bible at random three times and putting his finger on a passage without looking at it.

The first time he tried it, he turned to the Old Testament, Book of Machabees. He eagerly read the passage, then the passage on the facing page. Tom could not relate to anything he read on either side. He tried a second time. Maybe he did not ask properly for the message, he thought.

He was shocked at what he found. He had turned to the New Testament, Gospel of Luke, Chapter One, verse 20, and touched the passage, "you shall be silent" spoken by the Archangel Gabriel to Zachary, destined to be the father of John the Baptist, who questioned that his wife Elizabeth could bear a child in her old age. As the story goes, Zachary was unable to speak until the eighth day after the baby's birth when he wrote on a tablet that the child would be called John, the name that the Archangel Gabriel had told him.

Tom felt he was almost struck dumb himself. Tom tried a third time and got no message from the passage he selected. He suddenly realized that this was an act of insolence and that he should not have done such a daring thing. Now he would be obliged to act on it. He had feared the silent life of a Trappist, not sure he could live up to it. It seemed now he would have to pursue it. Tom began to see that his interest in the Baroness' work was really only an attempt to substitute for the vocation he had to the priesthood.

Tom thought about how definite John Paul had been about what he wanted to do. He was determined to fly planes, in or out of war. In September John Paul had gone to Toronto to enlist in the Royal Canadian Air Force. Tom put John Paul in his prayers under the care of Saint Therese of Lisieux, called the Little Flower. He had recently become devoted to her and often visited her shrine on the campus.

Tom still felt uncertain about his future, including his ability to sell his writing. Reading over a short story he had written in January 1941, he critiqued it in his journal as so dull it was almost a mortal sin, adding that "in hell, such stories are read aloud to the damned ... ."

Tom's yearning for a religious vocation persisted. He had developed a friendship with Father Philotheus who also lived in the college dormitory. Tom found him to be warm, personable, and scholarly. Father Philotheus, like Father Plassman, a German native and recognized scholar in philosophy as well as science, was much closer to Tom's age. Although not outgoing, he seemed very approachable. He was just the one to shed light on Tom's situation. He decided one evening to consult him about the question of impediments to joining the priesthood.

When Tom came to the door of Father Philotheus' dorm room, he suddenly felt some kind of force or energy stopping him from knocking. He decided to walk out to the Grove and say a prayer to the Little Flower, St. Therese. He found himself promising to be her monk if she could help him know what to do to be accepted. Then, in his imagination, he heard the bell in the tower of Gethsemani's chapel ringing just as he had heard it when he was there. He realized it was exactly the time for Compline. The bell would have actually been ringing when he thought he had heard it!

Tom immediately walked back to the dorm and found Father Philotheus in the Friars' common room. At Tom's request, they went to the priest's room where Tom recited his sad story. Father Philotheus did not react negatively to Tom's previous experiences. He gave Tom the answer he had hoped for. He must have perceived Tom's religious vocation that could not be dismissed. Tom decided to go again to Gethsemani on the Christmas break to see if he would be considered eligible to join there.

The Grove where Tom prayed was a secluded place on the campus. It held a shrine to Our Lady of Lourdes as well as the small shrine to St. Therese. With his decision Tom returned to the Grove to give thanks for this turning point in his life, relieved at last of the uncertainty. He prayed at the small red brick shrine that sheltered the statue of St. Therese with its overhanging barrel tile roof protecting her image. He would not forget her. He asked her also to protect John Paul, who was now in pilot training in Canada.

Tom immediately wrote to the Abbot at Gethsemani, asking for permission to come down there on December 18. Before he could receive a reply, on December 1 the mail brought Tom an order from the Draft Board to appear for a second physical examination. He called the local board to ask why, and he was told the restriction on the recruits' teeth had been relaxed and he would probably now be reclassified 1-A. That meant he would be immediately draftable. Tom now realized there was no possibility of either staying at St. Bonaventure's as an instructor or going to Harlem to work at Friendship House. If Gethsemani accepted him, he would not be drafted. If they turned him down, he would accept Army service. But he was determined he would not kill.

Tom wrote to the monastery again, asking to come before December 18. He wrote to the Draft Board, explaining his situation, and asking for a delay. A letter from the Draft Board notified him that a delay of one month was granted before he must have another medical examination. In the meanwhile, Tom had written to the Franciscans and asked for his documents to be returned so he could send them to Gethsemani.

He started giving away his books, manuscripts, and clothing. He gave all but five of his books to the St. Bonaventure College library. He sent a box of clothes to Mary Jerdo at Friendship House, including a favorite navy blue turtleneck sweater he had been wearing since his time at Oakham.

Father Plassman excused Tom from the remaining weeks of the semester, redistributing his classes to other faculty members. He gave Tom an enthusiastic letter of recommendation to take to the Abbot at Gethsemani and a bonus check to pay for his expenses. Tom closed his bank account and gave the remaining funds from his grandfather's estate, $167.43, to the poor.

On December 7, Japan attacked Pearl Harbor and President Roosevelt declared war on Japan. Tom wrote letters to Lax, the Baroness, and Uncle Harold and Aunt Elsie, and sent postcards to some of his friends. On December 10, Tom left for Gethsemani. He boarded the train on another desolate, rainy day. If he were not accepted at Gethsemani, he determined he would go to the Army, but after the war he would return to Gethsemani and ask for permission to stay.

The next day Tom arrived at a monastery that was stark in appearance compared to his memories from his first visit. He entered the gate that was still quite familiar, under the arch inscribed with the words, "Pax Intrantibus," or "peace to those who enter." Again Brother Matthew, the gatekeeper, met him. Tom told him that this time he would stay. The old monk told Tom he had prayed for him, that it would be so.

The Abbot, Frederic Dunne, accepted Tom on December 13. But first Tom had a preliminary discussion with Father Robert, Master of Novices, to explain his concerns. On February 21, 1942, he was accepted as a choir monk. This was a group who usually studied for the priesthood after their initial training. Being assigned to this group meant there had been no reason found why he could not eventually become a priest.

His personal possessions were put away. They would not be disposed of until he would make a profession of solemn vows at a time to be determined much later. Tom prepared a box for the few personal things he had brought with him. On a piece of paper he wrote his new name in Latin, "Frater Maria Ludovicus," the name that the Abbot gave him. This name only would be used by the monastery to record his arrival and eventual departure, whether in life or in death. In English his name translated to Brother M. Louis Merton, O.C.S.O., in honor of the sainted King of France. The M initial was given to all Trappist monks, in honor of Mary, their patroness. Tom later discovered that the Abbot sometimes chose French saints to name his novices since the Trappists were a French order.

Tom was happy for the Abbot's choice of this name for him, although he thought he would not have chosen it himself. He remembered he had occasionally prayed and lit candles before the statue of St. Louis in St. Patrick's Cathedral in Manhattan. He wondered at the coincidence.

Tom and two other novices were escorted into the Chapter Room wearing their own clothing. Father Abbot sat on the hard wood chair they called his "throne," a term that was a remnant of medieval times. Tom knelt before the Abbot on the monastery's stone floor and kissed his ring as a sign of pledged obedience. He and the other two novices made their simple profession and received the clothing they would wear from that day forward. Tom put on the clothing, or "habit," worn by the monks for centuries. Then his head was shaved to conform to the almost bald appearance of all the monks.

Tom could reflect that the change in clothes represented another metamorphosis for him, hopefully his last. As a boy in New York, he was an American child who still sang the French songs of his earlier years. Soon he was transformed into a French youth with an American background. Then he was a British student in a Peter Pan collared suit. During his teen years he wore the clothing of a young English gentleman, conversant in multiple languages in his travels as well. Later again in New York, he was an American college student and professor. Now he was exchanging it all for the French medieval clothing that was his ultimate transformation. He thought that this change required more courage than all the previous ones put together.

# BOOK TWO

"It would be an immense pleasure and relief to me if I simply did not exist for the world at large. Of course I just can't disappear like that now—I have a sort of responsibility and mean to fulfill it ... ."

Merton's letter to J. Laughlin, May 1, 1950

# Chapter 13

Tom Merton buried his past identities to blend into the uniform appearance and behavior of his new group. He was careful to observe all of the instructions given him about how everything was to be done, so that he would be accepted by the group and look as inconspicuous as possible. He assumed that the "high" he had experienced during his Easter retreat would return as soon as he became acclimated to the routine. It was not long, though, before he discovered how different it was to be on the inside of the monastery than as a visitor on the outside.

The tightly managed routine of work, study, and prayer kept even a self-disciplined man like Merton occupied. He soon found himself feeling comfortable in the daily life of the monastery. The quiet he had so dreaded actually had an appeal, since he did not know any of the monks and knew he could have never handled getting acquainted with so many people at one time. He assumed he probably would never know many of them since there was no conversation allowed. This was a lifestyle he could really appreciate. The quiet open landscape and prescribed schedule reminded him of his days at Montauban and Oakham as well as his most recent time at Olean. In fact, he found he liked the structured day because it freed him from his tendency to drift off course, which had caused him difficulty earlier.

The Trappist program is one that involves a life of work, prayer, and formal worship. A single leader manages the monastery and has complete authority over all aspects of the life and conduct of monks and their facility. His title is Abbot, and the monks address him as Dom, which translates literally as "lord" and indicates his absolute authority over the group.

Dom Frederic was a dynamic, no-nonsense man of 67 years with a bad heart at the time Merton arrived. He had the distinction of being the first native-born American Abbot in the Cistercian Order. He was proud of the role he had played in some fifty years of the Order's history. He ran his monastery like a benevolent dictator, and his monks loved him like a father.

Privileges at the monastery were granted in successive stages of the monks' development. First there was the limitation on the access to the monastery property. During the first seven years, a monk was not allowed to leave the strict enclosure other than to work out in the fields. As a choir novice, Merton was allowed only in the monastery church, the novitiate scriptorium, or library, with its 30 to 40 desks and wood stools, the novitiate chapel, and its even smaller triangular garden, and of course, the community sleeping area, dining room, and bathroom.

Merton's diet was even more limited than his space. No eggs, fish, or meat were ever served, except to those who were sick in the dispensary. The monks generally considered the food to be meager, plain, and boring. Once during Lent, the period before Easter, sweet potatoes were served on 39 of the 40 days. Choir monks, including Merton, fasted during Lent and the four weeks of Advent, taking only one meal a day.

The monastery was largely self-sustaining. The monks operated a full-scale farm, with crops and livestock, to provide all their food and most of their other basic needs. Horses were used exclusively for farm work when Merton entered Gethsemani. Tractors were only added about eight years after Merton arrived. The monks provided the revenue to pay for their other requirements by selling the tobacco and cheese that they produced.

The monastery maintained its own post office, designated Trappist, Kentucky. In fact, the monastery was like a self-contained town. It included carpentry, electrical and plumbing shops, shoemaking and clothing workrooms, classrooms, accounting and secretarial facilities, a bakery, photographic studio, printing shop, bookstore and gift shop, library, infirmary, and guest house.

Monks seldom left the grounds, except for serious medical problems or to conduct the monastery's business. In contrast, the Abbot traveled to Citeaux, France, the Order's mother-house for the Cistercian Order worldwide, to attend regularly scheduled meetings. Occasionally he visited other monasteries and traveled to inspect properties he was considering for acquisition to establish a new monastery. Medical and dental care were usually provided on-site by doctors and dentists who were brought in as needed. One or more monks ran a full time dispensary. They administered drugs prescribed by a visiting physician. The facility was also used to house elderly monks who were seriously incapacitated and near death as well as for monks who required temporary care, such as in flu outbreaks and accidents around the property or for post-operative recuperation after hospitalization.

The novices' day was more rigorously structured than for the rest of the group. There were periods of instruction, called conferences, four or five times a week, for 40 minutes. They also had lessons in singing the Latin music, or chant. Church services for the entire group who could attend comprised about one-third of the day, either for Mass or saying the offices, the prescribed prayers said by all religious worldwide. The novices went out to the woods or fields to work every day, walking in single file, usually to chop or split wood for the old heating system then in place and to help with the farm. Their contact with professed monks, who had already taken vows, was limited to having their confessions heard. The novices met weekly with the Master of Novices to discuss individual spiritual concerns. Meetings with the Abbot were rare.

Merton never expected to see the outside world again, for all practical purposes. At that time, when monks took their final vows, they expected to stay within the confines of the monastery for the rest of their lives. They would be buried there, next to the church, without a coffin. Merton was confident that this regimen would be enough to satisfy him for the rest of his life. It was a paradox that such confinement would provide the freedom he so desired.

Merton thought that the peace he would find at Gethsemani would provide a proper substitute for his writing ambitions. Adopting the penitential lifestyle was a sacrifice he was willing to make. Soon he found that the "highs" he expected to receive to carry him through his life of deprivation did not occur very often. He discovered that his greatest pleasure was in the structure of his day, even the chores and daily programs, and the privacy he was able to maintain in keeping his thoughts to himself.

Merton soon found that he was not able to suppress his creative spirit. He asked his Master of Novices for permission to compose a little poetry. His instructor agreed, provided it occurred only on his own time. After a while he asked Merton to let him read what he was writing. He noted that there was no interference in Merton's daily activities, so could see no conflict with his religious vocation. In fact, he was impressed with the piety that Merton expressed in his poems.

Soon Merton began to feel the urge to spend more time writing. Jotting down short verses of poetry only seemed to stimulate a greater need to express himself through his writing. He decided to ask the

Abbot to allow him to write some spiritual material for the monastery. To Merton's disappointment, Dom Frederic summarily told Merton he already had another writer who in fact was nationally published.

This writer was Father Raymond Flanagan, an Irishman a few years older than Merton, an outspoken and down to earth old-timer as different from Merton as could be imagined. He was an ex-Jesuit and held strictly conservative views. In Chapter meetings, the only occasion when all of the monks interacted, he would react forcefully when any monk differed with his point of view. Merton checked in the novitiate library for Father Raymond's publications. He assumed he had not heard of him because of his own limited knowledge of Catholic literature. He quickly found some of Father Raymond's books. A quick scanning told him the story.

Father Raymond had published a number of inspirational books and pamphlets with a sort of religious fervor that had popular appeal. Merton immediately realized that Raymond would be no competition for him. In checking with some of the older monks, Merton learned that Father Raymond's best-selling book was called *The Man Who Got Even With God*. Published in 1941, it is the story of a Trappist, Brother Joachim, the first American to enter Gethsemani. Joachim had been a Texas cowboy before he entered the monastery in 1885. At that time all the monks had emigrated from France to Kentucky. Brother Joachim was also known in the monastery for his temper. Merton thought to himself that Father Raymond's portrayal of Joachim was "the best description of the author." His blunt directness endeared him to some of the old-timers, but turned off many others, including Merton, who thought his manner was brash.

Father Raymond's writing style was simple and pious, and his output was prolific. He produced some 20 books and many more pamphlets. The monastery published his pamphlets, many anonymously, including "Running Off With God," "A Trappist Writes to Mothers Whose Sons Are in the Service," and "Father, You Are Leading a Dangerous Life." Father Raymond's books and pamphlets were pitched at a level that would appeal to a wide audience, primarily to stimulate conversions to the Church and recruits for the monastery.

Some of Father Raymond's readers did become prospective novices, and his mail brought news of some conversions or decisions to return to the Church. The monastery benefited from an unknown amount of revenue from Father Raymond's publications, which more than offset the cost of printing his pamphlets.

Merton was not intimidated by Father Raymond's status as the monastery's resident writer. His desire to write at this point was mostly a dream, he had to admit to himself. His previous efforts had brought only a few published poems and a lot of rejection slips from publishers, but he believed that with his determination, and some Divine help, he could succeed in getting his message out to readers.

Soon Merton learned that Dom Frederic was interested in writing and books himself, even though the Trappist Order did not have a tradition of engaging in or even encouraging publishing. His father had been in the publishing business in Zanesville, Ohio, where Sam Jenkins, Merton's grandfather, had originally operated a bookstore, by coincidence. Dom Frederic worked as a printer and bookbinder before he entered Gethsemani in 1894 at the age of 20. His father later joined him there as a lay-brother oblate and had brought along his small hand printing press and some type and bookbinding equipment with him.

Eventually Dom Frederic agreed to Merton's persistent requests to write, but only on subjects that he prescribed. These consisted of lives of saints and noted Trappists, aspects of the religious life, and texts to accompany books of photographs about the monastery. The Abbot also gave Merton assignments to translate various French and Latin documents into English. Merton was excited about the prospect of writing, but soon found the Abbot's assignments confining and unimaginative. The subjects themselves were only exciting to him as a learning experience because they filled in many of the blanks in his knowledge of church history. After all, it was his insatiable intellectual curiosity that brought about his spiritual journey all the way from Freud to Saint Augustine.

Merton was allowed to type his assigned work in a second library that he shared with another monk, Father Anthony Chassagne, who worked exclusively on translations. Once Merton was told to share the typewriter Father Raymond used while the one he had been using was being repaired. He did not sense any agreement on the part of Father Raymond to this arrangement, but decided to avoid any interaction with him.

Merton began to wonder if his desire to write might be a hindrance to his spiritual development. Dom Frederic allayed his doubts by placing him under obedience and his personal direction, therefore eliminating

Merton's guilt while controlling the subject matter for his own purposes. Merton continued to write poetry in his spare time, mostly composing it in his head and then writing it down later when he had the opportunity. In 1944, when Merton received his first offer from a publisher, Dom Frederic was surprised to find it would be a collection of thirty of his poems. The Abbot did not object, though, since he saw that it would bring in much-needed revenue for the monastery. With this success, Merton was convinced that he would eventually persuade Dom Frederic to allow him to select his own subjects for larger projects.

All the novices were given a small box in the novitiate scriptorium to keep their letters and library books. The monks were allotted only twenty minutes a week to select library books, which had to be pre-approved by the Novice Master. This required Merton to thoughtfully prepare in advance for alternative selections to maximize his use of the allotted time in case his first choice was not available. Then he could spend the remainder of the time looking at other books he might read in future weeks. This procedure was one of the most challenging disciplines Merton experienced.

Throughout the monastery there was little privacy or provision for solitude. The dormitories contained a small partitioned area for each monk. The beds were like wooden benches with a straw pallet and bolster, and a curtain of greenish brown fabric matching the bed cover enclosed the area. The monks were only allowed to occupy their beds during sleeping hours, except during the summer when they were given one additional hour of bed rest at the meridienne, in the heat of the day.

Dressing in the clothing of a Trappist monk was much like putting on a costume. The winter clothing consisted of a white robe, a long sleeve floor-length gown. It was covered by a sleeveless sort of long apron hanging from the shoulders, called a scapular, white for novices, black for the professed monks, with an attached hood. In addition, they wore a white cowl, or hooded robe in winter. Traditionally, Trappists were called White Monks because of the lack of color in their robes. They were made of a coarse wool and brought the weight of the winter outfit to about twenty pounds.

Professed monks wore a black leather belt over the scapular, anchoring it in place. Novices wore a white cloth band until they took their vows. Their underwear consisted of a long denim shirt, long drawers tied around the legs, stockings that tied to the drawers that stopped at the heel, and socks that fit like slippers. The drawers, stockings, and socks were all made of heavy duck cloth. Shoes were made at the monastery and were oversized to fit over the socks. They were much like military boots, often metal-shod.

The summer outfit was lighter. The shirts were a thin flannel, but as long as the winter shirts. The robe was of duck cloth, the scapular and cowl of cotton. Work clothes were a three-quarter length denim blouse, worn on top of the robe in winter. Straw hats with curled brims were worn in the fields for protection from the hot Kentucky sun.

The monks did not have nightclothes. Novices slept in the same clothing they wore all day. Professed monks, who had already made their vows, had a night habit or robe, with shorter length and sleeves than their daytime robe.

Wearing this clothing brought an additional penance: it was seldom clean. In winter, underwear was changed only every two weeks. The winter outer garments were worn from day of issue, December 8 each year, to Easter, the following spring, and were washed once a month. The summer underwear was changed twice a week, but the outer garments were worn from Easter to the following December 8 and were also washed only once a month.

Merton's major complaint was the temperature maintained in the facilities. The monastery was short of funds, and the heating system was old and inadequate. There was no cooling system. The climate in central Kentucky was punishing and made the medieval clothing adding an almost unbearable burden. In winter it was not unusual for the monks to suffer from bad colds and the flu or to faint sometimes in the summer heat. The clothing had all been prescribed by the Order's headquarters in France for uniform application at all monasteries without considering the Kentucky climate. It was not as cool in summer months as it usually was in France.

There were no bathtubs. The monastery provided only a single shower for professed monks to share, one for lay brothers, and one for novices. They were kept locked, to be used only with permission. Hot water was available only on Wednesdays and Saturdays. The bathroom, called the Grand Parlor, was used by all the community, and included a few tin cups and containers of bicarbonate of soda to share for brushing their teeth. Sharing these cups probably caused the rapid spread of colds and flu in the monastery.

All monks were required to have shaved heads, leaving a very thin fringe of hair like a sort of halo around the back, tonsured in the me-

dieval monastic style. Haircuts to maintain this style were given once
a month on Wednesdays and Saturdays to take advantage of the hot
water, half of the group at a time. The barbers were selected from the
entire group and received no training.

Life at Gethsemani was observed following the sixth-century Rule of
St. Benedict, interpreted by the Cistercian Usage in the eleventh century
and more strictly enforced in the seventeenth century by reforms begun
by Armand-Jean de Rance, the Abbot of La Trappe in France. Over
time many of the medieval hardships were relaxed from the original
prescriptions, but when Dom Frederic became the Abbot at Gethsemani,
he enforced the Rule with all its austerity. He eliminated the two fried
eggs previously allowed for Easter Sunday. He discontinued the wine
or cider that was universally permitted by the Order and replaced it
with a drink of barley or soybeans that he called coffee. It was served in
rusty tin cans. He eliminated the snuff that had previously been allowed,
along with the spittoons, which disappointed the older monks.

There were a number of restrictions involving the serving of food.
For monks assigned to serve the table, their food portion was reduced
if they spilled any food. Monks were reluctant to be rotated through
this assignment. Sometimes a monk would simply take from another
monk's place an item that may have run out before his place was served,
substituting what he had been given to the other monk's place. The
question was whether or not the put-upon monk would overlook the
violation as an act of charity toward the offender without reporting it
or whether he would wait for a payback opportunity.

One of the most significant Rules of St. Benedict was the Rule of
Silence. Instead of speech, the monks were required to use the Trappist
sign language, consisting of some 400 signs that slightly resemble those
used in sign language for the deaf. The signs were limited to provide
only for the expression of the monks' basic needs at times when they
were not allowed to speak. Normal speech was used in meetings, classes,
and in private conferences with superiors, in Confessions, and of course
in emergencies.

Merton mastered these signs in record time and enjoyed using his
imagination to invent some of his own. Not surprisingly, many of the
ideas Merton wanted to convey had no preordained sign, and in fact
it challenged him to devise extrapolations from these signs and to see
whether the monk he was addressing could read his message. Soon
the monks who shared Merton's sense of humor enjoyed exchanges

of the expanded sign language with him, although the monastery in fact had a rule against any use of sign language that was unnecessary. The practice reminded Merton of the word games he had played with his old group at Columbia. He found the whole procedure a welcome diversion, taking his old game to a new level.

There was no prohibition in speaking at the Abbot's regular meetings. To hold these meetings, all Trappist monasteries were constructed with a large Chapter Room, located off to one side of the church. At these meetings, the Abbot was seated on his special chair, called by tradition the throne, placed in the center of one wall. The monks sat on long wooden benches around the walls of the room, with the most senior monk seated nearest the Abbot. This actually gave a graphic picture to each monk of the passage of time, a reminder that if he did not leave the Order, as his position moved closer to the Abbot, he could see his own time nearing a natural end there.

At Chapter meetings, any monk could publicly criticize, or proclaim, a fellow monk for some fault he had committed in the opinion of the monk bringing the charge. This was called the Chapter of Faults. A monk could also proclaim himself, which was quite obviously not a common occurrence. A monk was not allowed to proclaim another who had just proclaimed him. He would have to wait until the next Chapter meeting to do that, so that he would have ample time to reconsider his decision.

The express purpose of this procedure was to humiliate the guilty party. The Abbot would give others an opportunity to comment and would then adjudicate the charge and either decide an appropriate punishment or merely admonish the charged monk. The penance could be perfunctory, such as reciting one "Our Father" or a few extra prayers, or could really be humiliating if the Abbot viewed the behavior to be a problem of pride. The monk being accused was required to take a demeaning position, up on his toes but with his knuckles to the ground while being charged. While they performed their penance, the monks were required to wear their hoods to exhibit a sign of shame. The offense might be anything from improper use of equipment to overusing the sign language.

The Trappists were not the only religious order to administer some form of fraternal correction to assist an individual in recognizing his faults. The purpose was to gain greater spiritual insight, particularly when one apparently was not aware of his faults. Going to Chapter meetings, a monk never knew whether he would be entertained by another monk's mistakes, or whether he himself might be humiliated, or even falsely accused. The silence and sign language could trigger misjudgment and animosity between two monks. The confinement of the group magnified their emotions and often exaggerated the significance of the behavior they proclaimed.

The Abbot had to find a resolution that satisfied both sides of any controversy. The Abbot knew that unresolved disagreements could plant seeds of discontent that might eventually lead to a general dissatisfaction with the monastic life. Ultimately this could lead to the destruction of the group.

Merton once admitted that he had been proclaimed for not turning in his outdoor shoes for repair when there were holes in his soles. This was considered a problem because it could cause the monk who repaired shoes to do more work later if the repair were delayed, and might require the shoes to be replaced sooner. Obviously Merton did not want to give up the use of his only shoes, even temporarily. Merton did not say what punishment he had received for this offense.

Many of the monks considered the Abbot's worst punishment to be the closet of shame. This was an old practice that was used for total control of the group, like primary school punishment. For some monks, like Merton, the public humiliation of having the complaint presented to the entire group was painful enough. Although the system was designed to provide a method for putting disagreements to rest and discouraging any continuation of a problem, it often had the opposite effect, because individual differences carried over from one incident to another and fostered grudges.

Merton's behavior did not always endear him to his fellow monks. He heard about it in the regular meetings of the Chapter of Faults. One time Merton's penance was to sit on the floor in the refectory and beg for his lunch and to eat it while seated there. Before ordination to the priesthood, he was required to beg for his food. By custom, all monks went through this initiation rite to remind them of their continued need for humility. Merton had to go before each monk in the refectory, sitting with their backs against the wall, on his knees and carrying a large bowl. Each monk would spoon some of his dinner into Merton's outstretched bowl. Dom James reported later that Merton showed unusual humility before the group when he performed this penance.

Merton also had to perform another humiliating task before he could
be ordained, by Cistercian custom. He had to kiss the feet of all the other
monks seated at the refectory tables, get down on his knees and kiss the
outstretched shoe. Sometimes the monks covered their shoe with their
robe to protect the novice, but often did not. In Merton's case this had to
be performed in two successive days to provide sufficient time because
of the size of the group. Dom James said later that Merton performed
this penance with a smile, because of his high spirits in anticipating his
acceptance to the priesthood. He was living up to Dom James' motto,
doing things for Jesus "with a smile."

Years later, Merton was on the other side of the discipline. As Master
of Novices he was required to proclaim a novice, if appropriate, during
his conferences. He would simply require the novice to say an extra
prayer or two for disrupting the class or for not paying attention. On
the other hand, the procedure also allowed the novice to proclaim the
Master of Novices, provided it was done in a private discussion. The
entire system gradually fell into disuse over time, but officially remained
in effect until the 1960's, when it was abolished by the Order.

The monks usually communicated by facial gestures as well as signing unless they were wearing their hoods up en route to the lavatory.
Unfortunately they could be easily misunderstood due to a lack of any
way to insure clarity. There was also a rule to avoid forming a Particular
Friendship, or close association with another monk. The belief was that
this might lead to a homosexual relationship. It was also intended to
keep all the monks as one integral group, eliminating both paring off
and forming cliques.

Another medieval practice was the use of a small whip of knotted cord,
called the discipline. Each monk had one hung on a hook in his cell, or
bedroom area. Every Friday after Chapter, the monks retired to their cells
in procession and gave themselves self-inflicted strokes with the cord for
the duration of the time it took them to say the "Our Father" or the 21
verses of the 50th Psalm, "Have mercy on me, Lord ... ." Exceptions to
the ritual only occurred at the Easter season and on major feasts when
they fell on a Friday. With the cord in each cell, the monk could use it
whenever he might wish to administer such self-discipline.

Merton did not require the adjustment to monastic practice that was
necessary for others. He fell into the routine even though it was more
rigid than either his French or English boarding school regimens. He said
once that he felt he had grown up in dormitories. Some of the novices

found this medieval program to be more restrictive than they could tolerate and soon left. Even some of the recent war veterans described the sensory deprivation as masochistic rather than inspirational and even more debilitating than military combat. For Merton, it was the penitential life he had wanted.

One of the biggest adjustments was the strict daily schedule. Designed by St. Benedict, the monks followed a rigid schedule of prayers called offices that were announced throughout the day by the ringing of the bell in the church steeple. They started the day at 2 a.m. after about seven hours of sleep. Prayers were organized around the seven canonical hours: Vigils, Lauds, Terce, Sext, None, Vespers, and Compline. Lauds, from the Latin, meaning praise, was at sunrise. Terce, or third, Sext, sixth, and None, meaning nine, were at around seven a.m., noon, and three p.m. Vespers were said at sunset; Compline, from the Latin, *hora completa*, meaning completed hour, was said before retiring.

These prayer interludes included the singing of Gregorian Chant, a medieval form of music that had its origin in ancient Greece and the pre-Christian synagogue. It evolved in the Catholic Church over time. Its name refers to Pope Gregory I, who supervised the organization of the Church's liturgical music in the sixth century. This music lent itself to the acoustics formed by the vaulted ceilings of the large European cathedrals and found wide appeal among medieval worshipers. St. Benedict required the regular chanting of the 150 psalms in his *Rule for Monasteries* in the sixth century. In the eighth century, the Emperor Charlemagne further developed the chant as a means of unifying his Empire by requiring uniformity in the singing of the chant, which was achieved by an enforced consistency in its documentation.

The people of both ancient and medieval times were fascinated with numerology. It played a significant part in developing the chant, which is considered a form of language regulated by number. The seven intervals in the octave were seen to equal a complete event, because the number seven was called the divine number, based on various Old Testament references beginning with the creation of the world in seven days. Chant is sung in Latin, free of harmony and often without accompaniment. Gregorian Chant uses a modal scale and sounds unique because of the differences in the distribution of tones and semitones within the scales, equivalent to not using the black keys on the piano. Each of the chants is determined by the choices of tonic and dominant notes. The only two modes that have survived in modern music are the major and minor keys, although the minor keys are more elaborate than ancient forms. When the musical notes first began to be recorded on parchment, they were written in square or diamond-shaped "neumes" or notes to indicate which tone was to be used as the predominant one and the direction of the sequence of notes to be sung, whether up or down the scale.

It was said that once some of the monks complained to Dom Frederic before Merton's time, because the monastery did not yet have an organ. All music therefore had to be *a capella*, or without accompaniment. The Abbot was said to have replied that no one ever died of not having organ music. It was the classic traditional point of view that deprivation is good for the soul.

Merton developed a special love of the chant and often enjoyed singing it alone in the woods as he walked, also reciting the psalms and contemplating God. While many monks had probably never heard serious liturgical music before they entered the monastery, Merton had a limited familiarity from Oakham in chapel services. It fit in perfectly with his artistic temperament.

For each prayer event, the monks were summoned at the sound of the bell from the monastery grounds to assemble in the church. Absolute punctuality was mandatory. Merton noted the paradox of the strict timing of all their activities considering the fact that their only purpose in life now was timeless.

These prayer times encompassed about two-and-a-half hours a day. The monks recited all of the 150 Psalms of the Old Testament on a two-week cycle. The daily schedule comprised a strict sequence of group prayer, chant, the Mass, study, and work, along with group meals. Novices who decided to leave the monastery often complained about the heavy requirement for organized group prayer. They had expected a relaxed monastery life primarily consisting of solitary contemplation. They viewed a strict schedule of activities as a distraction from their purpose for being there.

There was one period of the day that was given over to private prayer. It was called *lectio divina*, divine or holy reading. This involved reading a religious text and periodically stopping to reflect on its meaning and offering a prayer that would result from the meditation. Even this time was structured for the monk, so he was not left to drift off into private thought.

During the monks' group prayer, they bowed to God in unison at specific times. Even the medieval practice of bowing did not bother

Merton. At meetings with the Abbot, they also bowed to the Abbot in recognition of his position as God's representative on earth for them. There are three degrees of bowing, the profound bow being the deepest position, which is reserved for the most sacred times of prayer.

The monastery lifestyle was easy enough for Merton to adopt. He accepted the pace of the daily schedule without question. He had been on schedule all his life, especially at the two boarding schools he had attended. Even on the nine trans-Atlantic trips he had made between New York and Europe, Merton was accustomed to group activities and meals on schedule, and accepted the fact that he was cut off from world events and outside communication.

Merton certainly noticed the difference in the quality and quantity of the food served at the monastery compared with his past experience. On cruise ships an order could be specified to such a fine degree that one might ask for hot chocolate either as cocoa or as chocolate milk heated, along with a variety of gourmet foods at every course. Merton's digestive problems were aggravated by the monastery diet and eventually resulted in damage to his health. Merton tolerated the food good-naturedly, but found it impossible to adjust to the limitations in personal time for meditation.

Soon his frustration led him to seek transfer to another Order of more contemplative monks. Merton had been attracted to the Carthusians early in his search, but could not travel to their European location because of the war. Once the war ended in 1945, he could transfer, but only with the Order's permission. Dom Frederic summarily disapproved Merton's requests. He told Merton he did not believe it was necessary for him to leave Gethsemani in order to find sufficient solitude.

Merton's problem with shyness began to return. He was nervous about performing in front of the group, either in leading song, prayer, or speaking. He often requested he not be selected to lead any of the services. He thought he had conquered this problem when he was teaching at Columbia. Now that it had returned, he wondered about what was causing it, because it seemed uncharacteristic of his personality.

Later, after his writing began to be published, the Abbot required him to read his material at meals to the other monks. Father Raymond was also required to read his books aloud, and he found it equally distasteful. Father Raymond once said it was like water running down your ribs to read your own book aloud to others. This was in fact one of the few opinions the two writers seemed to have in common. Merton's shyness was so painful to him that he avoided mentioning his books to his fellow monks when they were published, other than in a passing remark made in another context.

There was no comparison between the books written by Father Raymond and Merton. Actually their work complemented each other, as Father Raymond's books portrayed life inside the monastery and Merton wrote from the point of view of the newcomer reacting to that life. The two exchanged views good-naturedly much of the time, stressing things they did have in common rather than their radically different paths.

Among the monks Merton soon developed a reputation for being a comedian. He used the events of the day to poke fun at whatever struck his fancy. He even mastered this humor in the form of the monastic pantomime. This seemed to be in contradiction to his shyness in church, which personally baffled him. He had felt this way before he became a Catholic when he was visiting churches in Italy and later in Manhattan. Then he feared making a gesture different from others and calling attention to himself as one who did not belong there, an intruder.

Chapter meetings included a talk or sermon by the Abbot. The monks sat with their backs to the walls of the Chapter room, while the Abbot sat on his special chair in the center of one wall. Dom James used this setting for influencing the monks to his point of view, as Merton saw it. He would put down any dissident opinions that were gaining ground in the group, or give reasons why he was imposing any decisions that may be unpopular, all interwoven within some other factual material to make his real message indirect. Merton saw through the Abbot's "hidden" agenda and often ridiculed the presentations. He did this by sign language, using hand signals the Abbot could not see but that were visible to the group. As Dom James pontificated, Merton presented a running commentary of his opinion of the message. The group immensely enjoyed Merton's game. It is unknown whether he was ever proclaimed for this behavior. Merton often found Dom James' tactics deceptive and hypocritical. He wrote in his journal that the Abbot could tell him what to do, but not what to think.

Sometimes in Chapter meetings there would be a discussion of theoretical questions involving moral theology. This would occasionally bring out a difference of opinion between Merton and Father Raymond. On one occasion, Dom James introduced the question of the degree of seriousness of the theft of a certain sum of money. Father Raymond complained that Merton was expounding his theories without any hesitation even when he lacked much knowledge in the subject and that Merton was no moral philosopher. In response, Merton said that Father Raymond attributed pettiness to God in determining how serious a sin it would be to steal a small sum of money. It was a typical standoff between the two.

Merton was frustrated by not being able to communicate with other writers so that he could exchange ideas. Although he was soon allowed the privilege of this type of relationship by correspondence, it was only some twenty years later that the Order relaxed the rules of confinement to the monastery to allow monks to attend meetings and visit with contemporaries for spiritual purposes.

Communication for monks with their relatives and friends outside the monastery was severely restricted. Mail could only be sent four times a year: Christmas, Easter, August 15, Feast of the Assumption of Mary into Heaven, and November 1, All Saints' Day. Each letter they wrote could only cover half of one page of the paper. Two of the four letters had to be to family members. All mail, incoming and outgoing, was subject to review by superiors before distribution or dispatch. All incoming mail was given out only the same four times of the year that outgoing letters were dispatched, except that letters received were distributed the day after Christmas and Easter.

For all the monks, visitors were rarer than the comforts of home. Merton was soon to be an exception.

# Chapter 14

Merton's first visitor was his brother, John Paul. It was July 1942, and John Paul was on embarkation leave from his training site in Canada. Tom thought his brother stood taller now, square shouldered and sharp in his Royal Canadian Air Force uniform. He was now a Sergeant and would serve as an observer on bombing runs. Tom asked him if he had thought any more about taking instructions in the Catholic faith. He said yes, he had thought about it but had not done anything about it.

John Paul asked Tom to instruct him while he was there, before he began seeing combat. John Paul would be there a week. Tom felt he did not have the knowledge, especially on such short notice. Father James Fox, the monastery's Guest Master, the representative to visitors, offered to talk with John Paul to determine if he could be instructed adequately in the faith in one week. He was willing to be helpful under these unusual circumstances. While Father Fox was speaking with John Paul, Tom literally burst into the room to plead for the monk's help. Seeing the sincerity in both their eyes, Father Fox believed the two brothers could work together, and he agreed to review the effort.

*"I was excused from all daily activities except to attend Mass and group services. Every day John Paul and I worked together in the retreat house library, going over all the subjects in Father James' instruction book. I would ask John Paul to repeat the explanation after each subject. He tried very hard, straining to concentrate like I had never seen him before.*

*He made up for my previous disappointment in him. Finally, after four days and nights of sessions, I told Father he was ready to be questioned.*

*I paced the hall in front of the big heavy wooden door of the Guest Master's study. I repeatedly said Our Fathers, Hail Marys, and please God, save John Paul. He needs this.*

*I need this too—to make up for so many years of neglecting my little brother.*

*John Paul came out about an hour later from behind the forbidding door, smiling the broadest smile I had ever seen. It reminded me of the old days when he enjoyed our success in blowing up johns with cherry bombs together in Douglaston. Father James followed him out with the good news and a firm pat on the back for me.*

*We automatically walked together over to the chapel, and we both thanked God he had made it.*

*It was July 26, 1942. I asked for permission to go to the Guest House. Father Master of the novitiate told me he had heard that John Paul might be gone for the Baptism. I went to the novices' chapel and prayed that it was so.*

*Father James had told us that I would not be allowed to attend John Paul's Baptism because of the Rules. Father James had called a friend of his who was pastor of a nearby church, St. Catherine's Church in New Haven, the nearest town to the monastery. I offered this as a sacrifice, not being able to witness the ceremony, in thanksgiving for the large gift of John Paul's faith.*

*My voice was still hoarse when John Paul came back with Father James from New Haven. After not speaking for most of the past six months, to speak almost continuously through the day was an unexpected strain. I didn't mind—nothing could dampen my utter joy in knowing John Paul and I were united in the faith.*

*I went to the Guest House after dinner. John Paul was beaming. He had pleased his big brother, and was finally accepted by his brother's group.*

*The next morning Dom Frederic allowed us to attend Mass together in the chapel at Reverend Father's private Mass, John Paul up in the gallery area and I down below, in front of the altar of Our Lady of Victories. When it was almost time for Communion to be distributed, I motioned to John Paul to come downstairs by going through the Guest House. There was no direct access within the church between the gallery and the main floor. He didn't move. I motioned again. He stood up, but didn't move from his place.*

*It was like a flash. I saw him as a little boy again, confused about whether he could come play with me or was excluded from the Clubhouse and proximity to "the big boys." Luckily, Father Robert, my Novice Master, saw the problem and showed John Paul how to come down by the circuitous route to the communion rail. We knelt together before the altar, he in his gray Royal Air Force uniform with ceremonial sword in its scabbard, I in my white monastery robe. Reverend Father placed the little white wafer on his tongue, then the same for me. The agony of a lifetime melted in my heart.*

*I was ready now to say good-bye to John Paul and release him to his destiny. Dom Frederic allowed us to spend the rest of the day together. Then*

*at dusk, I went to my dorm bed, he to the guest quarters. In the morning I
was allowed to walk out with him to the monastery gate. Another visitor at
the monastery drove John Paul to Bardstown. As the car started down the
driveway, John Paul turned and waved solemnly to me, and I waved slowly
back.*

*I had the feeling I would never see him again. But I believed now that
we would be together with God in eternity."*

After John Paul's visit, Tom wanted more than ever to proceed with
the profession of his vows. He wanted to feel more securely that he
belonged to the monastery. Christmas of 1942 brought a gift he never
expected. Reverend Father allowed him to make his vows privately to
him, a very special honor. It was the feast of St. Thomas the Apostle.
Tom was choked with emotion and felt a bond he could never have
imagined. At last he was at home. It was more than a year before he
was permitted to take the vows publicly.

His joy could not last. Tom's instinct was correct: John Paul did not
return from combat.

When John Paul left Gethsemani, he had gone to London, visited
the Bennetts and Aunt Gwyn. Then he went to Birkenhead to see his
girlfriend, Margaret Mary Evans. She was training to be a radio operator
with the British forces. They were married the following early spring
when John Paul got another leave.

On Friday, April 16, 1943, John Paul was in a bombing formation in
a raid on Mannheim, Germany. The plane he was in developed engine
trouble from icing on the wings. It crashed in the English Channel.
John Paul's back was broken, and he was in severe pain and in need of
water. After three hours in a rubber dinghy, he died. His buddies buried
him at sea. It was one week before Easter. The next day the survivors
were rescued five miles off the English coast, but it was a day too late
for John Paul.

John Paul's last letter to Tom was waiting for him when he received
the regular distribution of monastery mail on Easter Monday which
had been received at the monastery a month earlier. The day after Tom
received the letter, he got a telegram saying that ten days earlier John
Paul had been reported missing. After a few weeks, Tom received a
letter confirming John Paul's death.

Tom's grief was like a large cavity in his chest. He was now truly alone
in the world—the only survivor of his family. His only consolation was

the knowledge that John Paul was in God's hands. Tom did not know that the prayers he had chanted on Good Friday before Easter for the dead were also in fact for John Paul. He went to the woods, with the permission of Dom Frederic. During the mid-day rest period Tom was lying on his bunk, and a short poem came to him about John Paul's death. When the rest period was finished, he got up and wrote it on a slip of paper in its entirety. It helped.

The following Christmas, 1943, Tom's second visitor, Robert Lax, made a surprise appearance at Gethsemani. He had just become a Catholic. Tom was at Midnight Mass on Christmas Eve when suddenly he saw Lax there, unannounced. He couldn't believe his eyes. Tom received the Abbot's permission to visit with him as an exception to the monastery rule that only members of a monk's immediate family could visit them since he no longer had anyone from his immediate family living. Tom was thrilled to catch up on news from the old group and to spend some time with Lax, who always managed to keep him amused.

Lax had gone to work for Catherine de Hueck at Friendship House as a volunteer while he worked for *The New Yorker* magazine, and about a year later, his health would not allow him to continue. He had then taken a position as an English instructor at the University of North Carolina on a fellowship while pursuing graduate studies in philosophy. Ed Rice, the only Catholic friend in Tom's group at Columbia, persuaded Lax to return to New York and become a Catholic. He decided to take this step, which he had contemplated for years, then go to see Tom to tell him about it. He had just been baptized December 19. Tom too was gratified that Lax had finally made this decision.

Lax told Tom that Bob Gerdy had also recently become a Catholic and had gotten married, and was stationed with the U.S. Army in England. He reported that Rice was working in New York on *Time* magazine, and Lax was now returning to New York to work with him part-time and do freelancing. Rice had gotten married and now had children.

Before he left New York, Lax had visited Tom's agent, Naomi Burton, at Curtis Brown. He informed her that Tom had joined the monastery, so could not correspond with her. Lax told Tom that initially she was horrified, saying she feared his creative writing would stop.

Lax brought news of some of their other mutual friends from Columbia. Sy Freedgood was in the Army in India running a soldiers' newspaper. Lax told Tom that without thinking, Sy had swatted a fly, a major transgression to the Hindus working with him. The offended workers then went out on strike. Sy then quickly left the town as well as his job and went to look for their old friend, the Hindu monk from Columbia days, Bramachari, who he had heard was now back in India. He was unable to locate him, but wasn't really too surprised to find that he was still traveling around.

Tom gave Lax some of the poems he had been writing to take back to New York for Mark Van Doren at Columbia to read. Other friends of his who had copies of some of his poems began sending them to various publishers for Tom, knowing his correspondence privileges were limited and believing his work should be published.

Soon this effort bore fruit. Tom's poems began to be published individually from his friends' submissions in publications such as *Poetry* magazine in 1942 and *The New Yorker* in 1942 and 1943. Dom Frederic did not attempt to stop this activity.

Writing for Tom at this time was severely limited. His primary concern was proceeding to advance in the Order to the next step, the simple profession of vows. To qualify, the monks who had already taken their own final vows voted at a Chapter meeting on each novice's readiness. The ceremony was a traditional one. The Prior gave each monk different colored balls that looked like marbles, to be placed in a black container on a table in the middle of the room. It was made of ceramic porcelain and was shaped much like a chalice. For each novice in turn, the monk received three different colored balls, one color for voting in favor, one for opposition, and one for abstention. The monks hid the balls in the oversized sleeve of their garment to keep the voting secret. Two monks sat on either side of the voting vessel, collecting the two balls not used by each monk. When all had voted, Dom Frederic counted the balls in each of the three categories and announced the results. The vote for Tom was in favor of his profession. Those not voted favorably had to spend additional time as a novice before the Abbot would call for another vote.

Before the vows were to be taken, it was required that a novice make an eight-day retreat. On March 19, 1944, Tom completed his retreat and made his vows. He exchanged the white scapular, or apron, for a black one. He was thrilled to be dressed now the same as the senior monks. As a bonus, he didn't have to be so careful with a black apron as with a white one.

To make the simple profession of vows, it was also required to make a will. Tom's handwritten will, dated February 17, 1944, dictated that his shares in the Optional Saving Shares Account he still owned be divided equally between his sister-in-law (John Paul's widow) and "... my guardian T. Izod Bennett, Esq., M.D.,... this second half to be paid by him to the person mentioned to him in my letters, if that person can be contacted." He left his interest on the Grosset and Dunlap shares from his grandfather to Robert Lax. All other property was to go to the monastery.

The person that Tom mentioned to Dr. Bennett goes unnamed. According to Jim Forest and Edward Rice, Tom believed that he had fathered a son out of wedlock when he was under his guardian's supervision. One story is that the child and his mother were killed in the Blitz during a Nazi bombing of the UK. Jim Forest believed that these deaths may not have occurred. According to the biographer, Monica Furlong, Edward Rice claimed there was a "paternity case" that was resolved by a legal settlement out of court. The unnamed person that Tom mentioned to Dr. Bennett in his letters is a continuing mystery. Michael Mott, who researched the first Merton biography, explained that British legal practice in the 1930s prohibited any further contact between parties who enter into a legal settlement of this type. Harold Talbott, a friend in later years, claimed that in a conversation with Merton in 1968, Merton had told him that he believed he had had a son, but did not know if he had survived the Blitz.

The war was soon over, and many veterans coming back from combat were looking for a deeper meaning to their lives than society offered. The number of applicants to the monastery broke historical records. This mirrored the increase in the number of Catholics in the U.S., which almost doubled during this post-war period. Expansion of the monastery facilities was the only answer. Dom Frederic responded to the need.

It was the Feast of St. Joseph, and after the profession of vows, Father Abbot read aloud the names of those whom he had selected to go to Conyers, Georgia, to start a daughter house. Hopefully this would relieve the overcrowding and at the same time advance the Order in the U.S. Soon there would be additional monasteries opened in Utah, New Mexico, and South Carolina, as well as a convent of Cistercian nuns, and other English-speaking foundations begun in Ireland and Scotland

Tom realized quickly that this would create a demand for books about the Order and its history in English. He was eager to volunteer to meet this challenge. He hoped he would never be chosen to go to establish any of the new monasteries. Gethsemani was home for him in spite of its shortcomings.

Mark Van Doren passed Tom's poems that Lax had brought him on to James Laughlin. He was a wealthy young man who had recently started a publishing company called New Directions out of his family's garage. Having studied under Ezra Pound and an amateur poet himself, Laughlin sought to stimulate a modernist literary movement in the U.S. by publishing new *avant garde* writers. Van Doren was correct in his assumption that Laughlin would be interested in Tom's writing.

The Abbot fully concurred with Laughlin's desire to publish Tom's poems, undoubtedly encouraged by his need for funds to pay for the monastery's building needs. According to Laughlin's letter to Tom, the monastery was to get ten percent from the sales as Tom's royalties, minus any cost for permissions required if he used any copyrighted material. Laughlin published the collection as *Thirty Poems* in November 1944. The book would follow chronological order representing the development of thought at the time he entered the monastery. It included Tom's poem about the death of John Paul, which was considered one of his best efforts. Laughlin was not interested in publishing religious poetry, but he correctly recognized in Tom's early work a talent for expression that would fit his company's profile.

The book was well received. When Tom received his first copy of *Thirty Poems*, he walked out to the monks' cemetery by the church to contemplate its significance. The Abbot General, Dom Dominique Nogues, gave approval for the publication on the condition that Tom's monastic name not appear on the book.

Tom was disappointed to see that the cover showed the author to be Thomas Merton. He had wanted the identity of Thomas Merton to die when he came to Gethsemani, with his ego and interest in success and recognition. Now he knew the Order was on Thomas Merton's side, not on the side of the self-effacing Frater Louis who wanted to disappear, to erase the gap between himself and God. Thomas Merton rode on his shoulders, like the *doppelganger* in German myth, and he could not lose him.

One of the two has got to die, he felt. He was mortally afraid that Tom the author would reduce his vocation to a few ashes.

*To be as good a monk as I can, and to remain myself, and to write about it: to put myself down on paper, in such a situation, with the most complete simplicity and integrity, masking nothing, confusing no issue: this is very hard, because I am all mixed up in illusions and attachments. These, too, will have to be put down. But without exaggeration, repetition, useless emphasis. No need for breast-beating and lamentation before the eyes of anyone but You, O God, who see the depths of my fatuity. To be frank without being boring. It is a kind of crucifixion. Not a very dramatic or painful one. But it requires so much honesty that it is beyond my nature. It must come somehow from the Holy Ghost.*

*Entering the Silence*
Journal, September 1, 1949

# Chapter 15

This was not Merton's only burden to carry. He was now beginning his experience with the Church's censorship process. The system was instituted early in the Church's publishing history to avoid any heretical or incorrect interpretation of Church teaching, whether deliberate or inadvertent.

The censorship process was an involved system of multiple reviews plus a higher level review by two Church officials. It required two officials of the Order to give the "Nihil obstat," meaning no obstacle found, and Merton's Abbot General to give the "Imprimi potest," approval signified. Then the work had to be submitted for review outside the Order, such as an archdiocese, for a second "Nihil obstat" by a Censor Librorum, followed by an "Imprimatur," or let it be printed, from a designated church official at a higher level, such as a Bishop, Archbishop, or Cardinal. If there were disagreement between the two censors in the Order, a third would be added to help resolve it. The review and approvals signified that the Church was making an official declaration that the book or pamphlet was free from doctrinal or moral error. There was an added disclaimer to this approval, saying that it did not mean the church authorities agreed with the content, opinions, or statements expressed. In the Order's use of censorship, the release meant far more agreement than the procedure provided.

Before submission to the censors, writers themselves were under obligation to censor their own content so as not to embarrass anyone or glorify sin.

The system did not provide the writer with a personal dialogue with the censors other than in a formal written format. The writer could submit elaborate rebuttals of censored material, but had to accept decisions that were made by the censors. Higher church officials could intervene in the interest of the author to preserve the material or to expedite the decision process to get to publication. Dom Frederic did this, both for Merton's satisfaction and perhaps to expedite a financial return on the effort. The extent of the Abbot's influence in Merton's behalf is not known.

With Merton's work gaining attention, Dom Frederic became concerned about Merton's public identity and the effect it would have on curiosity seekers at Gethsemani. He asked the church censors for a policy on what name should appear on Merton's books. In September 1945 their decision was that his religious name should not appear anywhere on individual poems or any published books. He should proceed with the use of his former name. With this decision, the Church consequently perpetuated Merton's dual identity, and he was forced to live two lives, in and out of the monastery.

This policy was not imposed on Father Raymond, probably because his books were traditional in their presentation. Father Raymond did complain about the censors' judgments on his manuscripts. He was said to be more difficult than Merton in resolving disagreements.

The first book probably assigned to Merton by Dom Frederic was published by the monastery in September 1946. It is a translation by "A Monk of Gethsemani," of *The Soul of the Apostolate*, by Dom Jean-Baptiste Chautard, O.C.S.O. It is heralded as the first volume in a series of books on the spiritual and interior life by Trappist monks. It states that another volume in preparation is *The Spirit of Simplicity: Characteristic of the Cistercian Order*, which Merton first wrote as a pamphlet in 1946 under Dom Frederic, according to his journal. It was published two years later as No. 3 in the series, attributed only to "a monk of Gethsemani." Another forthcoming volume mentioned is *St. Lutgarde: A study in Cistercian Mysticism*. It was later published under Dom James' supervision by Bruce Publishing Company as *What are these Wounds?* with Merton as the author.[1]

Another book published in this series was *An Artist Soul* by Dom Andre Malet, OCR, the life of a French Trappist, Roger Durey, a convert from radical-socialism, published in 1947. Authorship is unknown, but Merton could have produced it. It relates the monastic journey of an artist who had wanted to correct the shortcomings of religious art. Even in his last days he demanded a crucifix without ornamentation and lectured his infirmarian on the beauty of natural and simple religious art. This theme would have certainly resonated with Merton's sentiments on the subject.

A 10-page "Biographical Note" about Dom Chautard, no author given, preceding the text of *The Soul of the Apostolate*, is undoubtedly Merton's work, as well as the translation of Chautard from the French, fittingly bound in black cloth with gold lettering. The sentence structure of this preface reads like the quality of Merton's work that Evelyn

Waugh tried to improve in *Elected Silence*, his re-write of *Seven Storey Mountain*. A sample follows:

> If this youth-club had been one of those more or less timid compromises with modern notions that make so much Catholic Action seem like no more than a Y.M.C.A. run by a couple of priests, Dom Chautard would have probably ended up by exporting nitrates from Chile. But here he found something more than third-rate amateur dramatics and the atmosphere of a secular social club. This was more than a tame and sheepish attempt to rival the attractions of the dance hall and the café by vainly trying to beat them at their own game of pleasing and entertaining human nature. ... (p. vii)

Reading Merton's early work only serves to testify to the laborious effort he made to perfect his writing style, which is witnessed by the incredible success of so many of his writings.

Merton's second volume of poetry was published August 25, 1946, after the war. The first volume of poetry was sold out, so the same 30 poems were added to 63 new poems and was titled, *A Man in the Divided Sea*. Now that James Laughlin had become his publisher, Merton was allowed to enter into a regular correspondence with him for purposes of the publishing process. In 1946, Laughlin also started sending Merton copies of other books being published so he would know what was being read and to help him improve his writing style outside the religious mode.

Laughlin and Merton did not meet in person until Laughlin's first trip to Gethsemani in June 1947. The friendship grew over the 23 years of their association. Laughlin received 403 letters from Merton. The publishing business was not the only subject they discussed. They exchanged ideas about other writers and their work, and Merton advised Laughlin about how to proceed on a spiritual path.

Merton was spending the two hours a day that he was allotted in the scriptorium working on the Abbot's writing assignments, lives of the saints, and a variety of material about the monastery. Having sold Dom Frederic on his determination to write, Merton proposed a new project that he was hopeful would meet with the Abbot's approval. He wanted to write his autobiography to portray the process of conversion to the Church and ultimately his vocation to the priesthood. He received the Abbot's approval in March 1946. Merton had done some autobiographical writing on and off since 1939 without success. This was an opportunity to devote all his efforts to produce a comprehensive product. He characterized the project as a cross between Dante's Purgatory and Kafka and a medieval miracle play in a poetic prose. It portrayed the journey of a spiritual seeker that resonated with readers everywhere.

The monastery was then heavily in debt, and Merton sought to maximize the profit he could make on this book to help Dom Frederic. He believed New Directions was not enough of a mainline publisher for this type of book. He decided to contact Naomi Burton at Harcourt Brace. Dom Frederic gave permission for Merton to submit it to her. He asked Naomi to read it and discuss it with Robert Giroux, his coeditor on the Columbia yearbook. Merton had heard that Giroux was now out of the Navy and had returned to Harcourt Brace. Giroux had rejected three of Merton's manuscripts before he entered Gethsemani, but this time Merton knew he had a winner.

Merton received a telegram on December 29, 1946, from Giroux saying Harcourt Brace had accepted the manuscript. Giroux had gotten approval to publish it only ten days after he had received it.

The book was to be called *The Seven Storey Mountain*. Merton wanted to portray the joy he had found in solemn asceticism, but he knew that readers could only identify with such a concept if he presented the story of how he had arrived at it. He knew it would be impossible to simply describe the mental processes he went through to reach his goal. He described his journey through the equivalent of the seven-circled mountain of Purgatory from Dante's *Divine Comedy*. He hoped his readers might follow his example and find their own peace in the discovery of God for themselves.

Merton felt inspired by the writers of the Old and New Testaments who, he recorded in his journal in August 1949, were " ... transformed by the white-hot dangerous presence of inspiration, for they looked at God as into a furnace and the Seraphim flew down and purified their lips with fire." In the last line of his autobiography, Merton called them the "burnt men" that he was to know. Later, in *The Sign of Jonas*, Merton referred to the white furnace of God

To get his story past the censors, Merton knew he might have to let his story be cut. In anticipation, he omitted many of the details of his transgressions. The Church required a writer to first censor himself before submitting a manuscript for review. Merton was amazed, though, when he received a rejection that advised him to take a correspondence course in English grammar before resubmission. Merton wrote a rebuttal that finally satisfied the censors. His sins were unnamed and unnumbered. As a consequence, the reader might wonder what drove Merton out of the world and into a monastery, other than the restlessness and extravagance of his youth. Merton accepted the censors' judgment about this point with few questions. He also had to delete social commentary because the censors considered it to be outside Merton's province to criticize anyone other than himself. Writing the book was an agony but a purging for Merton. It was a long, arduous process, but a great satisfaction to fulfill the desire he had had for several years to publish his story after his earlier failed attempts at publication. Compliance with the censors was a price Merton was willing to pay to get his story in print.

The Abbot informed Merton he was now considered ready to take his final vows. On February 16, he made the required will before taking his vows.

Merton was allowed to keep the leather wallet Tom Bennett had given him for his eighteenth birthday. Every other possession he had brought to the monastery five years before was to be given to the poor. He took one last look at his suitcase with the blue and white "Cuba Mail Line" sticker he had picked up in 1940 when he went to Havana. He wondered how he could have been proud to display such an insignificant thing.

Merton made his simple profession of vows of obedience, stability, and conversion of manners, including poverty and chastity, on March 19, 1947. It was the Feast of St. Joseph and the thirty-third year of his life. In the church in full procession, Merton lay face down in the middle of the sacristy in front of the altar to make his vows. He now swore to practice a life without material goods, without the physical love of another person, in complete obedience to the orders of his Abbot, never leaving the monastery of Gethsemani, and converting his life to the Rule of St. Benedict.

Ironically, Merton received the contract for his signature for publishing *The Seven Storey Mountain* after taking the vows. As a result, all royalties would go to the monastery during his lifetime as well as at his death. He wondered if the timing of this event had been planned, but quickly dismissed the idea. He was now unbearably happy to be settled in this home he had found for the rest of his life.

Since he was out of the novitiate now, Merton was free to move about the monastery grounds. The monastery was becoming extremely overcrowded, though, and Merton found it difficult to concentrate without sufficient opportunity for solitude. By 1944, Gethsemani was beyond its capacity of 50 to 70 monks. The new foundation, or additional monastery, at Conyers, Georgia, would only temporarily relieve the overcrowding. By 1946 the monastery was approaching 200 men, and costs were out of sight. Men returning from World War II were looking for an alternative to life's problems after witnessing the reality that involved the death of 15 million people. Eventually, many veterans heard about Gethsemani from *The Seven Storey Mountain* and came there to seek the peace Merton had expressed in his writing.

Dom Frederic was pleased with the success of Merton's work as well as in the growth of the Order, but there was no relief from the financial burden that the increase in applicants brought with it. His only hope for solvency was to establish a second foundation to move more monks to another location. He quickly accomplished this in 1947 with the purchase of some land and quonset huts in Utah, which he named Abbey of Our Lady of the Holy Trinity. Seeing this as only a stopgap measure, he was soon engaged in talks with Clare Boothe Luce and her husband, Henry Luce, about donation of their estate in South Carolina, called Mepkin Plantation. This would be a third foundation.

Dom Frederic's full schedule and failing health compelled him to let go of some of the control he exercised over his monks. In April 1947, Dom Frederic relinquished the guidance he provided through the Confessor-penitent relationship with Merton and a number of other young monks. He assigned them to be penitents of Father Anthony Chassagne.

In his journal Merton reported that he and Father Anthony went out to the fields together in commemoration of the Ascension feast day to bless the farm animals. Merton sprinkled holy water on calves, pigs, sheep, and rabbits, moving on after blessing each group. The chickens were more of a challenge—they ran away as soon as the monks approached them. Merton felt he could use the blessing himself, with the problems he had recently experienced while working in the woods. One day he said he nearly cut off both of his legs with an ax while he was trimming a pine tree they had just felled. He reported in his diary that the ax came at his knees like a fierce bird, and only his guardian angel saved him from the blade.

Merton's assignment began to evolve into one of writing on theology and canon law in the library. Father Anthony was anything but enthusiastic about the quality of Merton's writing. He expected Merton to write in the style of traditional Catholic dogma, and Merton tried to explain that he wanted to be frank with his readers without being boring. This did not resonate with Father Anthony's legalistic approach. He liked it less that Merton was interested in a transfer to the Carthusians.

The first project Merton received from Father Anthony was to write a pamphlet on contemplation. Father Anthony vigorously disapproved of Merton's product. He told Merton he seemed to have lost the manuscript for a period of time. He talked to Merton about his spiritual reading, and disagreed with the books Merton chose to read on the early Church.

Father Anthony told Merton he was a pedant and should be reading something modern. He also advised Merton to remember that he was a convert and should avoid problems with censors that he termed fights "in the family," even on contemplation. He objected to Merton's desire for more time for solitude and contemplation, advising that it was selfish and that he should resign himself instead to "a life of hard work." Merton concluded that Father Anthony did not like his writing, the books he read, and probably did not like him personally.

Ironically, Merton published a short article on contemplation in the winter edition of 1949 in *The Dublin Review*. It may have been a version of his manuscript for Father Anthony. He quotes Baldwin of Canterbury, a twelfth century English Cistercian monk.

The monastery allowed him to publish this article under his approved name, Thomas Merton. It is slanted to appeal to the readers of a British publication, in the syntax of his Cambridge days. For example, he says, " ... the last man who should be accepted in a contemplative monastery is a misanthrope! If you are anti-social by temperament, for pity's sake never enter a Trappist monastery: you will go crazy in ten minutes." He describes young American Trappists without identifying himself as one of the group, describing them as "vigorous and happy men, with all the energy and common sense and good-humour and sociability that characterize that nation." In the back of the publication there is a "supplement" of advertisements for other publications that includes an ad by Hollis and Carter for Merton's work. Ironically, it promotes Merton's *Seeds of Contemplation* on the basis that it is written " ... in the language of today and without abstruse technicalities."

Merton's full treatment of the subject, *Seeds of Contemplation*, was also published in 1949. When Merton was reading it serially in the refectory during meals, Father Anthony commented to Merton that "those who think they are intellectuals like it." Merton was probably happy to see Father Anthony depart two years later to serve as the superior of the new abbey in South Carolina.

For the Abbot, Merton's ability to write publishable work was considered a credit to the monastery, so there was no chance that Merton would be transferred to another location. Dom Frederic continued to encourage Merton personally in his writing, without regard to Father Anthony's opinions. While Merton's autobiography was being edited and reviewed by the censors, he continued to write other material for publication. In July 1947 he published an article, "Poetry and the Contemplative Life" in the serious Catholic periodical, *The Commonweal*. He was also busy composing more poetry for publication. In March 1948 New Directions published a miscellaneous collection of poems called *Figures for an Apocalypse*, largely about saints, about nature, and about Merton's days in New York City. In November 1949, Laughlin published Merton's fourth book of poetry in five years, *The Tears of the Blind Lions*.

In 1948 the writing that Dom Frederic assigned to Merton also began to be published. Early books did not include an author's name, but comments in Merton's journals about these works confirm his authorship of them. *Cistercian Contemplatives* and *Guide to Cistercian Life*, both published by the monastery in 1948, and *Gethsemani Magnificat, Centenary of Gethsemani Abbey*, in 1949, are assumed to be Merton's work. Concerning the preparation of *Cistercian Contemplatives: A Guide to Trappist Life*, Merton wrote in a letter to Laughlin, November 6, 1947: " ... my headache is to keep it from looking like a high school yearbook." In June 1948, a biography, *Exile Ends in Glory: The Life of a Trappestine, Mother M. Berchmans, O.C.S.O.*, was released by the Bruce Publishing Company.

*The Spirit of Simplicity, Characteristic of the Cistercian Order*, published by the Abbey of Gethsemani as "The Cistercian Library, No. 3" in 1948, was a product of "A Cistercian Monk of Our Lady of Gethsemani," according to the title page. It was comprised of translations of St. Bernard of Clairvaux and a report by the General Chapter, along with liberal footnotes and commentaries on both texts. Merton referenced his authorship of this work in his journal entry of April 25, 1948, in connection with getting the *imprimatur* and taking it to the printer.

There was also a sepia-colored insert of old photographs of four Cistercian monasteries in France which are cited for their simplicity in preference to "the frippery of second-rate art." Merton loved to study the pictures of the twelfth century Cistercian monasteries, commenting that this architecture, as well as the thirteenth century work to follow, was "true to the Cistercian spirit, combining the noble, expansive, sure taste of the man of quality with the austere simplicity of a true monk." He reminisced to himself about the ruins he and his father had visited together in France. Merton's name may not have been included in this work, but his imprint is all over it. For example, he comments in a footnote that Cistercian monasteries should "get rid of" "bad art" and other articles usually received as gifts so that they do not find themselves "at the mercy of the taste of their benefactors."

Bruce had also published Father Raymond's biography, *The Man Who Got Even With God* in 1941. Father Raymond's name, M. Raymond, and Cistercian Order affiliation, O.C.S.O., appeared on the cover of his book with no problem from the censors. This was also the way Father Raymond's name appeared in *Three Religious Rebels*, published in New York by P. J. Kenedy & Sons in 1944. On October 4, 1948, Harcourt Brace released *The Seven Storey Mountain* (by Thomas Merton). On the following December 8, Merton's *What is Contemplation?* was published by St. Mary's College, Notre Dame, IN.

Merton did not receive much feedback from his writing, except through his publisher and letters selected for him by the Abbot who screened them. As a consequence, he usually did not receive any negative or critical opinions of his work. At first, the monastery was receiving only a few letters a day. As the volume increased, one of the monks was assigned to open this mail and pass it on to Merton if it was of a routine nature. Finally, the volume became so unmanageable that the monk assigned to screen it stopped opening it and gave it to Merton directly. At this point, Merton realized he received a mixture of mail and was overwhelmed, especially since his time to read it was severely limited. He was deeply touched by many of the letters he received from readers who were inspired by the book. He only wished he had the time to write to all of them individually to thank them and encourage them in their spiritual life.

Dom Frederic was driving himself beyond his strength. Word came to Gethsemani that he suffered a mild heart attack while he was in Belleville, Illinois, for the consecration of a Bishop in late December 1947.

He ignored the need to slow down. His health was growing weaker, but he was more concerned about his abbeys as well as the monastery's preparation for their Centenary celebration.

The monastery received an advance copy of *The Seven Storey Mountain* in July 1948, and Dom Frederic eagerly presented it to Merton and shared in the pleasure of his accomplishment. He had brought Merton to the status of published writer with a growing national reputation. He couldn't resist commenting to Merton that this would not have occurred if Merton had left Gethsemani to join the Carthusians, the contemplative Order in Europe. Merton reluctantly had to agree that this was probably true.

Dom Frederic's work with Merton was at an end, however. The following month, the aging and exhausted Abbot died on August 4, 1948. He was on a train going to the monastery in Conyers, Georgia, that he had recently founded. Father Emery, the Prior, and second in command to Dom Frederic, announced the news at Chapter the following morning. The monks were sad but not shocked. The Abbot's poor health was common knowledge. Merton felt deep respect and affection for Dom Frederic, who had taken him into the monastery and accepted him without regard to his past. This was like the loss of another father.

Merton wrote a touching reminiscence of Dom Frederic as a memorial. He gave his manuscript to Father Raymond because he had heard that he had been selected to write a biography of the Abbot. The gesture was obviously not much appreciated, and in fact was probably forgotten by Father Raymond, whose viewpoint was as conservative as Merton's was free-thinking.

Father Raymond wrote two accounts of Dom Frederic's death. In 1949, his book, *Burnt Out Incense*, was published by P.J. Kenedy & Sons. This was a book Dom Frederic undoubtedly had assigned Father Raymond to write in anticipation of Gethsemani's upcoming anniversary. It covered the 100-year history of the Cistercian Order in America, tracing the story of Gethsemani back to its French roots and ending with an account of the Abbot's death. Father Raymond also wrote a separate 250-page biography of Dom Frederic, published by Bruce Publishing Company in 1953, *The Less Traveled Road*. In this book Father Raymond affectionately describes Dom Frederic as "cold steel sheathed in silk" and expresses his sincere appreciation of the Abbot as a man as well as a successful administrator. He cites the fact that Dom Frederic built up the American Trappist group from 70 to 270 men between 1935 and 1948.

In his Foreword to *Burnt Out Incense*, Father Raymond credits Merton's phrase, "the Christ of the burnt men," from *The Seven Storey Mountain*, which had just been published the previous year. But in the text, Father Raymond does not recognize Merton as one of the two choir novices who made their simple professions, along with a lay brother who pronounced his solemn vows, on March 19, 1944 before Dom Frederic announced the names of those who would be sent to Gethsemani's first foundation in Conyers, Georgia.

To elect a new abbot to replace Dom Frederic, Dom Gabriel Sortais, the Abbot General, was required to come from the Order's headquarters in Citeaux, France, to oversee the process. Actually, he already had a trip to Gethsemani planned as part of his visitation schedule. His official title was Vicar General. Only the professed monks who had taken Solemn Vows were allowed to vote. This automatically excluded Merton, but to his delight he was appointed to assist in the administrative process because of his fluency in French. Dom Gabriel did not speak or understand English well enough to manage without a translator.

Somehow in the process of the proceedings, a newspaperman slipped into the monastery garden and took a picture of the smoke coming out of the stove pipe as the ballots were burned before he was dispatched to the monastery gate. Merton was excited to witness the event. The procedure was conducted just as in Rome for the election of a Pope. The result was announced in Latin at the door of the Chapter, then at the church doors, and finally at the monastery gate. On August 23, 1948, James Fox was the newly elected Abbot. He took his seat on the throne in the cloister. The entry was unlocked for all the novices, young professed, and laybrothers to come in to sit with the choir monks for the investiture. Then all of the professed made their formal promise of obedience to him.

Dom James Fox until this time had been Abbot of Holy Ghost Monastery in Conyers, Georgia. He was known by most of the monks at Gethsemani because of his assignment as Guest Master before he was selected to lead nineteen other monks in founding the new monastery four years earlier. Merton was grateful to him for his help with John Paul's Baptism and eagerly looked forward to a relationship that could grow out of this momentous occasion in his life as a novice.

He was told to accompany the Abbot General to translate for him for the next several days. He was amazed and excited to learn that he and Dom Gabriel would go into Louisville to visit the Convent of the Good Shepherd. Merton was seeing the everyday world for the first time in almost seven years. He had not anticipated the shock of everyday changes he would notice. He also got an inside view of the way the Order's hierarchy conducted their affairs. Consequently he gained an insight that others did not have that he used to his advantage in future days. Many of the monks did not appreciate Merton's prominent position during Dom Gabriel's visit, especially since he wasn't even a professed monk yet. With Merton's natural ability to transform himself, he fell into the role of a French monk with ease. He won the attention and confidence of the Abbot General to the amazement of many of his fellow monks, to say nothing of their envy.

Dom Gabriel was a sophisticated, knowledgeable superior, appreciative of the finest Church architecture and art. His position required him to visit Trappist monasteries worldwide. Dom Gabriel told Merton once that he often had his guest room decorated at the monasteries he visited with all kinds of religious statues and pictures for his devotions. He confided to Merton that he usually put them all in the closet so he would not have to look at them because the quality of the art was so poor. He said he'd rather pray in a bare room than look at bad art. Merton couldn't have agreed more, and appreciated the Abbot General's confidence. He was thrilled to have a sympathetic contact at the Order's headquarters, especially considering his difficulties with censorship.

Merton, too, had been exposed to some of the finest religious art in his travels and had been trained by his father to differentiate in the quality of art he saw. The monastery at Gethsemani had an outdoor statue of St. Benedict that Merton considered a poor representation. He was delighted when it was finally moved to a location in the woods where he didn't have to see it. Merton was never shy about expressing his criticism of bad art, from churches to holy cards. Once Merton commented that he knew that God was patient because He tolerated so much bad art and music in His churches.

During the Abbot General's visit, Merton noticed a change in Dom James' demeanor from the days when he was at Gethsemani. He had seemed to Merton an unusually warm, approachable person when Merton had met with him and John Paul. Now Dom James seemed to take on an air of aloofness along with his new authority that Merton found troubling.

Reading press releases about Dom James and piecing together information from some of the old timers at the monastery, Merton began to learn more about him. Dom James had entered Gethsemani in 1927. He was a native of Massachusetts, and had graduated *magna cum laude* from Harvard and had additionally been awarded a Masters degree in Business Administration. He was in the Navy briefly in finance-related jobs and then worked for the U.S. Internal Revenue Service as a corporate tax examiner. He once admitted that his original ambition had been to make a million dollars. His values changed and eventually led him to the priesthood after his sister died unexpectedly just after she entered college. Now 52 years of age, Dom James was ready to assume the problems of the Abbey with plenty of energy, using ideas that had been successful in Georgia. His Ivy League education demonstrated itself in his polished and professional manner.

His wiry frame gave him an aura of efficiency that might have put one in mind of Ebenezer Scrooge. His smile seemed formidable, giving the impression of a grim determination to see to it that his instructions were followed with appropriate action. In fact, his smile was sort of a trademark for him. He got a rubber stamp made in French, for use on all the documents he distributed, saying "*Tout pour Jesus, par Marie, toujours avec un sourire,*" or "All for Jesus, through Mary, always with a smile."

Knowing the Order was headquartered in France and all his superiors were French, Dom James was sensitive to promoting his knowledge of their language even though it was limited. He used his ability to write papers in the French language that he read whenever he attended the Order's meetings at Citeaux.

As a strong leader, the new Abbot was confident of his control over Merton, who was under obedience to him. He would conclude that there could be no contest, only skirmishes with his talented novice.

### Note

1. The first book assigned to Merton by Dom Frederic, acknowledged in Merton's journal entry of December 13, 1960, was *The Soul of the Apostolate*, by Jean-Baptiste Chautard, O.C.S.O., translated by "A Monk of Gethsemani," dated September 1946. It was published by the monastery and heralded as the first in a series.

# Chapter 16

Dom James soon established his own image as the Abbot of Gethsemani and a notable reputation as well. He replaced the old, slow methods used by Dom Frederic with the efficient procedures he had developed in the past two years as Abbot at the Georgia monastery.

The monks were now to be shaved with electric razors. Soon they were issued their own razors, with brushes and soap, and their own mirrors. They would shave twice a week, which was considered revolutionary among the older monks. Within two weeks of his investiture, Dom James had a new heating system in the process of being installed in the cellar under the Scriptorium. Gethsemani was a project that capitalized on his business school training and was a welcome challenge to his management ability.

Dom James arrived at Gethsemani just in time to save it from a financial catastrophe. With the unexpected increase in postulants and the resulting costs, he instituted a stricter screening process before accepting new arrivals to cut down on the turnover of dissatisfied applicants. Secondly, he mechanized the processes used to farm and to operate the facility. He instituted an expansion of the living quarters as well as modernization of the church building, both of which needed major renovation. He also continued to seek properties for new foundations to expand the Order and at the same time reduce the size of the Gethsemani population. It was a labor of love for Dom James to apply the full range of management principles he had learned at Harvard's School of Business. His work mirrored the mechanization process underway throughout the country in the years following World War II. Gethsemani was a textbook case of an organization with problems mandating a solution.

Merton had fallen in love with the medieval peace and tranquility of Gethsemani in spite of its antiquated facilities and outdated practices. It was his enthusiasm for the place that captivated readers of his autobiography and made it a bestseller. Gethsemani's simple rural setting resonated with his memories of the countryside around Oakham and earlier at St. Antonin.

Merton's nostalgia was now interrupted. The sound of pneumatic drills and sledgehammers in the Scriptorium was deafening. Merton said it reminded him too much of New York City. Merton's peace was shattered. He resented Dom James' management style of bulldozing the monastery's atmosphere along with the buildings without regard to its effect on the group. Merton reinstituted his request to be allowed to transfer to the more contemplative Carthusians, as an exception to his vow of stability to remain at Gethsemani for the rest of his life.

Dom James was not particularly impressed with Merton's reputation as a writer, but he put the profits that resulted from sales of Merton's publications to good use. It was Dom Frederic who had successfully promoted them, especially *The Seven Storey Mountain*. Merton bristled to think that his royalties were paying for the noisy tractors and other heavy equipment that Dom James brought in to update the monastery. The new Abbot endorsed Dom Frederic's decision to deny Merton any request for transfer. Furthermore, he refused to send the request forward to higher authority for a review of his decision.

Merton's publishing success soon brought in significant revenues to the monastery. By the end of 1948, *The Seven Storey Mountain* had sold 31,000 copies. By September 1949, the figure was 275,000. It was the top bestseller of Giroux's career. The original edition eventually sold 600,000 copies before later editions came out. Giroux had obtained attributions for the jacket cover from prominent Catholic writers, including Graham Greene, Evelyn Waugh, and Clare Boothe Luce. Their praise for the book and its author may have increased its appeal to prospective readers since at that time Merton was an unknown writer. Monsignor Fulton J. Sheen said Merton's book was an echo of St. Augustine's *Confessions* in terms of the spiritual search that both works describe.

The honesty of Merton's story about how he had found meaning and peace in a world of materialism and anxiety was compelling for many people who were coping with the major changes taking place in the late 1940's. Other books about Christianity also spoke to the spiritual hunger evident at the time, resulting in bestsellers like *The Robe* and *The Cardinal*. In November 1948, the popular English author, Evelyn Waugh, visited Merton at Gethsemani to discuss his offer to revise *The Seven Storey Mountain* for his British readers. Waugh, too, was a convert to Catholicism. He had just acquired an international reputation for his best-selling novel, *Brideshead Revisited*. Merton acceded to the Abbot's decision to give Waugh approval to edit Merton's book. Waugh had said he particularly wanted to improve the sentence structure. Merton agreed that this would be helpful. But Waugh took additional liberties.

Merton was surprised to see he omitted passages in the text relating to descriptions of student life at Cambridge. Merton had tried to give the reader a graphic idea of the low moral level of his student life there by describing other students' behavior, since he was not allowed to describe his own activities. Waugh saw no need for Merton to describe any of the student activity, other than academic, in this prestigious British institution. He wrote only that Merton expected to be punished for his sins at the school.

Merton had already omitted any details he originally intended for the autobiography, assuming that the Cistercian censors would cut them out anyway. The manuscript had already been cut by about one-third when it was published, according to Giroux. In Waugh's version, only generalities were left to explain Merton's desire for a life of penance. Waugh also eliminated Merton's criticism of the Franciscan Order. Furthermore, he deleted Merton's touching poem concerning his brother's death. Overall Merton estimated that Waugh cut twenty percent of the book. He renamed it *Elected Silence*, taken from a poem by Gerard Manley Hopkins. Waugh obtained approval to publish his version of the book direct from the Order in London. Clonmore & Reynolds, Dublin, published it in 1949.

Merton acknowledged Waugh's reputation as a writer, telling him that he accepted his changes with gratitude. He claimed he agreed with Waugh that he had been too hard on Cambridge, especially for an edition to be sold in Great Britain. Regarding the poem about his brother's death, Merton said in a letter to Waugh that it was Giroux's idea to include it in the autobiography, not his own, but he was too late to get it removed. He thanked Waugh for all the changes, and said he believed the book was considerably improved. Merton continued his correspondence with Waugh after publication of *Elected Silence*, asking him for the next four years to review his manuscripts before he submitted them to publishers. Merton considered Waugh's comments very helpful to him.

Waugh had first received Merton's autobiography in galleys from Giroux, asking for his review and an attribution for the back cover, which he provided. After publication, Clare Boothe Luce, a popular American writer and promoter of Catholic publications, sent Waugh a copy expressing her enthusiasm for the work. At that time she had a hit play, "The Women," on Broadway. She was the wife of the wealthy magazine publisher, Henry Luce, founder of *Time*, *Life*, and *Fortune* magazines. She likewise was a convert to Roman Catholicism, having been instructed for five months by Monsignor Fulton J. Sheen. She publicized her conversion story serially in *McCall's* magazine, at that time the largest women's magazine in circulation. The Luces were friends of Cardinal Spellman in New York and moved in the most influential circles of their time. She traveled widely to lecture on religious and social issues.

After she became aware of Merton's work, she approached Dom James to see how she could assist the monastery. She donated a rebuilt typewriter and some of her books and recordings of classical music to Gethsemani, which Merton appreciated. In 1949 she donated her estate in South Carolina to the monastery, which became the third foundation for Gethsemani.

In March 1949 New Directions published *Seeds of Contemplation*, a major work that gained wide acceptance. Merton was not proud of it. He thought it to be too "clever," lacking "warmth" and revealing a "pride and contempt" for others that he thought he had eliminated from his character. A book club advertised it as a "streamlined *Imitation of Christ*." Merton recorded in his journal that he believed this work sounded more like Swift, the satirist, than Thomas à Kempis.

Merton's life changed radically after Dom James became involved in his publishing. Dom James fast-tracked the operation by providing Merton with office space near his own office to answer correspondence and to continue doing his writing. Dom James assigned other monks to type letters and manuscripts and assemble galley proofs, as well as to help manage the preparation and dispatch of manuscripts to publishers and censors. Merton's writing had become an industry, and Dom James set it up to run efficiently, like all the other activities he controlled.

Merton decided to apply for American citizenship in January 1949. He and another monk, Father Emery, went in to Louisville together to file the application form, called the first papers. They had both taken this step the previous summer, but had to repeat the process because they had failed to proceed to the final step before the deadline. On his application, Merton gave as his reason for not previously completing the process: that he was too busy with the pursuit of perfection to take the time. One would guess it was due to his forthcoming ordination and his assignment to prepare a commemorative book for the Abbey's centennial.

On their way to the courthouse, Merton and Father Emery dropped off Father Raymond at the Louisville Infirmary, where the monks were usually hospitalized. He was to undergo surgery for cancer, and the seriousness of his condition was unknown.

In spite of their differences, Merton felt sympathy for Father Raymond's condition and long absence from the monastery. Merton wrote to Father Raymond several times to cheer him up while he was away. He sent Father Raymond some clever limericks that poked fun at their habitual disagreements. Father Raymond's surgery was successful, and he earned the respect of all the monks by voluntarily taking on some of the most arduous work underway in the renovation project when he recovered. Merton had made gestures of friendship to Father Raymond on other occasions. Earlier, when Father Raymond suffered a broken tooth, Merton gave him a bottle of painkiller tablets he had been given when he was sick.

No matter how Merton tried, the relationship between the often-published senior monk and the outspoken young novice was not to be bridged. Eventually Merton accepted the public displays of their differences, demonstrated to the entire group at Chapter meetings, as inevitable. The depth of Merton's books met a need in his readers' spiritual life that devotional books like Father Raymond's did not even attempt. Although their audiences were different, their writing by comparison was consistently unfavorable to Father Raymond's work.

Merton progressed in the Order, but not in record time. Dom James appointed Merton as a subdeacon on December 19, 1948, four months after he had become Abbot. Merton was made a deacon on the following March 19, St. Joseph's feast day. His ordination to the priesthood had been delayed due to the death of Dom Frederic. His confessor, Father Anthony, recommended a postponement, saying that he believed Merton was not sufficiently mature in his faith to be certain about his emotional readiness for ordination. Better to delay this final step in his spiritual growth than to discover a problem later. Merton was not really surprised, considering his tenuous relationship with Father Anthony. The fact that Merton was a convert and freely admitted his difficulties in adapting to the religious life reinforced the decision. With a new Abbot in charge, it was not appropriate to argue the point. Merton knew that his study of Roman Catholicism was almost entirely self-generated, and there was no easy way to convey to his superior what he had learned about the Bible, Church history, and theology that prepared him for the priesthood.

Traditionally the Catholic Church has provided higher education in Rome for priests who are identified worldwide as having considerable potential for higher positions or for making special contributions. They receive formal theological training and advanced degrees in Church teaching at Gregorian University in Rome. From Gethsemani, both Abbot Flavian Burns, the successor to Dom James as Abbot, and Father Tarcisius Conner, O.C.S.O., were sent to Gregorian University by the Order. Father Timothy Vander Vennet was also sent to Rome for advanced studies. In contrast to Merton, most of the monks had had years of formal instruction in the Catholic faith before they entered the monastery.

As a very recent convert, Merton's only formal instruction had been the six weeks of Catechism instruction and his attendance at college lectures given by Maritain and Dan Walsh. He did attend the classes for novices at Gethsemani, but Merton obtained most of his knowledge through his own reading.

Later, in one of his own conferences with novices, Merton complained that one of his instructors at Gethsemani had only translated from a Latin text to the class, without comment, rather than teach anything. He told his students that he could have done that translation for himself. Merton acquired his comprehensive knowledge of Church teaching through his tried and true method of researching a subject that interested him until he was satisfied that he had acquired the knowledge he was seeking.

Merton also had learned Italian from his studies at Oakham and Cambridge, as well as from his travels, so he would have had a distinct advantage had he been sent to the University. In fact, the Abbot General discussed the possibility of such an assignment with Merton to get his reaction. He told Merton the building where he would study was near a park that had been closed and paved over due to frequent crime there. Merton could not imagine living or meditating in such a setting and told the Abbot General he would not be interested in going to Rome. He believed that acceptance would undoubtedly be viewed as preparation for an administrative assignment. This would not further his plan for a life of solitude.

Merton learned foreign languages much as he did Church dogma, by a tireless determination. After his childhood exposure and education provided knowledge of several foreign languages, he continued learning other languages by independent efforts. A study published by Virginia Bear in *The Merton Annual, Volume 15*, 2002, compares Merton's foreign language ability to the official scale used by the US Foreign Service Institute. According to the study, Merton had native fluency in English and French, and an equivalent knowledge of Latin. His Spanish was at full professional proficiency, almost to the point of native fluency. He developed a professional working proficiency in Portuguese and Italian, with an additional conversational ability in Italian. His German was limited to a working proficiency in the spoken rather than in the written word. He acquired a limited proficiency in reading Provencal and Catalan. His knowledge of Greek was a limited working proficiency.

He attempted a study of other languages primarily related to correspondents in other countries. He undertook Polish to correspond better with Milosz, Russian to correspond with Pasternak, and Chinese to enhance the quality of his correspondence with Suzuki and to study some ancient texts he had read in unsatisfying translations. He also explored Japanese, Hebrew, Arabic, and Persian, but never progressed in any of them, probably due to time restrictions and higher priorities.

Merton's ordination was finally set for May 26, 1949, the Feast of the Ascension of Jesus into Heaven. The title Brother was changed to Father M. Louis Merton. One other monk, Father Amandus, was ordained at the same ceremony.

Lying prostrate on their faces in the church, before the Archbishop of Louisville, John Floersch, the two monks vowed a lifetime of service to the monastery. Four additional monks were admitted into higher orders at the same ceremony.

*The ceremony was long, it was formal, and my emotions consumed me in a way I cannot describe.*

*I was consecrated to my God as a priest forever. I would spend the rest of my life as a priest at Gethsemani, without condition.*

*I told myself God Himself looked down on me at the moment I spoke my vows and accepted me as His servant. I felt a peace I never knew.*

*I began to realize that this wasn't the end I had been seeking. Rather, it was a beginning on a whole new plane of experience.*

*I had now arrived at the center of all existence.*

*I would begin again. Jesus, I nail myself to your cross.*

*Our Lady of Cobre, you prayed for me to make it to the priesthood.*
*Please help me to serve worthily, under your care.*

Following the ceremony, the six monks had lunch with the Archbishop who had administered the sacred sacrament.

Merton was successful in getting his old friends from Columbia days to come for the event: Seymour Freedgood, Robert Lax, Ed Rice, Dan Walsh, and Robert Giroux, as well as his publisher, James Laughlin, and from Douglaston: Nancy Hauck, his grandmother's Catholic companion, and Elsie Holahan Jenkins, who had married Uncle Harold. Tom nicknamed Elsie "Honily" at the ordination. Also some newer friends attended: Thomas Flanagan, a friend of Ed Rice, Rod Mudge, a friend of Dan Walsh, and George McCauliff. It was McCauliff who had sent Merton's first book of published poems to Clare Boothe Luce and introduced her to Merton's work. His only living relative, Uncle Harold, did not accompany his wife because it was said that he had severed his relationship with Merton when he entered the monastery. Merton did not record his feelings about his Uncle. Elsie's daughter, Patricia, later reported that Harold thought that for Merton, the monastery would be "a waste of a brilliant mind because it is a place of silence, of no words."

There was so much excitement among this group of Merton's friends while taking photographs that one of the monks proclaimed him on the morning of his ordination in the Chapter of Faults. The charge was for not preventing his guests from blocking the refectory door in the cloister when they were having their picture taken. It is unknown if Merton received a penance for this occurrence. It obviously could not diminish Merton's high spirits. The gifts his friends brought were most welcome: a newspaper of the day, a leather-bound copy of *The Seven Storey Mountain*, representing sales of 100,000 copies from Giroux, a hammered silver chalice from Dan Walsh, and lots of fellowship and news of the group. He was allowed to spend two hours with his guests, a precious privilege in the secluded monastery life of that time. Lax brought a movie camera and tried to record the whole event. He also received two gifts from readers. A Catholic high school in Mobile, Alabama, sent him three small altar linens and an amice, or linen cloth worn as part of a priest's vestments. A nun at a St. Louis, Missouri, hospital sent a cincture, or rope-like belt, also to be worn at Mass.

Merton's friends provided him with an update on world events, including the fact that the British no longer controlled India. Truman was now President in his own right, having been elected after serving out the deceased Roosevelt's term. Merton was equally interested in a report on various people's reactions to being mentioned in *The Seven Storey Mountain*. With great amusement Merton mimicked shock and amazement about the negative opinions of the parishioners at the Zion Church in Douglaston. His family had never really fit in to the conformist suburban group, being very much individualists and having other outside interests. Nevertheless, Merton later sent a letter of apology to the daughter of the pastor at the Zion Church for his remarks in the book and asked her to pray for him. Merton's guests noticed that he was much thinner now than his friends, and much more ascetic than they remembered. He was obviously comfortable with himself and happy with his lifestyle, as well as his new name. His friends immediately adapted it to call him "Father Louie."

It occurred to Merton that this small group of New York friends was the beginning of his spiritual community, united in something intangible that bound them together in fraternal brotherhood. Now, at the monastery, he experienced a slightly larger group that he felt he was now an integral part of, under the mantle of his transcendent Creator. He wondered if that concept extended to all humanity. In the eyes of God, perhaps we are all one, he thought.

After the ordination, Merton sat with his friends under the ginkgo trees. He told his friends about the phone call the Abbot had received at Easter, 1949. It was from Don Ameche, a popular Hollywood star, inquiring whether anyone had purchased the movie rights to *The Seven Storey Mountain*. He was interested in making a movie about Merton and thought he would like to play the part.

Don Ameche was a well-known movie star of the time, tall, dark-haired and dapper, with a thin black moustache. He usually played the role of a well-to-do gentleman of the leisure class who was neither serious nor intellectual. Actually, Ameche was a serious Catholic, educated at Marquette University and the University of Wisconsin, who played diverse roles in a number of movies in the 1930s and 40s. His real name was Dominic Felix Amici from Kenosha Wisconsin. Merton would not know that Ameche would later be recognized with an Academy Award for a serious role in 1986. Merton would have heard of his movies, "The Story of Alexander Graham Bell" and "The Three Musketeers" because of their wide popularity just two years before Merton entered the monastery.

Merton told his friends that his preference for an actor to personify him would be someone more like Gary Cooper. Cooper was usually portrayed as an intense, plainspoken man of purpose and firm resolve, obviously a much more complex persona than Ameche. Dom James rejected Don Ameche's overtures to purchase the movie rights, in spite of the monastery's financial needs. Merton was in full agreement with the Abbot, and was obviously relieved not to have his life portrayed as he could imagine it might be. He would not have wanted his life to be compared to either Alexander Graham Bell or one of the three musketeers.

The next morning, Friday, May 27, Merton said his first Mass, a low Mass dedicated to Our Lady of Cobre in thanksgiving for his priesthood. He was nervous and self-conscious and emotional about the mystery he was now part of. He firmly believed that Jesus Christ really appeared on the altar when he consecrated the host and then the wine. He made a few mistakes and a couple of omissions, immediately corrected by the monk who attended him at the altar. Once he lost his footing on the steps down to the communion rail, but luckily caught himself.

The following day, Saturday, he said his first High Mass, a much more formal observance than the previous one. He was still nervous, because he was required to sing many of the prayers. Those attending said his singing was beautiful, especially the Pater Noster, or Lord's Prayer.

The press was at the Mass to record the new popular author's singular exposure to the public. It was the one time that photographs of a cloistered monk were allowed, according to the restrictions prescribed by the Order. Paradoxically, it was because Merton was secluded that public exposure became newsworthy. An Associated Press photographer passed a message to Merton that he would like him to pose for a press shot at the consecration when he lifted his hammered silver chalice. Merton passed a message back, suggesting the news photographer go jump in a lake, and he could recommend a deep one two miles away.

Later that day, there was even more of an event underway for a secluded monastery. Preparations began for Gethsemani's 100th anniversary celebration. Merton's ordination was pushed out of everyone's thoughts when an Army helicopter flew in to deliver and set up a sound system for the event, five days in advance.

Gethsemani was the first Cistercian group in America, and the Abbey's church was now to be elevated to the status of a minor basilica in honor of the centennial. June 1, 1949, brought newspaper and radio news reporters as well as camera crews to produce the news clip that would be shown at movie theaters nationwide, along with the movie.

Merton had been commissioned to prepare a souvenir book. The monastery published Merton's tasteful product, called *Gethsemani Magnificat*, although Merton was not enthusiastic about it. He believed the end result was disappointing. •

The guest speaker was the noted Monsignor, Fulton J. Sheen, author, television personality, and the priest credited by Clare Boothe Luce and several other prominent figures for their conversion to the Catholic Church. He spoke over a microphone to the crowd gathered in the open field next to the monastery. Merton said that Sheen had praised the monks' silence at full volume. The local radio station, WHAJ, broadcast the event live, and Fox Movietone News filmed the monks singing some sacred music as well as Monsignor Sheen and Dom James giving their remarks. There were an estimated 7,000 people of all ages assembled, seated in folding chairs. Even though it was a hot summer day, the men wore suits, many with white dress shirts and ties, and the women were in their Sunday finest, many wearing straw hats and high-heeled shoes.

There was a press conference, and the reporters asked that Merton be included. Merton told the group that he was not allowed to speak or sign autographs, except that he had been given permission to answer questions from the reporters. He was asked for his blessing, and he gave it with some embarrassment, along with a blessing for rosary beads. Merton believed that he had been responsible for the extent of Gethsemani's notoriety at this solemn occasion, and that it was a most un-Trappist thing to have done. He had taken his vows only five days earlier, a remarkable coincidence, he thought, that it was just in time for his public appearance. Some thought Merton was being exploited and that his appearance at the centennial was used to further book sales.

Merton's status was now secure. He had eclipsed Father Raymond's reputation. Dom James assigned him space in the Abbey's rare book vault to work. He was given access to the manuscripts there as well, including original documents of St. Bernard, missals, and antiphoners dating back to medieval times. He loved to look at the manuscripts, and he applied himself diligently to translating them for the Abbot.

Merton felt there was a haunting beauty to the cloistered walkways and buttressed ceilings of the old abbey churches he saw pictured in the books. He found a cold beauty in the small arches leading the eyes

heavenward, a link to God. He didn't see this in his immediate surroundings. Looking at the parchment pages of the old books, he felt
privileged to have access to them and to get in touch with the transcendent spirit of the medieval abbeys. It brought back memories of trips
he had taken with his father to see the ruins of abbeys in France, and
he could now recreate in his mind's eye what they would have looked
like at the time the monks of those days built them by hand. They did
not have bulldozers, he thought.

He applied himself diligently to translating the old texts for the
Abbot. Merton called the vault area his cave, with its two steel doors
protecting him from distractions. Actually, it served as a first hermitage
for him. It was really a refuge, as the monastery exploded with growth
to a total of 270 men.

Dom James now organized the public persona of Thomas Merton with
the same efficiency he applied to the rest of the monastery. Five monks
now received and answered all of Merton's fan mail, with the instruction
to compose their reply letters in Merton's own writing style. Merton
was incredulous at the basic dishonesty to his readers, who sincerely
sought to share their spirituality with Merton. Merton saw no solution
for this. He let his vow of obedience prevail over his conscience, being a
reluctant party to this dishonesty. He would be allowed to write books
but not his own correspondence. He did not mind having help with the
mail that was arriving in bags at Gethsemani's' post office. Otherwise
he would have no time to read or do other writing. For Merton it was
a tough choice to make.

He described himself at the monastery as a duck in a chicken coop.
He began to believe that a complicated person caused more harm than
good in a monastery. He was not the most popular monk there. Merton's
self-consciousness continued to grow and make him uncomfortable.
He began to feel emotionally at sea again. He wanted to lose himself
in God, not by becoming public property.

What Dom James did not know was that Merton recorded his
activities in a diary, which actually became a repository of his feelings
through most of his monastic life. He found comfort in giving private
expression to what was happening to him to clarify his own thinking.
Only God would understand it all.

# Chapter 17

Merton's life did not change visibly for the next decade at Gethsemani. Inwardly his solitude and struggle to maintain his privacy were challenged. He wondered whether he should be publishing so extensively, or even writing at all, rather than leading a life primarily of contemplation.

Only a few weeks after his ordination, Merton sang a High Mass in honor of Our Lady of Mount Carmel. He had intensified his devotion to her in Havana and had promised her he would become a priest if she helped him to achieve this goal. Suddenly Merton fainted. Dom James was alarmed. He believed Merton had had a panic attack, although it could have been the hot July weather.

During this time Merton had been appealing to Dom James to extend the size of the monastery grounds that the monks were allowed to use. The increased number of novices mandated expansion of the living area. Dom James, being a pragmatist, and interested in a more productive operation, gradually relaxed the rules, which had been formulated when there were few monks. Acres were going unused. Merton was very pleased at the Abbot's decision, and his disposition improved noticeably when he could enjoy the natural beauty around him in all seasons of the year with the relaxed restrictions.

Merton was already working with Father Timothy Vander Vennet with the Abbot's agreement on building up their theological course to begin working toward establishing "a center of really first-class studies in spiritual theology." Merton assisted Father Timothy in outlining the coverage and structure of the classes which Merton hoped would lead eventually to a seminary building where canon law and other related subjects could be taught that are "so necessary for future superiors." Merton also recommended that the classes be taught in discussion groups to avoid "memory work" and "nervous tension"—a technique Merton himself employed later as Master of Scholastics.

As early as September 1949, Merton was at work attempting to influence Dom James about the way he would restructure the Gethsemani grounds in his comprehensive upgrade project. Writing to Dom James while he was still at Citeaux for a meeting, he reminded the Abbot that he had said that he wanted Gethsemani to become "a sort of West Point

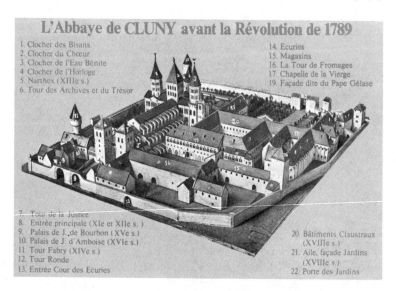

## L'Abbaye de CLUNY avant la Révolution de 1789

1. Clocher des Bisans
2. Clocher du Chœur
3. Clocher de l'Eau Bénite
4. Clocher de l'Horloge
5. Narthex (XIIIe s.)
6. Tour des Archives et du Trésor

14. Ecuries
15. Magasins
16. La Tour de Fromages
17. Chapelle de la Vierge
19. Façade dite du Pape Gélase

7. Tour de la Justice
8. Entrée principale (XIe et XIIe s.)
9. Palais de J. de Bourbon (XVe s.)
10. Palais de J. d'Amboise (XVIe s.)
11. Tour Fabry (XIVe s.)
12. Tour Ronde
13. Entrée Cour des Ecuries

20. Bâtiments Claustraux (XVIIIe s.)
21. Aile, façade Jardins (XVIIIe s.)
22. Porte des Jardins

The model, made in 1855 by Geugnon after the destruction of the 19th century, enables one to grasp the enormity of the monument at the same time as the beauty of its external dimensions, the tiered levels of which climax in the series of bell towers.

*Two views of the Abbey of Cluny (Saone-et-Loire), the largest church in the world until St. Peter's was built in Rome. It served as a refuge for Abelard in the twelfth century after the Pope condemned him for heresy, a charge that was later lifted. The two illustrations are the work of Francois Gueugnon, a 19th century Beaux Arts artisan. The upper picture is a relief plan of the Cluny complex before the French Revolution of 1789. From a postcard by Editions Combier, Macon, France. The lower illustration is from Gueugnon's model, built in 1855, depicting major destruction to the Abbey in the 19th century.*
*Alain Erlande-Brandenburg, Cluny Abbey. Edilarge S.A.*
*Editions Ouest-France, Rennes, 1996.*

or Annapolis for Cistercians." Merton undoubtedly hoped his Abbot would speak with the Abbot General while they were there together to get some preliminary agreement to make Gethsemani, in Merton's words, "a center of spiritual studies," including possibly a grange in the woods with a chapel "with a monk permanently in residence (guess who??) in the spirit of the Desert Fathers."

Merton was writing the history of the Cistercian Order and its significance in European history. He called it *The Waters of Siloe*, published by Harcourt, Brace in September 1949. Sales were attributed to the fact that it carried the name of Thomas Merton, not because the subject had appeal to a mass audience.

Merton's *Waters of Siloe* was dedicated to Evelyn Waugh. It may have been Merton's way of repaying Waugh for giving an endorsement on the cover of *The Seven Storey Mountain* as well as for his critique of Merton's subsequent manuscripts. This new book also included high quality black and white pictures of Gethsemani, other Cistercian abbeys in France, and the new foundations in the U.S. Some sign language is also illustrated.

Merton managed to get a few personal comments included in this book without distracting from the straightforward history. For example, he mentioned that Father Eutroprius, the first Abbot in Kentucky, " ... had more courage than physical strength—a common trait among Trappists." Then he mentioned that the Trappists baked their own bread on board ship to the U.S., before the " ... phenomenal menus of the modern ocean liner." This is one of the few references Merton ever made to his extensive experience in trans-Atlantic travel.

Merton also told the story of a major fire that destroyed the building where the monks had earlier operated a college on the monastery grounds. Their teaching obligations had gradually distracted them from their monastic vocation, it was determined by the Order, so it was not rebuilt. Merton sometimes did not hesitate to state his opinion as fact, adding that the building was replaced at the monastery's entrance by a "stocky, purposeful little statue" of St. Joseph, patron of the interior life. This was one of several instances when he could not resist the opportunity to pass judgment on the pedestrian quality of the artwork he had to live with. He concluded that a contemplative could become overly attached to his contemplation and " ... be as trammeled as a millionaire" in "complacent self-satisfaction." A love of ourselves is " ... the source of all boredom, restlessness, unquiet, misery, and unhappiness; ultimately, it is hell." Merton credits St. Bernard with this opinion.

Merton's book is strangely silent about his Abbot's death the previous year. He concludes his history of Gethsemani in July 1947, when Dom Frederic sent the monks from Gethsemani to begin the new monastery in Utah. This book was published only months after Father Raymond's book, *Burnt Out Incense*, was released. In Father Raymond's 100-year history of the Order, he had described Dom Frederic's contribution to the Order up to and including his death on August 4, 1948.

Merton would not have wanted to compete with Father Raymond's dramatic conclusion to his book. It provided a graphic description of Archbishop Floersh tossing the red Kentucky clay into the Abbot's grave. Father Raymond's final statement in the book was that some monks burn out while others must burn on, and eventually become burnt out incense. Merton could not have devised such a remark about Dom Frederic.

Merton's history is far more comprehensive than Father Raymond's, going back to the beginning of the Order in France, covering the same 100 years of Father Raymond's work, and then providing additional material about the foundations in the U.S. Merton also added a glossary of monastic terms and a bibliography that charitably included two of Father Raymond's books. On the other hand, Father Raymond's *Burnt Out Incense* did not include a bibliography and cited no works other than the four books he quoted directly in the Foreword (one of which was *The Seven Storey Mountain*).

The two books make an interesting comparison in other respects as well. Father Raymond praised Dom Frederic for his building and rebuilding programs at Gethsemani; Merton described the effect as like an armed camp, illustrative of the hard labor of men preparing for an approaching spiritual enemy. Additionally, Merton complained that the 160-foot water tower that Dom Frederic added to the monastery grounds challenged the viewer to picture a monastery in the tradition of the beautiful European ones. Merton said that the water tower made the monastery look more grim than before, but more alert and more American, he added diplomatically. He undoubtedly saw Gethsemani architecturally as a homely child of the Order in comparison with the European abbeys.

He was no doubt conveying a silent message in including pictures of some of the most picturesque Cistercian monasteries in France. The inside cover is a photograph of Fontenay, and inserts include photographs of Tamie, Aiguebelle, and Senanque. Merton commented in his journal (January 27, 1947) that "Cistercian architecture explains many things about our rule and life." He said that Senanque was " ... born of prayer and is prayer. Its simplicity and its energy tell us what our prayer should be."

Without fully identifying or describing it, Merton also included two pictures of only the interior of the Belgian abbey at Orval, which he commented on in *The Sign of Jonas*, published four years later. Merton said the sacristy in the rebuilt abbey resembled a circular bar on the promenade deck of an ocean liner. In *The Waters of Siloe*, though, Merton avoided such criticism. He stressed the beauty in the rebuilding of Gethsemani, although he certainly did not imply that it was comparable to the European abbeys. He obviously loved it because it was his home rather than for its architectural merit.

Merton described the day of his solemn vows without mentioning the event, saying only that it was the day Dom Frederic announced the names of those he selected to establish the foundation in Georgia. Merton added that it occurred after a matutinal Mass on March 19, 1944.

Merton gave ample coverage to Father Raymond's biography of John Green Hanning, who became Brother Joachim, termed *The Man Who Got Even with God*. Merton retold this story in his own words, and credited Father Raymond by noting the book went through twelve American editions and was translated into many other languages.

Father Raymond praised Dom Frederic's business dealings in founding the new monasteries first in Georgia, then in Utah to relieve the overcrowding at Gethsemani. He gave specific dollar amounts for purchases of the two properties. In Merton's book, he commented only that Dom Frederic spent too much money for the Utah property, and that Gethsemani could not afford it in 1947 when there was such a great need for repairs and rebuilding at Gethsemani. His interest in this aspect of monastery management may have been due to the fact that his own work was now paying some of the bills.

An interesting comparison to Father Raymond's book is a very readable article Merton published in *The Commonweal* magazine. It was his own version of the founding of the monastery in Utah, the second Cistercian foundation in the U.S. within three years. In Merton's down to earth style, he depicted the probable reaction of Mormons in Ogden to the 34 monks' arrival with cardboard boxes from Kentucky whiskey distilleries and coffee companies. Although the boxes only contained the monks' belongings, the Mormons would not know that and would object to what they saw, inasmuch as Mormons did not drink whiskey or coffee. In typical Merton style, mentioning his personal agenda in a passing comment, he ended the piece with the hope that a semi-eremitical order, such as the Carthusians, would come to America soon.

The article was later reprinted in *The Commonweal Reader*, published by Harper & Brothers in 1949, an anthology covering twenty-five years of publication of *The Commonweal* magazine. The book also included an excerpt from *Figures for an Apocalypse* and two of Merton's other poems.

As Merton continued to use different publishers, Naomi Burton began to encounter problems with legal entanglements from various contracts Merton was signing. He did not hesitate to give publishing and/or translation rights to various friends, associates, and charitable organizations who wrote to him seeking financial assistance.

Naomi got permission from the Abbot to come to Gethsemani in December 1949 to discuss the problem. She came all the way from Louisville in a taxi, to the amazement of the monks. This is about a 50-mile ride. This probably reflected a liberal travel budget, since her stature at the publishing company was based on her reputation as editor to some prominent writers, eventually including Ian Fleming and Ogden Nash as well as Merton. She and Merton sat together in the parlor of the gatehouse, the only building where females were allowed. Male visitors could proceed as far as the novitiate. When Dom James knocked at the door of the parlor to meet Naomi, Merton knocked back twice on the table to signal him to come in, a Trappist practice used to avoid unnecessary speech.

Naomi established and found it necessary to maintain a continuing dialogue with Dom James about the business aspects of Merton's publications, rights to translations, royalties, and contract amendments and clarifications. After all, the monastery owned the rights to Merton's work. Merton soon noticed that Naomi and Dom James had developed a rapport that excluded him. He gradually realized that he was not privy to all the decisions being made about his books, so he began to mistrust Naomi as his agent.

In one exchange of correspondence, Naomi told Merton to go to the barn and have a good cry for his self-pity. Later, after they reached a resolution of their communications difficulties, in one of several later visits, Merton took Naomi out to show her the barn where she had dispatched him for his good cry. Merton may have recognized his weakness at handling the business end of his publishing and resented Dom James' superiority. When he took the vow of poverty, he never expected he would be required to surrender control of his own work.

Merton was unfamiliar with copyright law. He saw his publishing activities as part of his own identity, and was reluctant to relinquish decisions about it to anyone. He wrote to Evelyn Waugh for advice about how to handle multiple publishers. Waugh advised him to reduce the quantity of his writing to reduce the problems. Merton felt obligated to help pay the bills for the monastery's much-needed renovation and expansion, so considered Waugh's advice as no solution. The situation resulted in the Abbot's encouragement and sanctioning of Merton's compulsion to write. He consequently maintained his vow of obedience, accepting the Abbot's decisions about his publications whether he agreed with them or not.

Naomi respected the Abbot's business sense as well as his ability to supervise Merton. Eventually Dom James became the conduit for Naomi's conversion to the Catholic Church. Merton was as surprised as anyone at this unexpected outcome of the relationship. Merton's spontaneity in granting publishing rights to worthy causes had started it all.

In 1950, *What Are These Wounds? The Life of a Cistercian Mystic, Saint Lutgarde of Aywieres* was published by the Catholic publisher, Bruce, which had also published Father Raymond's book, *The Man Who Got Even With God*. Merton had written the Lutgarde biography five years earlier for Dom Frederic and intended it to be published anonymously as a pamphlet for devotional reading. Merton later categorized the quality of his writing in this book as "awful." Dom James viewed it objectively as a thoroughly researched, sensitive description of a very devout nun and the convent life she led. Merton's name on it assured its sale through an established Catholic publisher.

Had this book not carried Merton's name as author, it would have had less than popular appeal to American readers. Dom James did not hesitate to release it for publication, taking advantage of the momentum of Merton's sales records. He had tractors to pay for and a monastery to renovate. To handle Merton's mail more efficiently, Dom James directed the monastery print shop to print reply cards. These cards contained general remarks to acknowledge the correspondence so that any of the monks could quickly address them to Merton's readers instead of a personalized response by Merton or another monk impersonating him. Merton was scandalized by the action but had to accept it.

Revealing some interesting things about himself in this book, Merton discussed a Church theologian's opinions about the meaning of visions of the dead. Merton stated dispassionately that it is " ... the least perfect kind of mystical vision granted to man on earth" but "most suited to our ordinary way of seeing." He added that theologians generally agree that " ... these bodies in visions can have an objective and physical reality." Merton was undoubtedly thinking of the vision he believed he had had of his father that he described in *The Seven Storey Mountain*. He added the counsel of Saint John of the Cross that these visions should be ignored because they could be from the devil or one's own imagination. Merton concluded that all Christian mystical theologians teach that " ... visions should never be encouraged or desired" since the devil likes nothing better than to take advantage of these things for his own purposes." Obviously Merton put considerable effort into researching this subject in light of his own personal experience, having no background in spiritual teachings on this subject, although obviously he did not mention his own experience in this book.

Another fascinating item in Merton's life of St. Lutgarde concerned stigmata, a wound that certain religious people have acquired mystically in the same location as the five wounds of Jesus Christ on the cross.

Merton remarked that medical science has investigated this phenomenon and has never been able to explain it. He added that in some cases "hysterics and maniacs have produced these wounds in themselves." Merton could well have been referring to himself and the scar he carried from the mock crucifixion he was apparently involved in at Cambridge. His fellow monks probably had no idea there could be a personal connection in this remark.

Merton's curiosity encompassed any type of endeavor. Shortly after Naomi's visit, during the Christmas season, the cellarer offered Merton the opportunity to drive the new Jeep to see the far side of the knobs. The cellarer is a title given to the monk in charge of a monastery's vehicles as well as other housekeeping functions. The cellarer assumed that Merton knew how to drive a Jeep. Merton apparently did not volunteer the fact that he had no driving experience other than a couple of lessons from a Father Roman at St. Bonaventure's in his old Chevie. Merton was thrilled to be allowed to try the new Jeep and assumed he could handle it. He drove it down one of the old logging roads, through puddles and ditches and eventually into bushes along the side of the road. When he returned the Jeep to the cellarer, it was covered with mud and debris. The cellarer was incredulous and angry beyond words. In sign language he told Merton never to take the Jeep out again. It is unknown whether he proclaimed Merton for this deception, if the cellarer were willing to admit his gullibility about Merton's driving skills to the entire group in Chapter.

In February 1951 Merton decided to apply for American citizenship for the third time. On this occasion he went alone. He was driven to Louisville by one of the staff to make application. He already had the textbook to master from his previous trips two years earlier. Merton was not the first monk at Gethsemani to apply for U.S. citizenship, since the monastery attracted postulants from many different countries over the years. This time Merton completed the process.

The following June 22, Merton was driven to the ceremony by two brothers, who were laymen living in the guesthouse and had not taken vows. Although Merton had never learned to drive a car, he would have been accompanied anyway in any trip from the monastery because it was a monastery policy that no monk would leave the grounds alone unless he were leaving permanently.

For the occasion, Merton was allowed to choose from the monastery's community closet of clothing. He selected a black suit, large black Spanish-looking felt hat, and a black shirt with white Roman collar. It was a very warm June day in Louisville, so he tilted the hat quite far back on his shaven head. It would have given him a unique appearance anywhere.

Merton's certificate of naturalization, dated June 26, 1951, issued by the U.S. Government, states under the heading, "visible distinctive marks," the following: "Scar palm right hand." On one of Naomi Burton's visits to Gethsemani in the 1960s, Naomi told Merton she had been studying palmistry and offered to read Merton's palm. When she examined his right hand, she asked him how he got the scar. He told her it was his "stigmata" and changed the subject. Naomi must have taken Merton's comment as an attempt at humor and did not pursue her question.

At the courthouse the candidates were seated together as a group and then questioned about any matter that might be a hindrance to eligibility for citizenship. Merton was asked to explain his membership in the National Students League at Columbia University. He undoubtedly answered the question to the satisfaction of the official conducting the procedure, although it must have been a very embarrassing experience for Merton.

After the naturalization ceremony, Merton returned to the monastery with a small American flag and a great deal of pride about the country that was now his. He was too shy to talk about his patriotic sentiments. From one who was homeless for most of his life and without roots, Merton was at last ready to declare himself an American. When he was asked why he had decided to take this step, he said it was because of his admiration for Emily Dickinson and Henry David Thoreau, both of whom were known to lead solitary lives, though not monastic.

Later Merton wrote an article about his own life as a hermit, "Christian Solitude," in which he said a solitary is not necessarily a monk, and might even be remote from cloistered life, like Dickinson and Thoreau. In the case of Thoreau, Merton may have also been thinking of Thoreau's essay on "Civil Disobedience." Merton was initially aware of Thoreau from his reading of Gandhi, who also practiced the principle of civil disobedience.

In his diary (December 27, 1957), Merton describes Gandhi as "in reality the most effective and trustworthy political thinker of our time," an opinion expressed by Einstein with which Merton completely agreed.

Thirteen years later, in 1964, Merton had second thoughts about his decision to become a naturalized citizen. He wrote in a letter to W. H. Ferry, a peace activist who became Merton's confidante, that he would not have become an American citizen if he had known more about the politics of Senator Joseph McCarthy (1950-54). He believed the U.S. Government, under McCarthy's influence, acted unjustly towards people who exercised their right to say what they believed about the Government's actions of that time. Through the influence of Senator McCarthy, a number of prominent citizens were labeled Communists, and many who were unjustly accused were then unable to find or keep meaningful employment. Merton was amazed to learn that Father Raymond supported Senator McCarthy's efforts to rid the country of Communism in this manner.

Anti-Communist sentiment was a prevalent phenomenon in the 1950's. Young men were dying or coming home wounded or emotionally damaged from combat with Communist troops in Korea who upheld the same ideology as the Communists in the Soviet Union. The resulting predominant sentiment in the U.S. was fear. History later revealed that there were in fact Russian spies infiltrating the U.S. Government at that time. However, they were not found to be the celebrities identified and accused by Senator McCarthy.

Merton believed the country was worth loving. He would not betray it. But he had a larger view of the world, based on his earliest travels and associations, through friendships, personal study, and formal correspondence. He saw the world as one. Ideally, citizenship in one country was not as important to him as world citizenship. Under God we are all one people, he maintained, without regard to the opinions of his fellow monks, his readers, or his friends.

# Chapter 18

The monastery was stressed with over-population and required repairs and rebuilding. There were 2,000 acres of monastery property, 400 of which were under cultivation or pasture. Even after the exodus to establish the two foundations in Utah and South Carolina, there were still some 270 monks remaining in 1951 housed in a facility that had accommodated 70. This growth in postulants followed a nationwide trend, the number of U.S. Catholic priests increasing 27% in the 1940s and 25% in the 1950s.

For two years Dom James housed fifty of his monks in a circus tent he was able to buy while buildings were being remodeled. The machines he brought in were ugly and noisy and continued to disturb Merton. The machine he hated most was the yellow Traxcovator, a powerful tractor that could perform a number of different operations and made even more noise than the other machines. Merton said it reminded him of a hippopotamus. As each new tractor or harvester appeared, Merton wondered if his royalties had paid for it. He found it ironic that his solitude that was disturbed was being marketed to acquire more of the same machinery that was distracting him, and, in fact, robbing him of the solitude he was writing about. He commented once that he estimated he brought in $20,000 to $30,000 a year from 1949 to 1951. He was apparently never told how much his writing earned for the monastery.

Merton's books could not have paid all the bills. Dom James organized the monks into a business he called Gethsemani Farms. They produced and marketed a Port Salut type of cheese, a variety of meat products, and bourbon-flavored fruitcakes, primarily through mail order shipments. They later added bread to sell to nearby stores. They also boarded thoroughbred horses and tended them. They even raised Belgian mares that they sent to the state fair. Gethsemani Farms was an ongoing business. A New York newspaper survey found their fruitcakes to be the number one fruitcake on the U.S. market.

Merton noticed Gethsemani was acquiring a "big business" atmosphere. The monks planted tobacco, alfalfa, and other crops at various times to experiment with the yield they could achieve. They began to use insecticide and other chemicals to increase production. They operated a 24-hour-a-day facility the Brothers called Little Pittsburgh, manufacturing alfalfa pellets for turkeys and race horses. The Abbot appointed Brother Frederic to manage the entire operation. He had come from the Ford Motor Company, and, like Dom James, had completed a college education in business administration. Dom James recognized Brother Frederic's talents and delegated the authority to him to put them to good use. The position of cellarer, or business manager, was a standard assignment in each of the Order's abbeys, but none had ever matched the scope and importance of the job as Dom James designed it.

Dom James then gave Brother Frederic permission to speak rather than be limited to sign language, since his new production responsibilities were so demanding. Merton loved to tease Brother Frederic, who would speak, while Merton replied in sign language as was required of him.

Each year, from September to December, the community made an all-out effort to prepare for the Christmas rush. Merton noted that there was no writing talent applied to the marketing effort. To advertise Christmas products, the monastery printed and distributed an advertisement that read, "Many porkers are called but few are chosen to produce our luscious hams." Merton was occasionally asked to write ads and other promotional material, but he avoided it when he could. Sometimes he felt obligated to make a contribution, although he said he would probably burn someday for helping with these ads.

Dom James instituted changes wherever he saw the opportunity to increase revenue for the monastery's expenses. Merton thought the monastery gift shop was an extension of Dom James' taste and management style. The monastery sold a religious medal on a cigarette lighter with a picture of St. Christopher on one side and the monastery on the other. The entire concept of financing the monastery through secular products drove Merton to distraction.

Dom James continued the marketing of Father Raymond's books that Dom Frederic had found profitable. In 1951 Bruce Publishing Company published Father Raymond's *God Goes to Murderer's Row*, a documentary about the electrocution of a Kentucky prisoner. Father Raymond was obviously being affected by the widening gap between his literary reputation and Merton's recent success. Father Raymond's Foreword pays tribute to other books "by or about the literati," ... telling brilliantly of the conversion of the learned. They run the full gamut: from the *Confessions* of St. Augustine and the *Apologia* of Cardinal Newman down to *Now I See* by Arnold Lunn and *The Seven Storey Mountain* by Thomas Merton. Marvelous though these testimonies be, they may lead some to forget that every soul is so infinitely precious to almighty God that He will spare no pain to save the least and the worst of us … from hell." Comparing Merton to Sir Arnold Lunn is amusing in itself. Lunn was an English author, Oxford educated, who published some controversial religious books and books on skiing and mountaineering before his conversion to Catholicism, when he produced his autobiography, *Now I See*, and several other religious books.

One of the reasons for the monastery's exploding population was that Dom James began taking postulants as young as fifteen. As a result, there was more turnover, particularly of the younger candidates. This marked the beginning of what Merton later termed the "Drop-out Phenomenon" in the population of the monastery. Monks began to leave the monastery in larger numbers than usual.

At the same time, some better educated applicants had arrived, including a physician, John Eudes Bamberger, a patent lawyer and linguist, Augustine Wulff, and a scholar and musician, Chrysogonus Waddell. These new arrivals were more consistent with the level of expertise of an earlier addition, Father Timothy Vander Vennet, a scholar and teacher with an extensive educational background in European universities. In earlier times there was also a broader range of backgrounds in the group, including lawyers, soldiers, and farmers.

Merton's sensitivity was masked by his determination to keep an emotional distance from these men who came to Gethsemani with open minds and hearts, thinking they were ready to give their lives to God's service. Merton learned from experience that the sooner he recognized those who weren't suited to the regimented lifestyle, the more charitable he would be in sending them back to secular life. He had to show a stern, detached demeanor to each of them to conceal his regret.

He refused to identify with the disappointed men, not daring to contemplate how he would have felt. He remembered too well how he was affected by his turn-down by the Franciscans. Of course, in the 1950's there was the possibility that some of the young postulants might be seeking a refuge to avoid being drafted to fight in the Korean conflict. The Abbot instructed the departing postulants that it was their obligation to register for the draft when they returned home.

It was the practice of the abbey that no one reveal his decision to leave, regardless of his length of time there. There were no good-byes even to those who were closest to the one leaving. Merton found this practice quite unnatural, and it bothered him through all his years at Gethsemani. To discover that a monk was no longer there without knowing why he had left was painful. There was no closure. The Abbot made no announcement about the departure, and never mentioned the departed monk or novice again, as though he had never been there. For reasons unexplained, this was considered the best way to handle the situation. For Merton it must have been a painful reminder of his mother's disappearance from his life.

One day Merton found some clothing in the woods near the road that had been worn by one of the monks. He knew it had to be someone who had left quietly, either temporarily or permanently. He did not know who it was.

Sometimes when Merton did not see one of the monks for a few days, he would assume that the monk had left. When he reappeared, all the monks would then learn the missing monk had been in the dispensary. All of this uncertainty and loss gave Merton a great deal of uneasiness and depressed him.

In September 1950 Merton was hospitalized at St. Joseph's Infirmary for surgery to remove a section of bone in his nose, due to his sinusitis. The 200-plus rooms of this hospital each carried a saint's name. To his surprise, Merton's room was named for a Saint Naomi. He wrote to Naomi Burton to tell her about the coincidence. The following month he had a repetition of the colitis he had suffered in 1936. An X-ray revealed calcified hilar nodes and scarring in his lungs, probably from old tuberculosis from his illness in 1927. Owen had never told him what this illness was. Tension and anxiety aggravated his stomach, in addition to the monastery diet, and Merton realized he now had chronic digestive trouble. His preoccupation about his health had begun to severely hamper his ability to write.

From the depths of depression caused by his physical condition, he suddenly found release from the writing block during the two periods in the hospital. He attributed this to Sister Therese Lentfoehr, S.D.S., a long-time correspondent. Sister Therese was a member of the Congregation of the Sisters of the Divine Savior, called the Salvatorian sisters, and an English professor. Later, she was designated Poet in Residence at the College of Racine in Wisconsin. She soon became a sounding board for Merton, beginning in his Columbia days, when she first wrote to him to compliment him on one of his poems that she had read in a magazine. It eventually developed into their lifelong correspondence.

In the view of Sister Jane Marie Richardson, Sister Therese was the sister Merton never had.

He sent her copies of his manuscripts through the years for her comments. She sent him some of the books that she had acquired that he did not have. When he could not get sufficient clerical support at the monastery, she typed for him from his handwritten manuscripts, including over 700 pages of notes for his lectures to the novices. She also typed his entire journal that Merton published as *The Sign of Jonas*. Dom James, recognizing her insight, wrote to Sister Therese and asked her opinion about the prudence of a monk publishing his personal thoughts. She of course endorsed publication of the book.

Merton was fortunate to have several women in his life, both single and married, who provided emotional support in his uphill battle to publish his ideas. Sister Therese Lentfoehr wrote to him frequently and visited him at the hermitage. There were also several married women he felt close to, some only by correspondence. They included Raissa Maritain, Carolyn Hammer, and Tommie O'Callahan, as well as their husbands. Naomi Burton was one of Merton's closest associates, both before and after her marriage in 1951 to Melville E. (Ned) Stone. Merton wrote her a letter of congratulation when he heard about the wedding, to give her the news of the Abbot's preliminary approval of his journal to be published as *The Sign of Jonas*. He enjoyed the privilege he gradually received to have picnic lunches on the monastery grounds with his secular friends, including Naomi, Tommie O'Callahan and her family, and the Hammers. These women were on the periphery of Merton's life, but nevertheless were loyal and dedicated friends and he depended on their emotional support.

Merton attributed the breaking of his writing block to a relic of St. John of the Cross that Sister Therese sent him. Merton called him the Mystic of Carmel. A relic is considered a very special gift for a person in the religious life. It is usually a piece of cloth that has been touched to the remains of a saint, called a second-class relic, or an actual fragment of their remains, called quite naturally a first-class relic. Merton had a deep devotion to St. John of the Cross. He was particularly fascinated with the saint's understanding of what God is not. Merton had been writing a book about his teachings and was having difficulty finishing it. He was amazed to find that he was able to complete it without difficulty in a few months after receiving the relic. Harcourt, Brace published it in September 1951, called *The Ascent to Truth*.

In an Author's Note, Merton credited the gift of the relic for the break in his writing block. He credited Sister Therese among others for supporting his efforts, although he did not reveal that she was the person who gave him the relic. He also strongly praised Jacques and his wife, Raissa Maritain, for their work that he believed contributed to his development of the book. Merton was grateful that the censors allowed this personal message to be published. He included a photograph of St. Martin du Canigou inside the front cover and one of the Abbey of Saint Martin du Canigou inside the back cover from Prades, his birthplace. The breakthrough from Merton's writing block proved more valuable to Merton than the success of the book. His confidence was back, and he hoped it would not elude him again.

Merton became notorious at the monastery for his clumsiness. Once he had an accident with an ax, and almost chopped off part of his hand when the ax slipped from his grasp. It was not the only accident Merton had while working in the woods. Merton had small hands, he readily acquired blisters, and cold weather aggravated the problem. Eventually Dom James excused Merton from participating in outdoor projects, at the same time relieving himself of worry about an unnecessary potential accident. After all, Merton must have the use of his hands to write.

Merton had escaped from the world of concrete and noise in Manhattan, and had returned to the natural beauty of an undeveloped landscape that echoed the beauty of God's creation. He would do anything to preserve the outdoors. When he was alone, he liked to walk barefoot in the soil, just as his father had done working as a landscape gardener. Merton wanted to be in touch with nature, to learn first-hand all he could about the plants and birds and other wild creatures, as well as the trees they were protecting. Once he came close to losing his temper when another monk inadvertently chopped down some fir seedlings Merton had planted, not knowing what they were.

The Kentucky landscape is rich with maple, beech, chinquapin oak, hickory, and cedars. Merton particularly liked the loblolly pines and, in Spring, the flowering apple trees. The limestone that builds the strength of thoroughbred horses in the famed bluegrass added to the rugged natural beauty. Merton felt it all mandated preservation.

Merton read the work of Rachel Carson and was excited by her initiative to protect the environment from the increasing pollution caused by insecticide. He believed that natural resources represent the visible presence of God because they are His handiwork. At night he liked to look up at the sky and identify the star formations on his way to chapel to pray in the pre-dawn hours. Since childhood he had been interested in astronomy, and wondered at the mystery of God's creation of the universe. He continued to check the local newspaper to learn the forecast of visible constellations.

Merton asked Dom James for more time for solitude, even though he was being allowed to walk freely in the woods behind the monastery enclosure for his meditations. Suddenly this privilege was threatened.

A Visitation was regularly scheduled at all Cistercian monasteries every one to two years, conducted by one of the higher authorities from France. It was now time for Gethsemani's review. One of Merton's fellow monks decided to use this occasion to complain about the use of the woods for prayer, since it was out of the enclosure. The visiting official reacted by banning the practice in his report of findings, and Dom James had no choice but to enforce it. Merton had been present as he was for all visiting officials from France to translate so that Dom James could understand the findings. When this decision was delivered, Dom James said later that Merton stood silently and obediently, showing no reaction other than tears in his eyes.

Dom James knew the catastrophic effect this decision would have on Merton. He knew that Merton needed his walks in the woods, almost like air to breathe, to maintain his serenity. Dom James was now able to demonstrate his managerial skills. He researched the history of the Order to find a precedent for assigning work in wooded areas for the benefit of the abbey. Although there was no monk currently assigned such a task, he found it had been done in the early days of the Order. Based on this precedent, he appointed Merton as the monastery's forester. Since Gethsemani included forest land, this would give Merton an opportunity to spend more time outdoors and therefore continue his periods of solitude. With his prevailing efficiency, Dom James would have Merton obtain information to improve the condition of the land. Many trees had been destroyed for firewood in the old wood furnace and boilers that previously had provided the heat for the entire monastery.

Merton was delighted at the Abbot's solution. He studied the subject diligently. He enthusiastically instituted a replanting program to replace the needed trees. Merton suggested that Nelson County, under the program of the U.S. Forest Service, be asked to build a fire tower on the monastery grounds to observe the frequent outbreak of brush fires. There were other fire towers already constructed in neighboring counties. The monastery could assist in identifying fires in other nearby areas by use of a two-way radio used by all the network of towers. The County would allow the monastery to staff the tower. The problem was that the optimum location of the tower would not be close to the enclosure and would require Merton to drive a Jeep to get back and forth to the monastery.

Merton tried again to drive. The monk who was the resident mechanic had just repaired and repainted one of the Jeeps, a two-week effort. He demonstrated how to shift the gears and step on the clutch and brake, and then gave Merton the wheel. Merton almost immediately stripped the gears, drove around the woodshed, and rammed the Jeep into a post that went right through the radiator.

The monk who had just witnessed the destruction of his labors could not control himself. Merton agreed that the event was a disaster. He cursed Merton aloud—no sign language was appropriate for this event. Dejected, Merton left the yard. That concluded the Abbot's plan to designate Merton as a full-time fire watchman. The tower was not accessible without a vehicle, and no one was sympathetic after his free-spirited disregard for the Jeep that provided a valuable service to many of the monks who depended on it. Merton must have certainly been cited in Chapter for this occurrence.

The tower was built on a steep hill called Vinyard Knob. It was a well-built steel structure of about 100 feet and part of a system of towers to observe fires in the area. It had a cabin with glass windows at the top and on all sides, a telephone, and short wave radio, with a trap door to enter it. In spite of the distance, Merton often hiked over to the tower and climbed up to enjoy the panoramic view and watch the hawks. Merton then got the idea that he might use the tower for a hermitage, and asked Dom James to seek permission for him to live in it. Dom James put in the request to his superiors in France, and it was approved on the condition that Merton be a full-time hermit. After three days, Merton informed the Abbot he would prefer not to do it. He had heard that the Master of Scholastics assignment would soon be open, and he said that he would like it to be given to him.

In 1951 another foundation was established to ease the overcrowding at Gethsemani, Our Lady of the Genesee at Piffard, New York. The current Master of Scholastics had been selected to go with the group to form the new monastery. Merton was appointed to replace him. He considered the opportunity heaven-sent.

Merton would now supervise the formation of junior monks who had so far only taken temporary vows. Merton had been voluntarily giving classes, or conferences, to seventy of the novices, students, and young professed before Dom James appointed him to the position of Master of Scholastics. In effect, this formalized what Merton had been doing *ad hoc*. Merton called his courses "Orientation in the Contemplative Life, Introduction to Cistercian Theology, and Mystical Theology." He probably drew on the material that he and Father Timothy Vander Vennet had begun to develop two years earlier. Merton was thankful for Sister Therese's help in typing, mimeographing, and binding his conference notes. Merton enjoyed conducting the classes, although he said he sometimes hated to hear the sound of his own voice. He held this position for four years.

Many of the group were young and came into the monastery with a great deal of spirit, and now without much of an outlet. Consequently, their behavior was sometimes lacking in the manners that were expected. Merton wrote a short pamphlet for his students to assist them in conforming their conduct to the decorum of the monastery. Titled "Monastic Courtesy," it cautions the students to avoid useless signs and to remember that "making one another miserable" can be considered "an offense against God." For those who may not have learned otherwise in their upbringing, he adds they should not eat with their elbows on the table or pick their teeth with their fingers at the table. Merton tells the students not to act as though they were in "a spiritual slum" only tolerating the "hoi polloi" around them.

As Master of Scholastics, Merton also served as a spiritual advisor to his students. He particularly liked the one-on-one counseling sessions, although some of the monks said that those who had some knowledge of literature impressed Merton too easily. He was sometimes able to use the subject matter he was teaching in his writing. At the same time, he used his classes as a vehicle for exploring material he was working on or planning to write about.

His further study of Benedict's Rule gave him another point of view about the Saint's original intent for the monastic life. The root meaning of the word "rule" was trellis in the original Greek and Latin. Rather than being a restriction, Benedict's plan was to establish a framework for the monk to grow within, finding his own path within a basic structure.

In 1951, Merton wrote a pamphlet called *A Balanced Life of Prayer*, which was published by the monastery. This was his only publication while he acclimated himself to his teaching and counseling responsibilities. He preferred to read and think about what he should write next. With the changes in monastery atmosphere, the solitude of the Carthusians beckoned him again. He had not forgotten his attraction to the Carthusians in England and France that had been inaccessible to him during World War II.

Merton's objection to the industry that had been introduced at Gethsemani was based on a philosophical difference he had with Dom James in the operation of a monastery. The Abbot's idea, backed by the Order's leadership, was that autonomy was paramount in the maintenance of the facility and did not violate their basic tenets of work, reading, and prayer. This was a considerable improvement over past systems that had weakened monasteries in the past. The medieval system of dependence on the nobility to support the monastery was tolerated until it degenerated into the compromise of their integrity and led sometimes to the appointment of the benefactor's son as Abbot. Later in Church history, some monasteries depended on donations from the public in exchange for offering Masses, so that liturgical activity took precedence over the monks' own monastic activities. The ability of each abbey to finance its own operation was considered imperative for its survival.

Dom James looked for ways to keep Merton satisfied, including authorizing him to spend some of the funds he generated for his own research. In the 1950's Dom James allowed Merton to receive books from Laughlin that he would not otherwise have access to at the monastery. Laughlin sent Merton a number of new books that he believed Merton needed to be aware of. Some books that Merton wanted to read were not available in Louisville, so he requested that Laughlin buy them for him and charge the cost against the monastery's royalties. Merton was amused by the fact that some of the books would not have met the Abbot's approval if he had known what Merton was reading. Occasionally Merton was surprised at the publications that Laughlin and some of his other friends sent him and even more surprised that Dom James had not intercepted them as a possible danger to his monastic vocation and even his faith.

At this time, correspondence with Laughlin centered on their mutual interest in Eastern philosophy. This stimulated an old interest Merton had had since Columbia days, part of the curiosity that had led eventually to his interest in Catholicism. Merton's pursuit of the meaning of life was insatiable. Although his study had given him a wealth of knowledge beyond his original expectations, he knew that he must look further for truth in other cultures anywhere in the world and throughout time. Rather than viewing this pursuit as inconsistent with his vocation, Merton saw it as a process of enriching his knowledge and faith and a testimony to his love for his Catholic religion. He knew that his journey was far from finished.

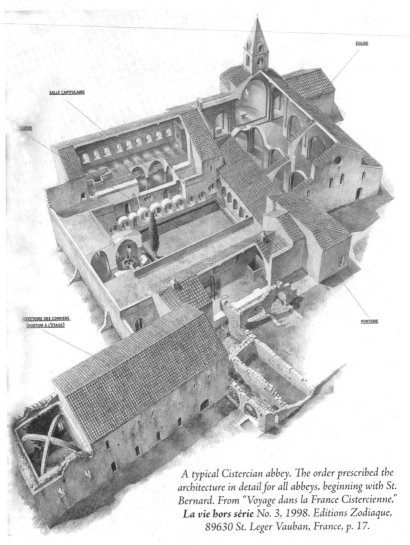

*A typical Cistercian abbey. The order prescribed the architecture in detail for all abbeys, beginning with St. Bernard. From "Voyage dans la France Cistercienne,"* **La vie hors série** *No. 3, 1998. Editions Zodiaque, 89630 St. Leger Vauban, France, p. 17.*

A computer reconstruction of the monastery of Cluny in the 11th century, the largest Christian church ever built until the 16th century. The magnificence of this structure symbolized the pride and power that had developed with the support of French royalty. The Cistercians under St. Bernard attracted those who sought to reform monasticism and return to basic spirituality. From Claude Wenzler, **Architecture de L'Abbaye.** Editions Ouest-France, Rennes, France, 1998, p. 4.

# Chapter 19

Dom James knew how to manage his assets and protect his investments, and that included Father Louis. He was aware of Merton's continual restlessness that always exhibited itself with his renewed attempts to transfer to a more contemplative religious order. Now that Merton had been serving as Master of Scholastics for a year, he could assume Merton would soon get bored again and want a new challenge.

He looked for other ways he could use Merton's talents. It occurred to him that Merton had never been off the monastery grounds except for a few brief occasions in the city. He had not forgotten Merton's disappointment at losing the assignment at the watchtower after the Jeep incident. An opportunity arose to acquire some property in Ohio, so he asked Merton to go and evaluate it as a possible site for another monastery. Merton had been doing a good job of organizing the replacement of many trees that had been lost when the monastery had used them to fuel the old furnace. This Ohio property was undeveloped, and an appraisal of its timber would be important in the decision to purchase it.

It was July 1952, and Merton had not left Kentucky in eleven years. He rode along in the monastery's truck with two Brothers who were going to Ohio to purchase hay. At first Merton did not notice too many changes in the landscape because they were on highways across Kentucky and Ohio, and he saw little but road signs and late model vehicles, which did not interest Merton. He believed they were overcharged for their meals at the restaurants where they stopped, but the Brothers reminded him that years had elapsed since he had come to the monastery and prices had risen over time.

Merton gave Dom James his favorable opinion of the property, although he feared the Abbot might have selected him to inspect the site as preparation to appointing him to head up a new foundation there. However Dom James did not share Merton's positive reaction for a number of reasons that were not obvious to Merton. While Merton did not appreciate the Abbot's difference of opinion, he nevertheless was relieved that this property would not present a threat to his security.

The trip back to Gethsemani was an exciting event for Merton: he and the Abbot had to be driven to Columbus, Ohio, fly to Cincinnati, then change in Cincinnati for a flight back to Louisville. This was Merton's first airline flight. The whole experience was an unexpected shock to Merton. Seeing women in the airport with clothing that was too tight or too short astonished him. Everyone seemed to be smoking cigarettes, even during the flight, and reading magazines he had never seen or heard of. He used to be familiar with a wide variety of publications, many of which had amused him. He concluded that the corruption he had seen in New York City had been flown into the airports nationwide.

It was surprising to feel so different when he was surrounded by things that used to be familiar to him. It reminded him of the time he went to France with Owen and again when they moved to England. Now in the U.S., these were his own people, but they seemed completely lacking in decorum and dignity. He felt like a foreigner again, and wondered where was home for him, at least on this earth.

Merton was mistaken to think the Abbot would consider him for a top management position. Dom James probably couldn't even imagine Merton coping with the trivia of running a monastery, even though a majority of the monks might vote for him to lead them. He had no intention of releasing a moneymaker like Merton to another monastery, even one of the foundations that would be under his overall direction. In 1952, royalties constituted 16 percent of Gethsemani's income, exactly double the proceeds at that time from its cheese and fruitcake sales. This was in a year when none of Merton's books were first introduced, the first year in which this had occurred. Dom James would not burden Merton with administrative work that would occupy the time he could otherwise spend on writing or nurturing his creative spirit. Merton could teach and counsel, but he could not be trusted to run things, in Dom James' opinion. Actually, Dom James held a deep affection for Merton, even though he suppressed it. Merton's intellect and spirit actually served as a bright light in the Abbot's dreary life. Competing with Merton's rebellious nature must have been an irresistible challenge.

Merton could not dismiss his distrust of Dom James' motives. He continually poured out his anger and frustration in his diary, while he prayed for deliverance from these negative emotions. His insecurities about what Dom James might decide to do with the power he had over him preoccupied his thoughts. He decided to use his connections to make overtures to the Camaldolese order as well as the Carthusians who now had been established in the U.S., as well as South America, the West Indies, and Cuernavaca. It was a frontal attack on Dom James' authority. Merton felt empowered. He persuaded Naomi Burton to write directly to Rome in his behalf regarding the Camaldoli.

Merton's sources reported that the Camaldolese Order apparently wanted both him and his typewriter. Then Merton received the unhappy news that Rome was interested in Merton continuing to write—at Gethsemani. It seemed the more Merton sought solitude, the more he was forced into a life of notoriety.

Merton's depression found a new low. He was set back but not defeated. He believed the call to a secluded life was from God, Who would not leave him enslaved to his Thomas Merton identity, he was sure. Be careful what you pray for, they say, but he did not believe it applied to him.

During this dry period of Merton's creativity, he unexpectedly received a request from Clare Boothe Luce to contribute to a collection of essays and sketches she was compiling. Merton wrote a piece on St. John of the Cross and contributed line drawings of St. John of the Cross and of St. Therese of Lisieux. These are his first drawings published. He created a total of about 800 drawings altogether. The book also included a sketch of St. John of the Cross by the noted artist, Salvador Dali. Luce's book was published in 1952, titled *Saints for Now*.

Salvador Dali's sketch of Saint John is a full figure, realistic representation of the saint (unlike the style of his well-known works). Merton's line drawing is a bust figure with a wide-eyed expression, outlined like a stark modern stained glass window. Merton's essay follows a biographical piece on John of the Cross. With due humility, Merton does not even reference his own comprehensive work on this saint, *Ascent to Truth*, that he had labored and prayed over so extensively as he contended with his writer's block. In the piece Merton even translates some of John's poetry from Spanish for the reader. At the conclusion, he calls his essay a prayer to the saint for a purpose the saint already knows, and which he asks John to share with Merton's readers. Merton leaves his readers to wonder what his purpose is for this prayer, although he describes the saint as "the maker of contemplatives wherever they may be found." Merton's sketch of St. Therese shows her eyes lowered to the point of possibly being closed. The drawing of Therese is dated 1951, and the one of John, 1952, a year after publication of his book on St. John.

Meanwhile Merton continued to have difficulty with the censors of the Order. They objected to the way he seemed to be writing about the Order like an outsider, that is, objectively, which had never been done before. In fairness, the censors were following precedent in disapproving some of the things that Merton submitted. Unfortunately for Merton, his writing was breaking new ground in enlarging the parameters for the material the Church would allow to be published. Approvals were slow to come and usually only after multiple submissions with laborious justifications for what he was writing. Merton viewed the entire process as painful and a real waste of his time to have to justify each submission.

In 1952 Merton wrote an article supporting the idea of hermits within their religious Order and backed it up with his research on early Church history. He published it only in French and Italian because he knew his American censors would not pass it. It was titled, *Dans le desert de Dieu.*

Ten years later Merton wrote in a letter dated November 17, 1962, to his fellow monk, Ernesto Cardenal, who had returned to Nicaragua, that he could only get his material past the censors quickly in England. The American censors would reject it, Merton said, if it contained more than statements such as "It is nice to pray, Good morning, Father, have some holy water. We never eat hot dogs on Friday, etc."

Merton was in a dry period and could not seem to find his way out of it. By October 1952, Merton was feeling ill again and suffering from emotional exhaustion. Merton called it a repeat of the illness he suffered in 1936, when he had the attack of gastritis on the train back to Douglaston and wondered if he were losing his mind. He thought again about the time just after his ordination when he passed out while saying Mass. He feared what might be happening to him.

He watched an old monk train some geese to walk in single file like the monks in the field. He even taught them to do tricks. Merton wondered at what point this old monk had retreated to a world all his own. Merton saw himself in the shadow of the path the old monk--and the goslings—followed.

Merton got permission to consult Dr. Philip Law, a psychiatrist from Chicago he had met and in whom he had confidence. Dr. Law emphatically advised Merton to leave the Trappist Order to gain the solitude he required. In fact, Dr. Law strongly advised Merton to leave and write a plan to start a new order of contemplatives. Father Bellarmine joined in this discussion with Merton and Dr. Law and agreed that Merton should take this radical action. Merton recorded his reaction in his diary on September 26, 1952: "For 37 years I have been writing my life instead of living it and the effect is vicious, although by the grace of God it has not been as bad as it might have been. But I cannot let myself become a hermit merely on the grounds that the thing looks credible on paper … .The Rule of St. Benedict put down on paper 1400 years ago is already quite enough. What I need to do is live *that*—something like the way he lived at Subiaco." Again at Christmas Dr. Law advised Merton to "go *now*." Merton ignored the advice.

Monks began to leave the monastery for medical reasons, including emotional problems more severe than had previously been seen at Gethsemani. This could have been due largely to the liberal admission policy of Dom James and his reluctance to allow anyone to leave precipitously. Merton now believed that as Master of Scholastics he shared responsibility for the success of the monastery with Dom James. He worried about the counseling he gave. He sometimes recommended that a novice leave the monastery in spite of Dom James' sometimes tearful insistence to stay. As Master of Scholastics, Merton held the fourth most important position in the monastery and had the opportunity to mold the future professed choir monks and develop a spirit among them for the overall good of the entire group. The positions of Abbot, Prior, and Master of Novices were above his, but he believed his responsibilities were critical to the future of the monastery. He had neither the inclination nor the aptitude to found a new monastic group.

In August 1952, Monsignor Larraona from Rome's Sacred Congregation of Religious visited Gethsemani. Dom James asked Merton to perform a concurrent translation of his talk from Italian. Merton also met with the prelate twice, and they spoke in Spanish, the Monsignor's native language, about canon law. He gave Merton information about forthcoming instructions from Rome on current interpretations of the contemplative life. He advised Merton to continue his writing. Merton took this as a message that Rome sanctioned his work.

Merton noticed that a clear split was occurring at Gethsemani that had never existed when Dom Frederic was there. The monks were not uniformly in agreement with Dom James' policies. The older, conservative monks did not accept the many changes that Dom James had instituted. Some of the younger monks thought his rigidity was unnecessary. Nevertheless, the Abbot held fast to his policies and succeeded in keeping the group together and working as a team. Merton found himself supporting the Abbot on many of his improvements because he actually agreed with him. Merton was often able to bring Dom James to a centrist position that a majority of the monks would accept, which maintained an equilibrium in the group that was essential for Merton's peace of mind.

One day Dom James asked Merton to be his confessor. This was the singular honor Merton believed the Abbot could give him. He accepted. Merton did not write anything about the Abbot's confessions because of the Church law of secrecy on anything said in Confession. It was known that every Monday Merton went to Dom James' office to hear the Abbot's confession, and Merton in turn, kneeling by the Abbot's chair, confessed his sins to Dom James for the absolution he was empowered to give Merton from the Lord. After all, this was Merton's superior and the only father he now had. It was an awkward relationship for Merton, although Dom James could be commended for selecting a monk with Merton's depth and understanding of the spiritual life. Nevertheless, the confessor role had to be difficult for both the Abbot and Merton due to their conflict over Merton's requested transfer.

When Father Timothy Vander Vennet returned to Gethsemani from his assignment to help establish a new foundation in Taiwan, Merton asked him to be his confessor. Father Timothy's positive relationship with Dom James was such that there was no difficulty in assuming this role from the Abbot. Father Timothy also had a warm relationship with his previous superior, who was normally very reserved in conversation with his monks. Father Timothy once told Merton that he and Dom Frederic had discussed the Abbot's love of Scripture, especially the Lenten readings. Father Timothy had made a significant impression on Merton since he had been his philosophy teacher in 1945. He remained Merton's confessor until Father Timothy left in February 1958 to serve as Prior of the new foundation in northern California at Vina, Our Lady of New Clairvaux. It was the second highest position at the abbey.

Another close relationship developed in much the same way as with Cardenal. Merton's special attachment to Saint John of the Cross somehow resonated in his acquaintance with a postulant by the name of Wasserman who took this Saint's name for his Trappist identity.

Merton was charmed from the time he met the Wasserman family in September 1952 and said Mass for them. Father John of the Cross soon became Merton's driver on a number of outings. In his journal, Merton particularly noted their drive to New Haven parish church for Merton's Baptism of Father Cyprian's mother in September 1956, and the trip to Bardstown in December 1957 to deliver a truckload of Christmas trees after Father John's solemn profession. Merton concluded in his journal entry for December 14, 1957: "we are stones placed together in this Church by the Providence of God."

When Father Timothy left to accept the Prior position at the California foundation in February 1958, Merton selected Father John of the Cross to be his confessor. Merton was a little shy about confessing to Father John since they had become such good friends. By November 1958 Merton described himself as "a complete phony" in confessing to his friend and believed the process embarrassed both of them. Merton found it curious that they actually had reversed roles, since he had been Father John's director when he was a postulant. Now Merton found his confessions no longer detached or "short and sweet," as he describes them in his journal. He added that Father John was "the person I most like and admire in the monastery and highly value his affection." He really trusted that their friendship would not ultimately get in the way of the confessor-penitent relationship.

As with other monks who had previously left the monastery, Father John began to show signs of the disillusionment process in stages that Merton recognized in others. First Dom James criticized Father John for reading *The Brothers Karamazov* in August 1956. The Abbot's formal approach to disciplining Father John occurred in March 1959 for what Merton termed his independence. Merton said in his journal that it made him "sick at the stomach" because "those he has helped continue to love him."

At this vulnerable point in July 1959, during a day of recollection, Father John agreed to seek permission to accompany Merton to Tortola, an isolated and primitive place that Merton had recently investigated for himself. At this time, Cardenal (Father Lawrence) was leaving Gethsemani for his health and wanted Merton to join him in Cuernavaca. Merton wanted to work with Cardenal and proceeded to apply for permission to join him there, hoping that Father John would accompany him. Merton was accepted by the Bishops of both Tortola and Cuernavaca, and thought he might possibly work in some combination of the two locations. For years Merton had considered the possibility of transferring to places he thought might be approved. He repeatedly tried, through direct conversation and correspondence with individuals both in and outside the church that he identified as influential, to accomplish a transfer. Instead he consistently met delay and ultimately disapproval. In July 1959, he wrote in his journal that his community was "like a convoy of ships in time of war, in which every vessel takes the speed of the slowest in the convoy."

Father John of the Cross told Merton that he had been elected on an early ballot to be Abbot at both New Clairvaux and Genesee in upstate New York. Dom James had declined the positions for Merton in both cases. It didn't surprise Merton that Dom James had never told him of these events. Merton never regretted that he had not been given either of these positions. At least he understood himself well enough to know they would have been a setback for him in pursuing his goals and certainly outside his vocation. Later Merton began using Father Flavian as his confessor until Father Flavian himself became a hermit at Gethsemani.

When the monastery renovations were finally completed, the yellow Traxcovator Merton so hated was used to haul a tool shed out to the woods at the far corner of the area known as the Petrified Forest. Dom James offered it to Merton for his use during certain hours of the day. This was obviously Dom James' attempt at offering a compromise for disapproving Merton's proposed transfer to gain more solitude. Even though other monks were allowed to use the little shed at other times, Merton felt a special attachment to it and named it St. Anne's. He made a little desk for it and would read there, with his watch that had no crystal placed in front of him on the desk. He knew otherwise that he would completely lose track of the time and miss the next scheduled event. Then he knew he would probably lose his privilege at St. Anne's.

Before Dom James provided this shed for him, Merton used to climb up into the loft of the horse barn where he had discovered he could read and meditate without interruption or distraction. This is probably the reason why Dom James found an alternative place, before Merton could fall and hurt himself. For Merton, it was no different than his New York balcony or the tree he used to climb at Olean to find a quiet place to read.

Merton decided he would like to publish some of his personal writing, in the tradition he had established with *The Seven Storey Mountain*. This was a five-year journal Merton had been keeping from December 1946 to July 1952, recording his impressions of life in the monastery. The Order's European censor disapproved it several times for being "inappropriate" and not reverent enough in describing the life of a monk. At Merton's request, Robert Giroux asked the eminent philosopher, Jacques Maritain, now teaching at Princeton, to write to the Abbot General, Dom Gabriel Sortais, in French, to support the book. Naomi Burton asked the British publisher, Tom Burns, to appeal to Father Bruno Scott James to persuade Dom Albert to withdraw his objections. Merton used the two visits of Dom Gabriel that year to make the case for its release over the censor's objections. Merton reminded him that St. Bernard of Clairvaux himself had written a journal, so there was no basis to allege that it was not in the Cistercian tradition.

Merton was successful in overriding the censor's protests, but only an English version was authorized in November. The following year the French translation was allowed. There were also now revised rules for censorship and translations. The General Chapter of the Order, which occurred annually at headquarters level in France, had finally acted, at Merton's suggestion, to approve it. Victory was not just sweet—it was delicious. The Sign of Jonas was published by Harcourt, Brace in February 1953.

Unlike his last book, The Ascent to Truth, The Sign of Jonas was immensely popular. It did not contain any heavy theology, so that the average reader could readily absorb Merton's message. It was the sequel readers were looking for to The Seven Storey Mountain. When The Waters of Siloe came out in 1949, readers had expected it to continue Merton's life story, but instead it only covered the history of the Order. The Sign of Jonas was the first of Merton's books to be reviewed by The New York Times, and his frank, pilgrim-like tone from The Seven Storey Mountain received a favorable endorsement. It concluded with a lyrical prose-poem, known now in its own right, called "Fire Watch, July 4, 1952," which described Merton's walk through the abbey after the other monks had gone to bed, checking for fire and punching the time clock at each station. The book was so popular in the U.S. that it was almost immediately translated into a number of other languages to be marketed worldwide.

Actually the censorship process had stripped out the real story of Merton's experience at Gethsemani. It glossed over the conflicts about his desired transfer, and portrayed life in the monastery as idyllic. Ironically, The Sign of Jonas was published when Merton was actively trying to transfer to another Order. There were rumors that a move had already occurred. Some believe that the book may have been approved to quiet the rumors that Merton was dissatisfied at Gethsemani and had left. Now Merton saw himself trapped there by his own reputation. How could he write about how much happiness and peace he had found at Gethsemani if he wanted to leave to join another Order? The Church authorities would never consent to this contradiction becoming a reality.

Merton was reading about the life of St. Benedict Joseph Labre, from southern France, who had tried unsuccessfully to join the Trappists, the Carthusians, and the Cistercians, and who lived a solitary penitential life, wandering around Europe and particularly Rome where he died in 1783. He was canonized in 1881 as a recognized saint, supported by 136 certified miraculous cures. He is considered the closest to being called the only Trappist saint due to his earnest desire to join them. Merton commented in his diary on March 10, 1953: "... it can always be a higher call to feel oneself to be, and actually to be, useless. Not however to be deliberately useless when you could be useful. Except on such terms as those of St. Benedict Labre." One of Merton's correspondents, a lady he does not name, sent him a relic of St. Benedict Labre, which Brother Alfred kept for him in 1953. Apparently the monastery exposed this relic annually on the saint's feast day, April 16, which Merton notes with appreciation in his diary on that day in 1964.

Merton was writing and publishing again. *Bread in the Wilderness*, a discussion of the Psalms, was published in December 1953 by New Directions. It is a lyrical presentation, revealing Merton's passionate love for the Psalms. "They become the Tabernacle of God in which we are protected forever from the rage of the city of business, from the racket of human opinions, from the wild carnival we carry in our hearts and which the ancient saints called 'Babylon.'" The book contains beautiful photographs of the crucifix, known as the Devot Christ, from the French Catalan cathedral in Perpignan. The British edition was published by Hollis & Carter, London, in 1954. Originally Merton planned to use some of his own drawings for this book, but decided instead on the photographs of the beautiful carved wood crucifix in the cathedral.

Merton's next publication was a book-length essay commissioned by the Order as a companion to a new translation of a Papal encyclical. It was called *The Last of the Fathers: Saint Bernard of Clairvaux and the Encyclical Letter, Doctor Mellifluus*, published in June 1954 by Harcourt, Brace. Merton did not want to write this book. He later said in a conference with his novices that he actually preferred Abelard, the

man of passion, who battled with Bernard on the application of logic
to questions of theology.

Abelard and Heloise lived in twelfth century France, a time and place
where Catholicism governed the careers and social mores of the people.
Heloise and Abelard lived in Paris and were secret lovers until Heloise
became pregnant. Abelard sent her out to Brittany to his family's home,
where she gave birth to their son.

Abelard was in his thirties at this time, and was at the height of his
career. Heloise, on the other hand, was a sheltered girl in her teens,
housed in a convent by her guardian uncle. The lovers were then secretly married so that Abelard's career as a teacher of philosophy in the
Church's schools would not be adversely affected should the relationship
be discovered. To maintain the secrecy of the marriage, Abelard housed
Heloise in a convent where he had conjugal visits with her. During his
visits Abelard insisted that she be dressed as a nun.

Incensed by the disgrace to his niece, Heloise's uncle directed his
servants to injure Abelard so that he would be physically incapable of
having sex with Heloise in the future. The attack was satisfactory only
to Heloise's uncle. After his castration, Abelard believed he had received
a religious vocation and decided to become a priest. He took lifetime
vows and persuaded Heloise to do the same, even though they were
married. Heloise did so against her will because she still loved Abelard
in spite of their problems. She said she had no vocation other than her
love for Abelard. Soon he rose to the position of Abbot. Eventually
Heloise became an Abbess. They maintained a relationship through
letters, with Abelard providing Heloise with spiritual guidance in
supervising her convent.

Bernard had become a leader in the Cistercian Order at this time.
He disapproved of a person acquiring knowledge for its own sake and
thought it should only be sought through contemplation. He saw it as
a hindrance to one's perfection. Abelard disagreed, advocating greater
freedom of education in the Cathedral schools. He did not believe
education should be restricted to monastic instruction in the cloister.
Abelard did not view knowledge as a secular pursuit for its own sake. He
said that knowledge served faith but did not hinder it, and he believed
in applying logic to understanding the mysteries of the faith.

Bernard sought to correct Abelard's teachings and philosophy by
bringing charges against him for heresy. After a hearing by a Church
Council, the matter was referred to the Pope. The Pope condemned

Abelard as a heretic, particularly for his teaching that Christ's death was not directly redemptive for man. He excommunicated Abelard's followers and ordered his books to be burned. Abelard was confined to a monastery in perpetual silence, but two high officials of the Church intervened and eventually brought about a reconciliation between Abelard and Bernard. The Pope's sentence was lifted, but by this time Abelard was in poor health. He died eighteen months after his condemnation. Later, when Heloise died, she was buried at her request next to Abelard in the abbey church.

It is believed by some that Bernard had unfairly influenced the Council against Abelard in advance of the hearing, that some of the differences were semantic in nature, and that there was good reason for the charges to be dropped. Merton was sympathetic to Abelard's misfortunes, although he readily acknowledged that Abelard had overstepped his bounds on Church teaching as well as in his personal conduct. Merton concluded that it was Abelard's own vanity and pride that caused his downfall.

Merton's next book was *No Man is an Island*, published by Harcourt, Brace in 1955. It is a book rich in Merton's practical ideas about leading a spiritual life and a departure from his romantic presentation of monasticism. It represented a clear turning point in his writing.

Merton was reading about the French Cistercian monk, Charles de Foucauld, who went to live among the Muslims in the Sahara Desert as a hermit. He was assassinated there by anti-Christian natives on December 1, 1916, and soon was considered by many of the French people to be a martyr. Merton was impressed with this monk's devotion to the eremitic life, and thought he would attempt to follow in his footsteps by renewing his efforts for a transfer to the Camaldolese Order in Europe. The Camaldolese, a Benedictine monastic group, was founded by St. Romuald in Italy in the eleventh century. Meanwhile, Merton continued to ask Dom James for more time for solitude.

Merton wrote to Dom Jean Leclercq, a Benedictine monk of Clervaux Abbey in Luxembourg and a noted scholar of monasticism. Merton knew him to be an advocate of the eremitic, or hermit, life from their exchange of letters in the past few years as well as their conversations during his inspections at Gethsemani. For Merton, Dom Jean had become a confidante by correspondence. Merton wrote to Dom Jean on April 27, 1955, in French, although he usually wrote to him in English. Merton told him that he knew that Dom James would read his letter before it was dispatched, so he wanted to limit what he would understand that it said. He knew that Dom James' knowledge of French was more limited than he generally admitted.

Merton's letter concerned the criticism in the last Visitation that Merton was not living in the pattern of the Cistercian Order because he sought an unusual amount of solitude. He begged Dom Jean to help him leave Gethsemani and join an Order of contemplatives, specifically the Camaldolese, in Frascati, Italy. Merton told Dom Jean that he had already found a friend (not named) who would pay his way to Italy to join this Order. In the letter, Merton said, with deep piety, that he was pursuing the hermetical life " ... with the sensation of having my hand in the hands of God ... .--the same feelings that accompanied my entry into the Church."

Dom James did intercept Merton's letter and held it for three weeks while he decided what to do in order to keep Merton at Gethsemani. Merton had committed the grievous "sin" of taking matters out of channel. Dom Jean was not in "the chain of command" and as a Benedictine, would be considered an inappropriate source of help to Merton. Unaware of this delay in dispatch of his letter, Merton wrote directly to Rome for permission to transfer. This was the ultimate disobedience to the Abbot, who was being ignored by his own monk. Merton's celebrity with his writing now selling across Europe aggravated the slight. It was a tacit statement that Dom James could not control the number one monk of the Order.

Dom James decided to write his own letter to Dom Jean, explaining his plan to give Merton more time alone. He also wrote to Archbishop Montini of Milan, later to be Pope Paul VI, stressing Merton's public image and the potential scandal a transfer could cause as well as the loss to the Church of the influence of Merton's books, which would no longer have credibility. He added that Merton was a recent convert, an extrovert, and as his Abbot, he believed he gave too much weight to his feelings over the will of God.

From the beginning, Merton had become acquainted with the French monks who came to Gethsemani on Visitations and needed his help in translating for them. His personal research and interest in scholarship impressed the visiting superiors, and as his publications came forth they recognized his real potential to influence the Church's policies. Dom Jean Leclercq developed an interest in Merton, recognizing their common cultural education and scholastic pursuits. Dom James, on the other hand, educated in the U.S. in business administration, soon built a noteworthy reputation as a manager of a very profitable monastic operation. Dom James was a deterrent to Merton's information base and spiritual development, but served as a stimulus to his rebellious spirit that gave Merton the energy to persist in his work. Merton sought and found in Leclercq a mentor and spiritual guide who could provide the understanding he longed for. Leclercq provided a broad perspective of the state of monasticism worldwide while at the same time guiding his study. Merton was able to produce progressively important writings based on a solid knowledge and current understanding of the issues. He would never have been able to formulate credible positions or to project remedies without the assistance of Leclercq and other correspondents over time that served to synthesize Merton's thought and positions. At the same time, Merton provided Leclercq with information and perspective on the American point of view in the Church, based on publications he received from his correspondents. The more significant material he mailed to Leclercq, and Leclercq did likewise for Merton from the material he accessed in the European press.

Merton received a direct reply from Rome denying his request. Archbishop Montini wrote to Merton on August 20, four months after Merton's letter to Dom Jean. He said he doubted that Merton would find the solitude he sought with the Camaldolese because they were currently going through a time of change. He said Merton's Abbot had a clearer judgment of the situation than Merton and that Gethsemani would offer him sufficient solitude for his spiritual growth and for his future work to flourish.

Dom James went to a meeting at Citeaux where the Order acted on Merton's request. They decided that Merton would be permitted to leave the Order only after five years of silence from writing. Dom James wrote to Dom Jean to explain the Order's ban, saying he believed Merton was an adventurer and a neurotic, and would probably not stay with the Camaldolese Order for long if he went, and would then become a "roamer" or "gypsy."

Dom James seldom missed an opportunity to instruct his monks on any subject high on his agenda when he had them all together at Chapter meetings. In one meeting he told the story, supposedly a true story, of a monk who had left his monastery and soon afterward fell into the Grand Canyon and died. He had first gone from his monastery to Guatemala and did not do well there. Because he had failed to keep his vows, he suffered the judgment of God, the Abbot concluded.

Merton wondered about the coincidence of his recent attempts to leave and the story related by the Abbot. It was on occasions like this that Merton believed the Abbot was poking fun at him and humiliating him without anyone else being the wiser of the game the Abbot played.

Another characteristic of Dom James' talks was the way he slanted his remarks. He spoke at the level of the majority of the monks, who were not highly educated. Merton could accept this, but the Abbot used expressions like "every cloud has a silver lining" and "day by day in every way things are getting better and better." He would tell the monks, "play ball with me all your life" to reach sainthood, "otherwise, baby … ." Having to sit for long talks at this level nearly drove Merton to desperation. Merton saw these talks as deceptive, controlling, and insincere. Merton knew that the Abbot laughed at him behind his back for his idiosyncrasies. One could assume that Dom James was equally aware of Merton's reaction to his ways.

Merton continued to have concern that he might be selected to head up a new foundation and become an abbot, if for no other reason than to keep him from transferring to another Order. He feared that his leadership ability would be misinterpreted as qualifying him to run a monastery. He knew that administrative work would destroy his chance of ever gaining more solitude and peace of mind. Merton asked Dom James and the Abbot General, Dom Gabriel, to let him take a private vow that "as long as I live I will never accept any election to the office of Abbot or Titular Prior either in this monastery or any other monastery of the Cistercian Order." Merton took this vow on October 8, 1952.

Merton believed this would give him protection from being assigned to head up a monastery and would hopefully leave the door open to being allowed to transfer eventually to another order with more solitude. He knew that a higher position in the order would eliminate any chance of getting the transfer he so earnestly believed he needed.

The position of Master of Novices opened up in 1956. Merton told Dom James he would rather have this assignment than become a hermit. Dom James was amazed, but probably thought God had answered his prayers for help in controlling the situation.

Merton knew that he could not stop writing, even if it meant losing the opportunity to gain more solitude at this time. Merton concluded it was better to express himself in his journal than to others, either personally or in letters. Writing in his journal almost daily for most of his monastic life was comforting, but writing for his readers was a mission. He would not be silenced.

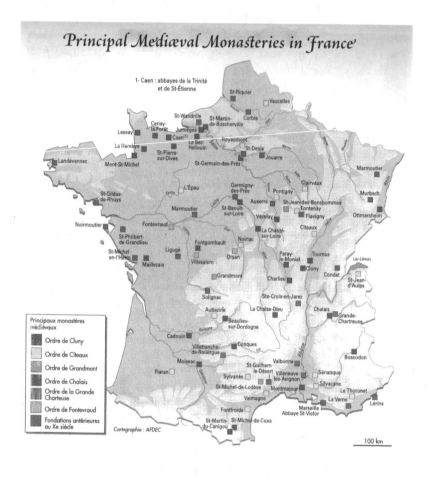

Principal medieval monasteries in France. *The large number of abbeys during that period greatly impressed Merton. He wrote of their beauty, including those now in ruins. From Claude Wenzler,* **Architecture de L'Abbaye**. *Editions Ouest-France, Rennes, France, 1998, p. 32.*

# Chapter 20

The air was now cleared. Merton would be the Master of Novices, and the Abbot knew that for a time the new position would be a challenge. Merton really had no choice but to find a role in the monastery he could accept. He certainly could not bear the thought of five years without writing, even with the possibility of a transfer after enduring the proposed silence. As it turned out, Merton discovered that training the novices actually served to stimulate his writing.

His next book was *The Living Bread*, a comprehensive treatment of the Church's doctrine of the Eucharist. It was published by Farrar, Straus, Giroux in 1956. Merton spoke of the Eucharist as a sign of the Parousia of the Son of God, the Second Coming and Last Judgment foretold in the Bible. He asserted his belief that eventually there would be a final union of mankind, which should occur through the Eucharist. He cited the Last Supper and Christ's prayer "that all may be one" as the forerunner of this event. He wondered if a visible union would be a political one, or whether that would be "one of the temptations of the world's final age." This was a theme Merton would continue to address in his writings.

The same year, *Praying the Psalms* was released by The Liturgical Press, run by the Benedictine Order. This is a short but comprehensive treatment of the psalms that reveals the depth of Merton's knowledge and devotion to these ancient prayers. At Gethsemani the monks were able to memorize all of the 150 psalms because they recited them so frequently. Merton recorded in his journal that his misery gave him insight into the Psalms, with their anguished appeal to God for help.

Also in 1956, *Silence in Heaven* was published in the U.S. by The Studio Publications Inc., in association with Thomas Y. Crowell Company. It was originally published in France by B. Arthaud Grenoble. It contains 90 photographs illustrating the cenobitic life of monks and nuns in French Benedictine and Cistercian monasteries. Merton's text, preceding the photographs, is titled "In Silentio." The book was tastefully assembled at the Abbey of La Pierre qui Vire, then the largest abbey in France, and head of the French Congregation of the Primitive Observance, an austere Benedictine order founded in 1850 in Burgundy.

Merton described the history of this order in *The Silent Life*, published the following year.

Merton's heavy assignment of writing projects mandated some relief, but he maintained that all he needed was solitude. Actually, Merton occupied a great deal of his time preparing lecture notes for his novices. He would not consider teaching from the notes of previous instructors. Merton discovered he thoroughly enjoyed training the novices. The mentor role seemed to energize Merton. He retained this position for the next ten years.

Merton was able to get feedback on himself from the novices' point of view. Most of them were young and expressive of their feelings and reactions. He did not tell his students that he was the author, Thomas Merton. Of course, most of them eventually discovered it, but he enjoyed the game of anonymity until they did.

One of the reasons why Merton could conceal his public identity within the monastery was a characteristic generally accepted by those who knew him personally. There was something about Merton's physical presence that did not give him the expected appearance of a successful author. His gestures were not polished, so that his demeanor was more like an overgrown boy from a boarding school than a man of reputation or manners.

Merton himself must have realized the disconnect, because he frequently played a game of hiding his identity from people he met. He employed this ruse in local restaurants and in doctors' waiting rooms, saying he was a farmer in the area. He dressed in jeans and other work clothes when he went into town, so his story had credibility. He did not exhibit the behavior of a priest, reading his prayers, or an author, deep in thought possibly about his next book. He laughed, not always softly, spoke in friendly fashion to the people he encountered, and generally presented himself as one perfectly at ease with himself in a rural Kentucky setting. He was universally disarming. In Merton's lifetime pursuit of trying to understand himself, it was probably a method he used to acquire information about himself by observing other people's reactions to meeting him.

When he went into Louisville for doctors' appointments or to use the University library, he liked to stop at the Cathedral near the center of the downtown area to say his Office. There he would only interact with God.

Merton shared his enthusiasm for the outdoors with his novices. He took them on walks and tree planting assignments. Twice on hot days he let them jump in a nearby pond to cool off. When someone told Dom James about the incidents, the Abbot put a stop to them. Merton sometimes went out with his novices when they were doing farm work. With his physical limitations, he would soon be sitting rather than participating. Brother Alban, a veteran farmer, said that one time Merton's face turned so red that he looked like he was having a heart attack. He told Merton that it wasn't the invasion of Normandy. Father Conner, Merton's Undermaster, or assistant, reported that the novices were often appalled at Merton's less than constructive ideas. They would give him the monastic sign language for "Boss" which in the secular world is an obscene gesture using the middle finger. The novices believed Merton understood they intended both meanings, and always took it good-naturedly.

Merton often digressed from his outline when he was teaching. He could not resist talking about literary works that related to the principles he was discussing. He often gave personal examples, too, from his own experience, even when they were sometimes a little embarrassing. He joked about his own weaknesses as well as recent incidents around the monastery. Merton knew how to hold his novices' attention and entertain them at the same time. To amuse his students, and probably himself as well, Merton sometimes coined expressions that blended the Cistercian sign language with his spoken language. He called the Louisville public library the "secular bookhouse," which is the transla-tion from three Cistercian signs: for "secular" or "layman," for "book," and for "house."

He attributed the success in his classroom to the example of Mark Van Doren at Columbia. Merton maintained a life-long friendship with Van Doren and credited him with his own development. Mark Van Doren visited Merton in January 1956 and again in September 1957. This was the ultimate joy for him to be able to exchange ideas with his mentor in person through the years. However, Merton's style did not even remotely resemble Van Doren's sophistication and traditional approach. Merton was himself, and Van Doren respected and encouraged that.

Merton did not realize that one of the aspects of his lectures that amused his students was his choice of vintage expressions long out of style in conversational English. His speech dated him as coming from the outside world in the 1930s and 1940s. In the 1960s young monks had never heard people say "for Pete's sake," "groovy," "beat it," and "ma-larky," except in old movies. Merton obviously colored his talks with such expressions in order to put himself on a familiar level with the young novices. Since the slang he used was intended to be entertain-ing, he did not realize that the quaintness of his expression was part of their amusement.

This phenomenon did not occur in Merton's written work because he did not write anything that included slang. His written English was formal, influenced by his reading, and, in addition, was edited by his publishers. One exception to this was his writing for secular magazines such as *Jubilee*, where he did use dated slang expressions. This was ac-ceptable because the level of sophistication of the magazine attracted readers of his age group.

Another reason for the disparity between Merton's written and spo-ken English was the imposed silence at the monastery. Since Merton's conversational English was limited for decades, his expressions re-mained largely static with the colloquialisms he used when he entered the monastery.

As Master of Novices, Merton now had the responsibility for de-termining the emotional fitness of the novices for the monastic life. Merton consulted the psychiatric literature in helping him prepare for this assignment. Merton was stunned at what he found. The American Psychiatric Association's *Diagnostic and Statistical Manual of Mental Disorders* (DSM), the psychiatrists' bible, listed religion as a delusion or evidence of immaturity, escapism, or neurosis. Religious feelings were lumped in with brainwashing and cultism. Transcendent experi-ences were considered psychotic and possibly calling for medication as a result.

It was not until 1994 that a new diagnostic category was added, called the "religious or spiritual problem." Before that time, psychiatrists had to use imprecise or inappropriate words of psychopathology when treating patients with spiritual issues in order to arrive at a diagnosis that would be billable for them. Later, as a result of further study, it was found that in the case of religious-related disorders, there was found to be an interface between the psychotic, the troubled one, and the mystic, the healed one, who learned to deal successfully with his mental state.

The only accepted instrument available to Merton to screen applicants was the Rorschach Test. Dr. Hermann Rorschach, a Swiss psychiatrist, published the instrument in 1921. It is a projective technique for personality assessment consisting of ten images to be scored on more than 100 criteria. However, it requires interpretation by the person administering it. It was originally called "an X-ray of the mind," claiming to predict success in psychotherapy. It was used worldwide until major limitations were identified. Critics said it tended to "overpatholigize," making some normal people seem maladjusted and even schizophrenic. The test's validity was attacked in the 1950s and 1960s, primarily due to its use by untrained persons. Systematic rules were not developed until the 1970s for giving and scoring it, which reinstated the test's acceptance.

A Dr. Kisker in Louisville taught Merton how to administer the Rorschach Test, better known as the inkblot test, but Merton felt inadequate in interpreting the results which would have a major effect on the future of the novices.

Merton knew instinctively that the monastery was operating by the seat of its pants in judging the fitness of its novices. There were several instances of seemingly normal monks exhibiting unexpected emotional problems that required the monastery to take emergency action. He suggested to Dom James that John Eudes Bamberger, the young physician who had entered the Order in 1950, be further trained to help the monastery better understand the psychological problems they were identifying.

Merton administered the Rorschach Test to himself and was concerned about his findings. He decided to begin an in-depth study of psycho-analysis on his own. In 1955 he wrote an essay titled, "Neurosis in the Monastic Life." He mailed copies to some of his friends for comment, including Robert Giroux. Giroux's reaction was to refer it to another of Harcourt Brace's authors, a psychiatrist by the name of Dr. Gregory Zilboorg, for comment.

Harcourt Brace had published an attribution by Dr. Zilboorg of Dr. Karl Stern's *Pillar of Fire* on the back jacket of Merton's *Ascent to Truth* in 1951, with or without Merton's knowledge or consent. Dr. Zilboorg was a Russian who had found refuge in the U.S. and had originally been an actor. He graduated from medical school at Columbia and, like Merton, was a Catholic convert. He then developed a practice as a psychiatrist working with prominent writers and artists, including Ernest Hemingway. He had read some of Merton's books and wanted to meet him.

Unknown to others, Dr. Zilboorg had already formed an opinion about Merton from reading his books. As a naturalized American and public figure like Merton both in and out of Catholic circles, as well as a published author, he apparently saw Merton as a rival. For Merton to cross over into the psychological realm, especially in a self-taught manner, was treading on his territory.

Naomi Burton was beginning to worry about Merton based on her correspondence with him. She recommended he get into analysis to offset the emotional effect she believed Merton was experiencing from his recent attempt to leave the Order and the threat of a five-year ban on writing. She sent Dr. Zilboorg a copy of Merton's essay on psychiatry with Merton's consent. Merton naively was looking forward to hearing the Doctor's comments on it. Merton wrote to the doctor to ask his professional opinion about what he should be reading, inasmuch as this was a new field for him to be involved in. Zilboorg replied that he gave courses in psychiatry for religious staff and recommended Merton attend one of them. He offered to visit Gethsemani to persuade Dom James to approve Merton's attendance, if necessary.

Naomi Burton, knowing of Dr. Zilboorg's reputation with other writers and Merton's current anxieties, recommended to Dom James that Merton be allowed to meet Dr. Zilboorg. Dom James agreed, and Merton was scheduled to attend an upcoming meeting concerning the practical application of psychiatry to the religious life. Father John Eudes accompanied him. Dom James would join them for the second week to follow up with Dr. Zilboorg to get a professional opinion of Merton's mental health.

The monks were housed at the abbey at St. John's University in Collegeville, Minnesota, where the workshop was held in July 1956. This was also the location of Liturgical Press, where Merton's book, *Praying the Psalms*, was being published. Liturgical Press had been founded by a Benedictine monk of St. John's Abbey primarily to provide Catholics with educational material about the liturgy. Later they also published Merton's *Spiritual Direction and Meditation* in 1960 and *Opening the Bible* in 1970.

Father John Eudes and Merton traveled by air to Minnesota. Merton again found it very difficult to pray in the airports or planes. It was vacation time, and there were many travelers to distract Merton. For the occasion, Dom James relaxed their Rule of Silence, and Merton was free to have discussions at conference breaks with other religious staff attending. He did not hesitate to use the privilege. He particularly enjoyed talking about the reading he had been doing on Zen and Eastern religions.

Merton and Father John Eudes spent one evening at the home of the novelist, J. F. Powers, who lived near the University and whose work Merton enjoyed reading. Merton found himself completely relaxed during this meeting. One day some of the attendees were surprised to see Merton sitting with his feet in a pond outside the living quarters of the Abbey after the session.

The following Monday, July 29, Merton had a private conference with Dr. Zilboorg. Merton felt uncomfortable immediately. The doctor was a short, husky man with a round, shiny face and large eyes that were magnified by his rimless glasses. His hair was quite curly, but he had a receding hairline that enlarged his high forehead. He had a prominent double chin and thick, bushy moustache. Merton stood before him, erect, trim, and clean shaven to the top of his head. Merton's *persona* was too much for the doctor.

*He said my article on neurosis in the monastery was dangerous, an amateur attempt into a scientific subject that would damage my reputation as a writer since I was not qualified in psychiatry.*

*I heard him saying I was intruding on his business as a fellow writer and Catholic convert. He thought Father Eudes and I were both in danger of becoming psychotic quacks. He said he had heard I was a gadfly to my superiors and stubborn in getting what I wanted from them, that I was afraid to be an ordinary monk in the community because I was neurotic.*

*He criticized my discussion about Zen with Dr. Rome at the conference break that he had overheard, and said I was using Dr. Rome to further myself. He accused me of wanting to be a big shot, of enjoying fame and publicity, and said I had trends toward narcissism and megalomania.*

*He also said my desire to be a hermit was pathological. If I were not in the monastery, I would be the type who would make money one day on Wall Street and lose it the next day on the horses.*

*Finally, he said I should forbid myself to write because my writing had now become verbological and I needed silence and isolation.*

*He said he had already spoken to Bob Giroux about this.*

For once Merton was speechless. He left Dr. Zilboorg with only the remark that he would see him later with Dom James.

When Dom James arrived at the conference, Dr. Zilboorg called them in together. It was as blunt and negative a report as the doctor had given Merton earlier. Dr. Zilboorg concluded, "You want a hermitage in Times Square with a large sign over it saying 'HERMIT.'"

Merton began to cry uncontrollably with shame in front of Dom James, and muttered, "Stalin! Stalin!" to Dr. Zilboorg.

At this point Dom James was willing to give Merton permission to go to New York to work with Dr. Zilboorg on his problems. However, Dr. Zilboorg could see, with Merton's outburst, that there was nothing to be gained by taking Merton as a patient, and in fact recommended that Merton not go into analysis.

Instead, Dr. Zilboorg referred Dom James to a Dr. James Wygal, a psychiatrist in Louisville, for Merton and other monks as well who seemed to need help. The following December, 1956, Dr. Zilboorg made a trip to Gethsemani and met with Merton, following up their initial consultation, to discuss Merton's work with novices and the use of Dr. Wygal's services. Again he told Merton that he did not need analysis.

Merton took Dr. Zilboorg's original recommendation to heart, if for no other reason than that he had not been able to control himself in the doctor's presence. He requested and received permission from Dom James to see Dr. Wygal for a limited number of visits. He may not need analysis, but he was convinced that a little counseling would help.

Merton updated Naomi Burton about his feelings in a letter dated May 2, 1956. " ... for me communication is not communication but a narcissistic gesture of some sort at which I happen to be quite clever. Do you think that I have ever in my life communicated with another person? Sacramentally I hope, but not in writing ... .Maybe that sounds horrible, or maybe I am exaggerating because of an ideal of communication that I know will never be attained on earth—or something. But I am trying to tell the truth ... ."

Dr. Zilboorg may have come to Gethsemani at the request of Dom James to review Merton's screening procedures, in view of the Abbot's thoroughness in overseeing the monastery's operation. Dom James had to be concerned about Merton's outburst even if Dr. Zilboorg had precipitated it. Nevertheless, Dom James had confidence in Merton's ability and knew from his own experience that Merton's ego was sufficiently in check to continue working with the novices and producing saleable books on a regular basis. He would employ Dr. Wygal to monitor Merton's emotional state as a professional check.

Dr. Zilboorg endorsed the idea that Merton had first suggested to send Father John Eudes for further studies in psychiatry. Dom James agreed, and Father John Eudes was sent to Washington, DC, for a one-year residency to qualify as a psychiatrist. When he returned, a screening team was set up for postulants that was composed of Merton as Novice Master, Father John Eudes as medical interviewer, and Father Matthew Kelty as vocational secretary. An inside joke among the old timers resulted, questioning who was screening the screeners?

As Novice Master, Merton received a great deal of respect from the group. He was more than a screener or a teacher. He provided valuable spiritual direction to his novices, and sometimes acted as a substitute father in times of a novice's distress. Some of his students later were selected for additional training or progressed to leadership positions at Gethsemani and other Cistercian abbeys. Merton further extended this role to many of his correspondents, serving as a spiritual advisor to those who expressed needs that he could identify from their letters.

*Scenes of downtown Louisville, KY, then and now, near the location where Merton had his spiritual experience at 4th and Walnut (now Muhammed Ali). From an old postcard and a photograph by the author in 1998.*

# Chapter 21

Merton had made a vow in Havana to Our Lady of Mount Carmel that he would live a life in solitude. Now his hopes were growing dim to ever accomplish this. He knew the incident with Dr. Zilboorg would be ready ammunition for Dom James when he received inquiries about Merton from other religious orders. He could readily say that Merton was emotionally too unstable to be a hermit. Merton was now determined to be a better monk, to live up to his own high standard of monasticism, and to prove his sanity through his writing. He believed he now had a broader view of his vocation since he had been studying the Desert Fathers.

Merton next wrote *The Silent Life*, published in January 1957 by Farrar, Straus and Cudahy. This was a treatment of different Cistercian and Benedictine models of monastic life, including cenobite, Benedictine and Cistercian Orders, and eremite, the Carthusians and Camaldolese. From his research he became interested in South America and thought he might like to transfer to an eremitical order there.

Some of his novices were Spanish speaking, and the information he acquired from them increased his desire to learn more. He began to read political poems from South America, and to follow current events in that region to supplement the chance information he acquired from correspondence and magazine articles. His concern expanded to include the significance and the global impact of the atomic bomb, U.S. civil rights problems, and the Church's place in the social and political structure of Latin American countries.

In March 1957 Merton published another collection of poetry, *The Strange Islands*, through Laughlin's New Directions. It was less than successful. It contained a play Merton had written for television, "The Tower of Babel, A Morality," which had been broadcast on the NBC television network on January 27, 1957. It had also been published in Ed Rice's magazine, *Jubilee*. This was the beginning of Merton's interest in writing morality stories to raise public opinion. Merton was undoubtedly fascinated by the Biblical story of the Tower of Babel, with his broad knowledge of languages. He could have easily imagined the confusion of builders trying to communicate in different languages.

Merton's writing was beginning to change focus. He wrote to Naomi Burton, June 4, 1956, that he planned to start over again, avoiding "a big smoke screen of double-talk." For the past ten years he believed that his writing had followed "the straight ascetic-mystic line" that got him nothing but pretenses that kidded a lot of other people. He told her that his current writing was "much rougher," "less publishable," but "more fruitful" and "more honest."

Toward the latter part of 1956, Merton became interested in studying the Russian mystics. The personification of Holy Wisdom as Hagia Sophia, the female image of God, fascinated him. He read that this image is said to have appeared to Russian pilgrims. His interest expanded to include a study of Russian writers and their philosophy from ancient to current times.

Dom James did not ignore his management of Merton's reading entirely. He intercepted and withheld two books that Laughlin sent Merton on the basis that they were inappropriate and that there was "kissing" in one of them. Merton was not really surprised. At the same time, Father John of the Cross, now becoming a close friend of Merton, told him that he had ordered a book by Gilson on painting that arrived "with all the nudes torn out."

Merton then wrote *Basic Principles of Monastic Spirituality*, published by the monastery in 1957. In this book, Merton states that the world's problems are not merely based on politics or the errors of Communism. The world is engaged in a spiritual war, he contends, and monks must be like trees, providing a vital presence and purifying the air. A much later edition added some photographs that Merton had taken around Gethsemani and three of his pen and ink sketches. This expanded edition was produced by Templegate Publishers in 1996.

In 1957 Merton was hospitalized briefly in Louisville for surgery due to hemorrhoids. A few months later, he had an impacted tooth extracted in the Flaget Hospital in nearby Bardstown. He was so upset by his surroundings, especially the canned music playing continuously on the intercom, that he just wanted to get back to the monastery as soon as possible. This was a sort of culture shock in reverse for Merton. The combination of physical and emotional discomfort continued to depress him.

When Christmas came, Merton was one of the volunteers who went out to cut and deliver trees from the monastery to decorate the Bardstown hospital. The weather was the official excuse, but Merton and his crew did not get back to the monastery until after dark, and long after the last prayers of the day. Dom James chose to ignore the violation in the spirit of the season.

In late 1957 a problem arose about the publishing rights Merton had given to the Baroness Catherine de Hueck years earlier to his manuscript that he called "The Cuban Journal." After Merton entered Gethsemani, she had married Edward J. Doherty in 1943 and moved from Harlem to Ontario to found Madonna House Apostolate. She now wanted to publish Merton's manuscript to help raise money for her sixteen houses in Canada, the U.S., and the West Indies.

Dom James readily gave his permission for the Baroness to proceed, but there was opposition from the four Cistercian censors. One of them, Father Maurice, turned the book down on literary grounds. He said that Merton's colloquial style was not appropriate for a monk. Merton was amazed at this reaction. Checking his sources, Merton found that this censor had been a Catholic high school English teacher before he joined the Order.

Throughout 1958 Catherine argued the merits of the benefit to the poor that this book's sales would bring. Believing approval was a hopeless possibility, Dom James repaid Merton's royalty check of $500 to the publisher out of monastery funds since he had initially given his consent to its publication. However, Merton was determined to honor the gift. He made numerous changes to satisfy the censors, except for Father Maurice's criticism of his literary style before the manuscript was approved for publication. It was published as *The Secular Journal* in February 1959 by Farrar, Straus and Cudahy. Merton said that the final product distorted the feelings he had had in 1940 and 1941 when he wrote it. Merton believed that the censors were too sensitive and insecure about the image of the Order and any adverse effect his work might have on it. He surmised that his readers would be disappointed that it did not contain any scandalous material from his pre-monastic life.

Merton was becoming compulsive about his production. He became a virtual writing machine in 1958. In quick succession he released *Monastic Peace*, a guide for postulants, with Shirley Burden's photographs of Gethsemani, and *Nativity Kerygma*, both published by the Abbey; *Thoughts in Solitude*, published by Farrar, Straus and Cudahy; and *Prometheus: A Meditation*, published by King Library Press at the University of Kentucky.

On March 18, 1958, Merton had another experience he considered to be not of this world. He was in Louisville to see the local printer about the postulants' guide he had written. Walking down a street in the main business and shopping center of the city, suddenly at the corner of Fourth Avenue and Walnut Street, he felt a love for all the people he saw. He experienced a realization that his vocation did not separate him from his fellow man. This experience permanently affected his beliefs and work.

(There is now a marker in downtown Louisville commemorating this occurrence by the Kentucky Historical Society and presented by the Thomas Merton Center Foundation in 1998. The intersection is now called Fourth and Muhammed Ali, since Walnut Street has been renamed.)

Merton had recently had a strange dream that he could not forget. It was about a young Jewish girl named Proverb. He had previously dreamed of this girl approaching him when he was living at Douglaston. He believed that the dream was sent to him by God. In this second dream the girl expressed her deep and pure affection for Merton by an embrace that moved him deeply. She complained to him about her name, saying that others mocked her for it. Merton assured her in the dream that it was a beautiful name. That was the end of the dream. When Merton had the experience at Fourth and Walnut Street, he said the people he saw there all looked like Proverb in terms of their purity and beauty and shyness, and that they were ashamed of their names and were mocked for them, just like the girl in his dream. Merton said these people did not realize they were the children of God playing in the world.

Merton apparently told only four people about this dream. One was Pasternak, which was related in a letter to him. The other three were probably his confessor and his publishing friends, the Hammers, who shared his fascination for Santa Sophia, Holy Wisdom, as the female image of God. One of the strangest features of this dream was the resemblance of Proverb to the picture Merton had sketched after he returned from his retreat at Gethsemani—the same beautiful face with the large, soulful eyes. Could he be deceiving himself? It was beyond his ability to understand.

Merton began to investigate the effect of drugs in altering the conscious level of awareness. He had received an article published by Aldous Huxley on "Drugs That Shape Man's Mind" (*Saturday Evening Post*, October 18, 1958), alleging that chemical mind changers could bring about a genuine religious experience and in fact make such experiences commonplace. In an exchange of correspondence with Huxley, Merton expressed his concern that there was a danger in both magic and drug use, which are based on manipulation, and therefore could not be true mysticism which is spontaneous, free, and transcendent. Merton was fearful that the nonviolent peace movement might inevitably become linked to drug use, and its reputation could be damaged. Merton compared drug use to a *Deus ex machina* (a god coming out of an artificial mechanism to save the day), devised by the Greek theater. Huxley's theories served to crystallize Merton's understanding that true spiritual experience comes as a gift of God, not through chemistry or an ascetic technique, and therefore cannot be gained by simply willing it.

Times were changing both in and outside the monastery. The Order relaxed the restriction on correspondence. The volume of Merton's letters to people he called his friends gradually increased to literally hundreds of men and women throughout the world. Some of these relationships developed after Merton initiated the correspondence to discuss matters of mutual concern, and others came about when people contacted Merton for a variety of reasons. He began to write about the social issues that were exploding throughout the country. He took an intense interest in world affairs, asking many of his correspondents to send him significant books and articles being published so that he could be adequately informed.

One of his most important correspondents of this time was Boris Pasternak. Merton had a letter to the editors published in *The New York Times* in September 1958 praising *Dr. Zhivago* when it was published. The two authors enjoyed a close, though brief, correspondence. When Pasternak died in May 1960, Merton said he believed he had more in common with Pasternak than with the monks in his own monastery.

Merton yearned for enlightenment to know the will of God in his monastic vocation. His attraction to South American locations and lack of direction in his writing often preoccupied and frustrated him. In July 1958, he again turned to the "sortes," or random opening, of the Bible for guidance. Just as he had found an answer about his Trappist calling, he hoped for new direction at this point. Now he found the passage, " … go rather to the lost sheep of the House of Israel."

Life in the world gradually began to play a more significant role in Merton's daily life. His frequent trips into town for medical appointments put him frequently into secular clothing. His choice of jeans and a jean jacket became stand-bys for him. The number of visitors who came to see him increased the frequency of his occasions outside the monastery because he was allowed to leave the grounds with his guests. Laughlin later said that Merton would ask him to pull over in a wooded area after they left the monastery so that he could change from a priest's black suit to his casual outfit before they came to a nearby town. They would often stop at a take-out store for cold beer, and he didn't want to be recognized as a local monk.

Outside the monastery Merton had developed a warm friendship with Victor and Carolyn Hammer, a couple who operated a small hand press, called Stamperia del Santuccio. Merton greatly admired the quality of their work. The Hammers released several limited editions for Merton on their press, which later became collectors' items. Carolyn Hammer was a librarian at the University of Kentucky in Louisville and helped Merton to locate books he wanted to read. Victor, although older and in poor health, was a teacher at Transylvania University in Lexington. Victor also painted in a classical style that Merton admired, particularly of religious subjects. Merton persuaded Victor to donate one of his original icons to the monastery for the novices' chapel.

Another of Victor's icons, part of a triptych of three panels, portrayed a beautiful woman, reminiscent of the woman in Merton's dream and in his sketch, but not exactly the same. Nevertheless, Merton was struck that it must be Hagia Sophia, a symbol of wisdom, or the mother of Christ. He asked Victor for an explanation, which was simply that he had painted an interpretation of a picture he saw in a book. Victor himself felt, though, that the woman in the triptych was nothing less than the manifestation of God's glory in creation. Merton was fascinated with the coincidence in his experience.

In December 1958 the monastery lost a good friend. Herman Hanekamp was a former monk who lived as a hermit on a few acres of woodland that the monastery gave him for his use. He had been a novice before the First World War and had taken Simple Vows before deciding to leave the group to live alone. Dom James sympathetically gave Hanekamp a house that was on a piece of property purchased to expand the monastery. The monks, including Merton, knew Hanekamp from his regular attendance at Mass. Merton also saw him when he went to inspect brush fires near Hanekamp's place. Merton had great respect for Hanekamp's choice of lifestyle, preferring to go it alone than stay at the monastery. His opinion was not shared generally by other monks, who thought the recluse to be lazy. When Hanekamp had not been seen for a while, a group of monks went to his house to check on him. He claimed to be ill, but some of the monks suspected him of pretending. On the next visit the monks found that he had died. Coincidentally at the same time, the monks were arguing a theoretical case among themselves at a Chapter meeting. The subject was the question of whether a dying man who is unconscious should be given absolution from sin.

As it turned out for Hanekamp, Father John Eudes, one of the group who discovered that he had died, gave him absolution. The monks buried him in their secular graveyard just outside the enclosure wall. Merton was one of the pallbearers. Dom James decided to give Hanekamp a formal funeral and personally sang the Mass for his intention. Merton said later that if he had known that the funeral would be such a big affair, he would not have attended.

In spite of the long, out of the way location, Merton's old friends loyally came to check on him after the rules for visitors were relaxed. Driving out of Bardstown, there was only a small, plain white sign with the one word, "Trappist," in small black letters pointing down the road toward the woods. Nevertheless, Merton's friends managed to find the monastery. In May 1959, Lax and Reinhardt came down from New York, with Bob Giroux arriving a few days later. Merton thrived on these contacts, which helped him to stay in touch with the reality of the world that he had left.

Merton enjoyed nothing better than his outings with his friends. With Laughlin, it was reported that Merton's lunch often consisted of almost a whole cold turkey, three-fourths of a bottle of wine, and three cans of beer. The Hammers also liked to come out to Gethsemani for picnic lunches with Merton. In cold weather he would wear a black wool French beret and join them in their car on the monastery grounds for lunch. On nice days they went to Dom Frederic's Lake, which was across the highway and some distance from the center of monastery life, in an extended part of the monastery's grounds.

Merton was in tune with the relaxation of the rules, and may have anticipated some of the liberalism before the Abbot was ready for it. He found himself soon being called Father Louie, and he liked that. It even sounded French.

In September 1959 two women admirers from California stopped by and were allowed to meet Merton on their way across the country. Another monk observed the two women in Dom Frederic's Lake with

Merton and then sunbathing to dry off. Merton knew that the Abbot had been informed, but for some reason Dom James never mentioned it. Sometimes Merton believed that the Abbot deliberately intensified his power over him by the absence of criticism or discipline. Merton would then be held in suspension wondering when or if the matter would be discussed and brought to closure.

In 1959 *The Selected Poems of Thomas Merton* was published by New Directions with an introduction by his mentor, Mark Van Doren. He and Merton had continued their friendship through a regular correspondence. At this time Merton was also working on a new version of *What is Contemplation?* which did not get republished until after his death. He was also drafting "The Inner Experience" which he would privately circulate, but not publish, he decided. At the same time, he was correcting the galleys of *The New Man*.

In October 1959 Merton went to Louisville for a rectal operation. He hoped he would not be put near the maternity ward again, as he had once before when the infirmary was full. Crying babies did not help his contemplation, except to pray fervently for his quick recovery so that he could return to the monastery. Only the snoring of some of the monks sometimes disturbed his sleep there.

To further increase the anxiety, Merton had spilled his suitcase in the middle of the street as he had approached the hospital. He reported this incident to his friend, Cardenal, in a letter dated October 24, 1959. Merton had taken the bag from common property, and had not noticed the defective fasteners. To make matters worse, it was raining hard when he had to gather up his clothing and books from the wet street, so all the things so carefully selected for his stay were soaked.

At this time Merton was hoping to become a hermit soon in some far-away place. Merton was in an all-out campaign, generating a great deal of correspondence to gain support for a transfer. Dom Gregorio Lemercier, prior of a small experimental monastery in Cuernavaca, had visited him twice during the previous summer to discuss a possible transfer with Dom James. Merton thought surely the pressure to release him would be effective. Later Dom James informed Merton that Dom Lemercier had gotten married. He showed Merton a photograph from a news article to prove it. This was another typical example of the mental combat between Merton and the Abbot, year in and year out. Merton told himself, though, that defeatism was a great temptation, and he was determined to resist (called "suadente diabolo," or diabolical persuasion).

Merton's efforts continued to be futile. He received a letter in December 1959 from Rome, four years after the last attempt to end-run a transfer. Merton went into the novitiate chapel to open and read it on his knees. Rome had sent him another rejection. He went outside in a light rain, selected some trees to be cut to give the nuns in a nearby convent for Christmas, and began to laugh at himself. Thomas was absurd! He was now free of his obsession to leave—free to be in solitude without geography.

One of the reasons for Merton's laughter was that the two officials from Rome who turned down his request had selectively edited one of his own writings to use as the basis for their decision. The passage, from *No Man is an Island*, was quoted out of context. It said Merton had claimed that he wanted to follow God's will for him. The passage continued to say that if there were an indication that God desired a change, he would change his vocation in an instant. Naturally, this part was not included in the passage quoted in the letter.

Merton believed that Dom James had squelched his request when he was in Rome a month earlier, probably using a report he had received from Dr. Zilboorg to substantiate his own opinions. Unfortunately, Dr. Zilboorg had just died a few months earlier the previous August, so there was no way to get his findings recanted. Merton confided to his journal that he believed he had a genuine dislike for Dom James, that he was being treated as the Abbot's personal property, and that Dom James simply could not envision Merton changing to a different superior. At the same time, he conceded that he felt a genuine affection for the Abbot. Merton believed that it was Providence that had brought the two of them together.

Merton's relationship with the Abbot had undoubtedly been strained over his appeal to Rome to transfer. Merton believed he had gradually broken with the community as the result of his attempts at isolation. He viewed monks as naturally individualistic loners. He fervently wished that he would not have to endure a long life there, ending in an old age with diminished faculties that would reduce his capacity to work or live a full life. He especially dreaded the possibility of being subject to a prolonged illness before death. He could not bear to think that one day he might die at Gethsemani. It would be a complete surrender to mediocrity, he thought, which he detested.

He walked barefoot in the pine needles wondering if the routine had destroyed his spirit. He worried that his writing was drawing men to an idealized lifestyle that wasn't real so would not materialize when they arrived at Gethsemani. Then they would become frustrated and confused and have to leave because it was not what they had anticipated.

Merton's artistic sense and incredibly persuasive writing were the formula for unintended consequences, he believed. For Merton, his artistic sense was boundless but shackled, he felt, by the daily regimen of group activities that broke up the day every few hours. He had to write at prescribed times, not when he was motivated. He frequently could not pursue an idea without interruption. He had little time to imagine, so his stimulus for expression was reined in. Furthermore, his subjects were sometimes chosen for him. He was forced into self-imposed censorship to curtail the rejection by the censors, which he knew was inevitable.

Merton could only confide in his journal:

"Monastery life is rigid, artificial, and culturally deprived. Mundane events become magnified in this atmosphere. Time is so controlled that there is no opportunity to deal with differences. Yet the monks have come here to prepare for eternity in a voluntary timeless waiting period. What is time to them?"

In December 1959 Merton gave Dom James a renewed promise of obedience and said he would no longer try to leave the Order. The words inscribed on the inside wall of the monastery, "GOD ALONE," expressed it.

*I read the prepared statement in Dom James' office. It was such a cold reception that I could hardly bear the experience. Then I walked out to the woods to make my personal vow to God.*

*Jesus, for Thee I live,*
*Jesus, for Thee I suffer,*
*Jesus, for Thee I die.*
*Jesus, I am Thine in life, in suffering, and in death. Amen.*
Did he hear a response?
Tom:
*For thee I lived,*
*For thee I suffered,*
*For thee I died.*
His soul was suspended between here and eternity.

Merton's dream to live the contemplative tradition seemed buried in the reality of the moment. Since the prophet Elijah, the contemplative life had survived intact. The Carmelites had memorialized him as their patron. The first Christians, in the East, had given birth to the Desert Fathers, who in the third century left the world of their time to maintain their true reality. In the West, Benedict had created the cloistered order more than 1500 years earlier and justified intercessory prayer as the answer to man's most critical needs. Now Merton wondered what was happening to the tradition in the world around him.

Merton had no choice but to continue working, the only way he could obtain some measure of solitude. The silent, gentle circle of hills around the monastery grounds comforted him.

Dom James continued to reap the harvest of Merton's efforts. His work in negotiating Merton's publishing contracts had become almost a full-time job. His responsibility was to keep Merton there and emotionally capable of writing saleable books.

Dom James continued to use Merton as his confessor. There was a continual discussion between the two in the privacy of the confessional, which could not be repeated. Merton could only listen to Dom James and had no way to express his feelings and frustrations to the Abbot in this relationship. Having the Abbot, his superior, in a subordinate role to him as his confessor, was difficult and awkward for him. Church law would insure Merton's silence. In effect, the Abbot was also in control in the confessional.

# Chapter 22

One of Merton's closest friends was his novice, Ernesto Cardenal, a distinguished poet from Nicaragua and, like Merton, an alumnus of Columbia University. He was known at Gethsemani as Brother Lawrence. In spite of the Abbot's policy against Particular Friendships, Cardenal and Merton shared their interests in literature as well as innovative ideas to improve monastic life. Cardenal informed Merton of the activities underway in his homeland to persecute the Church, and Merton was interested in finding a way that he could make a contribution. In 1959, Cardenal asked to return to Nicaragua because of his health. Dom James consented, although he suspected his health was not Cardenal's only reason to leave Gethsemani.

To Merton, Dom James was obviously resentful of Cardenal. The Abbot believed that Cardenal was concealing other dissatisfactions that he would not share with him. Actually, the Abbot was not completely inaccurate in his perceptions. Cardenal was a short middle-aged man who suffered from health problems. However, he found that he could not fulfill his vocation to serve the Church at Gethsemani, a place of prayer rather than of Catholic action. Catholics were being persecuted in his homeland and this apparently had increased while he was at Gethsemani, including the torture of one of his friends.

In correspondence Cardenal and Merton continued their friendship, with Cardenal persuading Merton to seek a transfer so they could work together. Cardenal's letters to Merton were marked "sub secreto," or "conscience matter," the term designated by the Order to insure that no one opened the letter other than the person to whom it was addressed. In the case of Cardenal's letters, Dom James ignored the practice and rejected Cardenal's letters out of hand. He returned Cardenal's letters unopened, commenting to an assistant that Cardenal should seek someone closer to Nicaragua to resolve his matters of conscience.

Usually Dom James disliked seeing any monk leave, considering it a personal failure. In the case of Cardenal, the Abbot had mixed feelings. Cardenal had become a very close friend of Merton's, which was a violation of Dom James' policy against Particular Friendships. He firmly believed such friendships could develop into homosexual relationships.

He was fully determined to shield Merton from any temptation along these lines.

In reality, Merton and Cardenal did have common goals to make a major contribution to the Church beyond the use of prayer and contemplation. In addition, they shared a creative ability: Merton with his writing and sketches, and Cardenal's poetry and sacred objects. In one project, Cardenal made concrete pourings for corpuses on crucifixes and placed them throughout the monks' dormitory. Merton was particularly impressed with Cardenal's artistic ability. In 1960, Merton translated into English part of Cardenal's poem, "The Jaguar and the Moon," which had been recognized with a prestigious award in Central America, and included it in his collection, *Emblems of a Season of Fury*, in 1963. In terms of Cardenal's writing, Merton once commented that if he ever included any instruction in poetry for his novices, he would have Cardenal provide the training.

The subject of relationships was an issue in the monastery. Merton described his ideas on this subject to his novices in one of the lectures he tape recorded by direction. He described a Particular Friendship as a sensory relationship for pleasure, not necessarily sexual, but exclusionary to the rest of the group. Merton characterized it as a relationship that does not end well, usually resulting in both parties on the bus leaving the monastery going two different directions, never seeing each other again. It can develop without conscious thought in the natural order of monastery life. Since one cannot select his fellow monks, and the group comes from diverse backgrounds, communication problems can easily arise, especially in sign language. Disagreements quickly arise and can be slow to resolve. On the other hand, when a fellow monk seems to relate well to another, an exclusionary relationship can readily form in the closeness of daily life.

The bond between Cardenal and Merton transcended the Abbot's suspicions. Cardenal was forthright and militant about working for souls in his native land and saw in Merton a man who could help him achieve his goals there. Merton thought the Abbot may have suspected a homosexual attraction, but concluded that this was probably Merton's over-active imagination working overtime. Actually, Dom James primarily saw Cardenal as a threat to Merton's continuation at Gethsemani. He believed Cardenal's persistent efforts to get Merton to follow him to a remote location in Central America would come to pass if he did not intervene. He believed he acted in good conscience to deny Merton this outcome for the sake of Merton's spiritual wellbeing in keeping his vow of stability at Gethsemani. And the monastery had something to gain as well.

In January 1960 Merton decided to put together a new course in Cistercian history for novices. Dom James was pleased at Merton's initiative and an apparently renewed interest in Gethsemani. Later that month Laughlin arrived at Gethsemani for a long-overdue visit. He told Merton that Cardenal had made all the arrangements for Merton to come to Cuernavaca and had also sent the information to the Hammers since his letters to Merton had been returned unopened. The Hammers told Laughlin that Merton had never received Cardenal's correspondence. Merton was overwhelmed at the Abbot's determination to keep him at Gethsemani. He resigned himself for the time being to accepting the Abbot's will, whether or not it was God's will.

In August 1960, Father John advised Merton to follow God's will and to continue seeking assignment to Cuernavaca, while Merton believed that Father John himself appeared to be leaving for destinations he had not revealed to Merton. In October 1962, he described Father John's current thinking as "an extreme interpretation of some of my own teachings." Merton at this point experienced intense feelings of guilt, since he had reinforced Father John's self-confidence, praising his superiority, particularly his sermons in Chapter meetings, and encouraging his dissatisfaction with the monastery's rigidity. Yet Merton believed firmly that Father John could "still be a saint," describing him in his journal entry of October 13, 1962, as "one of the most unusual and gifted people" in the monastery and with "the most profound effect on the people he advises."

In November 1962, Merton reported in his journal that he had discussed Father John's plan to leave the monastery with the Abbot, who told Merton that he would have elevated Father John to the Prior position if he had stayed. Merton concluded that this discussion gave him insight into the Abbot's character: "in some ways the best man in the house, and one who, in doing much good, hurts people incessantly and does tremendous harm – for which he will perhaps never be blamed and for which they also will receive merit and reward for their suffering. Yet to say that is for the monastic life would be unutterable blasphemy."

On Christmas Eve 1962, Merton faced the loss of Father John, "on a leave of absence," along with the merging of the two novitiates (described in Chapter 24), commenting in his journal that he now saw "absolutely nothing awaiting one here except death." He thought it was "like standing on the deck of a sinking ship and watching everyone else go off in a lifeboat."

One day Merton was allowed to go to Lexington to pick up the religious panel that Victor Hammer was donating to Gethsemani's novitiate chapel. En route he persuaded his driver to stop at Pleasant Hill so he could see the Shakertown complex which was now closed and abandoned. The beauty of the plainness of the Shakers' woodwork particularly impressed him. He soon researched the history of the Shakers and decided to write an illustrated article about them. He contacted Mr. Shirley Burden, a photographer he had worked with earlier on the preparation of *God is My Life* which was released at Easter, 1960. Burden had also provided photos for *Monastic Peace* two years earlier and for the cover of Merton's *Selected Poems*. Merton renewed his interest in photography and started borrowing cameras from his friends to try it for himself.

In March 1960 a fire broke out during the night in the Steel Building. Apparently some of the machinery ignited a pile of wood shavings. The monks on the firefighters team put it out, but the incident had additional significance. The Steel Building was considered the building least likely to be flammable. This pushed forward the issue of doing some major fireproofing around the monastery. The initial survey team of engineers who were called in refused to use the stairs in the three-story frame Old Guest House that the monks had been using for years. The entire project required a return of the heavy building equipment. Merton commented that the place was looking like New York City again. He wished they could do something about the heat—he wondered if Dom James thought he was a geranium.

The following month another fire broke out in the woods from sparks in some brush. Merton, one of the volunteer firefighters, was exhausted by the time it was brought under control. He had just developed an eye infection before the incident, which became irritated by the fire. For several months Merton suffered with conjunctivitis and had to wear dark glasses. Going into Louisville for treatment, Merton wondered if he looked like the "dark" philosopher he had been writing about in an essay, "Herakleitos the Obscure." It brought back memories of the disguises of Sy Freedgood at Columbia and the clowning around they had enjoyed.

Actually the fire brought Merton an unexpected gift. Dom James had a small alcove built in the process of the repair work for Merton's sleeping area. He had suffered with insomnia for years, and was thrilled to be allowed a quiet place to sleep. In daylight hours he had a great view of Rohan's Knob, which he said made him feel like he was sitting "on the edge of the sky." It was a little bit like his fire tower experience. He got a stool, an old desk from the scriptorium, and a bed, and added his three icons and a small crucifix that Cardenal made for him before he left Gethsemani. This was his second hermitage, in effect. He was so grateful and ashamed of his previous complaints about the lack of quiet. He told his diary that he sat on his bed in the alcove and cried.

Merton now had a solid reputation internationally for his spiritual books. Many of them were going into translation throughout the world. This did not miss the attention of the Church of Rome and its leader. In addition, Merton was making himself known at the Vatican personally. He wrote directly to Pope John XXIII shortly after the Pope's election to tell him about his idea for a monastery to conduct retreats for writers and intellectuals, possibly in Latin America. On February 11, 1960, fourteen months later, Merton received an autographed portrait of the Pontiff and a blessing for the novitiate. Merton responded in a letter reporting that he had received permission from his superiors to start a retreat project of both Protestant and Catholic theologians, psychiatrists, writers, and artists to hold a cultural dialogue that would be similar to what he had written about earlier.

On April 11, 1960, a representative of the Pope arrived at Gethsemani to see Merton. He was Lorenzo Barbato, an Italian architect and personal friend of John XXIII. He came to present Merton with an ornate gold brocade stole worn by the Pope at his investiture and, in addition, some medals he had blessed. The Pope wanted to recognize the contribution Merton had made to further the Church's work by his writings.

Dom James was dumbfounded. Merton was almost in tears, according to Father Matthew Kelty. The monastery was undoubtedly in a commotion of jealousy and amazement, all expressed in silence—a proverbial uproar spelled out in sign language and an embarrassment for Merton. The Abbot offered to put the Pope's gifts away in the vault with the rare books and manuscripts that had been donated to the monastery over the years. Merton declined, preferring to wear the stole on special days of prayer every month. Possibly it was a reminder to Dom James of his personal relationship with Church authority above and beyond the monastery and even of the entire Order. Merton gave Mr. Barbato a copy of his latest book, *The Wisdom of the Desert*, to take to the Pope. Merton had recently received permission from Dom James to organize a conference of local Protestant seminarians and pastors at Gethsemani. It had been successful, according to the feedback Dom James had received. Merton decided to write a letter to the Pope to tell him about it. He gave his letter to Mr. Barbato for the Pope.

This gift from a Pope to an individual priest was a unique event. Even more important, Pope John's gesture was a significant statement about the value he placed on Merton's contribution to the Church and a lesson for the hierarchy to contemplate. Merton soon saw the effect within the Cistercian Order. Two weeks later, Dom James received a letter from Cardinal Tardini, the Pope's Secretary of State, commending the ecumenical meetings that Merton had organized. The Pope at this time had just announced his decision to convene the Second Vatican Council.

Dom James invited Dan Walsh to come to the Abbey to help in the reorganization of the philosophy department and to assist in the instruction of the monks studying for the priesthood. Walsh accepted this assignment, which continued for ten years, until 1970.

A wide interest in ecumenical activities had begun throughout organized religion in the early 1960s. Other Church leaders were contacting Merton to suggest he participate in discussions of mutual interest. The need for a conference center at the monastery but away from day-to-day activities seemed obvious. Immediately after Dom James received the Cardinal's letter, Merton suggested a building be erected to hold these conferences--a hermitage was the answer. Dom James approved the idea.

Without delay, the low knob called Mount Olivet, the monastery's northernmost knob, just above and to the rear of the Church, was selected as the site. The plans for the retreat cottage were begun. Merton had found this site years earlier. He loved it particularly because of the view. There were miles of woods to the northwest, and because of the clearing on the knob there was a beautiful view of miles of Kentucky woodlands.

The stole was the gift of the Pope, but Merton knew the hermitage was a gift from God Himself.

Merton secretly dedicated the site to Our Lady of Mount Carmel. In Israel, Mount Carmel had been a place of contemplation for hermits and prophets. It was the place where Elijah confronted the false prophets of Baal, according to the Old Testament. Later, Mary appeared to Saint Simon Stock, a leader in the Carmelite Order in the thirteenth century, and gave him the Brown Scapular of Mount Carmel. Merton had been wearing this brown cloth scapular since he received it at St. Bonaventure College. Simon Stock was known for his reform of the Carmelite Order, combining the apostolic mission with the life of solitude, which probably resulted in saving the Order. Merton saw John of the Cross as a follower of Simon Stock three centuries later in attempting to reform the Carmelites by advocating the combination of contemplation with the direction of souls.

Merton dedicated the hermitage to Our Lady as a fulfillment of his promise to her in Havana and again at his ordination. For Merton this tied together his experience at Cambridge, where Simon Stock was visited by Our Lady, Merton's lowest point, to the height of his spiritual accomplishment in acquiring the hermitage. He saw this place as the answer to his question about how he should live the remainder of his monastic life—to remain contemplative but to reach out to all humanity by writing and speaking on subjects relevant to contemporary society.

On the feast of Our Lady of Mount Carmel, Merton would put a gardenia before a statue of Mary in her honor. This feast occurred in July when gardenias were in bloom. Merton loved the structure of this flower as well as its scent.

Merton was allowed to attend meetings then being held in Louisville at Bellarmine College to plan a conference center for this site. The ambitious original plans were eventually dropped, probably due to Merton's persuasion. He was successful in getting a simple structure approved that could double as a hermitage for him. He used the argument that the structure should be consistent with the Cistercian vow of poverty and style of simplicity. Merton certainly believed a more substantial building would kill his chances of ever being given the place for his exclusive use.

In November a single-story cinder block cottage was constructed. It consisted of only two rooms, one behind the other. The front room had a large stone fireplace to heat the cottage. The bedroom was in the rear. There was no electricity. A long, open porch ran across the front. The structure had no plumbing, so an "outhouse" of plain wood boards was constructed, the size of a portable toilet. Merton termed the cottage "Mount Olivet Hermitage." He and two of his novices helped the local work crew pour cement for the foundation to get the job done more quickly. Merton then started calling it "St. Mary of Carmel."

A fifteen-minute walk from the main buildings, and less than one mile away, it was worth the trip just for the view of the bottom lands and the hills south of it after the morning fog lifted. There were pine and cedar trees already growing there, and with some help Merton planted maple saplings on one side. He got a pink dogwood tree and a red bud tree for either side of the cottage near the porch. In the immediate area, he had locust, oak, juniper, hickory, sycamore, and black walnut trees. Eventually he had crocuses and day lilies as well as a rose hedge that the birds loved to inhabit.

Merton loved to sit on the porch in his simple wood straight-backed chair, staring across the landscape, like Saint Exupery's well-known figure, "the Little Prince," perched on the same type of chair looking out from his small planet, Asteroid B-612, across the horizon. Merton may have been familiar with this classic imaginary figure. He wrote in *The Last of the Fathers* in 1954, "what is not seen is the essential," a similar statement to one in *The Little Prince*, published in 1943.

Merton was the first American Trappist allowed to live alone. By December 1960, Merton was building fires in the hermitage fireplace. He arranged with his friend, Victor Hammer, to get a redwood table built, a copy of one Victor had built for himself, that Merton could use as a desk. It was modeled on a Shaker schoolboy's desk. From old furniture around the Abbey, he found a plain wood chair from the library. He acquired a wood rocking chair with a simple pattern in the back that could have been a copy of a Shaker chair. From the library he got a small wood bookcase to put his current reading material on, and another old piece with open shelves for miscellaneous supplies. His bed was similar to an Army cot. He used a kerosene lamp for light.

Merton was the only monk at Gethsemani who was allowed to use the cottage, even though he was only permitted to be there part-time at first. He could spend a few hours there in the morning or afternoon, but never at dinnertime. Later he was allowed to stay there throughout the day occasionally but not overnight. Then he was allowed to stay overnight, but not say Mass there. Soon he was allowed to say Mass there, but never with the Eucharist reserved there in advance. With these incremental concessions, Merton concluded that Dom James would eventually give him what he asked for, so long as he stayed at Gethsemani. He was thankful and at peace for the time being.

Some of the monks, including some in authority, began to register disagreement with the notion of any monk in their group living on monastery grounds as a hermit. Merton once said that if they did not want him there, he could go to other places where he believed he would be welcome. It hurt him to be criticized by some who were not trying to live up to the monastic ideal, in his opinion. Unfairness of any kind bothered him. His solution was to reflect the events that most affected his sense of fairness in his journal. Merton was particularly troubled by the groups' emphasis on observances and meditations on spiritual books rather than contemplation to reach a deeper level of spirituality.

Monks were now being assigned to help Merton with the paperwork he generated. Some of the monks reacted jealously to Merton's whole operation, but they could not accuse him of acting differently after his work made him "a name." There were even some monks who were not aware of how well known Merton had become. He always took pains to act and be treated like any other monk. He particularly relied on his schooldays pranks and humor to help him to relate to his fellow monks.

Merton was extremely conscious of time, which was consistent with the monastery's strict scheduling of prayer and work throughout the day. He saw to it that he safeguarded the precious little discretionary time he could devote to his writing and attendant correspondence. Some monks thought him to be short-tempered in their dealings with him, but meaningless talk or extraneous conversation that had no particular value easily frustrated him. His time was so limited for the amount of work he attempted to accomplish that he used whatever isolated minutes he had either to write or to think about what he was currently working on, as well as to perform his own spiritual practices.

He resorted to writing essays and book reviews as well as poetry rather than full-length books, because it was easier to complete in the short periods of time he had allotted to do his work. Longer works more frequently became compilations of the essays. With the increasing popularity of magazines, the shorter works could get published in a more timely fashion and then be batched and reprinted later in books. This strategy led to the complications that developed with his publishers when he had to request republishing rights.

Meanwhile, Merton's business with publishers had grown more complex. Naomi Burton had left Curtis Brown, and Merton assumed more of the work himself. Naomi had moved to Doubleday for advancement, and Merton did not want to interfere with her own career move. Soon he had to appeal to her to help him unofficially. Unfortunately, his system of multiple publishing and the provisions of various contracts became too much for him. At his request, she then took over the problem he was currently having with his English publishers, Burns and Oates. He appreciated her generosity and had no qualms about accepting it. He knew how quickly he could get into difficulty with the legal requirements of publishing.

Merton organized both his work and his study for ready access to it. He read extensively and kept numerous notebooks of detailed comments, often with the dates he read the material, so that he could make reference to his ideas at an appropriate time in his writing. He often copied long passages from works he wanted to think further about because the books had to be returned either to friends or to the library at the University of Louisville or the Library of Congress. He also wrote extensive marginal notes in books that were gifts to him. He had no technical method for making copies, so handwritten material was his only recourse.

Merton's linguistic ability is evident throughout his journals. He also demonstrates a familiarity with an immense range of literary works. He references ideas or quotes from literally hundreds of non-fictional and fictional works, including many in foreign languages. This is an amazing phenomenon when viewed in the context of his daily life, absorbed in hours of ritual, group meetings, and demanding assignments of either physical labor (in his younger days) or teaching, coupled with impositions of conditions that were humiliating. This included denial of indoor plumbing, of speech, of fraternal association, and of balanced meals, representing the gamut of deprivation.

Merton's personal correspondents soon numbered in the hundreds. Eventually it grew to thousands. He began to keep copies of his own letters to maintain the continuity of his correspondence. He described his typing as like a newspaperman, using only two fingers on each hand, but working rapidly, even though his typewriter was for a long time a manual one. Many of Merton's manuscripts were in longhand.

In April 1960, Merton got a new electric typewriter. He was thrilled at the possibilities this would provide in terms of time and quality of product. Dom James arranged for him to designate extra keys he preferred for foreign languages. Merton reported to Naomi Burton that he got the French accent marks added but accidentally lost the question mark. He couldn't believe he had overlooked such a basic key.

Merton's manuscripts soon became a major maintenance project. He was careful to date all his drafts, to be able to identify the latest one. He scrupulously used different colored inks to indicate the sequence of his revisions on a manuscript, since he sometimes made changes to a published work before republishing it in another format. This led to numerous incidents of sorting out which publisher he had to seek permission from in order to republish a work, either in a collection in the U.S. or in a foreign country.

He also got involved with translators and their versions of his works. He preferred to publish his own translations when he was sufficiently comfortable with his ability in the given language. Sometimes he composed only in a foreign language, particularly French and Spanish, with no English language version. He translated poetry from Greek, Spanish, Portuguese, French, and Chinese, sometimes for his own pleasure or to use in his lectures, as well as to be published. He was as compulsive in acquiring foreign language ability as in maintaining relationships with his correspondents.

Early in his publishing experience he had donated publishing rights to various charitable organizations to help them financially. These groups sometimes sold their rights to various publishers for the money they needed, often without notifying Merton of the sale. Merton would hear from publishers themselves who had purchased the rights without his knowledge.

Merton managed his own marketing activity, using his publishers to implement his suggestions. He often promoted his image by suggesting ideas for ways to publish both his essays and poetry in combinations to make a book. He also suggested particular publications that might be appropriate to publish individual essays or poems to keep his name before the public while he prepared to combine them in a book. He had a good sense of timing in submission, such as what books are coming out and when for sequencing purposes. By spreading out his publications that were in process with different publishers, he could insure that one book did not compete with another, and thus obtain maximum sales. He suggested titles for all of his works, most of which were used. He also suggested pre-publication of material in magazines as a promotion for forthcoming books and wrote the copy for ads.

Merton had learned early, consciously or not, that it took more than creativity to be recognized. He had seen his father spend a large proportion of his time marketing his paintings as compared with creating them. He had to pursue dealers and attend shows, as well as submit textual material to be published in program notes and advertising copy describing and praising his work. Merton was surely grateful for this early lesson. He knew how many good books were not read because the intended audience had never heard of them.

Dom James' overseeing of Merton's publishing activities was a major bone of contention between them. Merton believed he had proprietary rights over his work in relation to the choice of publishers for his books and articles. He believed the monastery's role should be limited to their receipt of the royalties he voluntarily surrendered under his vow of poverty. All of this paperwork was a burden to manage for both of them, considering the volume of Merton's correspondence and compositions, all prepared using only typewriters and a mimeograph machine. Merton had only carbon paper to make copies of any correspondence. Eventually Merton lost most of his clerical assistance. As vocations fell off, there were fewer monks available to help him, and the difficulty of Merton's complex materials and often illegible handwriting eliminated many who might have been willing to participate. The process took its toll on his patience as well as on his health.

In July 1960 Merton went to St. Anthony's Hospital in Louisville for X-rays. His back was a chronic problem. The doctors decided to run a comprehensive series of diagnostic tests. He was admitted to the hospital, under protest, for five days. He was eager to get back to the monastery and to his work.

One of Merton's prominent correspondents was the Polish author and poet, Czeslaw Milosz. In 1960 he had accepted a teaching position at the University of California, Berkeley. Merton was impressed with Milosz' anti-Nazi books that he had published secretly during the Nazi occupation of Poland. Milosz' subsequent defection from the Polish diplomatic service and ten years in Paris stimulated Merton's interest in him as a man of principle as well as a poet. Milosz exchanged very frank remarks with Merton. He questioned Merton's desire to stop writing about contemplation and instead turn his attention to activism in the peace movement. He also asked why Merton wrote only favorably about nature, and negatively about institutions and people. Being questioned stimulated Merton to develop his ideas. The work he now planned was to address the social problems of the world and hopefully to make a contribution to their solution.

In November 1960, John F. Kennedy was running for U.S. President, and was the first Catholic to be elected to this office. An interest in current events suddenly became acceptable in the monastery. "Vote Democrat" stickers were seen on the wheelbarrows at Gethsemani for the first time in history. After the Kennedy election, the monks were regularly briefed in Chapter on current events. News of the standoff between Russia and the U.S. reignited Merton's militancy. He believed it to be his duty to use his name to influence public opinion against the possibility of a nuclear war and the possible destruction of the human race.

Merton used the Hammers' press to produce limited editions of quality publications that would not have commercial appeal at that time, as well as to bring out unorthodox material that was not politically controversial. They had earlier done a limited edition of *Prometheus: A Meditation*. In 1960 they printed sixty copies of *The Solitary Life* on their press, Stamperia del Santuccio. *The Solitary Life* had originally been printed in France at the Abbey of La Pierre qui Vire, but the censors stopped publication in the U.S. Also in 1960 the Hammers published *The Ox Mountain Parable of Meng Tzu*, from a Chinese translation Merton revised. In 1962 the Hammers produced the limited edition of *Hagia Sophia*, which later became a collector's item.

Merton was beginning to seek ways to express his pacifist philosophy in a subtle way that would not involve him in a political way. He had read the Russian mystics' earlier treatment of Sophia as the personification of Holy Wisdom in the world. In the spirit of their message, Merton reflected on Sophia as the great stabilizer for peace and man's basic hope to survive his complete destruction. He recorded this concept in his journal in 1961.

Merton found that he could use the private publishing technique that the Hammers provided without repercussion. He assumed that Dom James might have discovered what he was doing, but did not stop him because he did not consider it a problem. While the process was harmless in itself, it nevertheless encouraged Merton to proceed with his writing without regard to the restrictions of higher authority. This emboldened him to seek avenues of interest without regard to the Order's probable opinion about publishing such material. He believed it was his moral duty to explore these subjects because no other Catholic writer was effectively doing it.

Merton now wanted to disown his reputation for his early work. He said the two religious biographies he had written were embarrassing to him with their piety. He characterized himself as "a sort of stereotype of the world-denying contemplative—the man who spurned New York, spat on Chicago, and tromped on Louisville, heading for the woods with Thoreau in one pocket, John of the Cross in another, and holding the Bible open at the Apocalypse." He published this description of himself in his essay, "Is the World a Problem?"

The man who wrote *The Seven Storey Mountain* and *The Sign of Jonas* was dead, Merton said.

In the Japanese Preface to *The Seven Storey Mountain*, he offered this reflection: " ... Therefore, most honorable reader, it is not as an author that I would speak to you, not as a story-teller, not as a philosopher, not as a friend only: I seek to speak to you, in some way, *as your own self.* Who can tell what this may mean? I myself do not know" (p. 67).

# Chapter 23

The 1960s added a complexity to Merton's life that he could not have anticipated. As the Order liberalized the restrictions on its monks, Merton was immediately affected. He had continually fine-tuned his ideas from speaking with the people he met as well as from his reading. His compulsion to know what was going on in the world and how people were reacting to it intensifed when his visitors and his access to information about current events were no longer limited. At the same time, social and political changes were wreaking havoc in the U.S. Merton rapidly became engaged in analyzing and speaking out on the issues of the day. His self-awareness brought him to the unmistakable point of knowing that he was now becoming involved in highly controversial issues, and that there were people who might wish him harm without regard to the fact that he was a monk.

He wondered if he had the courage to withstand public criticism, but the challenge of contributing to the problems of the day energized him. He had been wrestling with a possible role in the troubling events of the day for some time. At the same time, he knew that this meant to risk endangering himself physically. Leaders on both sides of current issues were being attacked and sometimes murdered. Merton's hermitage could be accessed from a back road off the highway. Merton began to fear for his personal safety when his name became associated with the controversial issues he felt compelled to speak out on.

He believed that he had been "a guilty bystander" to witness world events without taking a public stand. Ten years earlier, in 1951, Merton had written in his *Ascent to Truth*, "If you are looking for the Atomic Age, look inside yourself, because you are it. And so, alas, am I" (p. 6). He felt he was called by God to speak out against nuclear weapons and the moral breakdown in society, especially since no prominent voices could be heard in the Church hierarchy. He now believed his name recognition could serve as an influence and give his works a voice in the places where decisions were being made. He was determined to influence public opinion against the trends he saw in the world that violated all he believed in. Merton once said that he had not yet caught up with the twentieth century because he still held the primitive belief in protest.

Merton's friends and other correspondents were sending him publications that inflamed his sense of justice. One of his closest friends from
college days, Ed Rice, still living in New York, kept Merton up to date
with his publication, *Jubilee* magazine. It had been started by Bob Lax
and Ed Rice in 1953, with Merton as their sort of unnamed collabora-
tor. Lax and Rice had been inspired by the success of Merton's *Seven
Storey Mountain,* recognizing the need for bringing the Church to the
laity in twentieth century terms. The magazine contained top quality
photographs, articles, and art layouts. It lasted 15 years, until 1967, with
peak circulation estimated at 72,000. It was a sophisticated publication
for Catholic readers analyzing current events. It did not mince words in
disagreeing with ideas that may be enjoying popular appeal.

Merton's first contribution to *Jubilee* was an article on St. Bernard
in August 1953. Merton contributed heavily to *Jubilee,* both to help
keep the magazine going, as well as to reach a wide audience of thinking Americans. He also interceded with many prominent figures to
contribute material of current interest. In addition to Merton's articles,
there were reviews of Merton's books and articles about him, such as
Maritain's visit to Gethsemani. Some of Merton's major articles included
"The Tower of Babel" in 1957 before its publication by New Directions,
"Boris Pasternak and the People with Watch Chains" (July 1959),
"Mount Athos" (August 1959), and "Nhat Hanh is my Brother" (August
1966). In "The Death of a Holy Terror" (June 1967) about Frere Pas-
cal, Merton compares him to Charles de Foucault, both contemplative
monks in France who left their monasteries to live, and die, among a
remote group of suffering humanity. In this article Merton argues the
need for monastic renewal. He states that one who feels a call to change
his vocation from contemplative to apostolic service should be allowed
to do so without difficulty.

*Jubilee* did not hesitate to cover controversial subjects, including divorce,
birth control, and Catholic politicians, subjects not viewed favorably by
the Archdiocese of New York during Cardinal Spellman's tenure. It was
said that one of the Cardinal's spokesmen told Rice that the Church
would have a picture magazine if it thought it to be needed.

When Merton did not want to ask permission or thought he would
not receive approval, he submitted articles using an alias. According
to his friend, Jim Forest, Merton published under numerous aliases,
including Benedict Monk, Marco J. Frisbee, Joey the Chocolate King,
Frisco Jack, R. Higden, Harpo, and Moon Mullins. Some believed to

be Merton's include "The Loyalty Oath of Henry VIII" (June 1964), "The Voice of the Turtleneck" (March 1965) about free speech in college newspapers, "My Life in the Middle Ages" (July 1965) about inferior Catholic pamphlets, and "Mother was a Coat Hanger" (December 1965) by Richard P. Frisbie.

This last article discusses a woman's role as a mother and the effect she can have on her son's contribution to the world. It is written in the context of a book review of *The Flight from Woman* by Dr. Karl Stern (Farrar, Straus and Giroux, 1965). Dr. Stern discusses the lives of six men, Descartes, Schopenhauer, Sartre, Tolstoy, Goethe, and Kierkegaard, who he says were maladjusted due to a cold feminine image. Merton's disagreement with Dr. Stern's position may imply a questioning of any ill effect his own mother might have had on his life.

Merton well understood that the Order could not associate its name with material that contained controversial views, either on Church matters or a secular subject. It amused Merton to publish under his contrived names. Two of his names for articles in *The Catholic Worker* were Benedict Monk and Benedict Moore. He also wrote letters to the editor using aliases that were published in these magazines.

In July 1959, Merton began corresponding with Dorothy Day, a fellow convert and activist working and living with the poor on New York's Lower East Side. He sent her a number of articles that she published in her newspaper, *The Catholic Worker*. It was a popular anti-establishment paper in the 1960s that championed the rights of the individual. It sold for a penny a copy. It also passionately called for an end to war. Dorothy Day and Peter Maurin had founded the Catholic Worker Movement in 1932, providing soup kitchens and housing for the needy in New York City. The paper was a significant outreach effort to promote social justice throughout the U.S.

At the time that Merton became involved with this program during the Vietnam war, Day's work was considered a radical social movement and did not have the support of much of the American Catholic hierarchy. In fact, it was alleged by some that the *Worker* was a Communist paper.

Earlier, in the 1930s, Jacques Maritain contributed material to the paper opposing Franco in the Spanish Civil War, a position not held by most Catholics of that time. The Berrigan brothers, Philip and Daniel, both Catholic priests, were active in supporting Dorothy Day's policies, particularly concerning nonviolence and peace. Through Dorothy, Merton became acquainted with Jim Forest, who worked for her in 1961 after his military discharge. He founded the Catholic Peace Fellowship in 1965 to educate Catholics on the pacifist traditions in the Church and to counsel men who wanted to resist the draft. The Fellowship eventually had 800 members. The Fellowship of Reconciliation (FOR) was an affiliate of the Catholic Peace Fellowship. FOR's magazine, *Fellowship*, published several of Merton's essays and poems.

In the summer of 1961, Merton wrote a poem about the Nazi persecution of the Jews in the 1940s, "Chants to be Used in Processions around a Site with Furnaces." Dorothy Day published it in *The Catholic Worker*. Merton had never recovered from his horror of the holocaust. He recognized that in World War II civilian casualties came to be viewed as collateral damage. The development of nuclear weapons reinforced his fear of history repeating itself in mass exterminations.

In June Merton had a visit from Tashi Tshering, a young Tibetan monk studying in the U.S. He told Merton that the Dalai Lama might send one of his 1500 monks to the U.S. to study Christian monasticism. Merton admired the courage of the Tibetan monks to persevere against the Communist overthrow of their country and the ability of some 60,000 Tibetan refugees to survive in India in exile. In his journal, Merton told himself he would be willing to be shot for taking a moral stand against issues. In fact, he mused in his journal that he probably would get shot some day. He viewed the times as a post-Christian age. The world as a whole used to be Christian, Hindu, Moslem, Buddhist, but was now "going to be not pagan, but irreligious."

Merton's prose poem, *Original Child Bomb*, published in October 1961, criticized the U.S. bombings in August 1945 of Hiroshima and Nagasaki, Japan, which were credited with accelerating the end of World War II. The Hiroshima bomb was said to be the equivalent of 15,000 tons of TNT. At Nagasaki alone, the body count finally totaled 73,884 killed by a single bomb in August 1945, with an additional 76,796 injured or missing, according to published reports. It was provocative and naturally became controversial, although many cheered at the news a few days later when the war ended. As a gesture to offset the negative public reaction of some people, the U.S. Post Office offered to waive postage on letters sent to the region that had been bombed.

Lawrence Ferlinghetti, publisher at City Lights, had been a witness to the Nagasaki attack when he was a young sailor. The counterculture writers he published in the 1960s resonated with anti-war activists. He published "Chants to be Used in Processions around a Site with

Furnaces" in 1961 in a collection of *avant-garde* pieces. It was published by the former Unicorn Press, located in Santa Barbara, CA, as was City Lights. Unicorn published limited editions of 20th century poets until 1984. *Child Bomb* was released as a paperback with an irregular cover about two inches smaller than the book. It had no publishing date. Merton learned that some booksellers, not knowing what his book was about, shelved it in the children's section of their stores. Merton ironically termed it his comic book.

Merton's idea was that God gave man dominion over all things, but not absolute dominion. Merton did not specifically make the comparison, but from the beginning, this was shown in the Garden of Eden, where man had no control over the tree of the knowledge of good and evil. Merton believed that man is participative with God, but not in complete control over all things. Therefore man would have no right to destroy the earth with nuclear weapons and in fact had a profound responsibility, as stewards of creation, not masters. Merton saw the self-righteous attitude toward use of such destructive power to be faulty logic: the end (world peace) would not justify the means (use of nuclear bombs).

In one of the pieces Merton wrote for *The Catholic Worker*, he said the love that unites people brings suffering by our contact with each other, because it is "the resetting of a Body of broken bones" from a dismemberment of the Mystical Body of Christ.

Merton's newly acquired controversial reputation among conservatives showed itself within the Order as well as the reading public. He was formally denounced by a Japanese monk at the Trappist mother-house at Citeaux because of a misunderstanding of his work. The monk mistakenly believed that Merton was glorifying atomic war. His confusion probably arose from the difference in language and a lack of familiarity with satire as a means of expression. Problems with Merton's statements frequently occurred now that Merton was expressing himself on controversial issues. Some writers argued that a cloistered monk does not know enough about world affairs to know what he is talking about, and anyway should not be expressing himself publicly. Merton said he believed he was on everybody's black list, but he was determined to do what he could to stop the Nazi mentality he believed was taking root in American attitudes. He submitted letters and articles to any Catholic magazines that he believed would welcome his writing as part of what he felt was now his calling. Merton also contributed material to another popular magazine, *U.S. Catholic*, published in Chicago.

Merton had difficulty and impatience with the pace of the Church in making changes and responding to current events. He was especially annoyed at the silence of Church leaders in his Order, in the U.S., and in Rome. He had been one who responded to change all his life, did not feel any fear of it, and saw it actually as a benefit, not a threat. If he had not accepted change and dealt with it, he knew he would have never graduated from Columbia, become a Catholic, or joined the Trappists.

Merton did not view all change as good, however. The social changes rapidly taking place in America concerned him deeply because of the deteriorating effect they were having on unsuspecting people. Mark Van Doren's son, Charles, starred in a popular television quiz show, "Twenty One," and was awarded large sums of prize money to give answers furnished to him in advance by the show's sponsors. From the notoriety of being honored on the cover of *Time* magazine for his intellect to the humiliation of admitting to a Congressional committee (also televised) that he had consented to deluding the American public was a national scandal. In November 1959, Merton wrote to Charles expressing admiration for his honesty and congratulating him " … on being instrumental in the death (?) of an important illusion." Merton wrote several letters to Mark Van Doren during this episode, emphasizing the event as symbolic of the country's "uggsome image" of a false self that revealed a lack of belief in God and His forgiveness. The incident was later portrayed in the movie, "Quiz Show," produced by Robert Redford, and was among those nominated as "Best Picture" of 1994. Merton is mentioned in the script as a friend of the family.

Merton's work was making him more visible than before. In 1961 Columbia University awarded him a Medal of Excellence. By the Order's rules, Merton was not allowed to go to New York to receive the honor. He would have been embarrassed at the public recognition anyway. Merton did not indicate how this honor came about, but he asked Mark Van Doren to accept it in his behalf and mail it to him. He may have recommended Merton for this recognition.

In February 1961 Dom Gabriel came for the annual Visitation to Gethsemani. Merton braced himself, fearing the Abbot General might order them to demolish the hermitage. Merton walked out with Dom Gabriel to see it, and he told Merton it was a good place to visit a few hours a day, since he was Novice Master. Merton was greatly relieved he did not bring up the subject of his previous efforts to transfer to another order or Cardenal's attempt to get Merton to Cuernavaca.

Merton had the opportunity to spend private time with Dom Gabriel on the long drive into Louisville to translate for him while he purchased a pair of glasses. One of the monastery's volunteers drove them to town. Merton used the occasion to discuss his latest book, *The New Man*. Merton was having difficulty getting past the censors again. Dom Gabriel agreed to use his influence to get it approved as written. It was published by Farrar, Straus and Cudahy later that year.

Again it was a problem of censors disagreeing with Merton's choice of subject or style when their authority was supposed to be limited to doctrine and morals. Merton complained to Laughlin about the delays he continually encountered. Once he wrote that he was having "a difficult time with these people and their Byzantine formalities." Another time, he complained that if he wrote the statement, everyone ought to say The Lord's Prayer, one of them would ask for changes. Merton was practical, though, about his attitude. In another letter to Laughlin, Merton said he didn't want to offend the censors because they had "the power to shut me up completely" and he wanted "to retain some power of expression in case I might need it some time."

Merton was well aware of the importance of getting his message out in a timely fashion through magazines. At this time periodicals were the most popular sources of information for the general public. Television was still in its infancy in the arena of public affairs. Newspapers carried the current news, but magazines provided the depth of the story through commentary and analysis of the news that molded public opinion, so they exercised a powerful influence. This resulted in public reaction in the form of protest marches and other demonstrations of reaction to the events in order to influence Government policies and practices.

Merton decided to make use of the popularity of magazines as well as to apply the rules of censorship to his own advantage. The Statute of Censorship of the Order required that brief articles for periodicals of limited circulation and influence required only permission of the local superior. It was at this point that Merton began to use magazines of this type to get his message of social change out. He published his criticism of nuclear war in the English periodical, *Blackfriars*, in the November and December 1963 issues. He sent his writing on the racial question to *La revolution noire*, a French publication in 1964. Both were published almost exactly as he had written them and were immediately popular with thoughtful readers. He once advised the peace activist, Jim Forest, in a letter (Nov. 14, 1961) to get Merton's articles first published in *Pax* or *FOR* (Fellowship of Reconciliation), because they were small publications. Then Forest could write something for *The Catholic Worker* quoting Merton's material liberally from the other publication. This would take advantage of the loophole in the censorship statute of the Order and keep Merton from violating the Order's restrictions. Actually Merton told Laughlin in one of his letters that the Abbot or Abbot General could have forbidden him to publish in small limited circulation publications if they had wanted to, but neither ever did.

Father Paul, the chief censor of the Order in the U.S., was not actually the chief source of Merton's frustrations. Dom Gabriel made the negative decisions himself. Father Paul had protested to Dom Gabriel when he was appointed to review Merton's work that Merton "knew more about the Cistercian Order than I do." Father Paul considered his role more of a copy-editor than a censor. He only corrected mistakes that he pointed out to Merton, and Merton had thanked him for catching them. He regretted that all of his talking with Merton had to be by mail, due to the Order's required silence. Actually Father Paul was himself a world traveler before he entered the Order and had known intellectuals in the Church as well as in secular circles, including Picasso when he lived in Paris.

Merton was also producing books at the same time he was writing for periodicals. *The New Man, New Seeds of Contemplation,* and *Original Child Bomb* were all published in 1961. At the same time, Merton was assembling already published material for the *Thomas Merton Reader.* Thomas P. McDonnell, also a writer, suggested this collection to the publisher, Harcourt Brace and World (Jovanovich later replacing World). McDonnell made two trips to Gethsemani, in May and October 1961, to work with Merton in selecting the material. The publishing rights to the selections were held by various publishers and required their prior approval, which in some cases was easier to obtain than others. Farrar, Straus and Cudahy (later renamed Farrar, Straus and Giroux) refused to grant reprint rights. After a futile attempt to get their release, the book was published in October 1962 without the material they controlled. McDonnell believed the resulting major loss to the book was *Thoughts in Solitude.*

Merton compiled another book using some material previously published, called *Life and Holiness.* The dispute over publishing rights to this book almost went to court, and was finally published in the spring of 1963 by Herder and Herder. Merton dedicated it to the late Louis Massignon, one of his correspondents who had made an in-depth study of Islam and Sufism and had led a movement of non-violent resistance to the recent war in Algeria.

In September 1961, Merton heard of the accidental death by drowning of Pere Francois de Sainte Marie, a French Carmelite. Merton had just recently written an Introduction to the English language translation of his *The Simple Steps to God*, published by Dimension Books, Wilkes-Barre, PA, in 1963. Through correspondence Father Francois had helped Merton with the French edition of *The Ascent to Truth* when he was researching John of the Cross for this book, published exactly ten years before Father Francois' death. Merton had been attracted to Father Francois' book because it was based on conferences given to French lay people during the Nazi occupation of Paris. It referenced the contributions of John of the Cross and Teresa of Avila, as well as Therese of Liseaux, in all of whom Merton had an intense interest.

Before the year ended, Merton had a visitor that surprised and disarmed him completely. Aunt Kit arrived from New Zealand in November 1961, leaving the summer weather in New Zealand to travel to the U.S. at the opposite season. She arrived at Gethsemani on a cold winter day. After more than 20 years of isolation from any of his family, Merton was happy to see her again. He had not seen her in 42 years. It was nostalgic to talk about the family's members. It brought back all the old memories, good and bad, that Merton had suppressed. Ironically, Merton discovered that his aunt's memory was colored by what she wanted to remember. He wondered if it was better to forget or to fantasize about the past.

Aunt Kit had never lost her affection for Merton as a motherless child. The trip to Louisville was a big effort for her at her advanced age, but she wanted to see her nephew one more time while she was traveling in the U.S. After seeing his wardrobe, she knitted a pair of socks for him when she returned to New Zealand and mailed them to him. In March he received the little package. Merton was surprised and touched by her loving gesture. He could only bury his feelings and move on in his secluded life. He knew he would never see her again in this world.

The New Year, 1962, brought an increased number of visitors to Gethsemani to confer with Merton about the peace movement. Merton asked Jim Forest to come down to update him. In February, Forest and his friend, Bob Kaye, hitchhiked from New York, a trip of three days. Up to this time, Merton and Forest were only acquainted through correspondence and their mutual friend, Dorothy Day, whom Merton only knew by correspondence as well. Jim was a young, handsome intellectual who, with his friend, Bob, took an active role in anti-nuclear war efforts. They were determined to make a difference. Merton and his visitors enjoyed the occasion. Their laughter could be heard around the monastery grounds. At one point Merton was rolling on the floor in the guest house laughing. He told them that after three days on the road, Bob's socks smelled exactly like those that Merton's friends used to wear in New York.

Two weeks later Forest and others from the newspaper staff were arrested for demonstrating against the U.S. Government at the Atomic Energy Control Building in Washington. Merton supported the peace movement generally, but did not condone burning draft cards or damaging Government property. He preferred activity of a more positive nature. He donated blood whenever the Red Cross truck came to Gethsemani, even though it cost him dearly in energy to get through the remainder of the day. He never wrote or spoke of his donation because he simply considered it a basic patriotic duty.

John Laughlin came to see Merton again in January 1962 to discuss what came to be known as *Breakthrough to Peace: Twelve Views on the Threat of Thermonuclear Extermination*. It was edited and included an introduction by Merton, and published by New Directions later that year. Merton's essay, "Peace: A Religious Responsibility," was included in the compilation.

Laughlin asked Dom James privately about his restriction on Merton's writing about political matters. He reported that the Abbot told him that the work of monks was to pray, and God would hear their prayers and solve the world's problems.

W. H. (Ping) Ferry came from California in April to meet Merton in person. They had become acquainted through Laughlin and soon developed a regular exchange of correspondence. As events unfolded, there were increasing rumors of intercepted mail as well as tapped telephones of peace activists. It was a lot safer to discuss Ferry's peace movement activities on an outing than in letters. Ferry was a Fellow and Vice President for the Center for the Study of Democratic Institutions in Santa Barbara, California, an organization that advocated social change. He once commented to Merton that he was disillusioned with America's preoccupation with aggression, commenting that this country's "frailties have become its strengths." Ferry was a tall man, with a high forehead, soft dark eyes, and a quiet but strong way of expressing himself. He and Merton found their common interest in peace served to form a bond of friendship without regard to the geographical distance between them.

Merton began to wonder if he could find a way to enrich the simplistic notion of monasticism that continued to prevail in the Church. He was concerned about the death-of-God movement that had gained popularity in the 1960's. Nietzsche had spread his idea that the God of Theism was dead and that man must find a God beyond this God. Paul Tillich, a Protestant theologian, echoed this philosophy, reflecting on the meaninglessness of existence to modern man. The movement's purpose was to strip away the mysticism of the deity and to focus instead on the ethical behavior of an historical Jesus. In that way, Christianity would make more sense.

Merton referred to this subject in a letter to Lax, August 12 1966, jokingly saying in his fractured English, "Thus you never heard such a rush of people running and falling over each other to say God is dead. Norman Vincent Peale etc is all God is dead, and positive thinking killed him ... ."

Merton was deeply concerned about this philosophy and turned again for answers to traditional thought, going all the way back to antiquity. Merton renewed his interest in Eastern thought. He began studying Chinese on his own to better understand translations of books he was reading. He soon discovered this language was not one he could master as he had learned Western languages. John C. H.Wu, the Chinese philosopher, came to visit him in June 1962. Wu had been helping Merton with difficulties he was having trying to translate the writings of Chuang Tzu from Chinese.

Wu had a great deal of respect for Merton and his grasp of Eastern concepts. A few years later, he asked Merton to contribute an Introduction to his book, *The Golden Age of Zen*. Merton wrote a clear, comprehensive treatment of Zen from the Christian's point of view to give the reader "a healthy natural balance in our understanding of the spiritual life." It was obvious to him that there was an innate unity in the spiritual experience for people of all faiths. In December 1965, Merton learned from John Wu that his name in Chinese, Mei Teng, meant "silent lamp." Merton wrote the introduction for Wu in July 1966, and the book was published in 1967. Wu once said it would not be known until eternity why Merton was so Chinese in his way of thinking.

Merton believed that secularized society had stripped Western man naked and left him no security to lean on. He found in Buddhism an answer in seeking the Great Emptiness, that he termed an elaborate form of spiritual psychology. Rather than fear it, he thought that Western man should absorb it. Merton began reading Meister Eckhart, the 13th century Dominican theologian and German mystic, who described a "wayless way" that bridges East and West. Eckhart wrote of detachment as a virtue. Merton added in *Seeds of Contemplation*, "Attachment to spiritual things is therefore just as much an attachment as inordinate love of anything else ... that only makes it all the more harmful because it is not so easy to recognize."

Merton also had a visit from Dr. Paul Sih, who headed up an Asian Studies Center at the University in Jamaica. He tried to teach Merton how to use a Chinese dictionary. Merton also began a study of Islamic culture. He was fascinated by the fact that Sufis wore undyed white wool clothing like the Cistercians. He saw the Sufi concept of God as being close to early Christian tradition. Merton approached Eastern philosophies as having a seamless connection to the West's Judao-Christian beliefs, all developed in a continuum of time in history. The conceptual leap from one era to another, along with its accompanying belief systems, was no problem for Merton. He respected all of their beliefs.

Lax once explained that Merton spoke to Muslims or Buddhists as they would talk and they recognized it. He was not trying to make bridges to them. He had arrived. As Lax saw it, Merton understood that there was much wisdom all over the world and he felt compelled to gather it and learn from it. Lax said that Merton believed he had been born to communicate the Divine message, and people could recognize this as a fact and paid heed to what he said, without regard to criticism from skeptics.

Merton was following his tried and true technique of relentlessly pursuing subjects that aroused his curiosity. It had always worked for him. He had been curious about philosophy, about the Catholic Church, about the Trappists, and everything he had ever accomplished. Why not study Eastern religions? He had been curious about them since he met Bramachari at Columbia. After all, hadn't that led him to the Church and his vocation to the priesthood? What harm could it do?

Merton was aware that there was a connection between the physical aspects of higher levels of consciousness and the spiritual concepts of ascetic experience. It is not surprising that he wanted to investigate Eastern spiritual practices, as well as that of the Native American, to build on the knowledge he had acquired from his own ascetic experiences in Havana, in the hotel in Rome, and at St. Bonaventure's. He wanted to find out more—the existential basis of it all. After all, the Greek word for asceticism is training.

Merton began to experiment with Eastern methods of prayer. One day he was seen standing on his head with another monk, Father Augustine, practicing Yoga. The scene was even more bizarre because Father Augustine had an artificial leg and had removed it for the exercise. Dom James was incredulous at Merton's performance and refused to allow any more Yoga at the monastery. Merton, however, continued to pray with his legs folded on the floor in private meditation.

Dom James did allow Merton to design and supervise the planting of a Zen garden for the monastery, with the help of his novices. This would involve using specially designed rakes to move white sand in a whirling pattern to look like water. The sand was to be moved around large rocks. The garden was supposed to represent the art of suggestion for purposes of meditation. This was a project Merton could put all of his energy and imagination into. He probably relied on the principles he had picked up from his father, whose landscape gardening was considered exceptional. Merton had found an old bell on the monastery grounds that he was using in 1952 to call in his novices from their free time for vespers on Sunday afternoons. He decided to add the bell to the Zen garden, which was next to the novitiate. Later, after Merton's death, the bell was donated to a monastery in Thailand.

Dom James also encouraged Merton to pursue his interest in the Oriental art of calligraphy. He thought it would help Merton to relieve tension. The monastery already practiced a ritual that reflected an ancient religious practice. The monks spread flower petals in intricate religious designs on the walkway leading to the church each year on Corpus Christi Sunday. This practice typically requires many hours of community labor. After the ceremony they remove it and offer it as a gift to Christ. This is similar to a Buddhist practice of the sand mandala (Sanskrit word for circle), designing intricate patterns in millions of grains of sand dyed in an array of colors and laid into place on a five-foot square wooden platform. After several days of work, it is destroyed and the sand is poured into a stream to demonstrate the impermanence of all that exists.

Merton's workload was undoubtedly a basis for tension. In addition to his own writings, Merton was often asked to write introductions to other authors' books on peace or on religious topics. Sometimes he was approached directly by the authors, and sometimes his publishers asked him to endorse or contribute to another book they were producing to enhance sales. Merton was more than generous with his time in reading others' manuscripts and often complied with their requests for material. Over time, the requests became so numerous that he had to decline to read or to contribute to all but his most cherished subjects. Writing for others deprived him of time for his own work. He confided to his journal, "everyone believes I secrete articles like perspiration."

Later in January Merton attended a conference at Asbury Theological Seminary in Wilmore, a small town south of Lexington. He persuaded his driver to make a side trip on the way back to Gethsemani through Shakertown, since it was nearby. This was Merton's second visit to the place, and this time he brought a camera he had borrowed to photograph some of the 30 restored buildings. The entire complex covered 2700 acres. His pictures eventually became part of an article published in *Jubilee* two years later. Merton made a number of visits to Pleasant Hill to see the Shaker structures on his way to and from Lexington to visit his doctor, just for the joy of it. The simplicity of the architecture appealed to Merton's aesthetic sense. At the monastery he was obviously culturally deprived. Merton had a refined sense of what he considered to be good art, since his extensive travel with his father. Merton was never shy about expressing his criticism of inferior art, no matter how highly regarded by others.

Merton wrote in a letter to his friend, Cardenal, November 18, 1959, concerning an illustrated news article he had seen about the dedication of the new National Shrine of the Immaculate Conception in Washington, D.C. Merton said that in his opinion it looks like "a big substantial bank, strictly official" with an "evident Soviet quality" or a bank on Wall Street, inasmuch as "Soviet and capitalist materialism are more alike all the time." In his journal he recorded that it had a "blank splendor of what is expensive and big and expressionless" (November 18, 1959). Merton's journal was a welcome refuge for him to vent his negative feelings on a wide variety of subjects.

Merton often assumed his friends would protect his privacy when he shared his opinions with them. In fact, Merton's letters had become an intrinsic part of his literary work. Over the years they were necessary to substitute for meetings and phone calls and circumvented the rule of silence. Merton was in fear of being misrepresented by some of the activists he had developed an association with, even if it might be unintentional. Merton sent Dorothy Day and Jim Forest a draft of an article about pacifism that he had not yet cleared with his censors. Instead of protecting his confidentiality, they published the article in *The Catholic Worker*. They apparently discounted the importance of the Order's approval process in the interest of putting out Merton's powerful message to their readers. This intensified Merton's problems with his censors and Church superiors. Merton had been reluctant to take any active role in the peace movement up to this point, and this occurrence confirmed his opinion.

Not all of Merton's readers agreed with his social philosophy. Some conservative Catholics were reluctant to accept Merton's position or his right to express it. His credibility was in question by some who rightly believed he was not fully informed behind the monastery walls. Actually Merton was limited in his exposure to the full story of some current events. He had no subscriptions to magazines or newspapers. Dom James read the *Wall Street Journal*, but it is doubtful that Merton ever saw it. Merton received secular publications occasionally from friends or from one of the other monks who received them from their correspondents. There was no radio or television, so breaking news was only received when someone called the monastery to report it. The monastery routinely received religious magazines. Ironically the monks were often informed of significant events by reading an analysis of them in the liturgical publications.

In June 1961 Merton recorded in his diary that he was reading the letters of Fenelon, undoubtedly for his Introduction to John McEwen's *Fenelon Letters*, published by Harvill Press, London, and Harcourt, Brace and World, Inc., New York, in 1964. Merton saw a similarity in Fenelon and John Henry Cardinal Newman as men not "ahead of their time, or of it, or behind it," but rather "above it" and therefore able to "survive indefinitely." Merton was fascinated by Fenelon's courage in declaring his opposition to unjust wars and other violence under the reign of Louis XIV. As a result of speaking out, Fenelon was banished from Court and his writings on mysticism condemned by Rome, because they were thought to represent a morbid subjectivism. At that time, spontaneity in prayer was considered dangerous. Merton concluded his Introduction with this comment about Fenelon and Newman: "Even though we cannot altogether think and write as such men do, we need their spirit and their music." Merton added in his diary entry of June 22, 1961: "And they both have, above all *style*."

Merton had been particularly attracted to Cardinal Newman since his initial influence on Merton's conversion to Catholicism. From his own later experience in speaking out on subjects not always welcome by Church authorities, he came to admire Newman for his courage in expressing himself while not wanting to engage the Church in another Galileo incident.

Gradually world news began to reach Gethsemani in more detail and became increasingly troubling as the 1960s progressed. Merton decided to take a strong public stand against war. He believed time was critical in influencing public opinion against the Government's policies. No one in the Church to Merton's knowledge was writing or speaking out against nuclear war or the Vietnam conflict. He believed it to be his calling to take a stand and hopefully to lead others in this effort, but in a less direct way. It occurred to him that letters were his primary means of communicating personally and effectively with his friends and associates. Why not extend the vehicle to include his serious readers?

In October 1961, he began the *Cold War Letters*, a series of letters about his position on war. Letters were not considered publications, and therefore not subject to censorship. He used the monastery mimeograph machine to produce the copies. He carefully chose the people he sent them to, those who could and would effectively spread his ideas. Pacifists were in the minority in the Church in the early 1960s, and Merton knew that his work would never pass the censors. In his opinion, good censorship was strictly theological. He called it silly for them to censor things they didn't like the sound of, when in fact they were out of touch with contemporary thought. Merton may have gotten the idea for his *Letters* from Teilhard de Chardin, who was prohibited from publishing in Eastern Europe.

Merton dispatched 49 letters individually, for a total of 62 before they were published as *The Cold War Letters*. In his first "Letter," published in *The Catholic Worker* in October 1961, Merton said he feared the unknown in starting on this journey of social protest, joining a vocal but unknown minority. Unable to work with freedom from the confines of the monastery, he knew his information would be limited, that he was chancing his future reputation, although he was more than ready to destroy his image as the devoted monk at peace with his surroundings.

This image had deprived him of the transfer to an order where he could live as a hermit. Now he hoped he could find God's will in taking up the cause of social protest.

In another of these letters, Merton commented on the U.S. policy on Cuba. He did not want to hear more about the righteousness of the U.S. Government in attempting to overthrow Castro at the Bay of Pigs. He believed action should have been taken earlier when Castro initially overthrew the government of Batista, Cuba's previous leader. Merton said he guessed that he would now be considered a security risk for saying this. He said he would throw a bowl of soup at anyone who spoke to him about the U.S. policy in Cuba favorably.

Merton received severe criticism in an editorial published in the *Catholic Standard* magazine in March 1962, which called him a pacifist and anti-Catholic. This was difficult for Merton to accept, but he knew it was the price he had to pay to reach a wide audience. Merton told himself that not all readers agreed with that publication's conservative position. From his extensive correspondence with Catholic priests and nuns, he had been responding to the concerns of his fellow religious as well as expressing his own ideas about successfully following a religious vocation in that turbulent and confusing era.

Merton, fearing he was acquiring a siege mentality, wrote to Naomi Burton to ask her to take over his publishing affairs again, although he doubted she would agree with what he was now writing. She replied that as an Anglican in 1947, she had disagreed with Merton's remarks about religion in *The Seven Storey Mountain*, but that did not stop her from handling the book as his agent or from being a friend. She never refused to help Merton whenever she could.

Merton received a request from U.S. Representative Frank Kowalski, Democrat of Connecticut, which provided Merton with an opportunity to speak out publicly on peace. He was asked to write a "Prayer for Peace" for the upcoming Easter season. The Congressman read Merton's prayer in the House of Representatives, then published it in the "Congressional Record."

Merton believed he had found the solution to the censorship problem by mimeographing his material, thereby sidestepping the need for censors to review and approve it. So long as he was not forbidden to do this, he believed he was free to use this outlet for his social commentary. He regretted that the Vatican had not come out with a statement against nuclear war. He hoped to influence the forthcoming Second Vatican Council to his position when they convened in October 1962.

Dom James received several letters and reports from Dom Gabriel, officially registering the Order's opposition to Merton's writings against nuclear war. Although the letters were dated back to January, Dom James did not give them to Merton until April 1962. Since the correspondence did not actually forbid Merton to continue, he ignored them. Merton strongly disagreed with Dom Gabriel's view that his peace efforts were falsifying the message of monasticism, detached from the world and living in the eternal rather than the temporal world.

Merton's book, to be titled "Peace in the Post-Christian Era," was scheduled to be published by Macmillan, and had already been approved by the censors. At the last minute the Abbot General cancelled its publication. Merton received a letter from Dom Gabriel in May 1962, directing him to stop all publishing on war and peace. There was a rumor that Dom Gabriel had acted at the request of an unnamed agency of the U.S. Government, but this has not been confirmed. In his letter to Merton, Dom Gabriel said that a monk's role is rather to pray and live the withdrawn life on behalf of peace rather than to write about it. Merton then issued the book himself in mimeographed copies.

Before Merton was banned from publishing on war and peace, he sent a long article, "We Have to Make Ourselves Heard," to *The Catholic Worker* that was published in two issues (May and June 1962). He chose to bypass the censors on the basis that it was an expansion and clarification of an article he had published in *Commonweal* (February 9, 1962) which had passed the censors. He said it was important for him to clarify his position on nuclear war, since he had let it be known that he had been silenced on this subject. He did not want the Church to repeat a misjudgment in this critical area of nuclear war such as occurred in not recognizing Galileo's revolution in astronomy.

Part of Merton's banned "Peace Book" was adapted into an editorial titled "Religion and the Bomb," published in the May 1962 issue of *Jubilee*. Merton commented in a letter to his friend, Ping Ferry (May 8, 1962) that this piece was "strident" and "will set a whole lot of people right on their ear … .I lash out with a baseball bat. Some professor of non-violence I am. Oh well."

Daniel Berrigan, the activist Jesuit priest at Cornell, came to visit Merton for the first time in August 1962. Merton was not surprised at Berrigan's appearance, a slight build with dark, searching eyes. Merton had seen his picture wearing the familiar black turtleneck sweater and wool beret that were popular in France. Their relationship had matured through their exchange of ideas in their correspondence and mutual respect. Berrigan had published a favorable review of Merton's *New Seeds of Contemplation* for *America* magazine. Merton called Berrigan's work Zen-like and a spirit of the church he could believe in. He supported Berrigan's efforts in the peace movement, but could not be persuaded to take such an active role himself. Merton was steadfast in his position that he belonged at the hermitage and that his role could be most effective with prayers, fasting, and his pacifist writing.

Merton was six years older than Dan Berrigan and with his own personal experience, he advised Dan to handle his problem with Jesuit authority "with delicacy and understanding." Merton said the Church needed "a real renewal, not just an explosion."

Just as the Second Vatican Council was convening, in October 1962, Merton composed a powerful Introduction to *The Prison Meditations of Father Delp*. Like Merton, he was a convert. He became a Jesuit priest, then was imprisoned and executed by the Nazis at the age of 38, nine years younger than Merton at the time of this publication. Father Delp composed his diary just before the Nazis executed him on trumped-up charges of being a traitor to his country in time of war. The book contains only excerpts from the diary, and there is no editor named and no indication of what was omitted. Only Merton's name is given as the author of the Introduction. It was published in 1963 by Herder and Herder.

In his Introduction, Merton makes the point that the world has not changed since Father Delp's time insofar as the need to overcome the power of government over the rights of the individual. Merton cites Pope John XXIII's encyclical, *Mater et Magistra*, in support of his view that the world is again risking the possibility of annihilation of innocent people by allowing the proliferation of nuclear weapons. He agrees with Father Delp that the spiritual condition of modern man is fragile: "alienated, void, internally dead, modern man has in effect no capacity for God." This leads to a "dehumanized bureaucratic conscientiousness" such as exhibited by Eichmann and others in the operation of Nazi concentration camps. Merton emphasizes the message of

Father Delp, charging that the church has not yet gotten in touch with "the spiritual hunger" of modern man. Merton says that "true worship" is not "a matter of standing aside and praying for the world, without any concept of its problems and its desperation." A contemplative and cloistered religious "must understand the world's anguish and share it in their own way, which may, in fact, be very like the experience of Fr. Delp." Merton commented in his journal at the time of this writing (September 26, 1962) that (sadly) the monks who seemed to him to be taking the monastery seriously were mainly the ones involved in the business end of the operation.

Merton's uncanny ability to see through events to their reality required a continuous battle against cynicism for him. Merton had a wide range of feelings about pacifists. Some he highly respected, and others he believed were too militant. Merton wrote to his old friend, Catherine de Hueck Doherty, (November 12, 1962), that he felt a lot of people working in the peace movement were "wacky," but thought they were being used by God for His purposes. He wanted to extend an arm around them on behalf of the Church to encourage them, since no one else in the Church was publicly supporting their efforts.

Merton was also working on new poetry to express his position on social issues. At the same time he was translating the poetry he liked in foreign languages into English versions. He combined a collection of both his own and others' poetry on contemporary subjects in his *Emblems of a Season of Fury*, published in December 1963 by New Directions. This was his fifth book of poetry.

Meanwhile, the Second Vatican Council was underway. Merton was excited about the possibilities for change in the Church's administration through the work of this group. He saw John of the Cross as a forerunner of Vatican II. He thought the Council's universal call to holiness would result in a unity of all activity to get closer to God through the Catholic Church.

The Cuban missile crisis strongly influenced the representatives convened by Vatican II. Merton was asked to submit his writings on nuclear weapons for consideration by the Council in developing their position. The Pope had issued two encyclicals, *Mater et Magistra*, in 1961 on social justice and *Pacem in Terris*, on peace, in 1963. The latter called for moderation in the use of nuclear weapons. Merton felt vindicated. He again requested Dom Gabriel's permission to publish "Peace in the Post-Christian Era" that had been suspended. In May

1963, Dom Gabriel refused him again on the basis that the Encyclical spoke only of aggressive use of nuclear weapons, and not of their use for self-defense. Merton's position was considered to be more far-reaching than the Pope's and therefore not acceptable. Merton commented privately that it was well that Pope John did not have to get his Encyclical through the Cistercian censors. Otherwise it also might not have been published.

Dom James counseled Merton that it was not his place to write on such controversial topics. It was a subject for bishops. Merton's position was that the Church's theologians were sitting it out and "preserving their reputations," keeping the Church "half dead."

In June 1963, Pope John XXIII died unexpectedly. Merton believed he would be declared a saint one day. When Paul VI was elected to replace him, Merton wrote him a letter of congratulation. In July, he was gratified to receive a personal letter from the new Pope in response, along with his Apostolic Blessing for Merton and his novices. Merton must have been encouraged by this attention, as well as the one-upsmanship it represented.

Another form of recognition came to Merton as well. The Pax Medal was awarded to him by the Massachusetts Political Action for Peace organization in recognition of his contribution to world peace. This was a pacifist group associated with the *Catholic Worker* paper. The medal was awarded by H. Stuart Hughes on April 26, 1963. Merton naturally did not attend the ceremony..

A few months later, in November, Dom Gabriel died after a period of ill health. It was the end of an era. Dom Gabriel's traditional policies that followed the centuries-old way of doing everything would inevitably be modified by the Order's next leader. Dom Gabriel had been unsupportive of many of Merton's ideas. Nevertheless Merton respected him because he was straightforward in his opposition as compared with Dom James' surreptitious actions towards his activities. Merton would wait now to see how all this would affect the release of his writing.

Soon Merton found that the new Abbot General, Dom Ignatius Gillet, would prove to be tolerant of Merton's writing on peace.

# Chapter 24

Merton's physical problems were increasing. Now at 48, Merton was not so trim, up to 185 pounds. Some of his friends thought he resembled a good-natured truck driver, as compared to the thin, fragile monk they first knew. By September 1963, he was frequently experiencing discomfort in his digestive processes. He suffered with a chronic pain in his left arm and at the base of his neck. His doctors decided to institute a thorough investigation, so hospitalized him at St. Joseph's Infirmary in Louisville for two weeks for tests. They found a fused cervical disc.

Merton dreaded being in a hospital. Besides the obvious reasons for fearing confinement, he also dreaded the loss of freedom to escape the people who tried to meet him. He often used his Latin name on his hospital records, Father Ludovicus, to reduce the number of curious people dropping in on him. He loved playing games with names, and even more, he loved his privacy.

Meanwhile, reform in the Order was having unintentional effects at Gethsemani. To comply with Vatican II, the Order prescribed reforms of some of their medieval Cistercian practices to appeal to the incoming postulants. Some of the old-timers reacted negatively to the changes: two monks left Gethsemani to become hermits and another took an extended leave. Some 2,000 postulants entered Gethsemani during a ten-year period in the 1940s to 1950s. Merton noted that most of this group left, and did so early in their novitiate. Merton believed that modernization did not solve the problem of turnover of the postulants and in fact stripped out the solemnity of the life they were seeking. In his view, they could not adapt to the "complex and fatal machinery in which one was finally exhorted to renounce even what he had come to the monastery to find." This was later published in "Problems and Prospects" as a chapter in *Contemplation in a World of Action*, first published by Doubleday in 1971, then by the University of Notre Dame Press in 1998.

One of the major changes in procedures was the elimination of the two disparate groups within the monastery. The brothers and choir monks were now combined after hundreds of years of their separation as distinctive groups. Merton strongly disagreed with this decision, believing the brothers would lose the distinction of their own group and suffer the loss of morale from the result. The brothers were involved in primarily physical rather than mental tasks. Merton did not consider the difference between the two groups as snobbery, but a clear distinction between two types of monks. They had voluntarily chosen the group to which they belonged, depending on the pursuit of the lifestyle they had come to the monastery to follow. There were intellectual monks who chose for their own reasons to belong to the brothers' group. Combining the two groups was probably an attempt to form the monks into a homogeneous organization. Merton thought it might instead have combined two content groups into one very dissatisfied organization.

Much of the medieval liturgical music was eliminated by these changes. The chants sung in Latin were replaced by ordinary hymns in English to appeal primarily to the younger monks and to avoid instructing the Brothers, since they did not sing the Latin chant. The choir monks were sure it would not be reinstated, now that it had been discontinued. The new music distracted Merton. He said that some of the hymns reminded him of the Anglican services he had attended in his youth. He considered this change a severe deterioration of the liturgy. Dr. Wygal thought that Merton's singing of the chant had irritated his stomach disorder. In fact, Merton admitted a nervousness often occurred when he sang during the services. Now that he was deprived of the Latin chants, he confined himself to reading his daily Divine Office in Latin rather than in the now approved English translation.

Merton resorted to singing the Latin chant on his walks in the woods. Some of the monks reported they also heard him singing excerpts from the operas his grandfather used to teach him. He was more comfortable singing with the birds and other wildlife than with his fellow monks. He treasured the natural beauty of his surroundings and researched preservation methods to insure its maintenance. He was concerned about the effect that DDT was going to have on all the wildlife. The monastery had begun using pesticides to enhance the growth of its crops. Merton noticed, though, that some of the plants and wildlife were already experiencing a gradual deterioration that was noticeable to one who, like him, moved around close to nature. For the wrens, screech owls, and even the cawing crows, Merton felt the responsibility to protect them.

Rachel Carson had just published her book, *Silent Spring*, which publicized the destructive effect of insecticides on wildlife and other natural resources. Merton heard about Carson's book in the December 1962 issue of *The New Yorker* magazine that he saw in his doctor's office. He was alarmed. The nature around him was part of his world, and he respected it. He wrote in his journal, "we are destroying everything because we are destroying ourselves." Merton was beginning to view the changes around him as being counterproductive to the monastic life. He saw the religious life as becoming irrelevant in a world that was battling with basic survival.

Merton once wrote a poem taking aim at the monastery's emphasis on commercial endeavors. As a parody of Kilmer's poem, "Trees," he put this rhyme on the monastery's bulletin board, entitled "Chee$e," beginning:

"I think that we should never freeze
Such lively assets as our cheese."
He ended with the sixth couplet:
"Poems are nought but warmed-up breeze,
*Dollars* are made by Trappist Cheese."

"Signed: Joyce Killer-Diller"

War and peace were not the only issues being ignored by the Church. Merton saw the segregation problem rapidly spinning out of control.

With the advent of television, the unfairness and persecution of black America came into every home. It energized people on a large scale by raising their awareness and encouraging them to participate, either for or against the issues. Protests were telecast nationally and shown in movie theaters in newsreels. Local problems of racial discrimination could no longer be passed off as nobody else's business. They had moved to the national stage.

He decided to turn his attention to the matter of racial discrimination. He had always supported Gandhi's principle of non-violence since his student days at Oakham. He saw Martin Luther King, Jr., as a leader in that tradition. Merton believed that his writing could be an asset to the civil rights movement, expounding on the Christian principle of the brotherhood of man.

In August 1963, he published a poem in *The Saturday Review* magazine, "And the Children of Birmingham," concerning the murder of black children there by a white mob. Merton was especially touched by a photograph he saw in *Look* magazine of a little black girl, one of the bomb-murdered children, clutching a white doll. He composed the poem, "Picture of a Black Child with a White Doll" and sent a copy to the girl's father, Chris McNair. In his letter, dated October 12, 1964, Merton said he related to black children because of his own experiences as a child of a minority group. He explained that he had fortunately been able to speak with the right accent and assume the right "protective feathers" within a few months to survive as a foreigner in France and England. Now he was having nightmares about the discrimination against blacks that was erupting in violence all around him.

Merton believed the Catholic Church had failed its black American members by its inaction and official silence. He said that white Catholics were treating blacks like incurable infants, holding something against them that was out of their control. He also saw the white population in need of healing so that they could accept blacks as their equals in God's eyes. With his international background, he found it impossible to accept the status quo of segregation or to understand the Church's hands-off policy. Merton believed the non-violent campaign was a miraculous opportunity in the U.S. that was being wasted. He thought it would serve the Church well to support a moral stand on the issue that would free whites as well as blacks from the oppression of their prejudice.

Critics of Merton pointed out that he lacked knowledge of the full situation since he lived in a secluded monastery in Kentucky, a state that was not really even considered a Southern state. They believed he was not personally familiar with the problems of the South and therefore not qualified to express his opinion or judgment of the situation publicly. Merton was disappointed to find that he did not have a unified audience in his readers on the civil rights issue. There was no common prevailing position as there was in the matter of nuclear weapons. Even within the Church, he found it difficult to win support on civil rights.

Merton was also sympathetic to the Black Muslims, seeing that organization as primarily focused on building up the black man's self-respect. He wanted to help the group to find ways of changing the black self-perception of having no choice but to live lives inferior to whites. Eldridge Cleaver, a leader of this group, paid tribute to Merton in his autobiography, *Sand on Ice*, for the support of their cause as well as in speeches he gave to Black Muslim supporters before he was killed in 1965. Later Merton wrote an article about Malcolm X after he was assassinated that same year. Merton recognized his sincerity and his attempts to further the rights of blacks in American society. Merton regretted these untimely deaths and their negative effect on their efforts.

Merton's name was becoming more familiar, but his actual identity remained largely a mystery because his photograph was never included on his book jackets. As a result, occasionally unscrupulous people impersonated him to raise money. Sometimes they even gave lectures, collecting money from unsuspecting people who thought they were contributing to a legitimate cause. With the Order's continued policy of concealing Merton's identity, it was easy for con artists to profit from the situation. Often it was rumored that he had left the Order or that he had been seen in various places throughout the world. Merton usually found this amusing, and sometimes annoying, but felt powerless to stop it.

In June 1963, the University of Kentucky awarded Merton the honorary degree of Doctor of Letters. Victor Hammer accepted the diploma for Merton, and may well have been influential in the school's decision to award it. Dom James did not allow Merton to attend the ceremony. Even if the Order had not forbidden it, Dom James would have concluded that Merton already had enough notoriety.

In July 1963, Swami Shivaprem, a yogi from Rishikish, India, visited the monastery. Since Dom James was away, Merton encouraged him to stay for three days. The Swami was teaching yoga in Milwaukee and was interested in learning more about Christianity. Merton let him speak to the novices. He commented in his journal that he believed he had more in common with this Indian monk than with the average American secular priest "as far as the spiritual life is concerned."

In August of 1963, he was wondering where Father John of the Cross now was, as he contemplated his feelings of being untrue to himself. In December Merton learned that he was teaching at Portsmouth Priory, according to Dom Aelred. The following November, Bellarmine College, a progressive Catholic liberal arts college in Louisville, requested the privilege of becoming the permanent repository of Merton's original manuscripts. Merton had developed some professional relationships with clergy on the faculty in addition to his old friend, Dan Walsh. A committee chaired by Father John T. Loftus headed up the project. They had picked up on the concern Merton had that the Order may not be too interested in preserving his material. Some of the local Catholic families agreed to create a fund to establish and maintain a Merton Collection at the school library. Merton was a little embarrassed about the project, especially at such an early time in his life, but could not deny that he was relieved to know his papers would be taken care of when he wasn't there anymore to do it himself. Now that he was cleaning out his files in preparation for his move to the hermitage, the timing was right to arrange for the disposition of this material. There was no opposition to this plan from any of Merton's superiors, and it was rapidly arranged.

Again, Merton was not allowed to participate in the dedication ceremony. He asked Dan Walsh to read a paper for him to acknowledge the honor. Soon the College opened a Merton Room at the library for scholars. Merton began to wonder if he was becoming the object of a cult.

Merton once said that anyone who imitated him would experience some fine moments of naked despair. Merton said that if he wished that others should repeat his life, it would be a mortal sin against charity for him to wish such misery on them. At the same time, he freely acknowledged that he loved the recognition of his work and could not resist continuing to preach, orally and in writing. But, on the other hand, he said that he felt like a canary in a cage. He recorded in his journal that it would be easier for him to get permission for a mistress than to leave Gethsemani for meetings and to respond to invitations.

Times were changing more rapidly than even Merton realized. He came close to appearing at the White House during the Kennedy presidency. Dan Walsh had been invited to give lectures there for top members of the Administration. In March 1963 Robert Kennedy requested that Merton be included. It was not to be; President John Kennedy was assassinated in November, before the final arrangements were made.

The assassination was a pivotal point in Merton's experience that moved him to take action. It caused Merton to grow more skeptical than ever about the state of the country, and even cynical about the American government. The subsequent rise to power of Lyndon Johnson and the escalation of the Vietnam war during his Administration troubled Merton tremendously. By this time, Merton did not hesitate to speak out about his ideal of pacifism, the principle that he associated with his love for the country.

With his mental processes in so much flux, Merton used his correspondence to encourage a wide variety of people to feed his insatiable thirst for information about what effects the events of the time were having on the public. He needed an audience to test his ideas before he drew any conclusions he would publish.

In a letter to Dan Berrigan on June 25, 1963, Merton said that some monks have an obligation "to shout very loud about God's will, God's truth, and justice of man to man" in the tradition of the prophets. A few months later, in a letter dated February 23, 1964, Merton wrote to Berrigan that they should not be discouraged. "The Holy Spirit is not asleep … God writes straight on crooked lines … .The lines are crooked enough by now. And we I suppose are what He is writing with, though we can't see what is being written. And what He writes is not for peace of soul, that is sure … ."

Berrigan once commented that Merton was like a tightrope walker because he could maintain balance by moving forward.

Merton was now becoming aware of a shift in the pace of his life from managing the events and even the thoughts he had, to one of being now somehow disassociated from his own reality. It was suddenly as if some cosmic force had relieved him of control and was orchestrating the experiences of each day in a preordered sequence of events. He did not understand it, but he was definitely conscious of how he was being swept along in the destiny of his time.

Ironically, Merton wrote some thirteen years earlier in his biography of St. Lutgarde, *What Are These Wounds?*, a description of how the nun differed from the Cistercian model. It sounds like a prophecy of the image that Merton came to display:

" … she lacks this Benedictine plainness, and this Cistercian technique of humility which consists in a kind of protective coloring, by which the monk simply disappears into the background of the common, everyday life, like those birds and animals whose plumage and fur make them almost indistinguishable from their surroundings … .It was not her fault that Christ singled her out, by means of extraordinary graces and sufferings, from the rest of her sisters and from the rest of the world."

Cover of **The Critic**, December 1965–January 1966 issue, Vol. XXIV, No. 3. Merton appears on the far left of the bottom row. Not arranged in order of importance, those selected by the magazine's Editor, Joel Wells, are John Courtney Murray, SJ, Dorothy Day, The Most Rev. John Patrick Cody, Robert Kennedy, Richard Cardinal Cushing, Philip Scharper, Phyllis McGinley, William Buckley, Jacqueline Kennedy, Robert Hoyt, John Cogley, Merton, The Honorable Richard J. Daley, Sister Mary Luke, SL, and the Most Rev. John J. Wright. This magazine is no longer in publication.

# Chapter 25

The 1960s in America were difficult for every thinking person. Merton could have taken honors for the extent of his concern about everything: his life, his monastery, his Order, his Church, his friends, and his country. He involved himself in discussions of public events and commented on the morality of what he viewed to be wrong directions. At the same time, Merton was experiencing the period in his life when his monastic vocation was evolving from idealistic illusion to practical reality. He knew that as a monk he was marginalized by society, and willingly so, but that did not mean that he and his ideas were irrelevant. He decided to dig in his heels and devote his life to a substantial improvement in 20th century monasticism as he thought it was appropriate for him. He nurtured friends and involved himself in activities to expand his worldview so that he could have a realistic basis for his literary contribution. He researched, analyzed, and put forth proposals to update the monastic life without sacrificing the integrity of the traditional spirit. And he would not step aside in the face of criticism or any other impediment in his path.

The turmoil of these times brought Merton more frequently to the isolated places behind the monastery where he knew he would be alone with his thoughts and with his God. He could compose himself, put things into perspective, and make decisions about what he would do to assist in the repair and rebuilding of a now fractured adopted homeland.

On the monastery grounds, Merton often found bullet shells. He had seen hunters nearby with dogs hunting raccoons. Once he found a discarded package for shells with a one-mile range. To Merton's disgust, the Abbot made no effort to discourage or stop hunters from killing the wildlife on the monastery's property, so an accident could occur at any time.

The woods that Merton had found so comforting and even inspirational as he meditated on the beauty of God's creation had now become something dark and physically threatening. Eerily Merton remembered how the same phenomenon had occurred to him in New York, when the bustling city that represented so much about possibilities had become a sinister, frightening place to him. Walking in the woods as Merton loved to do had in fact become risky, especially since he had no brightly colored clothing that would identify him to hunters. He hoped they were only hunters who were trespassing, but he was afraid that some might not be there only seeking wildlife. Now that his image had become controversial, his fear of personal danger seemed a very possible reality.

Just days before the Kennedy assassination, a young woman came to Gethsemani to see Merton, telling the gatekeeper that she was a distant relative. Merton came out, wondering who she might be. Suddenly she lunged at him and attacked him with all her strength as one who was deranged. He had to overcome her to stop her. He then tried to talk to her, but it was useless and she left as suddenly as she had come. Merton later described her to the other monks as a beatnik-type, with her hair in her face. He said he thought she might have been a nymphomaniac. Merton was shaken by the experience and afraid that this might be only the beginning of similar occurrences. Events were pushing people with fragile emotional states over the edge--they could not foresee an end in sight to the unsettled mood of the country. It had its effect within the monastery as well.

In February 1964 Merton had an even more frightening experience. He went down from the hermitage to the gate house to be driven into Louisville to see his dermatologist. One of the monks gestured to him in sign language that a man had just been there with a gun, threatening to shoot Merton. The visitor had been subdued by several of the monks and taken away before Merton arrived at the scene. Merton was visibly shaken. When he tried to get more details, the monk who had given him the alarming message said that Merton had misinterpreted the sign language, and that the man had threatened to kill his family and himself, not Merton. Merton could not establish whether this had actually been a threat on his life or a mix-up in communication, or whether the monk thought it was wiser to deceive Merton about the event, seeing his alarm. John Howard Griffin, Merton's friend and later his first biographer, believed it was an actual death threat. In fact, Merton received hate mail in his box the same morning. He knew that he might pay a price for his controversial positions on issues so personally important to people, especially in a rural area. He had been told that monks were expected to be neither seen nor heard, but he could not accept it in such troubling times.

Merton had been disturbed all his life by gunfire. When he was an infant, his parents lived close enough to the beginning of World War I to hear the canons of the invading German army moving through western France. During and after World War II, Merton could hear the guns at Fort Knox during practice maneuvers. He thought, it wasn't enough to use the place to store all of the U.S. gold; they had to train pilots for war there, too. The planes flying over Gethsemani created an almost deafening noise, especially contrasted with the earlier silence. The Vietnam conflict brought renewed activity at Fort Knox. The monks could hear the gunfire almost every day. It was especially loud at the hermitage. Merton learned that the atomic energy facility at Oak Ridge, Tennessee, was only a couple of hundred miles away. He calculated that an atom bomb exploded there would burn his eyes out at Gethsemani.

The general public's opposition to warfare was intensifying with each succeeding conflict. The public was increasingly becoming directly involved in the conflict with each successive war. An analysis of the ratio of soldiers to civilians killed illustrates this phenomenon. In World War I, there were 90 soldiers killed to every 10 civilians, and the war directly involved only soldiers. In World War II, the ratio rose to 50-50, due to mass bombing, the use of the atom bomb, and genocide. After World War II, 10 soldiers were killed to every 90 civilians, with use of child soldiers, chemical weapons, inhumane terrorism, and mass murder of civilians (as in Cambodia). Merton recognized this trend, and believed that the just war theory was now outdated. War had now become morally unacceptable. He therefore had a moral obligation to speak out against it.

Merton was shocked by a series of articles in *The New Yorker* magazine by Hannah Arendt on Adolf Eichmann published in 1963. He learned that in the investigation of Nazi war crimes, the doctors who examined Eichmann had found him to be perfectly sane. He was merely carrying out orders in killing Jews. Merton decided this fact demanded public visibility to try to prevent the recurrence of this kind of horrible event. People must become part Jewish at least by imaginative identification, he wrote in his essay called "A Devout Meditation in Memory of Adolf Eichmann." It was first published in Laughlin's annual collection of essays and poetry, *New Directions 18*, in 1964.

Merton spoke compassionately about the abuse of Jews and called himself a complete Jew in his *Cold War Letters*. Merton pointed out that oppression is another form of violence. In a letter to Rabbi Steven Schwarzschild, included in a *Cold War Letter*, he said the Jews in Israel have a legitimate right to protest and self-protection. He wrote that non-violence was the best solution in America, but he did not know if it would be possible to implement it anytime soon. He began to have doubts that King's movement would be successful, and it depressed him that he saw it that way.

One of the places that most comforted him was the Zen garden that he and his novices had recently built. In collecting rocks for the project, he had discovered some large boulders outside the wall of the main buildings that he believed would add a considerable depth to the appearance of the garden. Unfortunately they were much too heavy to be moved by the monks. Merton thought that the powerful earth-moving machinery being used for renovations could lift them. He mentioned it to the novices, but didn't dare ask Dom James. He would never open himself up to the Abbot's ridicule for having found a personal use for the machines he had complained so bitterly about.

While Merton was back in the hospital for the tests that found his cervical disc problem in September 1963, the monks planned a surprise for his return. The cellarer used the machines to move the rocks to the garden, hoisting them over the wall and setting them in place according to Merton's design. When he got back to the monastery, Merton was as much surprised as overjoyed, but some of the monks did not let him overlook the fact that the machines he so despised had done the job. He raised up a Chinese red fish kite that made the scene complete.

Merton's interest in the arts seemed to widen with his every exposure to a different type of creative work. Merton was drawn to the design of Shaker furniture, because he believed it reflected the simplicity of the monastic life. Edward Deming and Faith Andrews were preparing a comprehensive book on Shaker furniture, to be called *Religion In Wood*. Dr. Andrews asked Merton to write an introduction for it in 1964 before his death. It was published in 1966 by Indiana University Press. Merton recognized Dr. Andrews as a foremost authority on Shaker philosophy, and pointed out its relationship to the work of William Blake, who was a contemporary of the first Shakers. Merton saw in the furniture's design a reflection of an integral world-view of man's relationship with the eternal. In his introduction, Merton questioned if it would be possible for such simplicity to survive in a technological world. Merton probably met Dr. Andrews through Mark Van Doren, who wrote an attribution for the back cover of the book.

Merton continued to write moral essays to keep his readers' opinion on current issues in perspective. In April 1964 Merton compiled a collection of Gandhi's writing, along with an essay applying his principles of non-violence to the nuclear age. *Gandhi on Non-Violence* was published by New Directions in 1964.

In May 1964, Laughlin visited Gethsemani and saw the final material on Gandhi. He also took a look at some translations of the Chinese philosopher and poet, Chuang Tzu, that Merton had just finished, and was enthusiastic. New Directions published both the Gandhi book and *The Way of Chuang Tzu* in 1965. Merton's translation of Chuang Tzu became the favorite of all his books, probably because it reflected both his sense of humor and interest in paradoxes, and dealt with subjects of obviously lasting appeal, especially involving human nature. He once said that the parables in the New Testament are much like Chinese stories. He noted that the early Church Fathers also had used stories to bring home their messages.

Later that month, Archbishop Thomas Roberts, a pacifist and acquaintance of Gandhi, made a surprise visit, along with a group of Japanese survivors of the Hiroshima bombing. Merton wrote to Laughlin that the visit was not long enough, a sentiment he often expressed. Merton once said that with his associations now worldwide, he traveled vicariously. Laughlin purchased an atlas for him to study all the places that caught his imagination, and Merton put it to good use.

Meanwhile, the Cistercian Rule concerning stability was modified to allow some monks to attend out-of-town conferences, but Dom James told Merton there would be no relaxation of the restriction for him. Merton could only accept the decision in obedience, but his private reaction was that Dom James probably thought he'd run away and never be seen again, like the priest who supposedly fell into the Grand Canyon. Merton concluded that the organized artificiality of monastery life was now actually good only for new and for very old monks. As for himself, he was finding organized prayer and activity to seem artificial to him and therefore more of a penance than a consolation. He thought travel to meetings might be beneficial.

In June 1964 Dom James made an exception to Merton's restriction. The Buddhist monk and noted Japanese Zen scholar, Daisetz Suzuki, was to be in New York and invited Merton to come for talks. They had carried on an extensive correspondence during the past few years and had a mutual desire to speak face-to-face. The 94-year-old monk's health was too frail to allow him to travel to Gethsemani. It would be Merton's last opportunity to speak with him about the connection between Eastern and Western philosophies. Suzuki had left Japan and moved to New York after Merton had entered Gethsemani. He had been teaching at Columbia and lecturing throughout the world, spreading Zen Buddhism in the Western hemisphere, a process he described as similar to "holding a plant to a stone." Suzuki's following now included a number of prominent thinkers, including C.G. Jung and Aldous Huxley. He had become one of Merton's favorite correspondents.

Dom James reluctantly gave Merton both the permission and the funds to fly to New York, but on condition that he would not contact any of his old friends. He was put on a very limited budget, so there would be no temptation to do anything else. Merton readily agreed to the Abbot's conditions.

Merton arrived in a rain that lasted the first two days of his visit. He got his first view of the New York skyline in twenty-three years. From the air, he noted in his diary, he could even recognize the chimneys of the Elmhurst crematorium where the remains of his mother and grandparents had been taken. Nevertheless he was thrilled to see New York again after so many years. He stayed in a dormitory room alone at Columbia for the first two nights. He was happy to have the privacy to do his yoga on the floor of the room just as he had in his old apartment. On the third night, he stayed at a hotel to be more conveniently located for his departure in the morning. He said Mass twice at Corpus Christi Church where he had been baptized, but he did not identify himself there to avoid recognition or any discussion. He did not even ask anyone about Father Ford, who had wanted him to become a secular priest. He was surprised at his disengagement with his past. He ate alone, once in a Chinese restaurant. It was enough for him just to take in all the changes in people and places he saw around him in his old familiar surroundings. It was a bittersweet experience, but he was grateful to be there.

Merton and Suzuki had two meetings. Suzuki's female attendant, dressed in a proper Japanese kimono, served tea and handed Merton an ear trumpet to speak through so that the elderly monk could hear him. Merton had never even seen one before, but tried to conceal his absolute amazement and embarrassment in using it. Suzuki told him that his *Ascent to Truth* was popular in the East among Zen scholars and monks. Merton could not have been more pleased at their free exchange of ideas. Considering his advanced age, Suzuki would never be able to travel to the U.S. again and provide this opportunity for Merton to learn about the East directly from this preeminent figure.

In spite of the restricted budget and time for the trip, Merton managed to visit two museums while he was in New York. Merton's interest in art had been rekindled since he had recently met Ulfert Wilke, a calligrapher in Louisville, and had visited his studio. With his encouragement and assistance, Merton had started creating calligraphies himself, using black ink on white paper. Dom James had encouraged Merton in this activity, probably as a relief from his tension and frustration.

Merton had received some thin Japanese paper from his old friend, Ad Reinhardt, one of his old friends from Columbia, probably as a birthday gift, in January 1964. Merton was very much in tune with the influences he and Reinhardt had shared: a minimalist view of art without emotional excesses. Reinhardt's paintings were a major contribution to the art of his time. His works are said to suggest a contradiction between the material and the intangible to lead the viewer to a meditative state. His famed black paintings with faint tracings of Greek crosses were judged by critics to be quasi-mystical and some of the most radical art of the 1960s, subtly combining notions of completeness with an Eastern concept of the cosmic "void."

Of course, Merton's first influence in the field of art was his father's work, even though pastel scenes like his father's could never be expressive of his sentiments. Merton, like Reinhardt, decided to express himself visually only in black and white. Merton also used only black and white film for his photographs, unless he could buy only color film. He knew the contrast would be more distinct and that he could make a stronger statement in black and white. It reflected his point of view generally, that a statement should be clear cut and discrete and in stark contrast to the ideas he opposed. Merton would not produce any rosy pictures.

When he returned from New York, he learned that his manuscript, "Peace in the Post-Christian Era," had been approved for inclusion in his forthcoming book, *Seeds of Destruction*. Merton was told that the new Abbot General, Dom Ignace Gillet, had approved it on the basis that it did not say too much about war. The book was published in November 1964 by Farrar, Straus, and Cudahy. Merton also included in this work a portion of the mimeographed *Cold War Letters* he had distributed in 1961 and 1962.

Merton had been dealing for years with Marie Tadie as his agent in France. While Merton believed that she took an overly materialistic view of getting his works published in France, Merton occasionally believed she overstepped her authority in publications of his works, including some translations in his behalf. In November 1964, Merton complained in his diary that she was "unreasonable" and "very trying." She opposed his giving copyright authority as spiritual gifts to requestors. He considered this his prerogative and really not any of her business. At times, through the years, there were occasions when Merton wished he could control Marie Tadie legally. He always concluded that it was impossible, however, since she was located in France and he had given her a great deal of leeway from the outset before he knew how extensive his international publishing would become.

During the summer of 1964, Merton wrote a script to accompany a film shown at the Vatican Pavilion of the New York World's Fair. It was called "The Church is Christ Living in the World Today." He received a warm thank-you note from Cardinal Spellman of New York, who had given the final approval for several of Merton's books in the censorship process. Initially Cardinal Spellman rejected Merton's film script. He asked Merton to revise it to emphasize charity, peace, and social justice, and to clarify that the Catholic Church is the one true Church. He said he wanted to dispel any confusion that may have been caused by the ecumenical movement. He obviously took exception to Catholic churches holding joint meetings and services with other denominations. It was said that Cardinal Spellman was a close personal friend of Pope Pius XII from earlier days when the Pope had served as Papal Nuncio and represented the Vatican to the United States. Merton did not challenge the Cardinal.

He prepared the requested revision, although he obviously could not have disagreed more with the Cardinal's sentiments. Merton wondered if Cardinal Spellman had heard about the recent recognition he had received from the Vatican for his ecumenical work. He complained about the assignment in one of his taped conferences with the novices. He didn't tell the novices he disagreed with the guidance, but only that it was something he had to do under an almost impossible deadline.

He wrote to Dan Berrigan in a comical, but soul-searching letter on August 4, 1964, about his recent workload and its effect on him. He described himself as "a burnt-out case" just standing there saying Mass where I was hit by the bullet and shot dead. He said, "word will go round about how they got this priest who was shot and they got him stuffed sitting up at a desk propped up with books and writing books, this book machine that was killed. I am waiting to fall over and it may take about ten more years of writing. When I fall over, it will be a big laugh because I wasn't there at all." Merton had few correspondents with whom he could share such personal feelings and trust that his confidence would be respected.

In October 1964, Gethsemani hosted the second annual meeting of all the Abbots and Novice Masters of the Cistercian Order. Decisions would be made about what changes the Order would make to conform to new Church guidance resulting from Vatican II. Dom James appointed Merton to set up the program. It made him nervous to be thrust into the center of the activity, but he was being allowed to read a paper of great importance to him. He was requesting the Order's approval of a hermitage at the monastery for monks who might wish to follow either a temporary or permanent vocation to solitude. If this were approved, he could probably get permission to move into the hermitage, so long as the group voted to allow hermits to be located at that abbey. Approval of the concept would not mean automatic approval for any individual monk. The Abbot would make an initial determination as to whether the individual were suited for this solitary life, then recommend approval to the Abbot General. Merton was determined to win approval for the eremitic lifestyle as an alternative to the life in community. Now that he believed he would never be allowed to leave the Order, he hoped to be allowed to lead a contemplative life while still remaining in the group.

Merton's presentation had the desired results. The group approved Merton's proposal in principle. In December Dom James authorized a cot-type bed to be moved into the hermitage for Merton to use overnight occasionally. He further requested permission from the Abbot General for Merton to reside there permanently.

Although Merton knew he should be happy, he could not put aside his suspicions of Dom James' motives. Merton believed the Abbot would now control the number of his visitors as well as use the hermitage as a basis for denying him attendance at out-of-town meetings. He also guessed his writings on social issues would be curtailed, since some of the Abbots at the meeting commented that Merton's recent work had been dividing Catholics. Some thought he was even an embarrassment to the Order. He knew he would now be expected to limit his writing to devotional subjects. He dreaded the prospect of further restriction as much as he longed to move into the hermitage.

Fortunately, the negative attitude toward Merton's work was not universal by any means. Archbishop Paul Philippe asked for material on Merton's monastic views to circulate to other Orders in Europe, to the Pope, and to those attending the Second Vatican Council. The Church began to experience an exodus of good monks after the Council got underway. There were at the same time fewer applicants, and it soon became obvious that these young novices were different. Merton's experience as Novice Master for the past ten years was seen as very valuable. Merton was perceived as being quite able to adapt to the changed attitudes and Church practices, and in fact he was ready for the adjustment. He reinterpreted the Order's concept of obedience as a free changing of the will as opposed to the traditional idea that monks had to suppress their rebellion, which he called a deception.

So much change in Merton's routine was a challenge, though it was welcome. A rash broke out on his hands, and he assumed that it was an emotional reaction to all the recent events and would eventually pass. When he could no longer delay getting medical treatment, he learned that he had a skin disease. His hands had become so irritated that he was required to wear white gloves to minimize infection. As a consequence, he was unable to type and handle his papers most of the time for more than a year. This caused Merton a degree of frustration that was almost unbearable.

The following month after the meeting, November 1964, Merton had a visit from a Buddhist scholar, Marco Pallis, accompanied by a Dominican monk, Brother Antoninus, whose poetry was also published by New Directions. Laughlin probably set up the get-together. Clergy of many faiths were becoming interested in Merton's ecumenical overtures and were excited about the Catholic Church's new policy on inter-faith matters.

That same month, Merton hosted an ecumenical conference at the hermitage organized by the Fellowship of Reconciliation (FOR), an interdenominational religious pacifist organization founded on Gandhian principles. Members of a number of different religious groups and liberal organizations assembled to discuss non-violence, including Philip and Dan Berrigan, Jim Forest and John Oliver Nelson from *The Catholic Worker*, and Ping Ferry. Brother Simon (Patrick Hart) distributed copies of Merton's newly released book, *Seeds of Destruction*. Hart was soon to become invaluable to Merton as his secretary. He had just returned from an assignment in Rome, and Merton welcomed his assistance. It rained heavily throughout the meeting, but that did not dampen the spirits of the group.

Merton had a special fascination for rain, which was not always positive. He noted that throughout his life, momentous events often occurred during rainy weather. Many of his saddest experiences were on rainy days. He said that rain made the solitude much more tangible, especially on stormy nights. Merton wrote an essay called "Rain and the Rhinoceros" in December 1964. It describes the disease of "Rhinoceritis," an illness of those who do not have a desire for solitude. He used the imagery from Ionesco's play, "Rhinoceros," to show a connection between the hermit life and contemporary existentialism. It was first published in *Holiday* magazine in 1965.

By now Merton had completed enough calligraphies to have an exhibition, and he wanted to use them for some positive good. With his friend Wilke's help in framing them, Merton organized a showing of his drawings, with the proceeds to be used to establish a scholarship fund for a black female student to attend Catherine Spalding College in Louisville. Unfortunately, the event did not raise enough money. Some of Merton's friends arranged to send the calligraphies on tour, which was mildly successful. An anonymous donation of stock completed the difference needed. Merton was relieved when enough money was finally raised to begin paying for the scholarship.

Merton began to take a greater interest in photography now that he was spending more time at the hermitage. John Howard Griffin, a civil rights activist and author of the best seller, *Black Like Me*, began to visit Merton to discuss civil rights issues. He was also a photographer. He loaned Merton a good camera and offered to develop his film for him. He taught Merton a great deal about shooting black and white pictures. One of the pictures Merton took was used for the cover of his book of essays, *Raids on the Unspeakable*, published by New Directions in 1966.

Merton started photographing his friends when they came to visit, and sometimes they photographed Merton as well. Jim Forest and John Howard Griffin took many of the pictures of Merton that have been published. They said that to them Merton had facial features resembling Pablo Picasso in his later years, particularly with Merton's shaved head (now without the monastic hair band) that emphasized his heavy eyebrows. Merton himself found the similarity amusing.

By Merton's fiftieth birthday, January 31, 1965, the hermitage had been wired for electricity. He had been working only with a kerosene lamp up to this time. His only heat was from the fireplace, so the bedroom was extremely cold. One night he found the water frozen solid in his cup near the cot. Soon he was given a small refrigerator. This enlarged his options for preparing his own meals, and Merton noted that it also provided a means for keeping beer cold.

His friends began to send him gifts for his hermitage. He received a beautiful scroll from Suzuki, hand painted and enclosed in a special box. Merton hung the scroll on the wall near his desk. Suzuki did not tell him what the message said on the scroll, so Merton asked one of his Chinese visitors to translate it. He guessed that Suzuki was too polite to offer a translation, which would have assumed that he thought Merton could not translate it himself.

Dom James told Merton he could move into the hermitage full time in the coming summer, 1965. He would only be required to come down to the monastery once a day for his main meal and to say Mass, which was agreeable with Merton. He was overjoyed at the prospect of finally moving out of the monastery to his own place of solitude.

Dom James had also changed his mind about hermitages on the monastery property. He was considering an opportunity to acquire an 800-acre property called Edelen Farm that adjoined the monastery grounds, so that other monks who might like to adopt this lifestyle could have space for hermitages. He asked Merton to explore this property for him. Merton exhausted himself one day looking it over. He was happy to think of the prospect of the hermitage concept being enlarged so that others could follow his example. Dom James indicated he might like this lifestyle himself when he retired, but Merton did not take the comment seriously.

Although the hermitage was his heart's desire, Merton often worried about the physical danger of being out there alone, now that Dom James was allowing him to stay overnight. Often when he couldn't sleep anyway, he would become anxious when he heard sounds near the hermitage that he thought might be an intruder. Sometimes he tried to see with a flashlight, but with wild animals it was usually impossible. He prayed for protection and for deliverance from his terror. In the morning he would find a deer's footprints or some other animal he had not been able to identify from hearing only its sounds in the dark and not being able to see it.

Merton now began to be concerned about the frequent B-52 SAC bombers overhead. While he was walking around Edelen Farm, he saw five bombers flying only two or three hundred feet above the place, so close that Merton could see the trap door of the bomb bays of the first and last of the group. The fifth plane went over twice. Merton knew he was looking at the place from where bombs would drop and kill many innocent people. Then Merton realized he was standing on the site of a former house for slaves. Loose bricks were still there from the foundation. He was struck by the incongruity of the place. With the added threat of Oak Ridge and its H bombs nearby, he believed he was looking into the very face of evil. Then he accidentally hurt his eye with a twig. The doctor found that he had seriously damaged the cornea and required him to wear an eye patch, then dark glasses, for some time until it healed. Actually the doctor told him he was fortunate that he did not lose his sight. This accident curtailed his reading, and consequently his work for several months. Merton reflected that it was all part of the price he paid for being there.

In March he had an opportunity to visit with Mother Luke, the superior of the Convent of the Sisters of Loretto at the Foot of the Cross, in Nerinx, Kentucky. She came to Gethsemani to attend their annual retreat. Jim Wygal had spoken to Merton about her because he was certain that he would like her. Merton had been to her Convent several times during the past two years to give talks to the nuns, but they had never conversed. He was happy to have this opportunity to speak with her at greater length, because Mother Luke had been selected to attend the Vatican Council as an observer and was assigned to work on Schema Thirteen concerning nuclear war. Merton congratulated her on her selection. She agreed with his position on war, but realistically knew that as a nun she would have little influence at the Council.

In May 1965, Dan Berrigan came down from New York with two of his friends from the peace movement to consult with Merton about the amendments to Schema Thirteen. They were all equally concerned that the Church might decide to support the use of nuclear weapons. Merton was afraid that the U.S. Government might eventually employ nuclear weapons in Vietnam. Merton thought that the U.S. policy of attacking civilians who seemed suspicious but not confirmed as combatants implied that the Vietnamese people were inferior and therefore could be treated like pests being exterminated. Although nuclear weapons were not used in Vietnam, Merton was rightfully concerned about the heavy casualties that eventually resulted, estimated as about 58,000 U.S. and 1.3 million Vietnamese by the time the conflict ended.

In one of his *Cold War Letters*, he said that he himself would never kill another human being even in self-defense. He was seriously concerned about the evil influence he saw in the events of the time. He later wrote in a letter to Dan Berrigan that he believed demons were influencing some of the Church's leaders.

In June Merton saw the pictures on the cloister bulletin board of the astronaut, McDevitt, in space over the curve of the earth. Considering the events that were literally tearing the country apart, he thought that space exploration was also an insidious event. Merton commented in his journal, "Space flights are after all a rather expensive way of convincing oneself that one is free from mother."

Merton's negative attitude permeated most of his thoughts, probably because Merton's health was deteriorating. The skin problem on his hands worsened, requiring him to wear dermal gloves full-time. Finally, he spent one night at the monastery infirmary. When he returned to the hermitage the following day, he collapsed. He could no longer ignore his health. Merton asked the Abbot to relieve him of his assignment as Novice Master. Dom James agreed, but asked Merton to prepare an updated postulants' guide first. Using about half of what he had written in 1957, he rewrote and patiently finished the guide in August 1965.

Merton was preparing a collection of essays, to be published as *Seasons of Celebration* in December 1965 by Farrar, Straus and Cudahy. Two other collections were readied but not published until later. *Raids on the Unspeakable*, with the essay, "Rain and the Rhinoceros," was published in August 1966 by New Directions. In the fall of 1965, Merton could not resist rewriting many of the short pieces he included in the *Raids* collection. He included 15 abstract calligraphic ink drawings in the collection, his first publication of drawings since 1952 in Clare Boothe Luce's *Saints for Now*.

Philip Berrigan asked Merton to write the introduction to his book, *No More Strangers*, published by The Macmillan Company in 1965. In this stirring piece, Merton references the tradition of Teilhard de Chardin and Charles de Foucauld, and ties in the Second Vatican Council's call for renewal with the civil rights issue. He says reform is needed both to establish racial justice as well as to abolish war. He makes the point that Christians need an awakening to live their religion through love of their fellow man. The Church belongs to the layman, not the clergy.

He cautions against a Madison Avenue style of religion and concludes there is "more to do than sing hymns while the ship goes down."

Like the Berrigan brothers, Merton took an activist position toward the work of Vatican II compared to most church figures of his time who largely adopted a wait and see attitude. In the September 1965 issue of *Worldview*, Merton published a letter to the Bishops who were returning to Rome for the Council's final session. He said that the American Hierarchy could be identified with a nation that would escalate warfare to involve the entire world in a global conflict. His pacifist position drew criticism from enough readers to elicit an editorial in the November issue that accused Merton of favoring Hanoi in the war. Merton rebutted the charge, but there were many Church leaders who considered Merton a meddler who had overstepped his authority in speaking out.

*Mystics and Zen Masters* was published in May 1967 by Farrar, Straus, and Giroux. This was Merton's comprehensive treatment of Eastern philosophy presented in a context of how it is perceived in the West. He makes the point that the Church is not identified with any one culture, nor is it one with Western culture, and in fact was an Eastern religion before it came to the West. He viewed the Desert Fathers as the linkage between East and West. He had first been led to study the Desert Fathers when he read that Cardinal Newman had discovered them and attributed his conversion from the Anglican Church to them. In the 1960s, there was a renewed interest in the early Church Fathers in France to go back and study them. Merton picked up on this trend. He said there was a "Zen quality" in the work of the Desert Fathers.

In *Mystics and Zen Masters*, Merton discusses the thought of a number of mystics throughout history and around the world and pulls together ideas that he had been exploring for decades. He concludes that the Christian existentialist warns us against the perils of institutional complacency and acceptance of the *status quo* in Western religion. Something could be learned from the Buddhist principle of being realistic about dealing with problems without pretense. Merton once said that St. Therese, called the Little Flower, was a sort of Christian Sufi because of her personal relationship with God. Merton typically saw a seamless relationship between East and West in religious practice.

Merton thought that with his deteriorating health and seclusion at the hermitage, he should probably curtail his writing to enter more fully into a solitary life. Ironically, he soon found that extended hours alone were difficult for him. He wrote to several of his regular correspondents, including Naomi Burton, about his problem in adjusting to his new lifestyle. She responded immediately that she wondered if Merton's greatest paradox might be that he had fought for years to be given a place of solitude, and when he got it he didn't want it because he missed contact with other people.

Merton admitted to himself that he feared being without a support system. The Abbot, representing authority, caused him insecurity and anxiety, but he soon found that he felt even more alone and unprotected without his direct supervision. He admitted to his journal that he substituted papers and books for personal relationships. The monastery had removed his ready access to any friends, but he studiously sought and maintained real friendships with his correspondents who cared for him deeply. The only problem was they did not eliminate his loneliness.

In July Merton was frightened by a storm that almost took his life. A bolt of lightning struck him, like a wave of electricity coming out of his feet. He told some of his fellow monks later that he doubted it was a religious experience, but said he found it exciting to see the lights in the hills. This was obviously said "tongue in cheek." He thought it might please Dom James to know that living alone in the woods was a penance for him as well as a relief from the community life. He probably pretended the bravado reaction to avoid any risk to losing his hermitage privileges.

Merton was determined to adapt to both the dangers of the natural phenomena that occur at night as well as the safe, quiet time, of the early morning. From the first minutes of his day, Merton's regular companions at the hermitage were the wildlife, and he annotated in his journal their place in his life. Beginning at sunrise, he fed the birds on his porch, including juncos, cardinals, robins, mocking birds, titmice, and myrtle warblers. He counted fifteen pairs of birds that stayed close to the cottage. Even whitefooted mice would come up to eat the breadcrumbs he put out. He saw finches, humming birds, blue jays, ground hogs, frogs, a crow, and occasionally a bald eagle. He found it amusing to watch and learn the behavior patterns of the squirrels and other creatures he shared his life with. He once said that he did not need to know the structure of a squirrel's circulatory system to experience the uncomplicated joy of the little creatures playfully darting around the bushes seeking their next nut.

Merton loved to observe the wild animals. They were free. He was the prisoner in the sense of being under obedience, and he undoubtedly envied them their freedom to come and go without hindrance on their own instinct. He idealized their life activities, undertaken without supervision or evaluation. He remembered reading in the Old Testament that the animals and nature are our teachers. They reminded him of their Creator and His benevolence to them all. He sometimes wondered if God had not blessed the animal world by not giving them intellect. They were obviously so much more content than he was!

Merton began to suffer severe digestive problems beyond anything that could be caused by stress or poor diet. In June he went to Lexington to a Dr. Fortune for tests that were so rigorous he stayed overnight at the clinic. As it turned out, he found he had a severe staphylococcus infection in his intestines, caused by drinking the water at the hermitage that was not sanitary, and washing his dishes in it as well. The Abbot had delayed getting a well dug to put running water in the hermitage, and Merton had resorted to using rain water to minimize the water he had to carry up to the hermitage from the monastery. He would not ask another monk to carry water for him. And he certainly did not want to risk losing his privilege of living at the hermitage. He thought it particularly ironic that his zodiac sign was the water bearer.

Meanwhile, at the monastery changes were slowly but surely being incorporated into the community's daily life. Dom James decided to have a vote on whether the monks wanted to continue to shave their heads with the crown remaining. Merton was amused that Dom James would relegate such an unimportant detail to the democratic process. He found it typical of the Abbot to put forth some relatively insignificant issue that he could later point to as proof of his desire to give the monks a say in the changes to be made in the spirit of the Church's reforms.

The Abbot employed the old system of voting at the Chapter meeting. Each monk was given a black and white ball and was to place one of them in the receptacle according to his preference for or against the tonsure, or hair crown. Merton's protest of this was to place both the black and white balls given him in the container, thus not voting at all. The community voted to shave off the hair completely. Merton and Father Raymond both preferred the tonsure for reasons of tradition, but accepted the new plan.

Dom James also had the monks vote on whether or not to have Sunday Mass in concelebration, which is offering the Mass in groups rather than individually. Merton agreed with this idea because it made sense to him. The community by majority voted the same way. Merton participated in the Sunday concelebrations and found them fulfilling. He may have favored the group Mass because of his nervousness in ceremonies that brought attention to him personally.

In August Merton spent a week in the hospital for more tests. When he returned to the monastery, Dom James' private council met on August 17 and voted whether the monastery should have a hermit in its group. The vote was favorable, thanks to Dom James' personal support. Merton retired permanently to the hermitage on August 20.

Merton was no longer to participate in work around the monastery. In fact, with the mechanized system in full effect, less work was available for any of the community in planting, cultivating, and harvesting the crops they grew, principally potatoes, tobacco, and corn. Merton's only official role at this point would be a conference he would conduct every Sunday for those who would like to attend. Individual monks could request permission to go to the hermitage to visit him and seek his guidance, but Dom James did not encourage it.

Merton went to the clothing room and selected some of the oldest work clothes with patches for his wardrobe at the hermitage. These were the clothes he typically chose to wear when he went into town for his medical appointments. On trips outside the monastery, he displayed no indication of his religious affiliation. Some of the local people he met in Louisville, seeing his denim work clothes, considered him a "well read farmer," according to his friend, Jim Forest. In one of his recorded conferences, Merton explained that it was better to be hidden or invisible in town. With only a Roman collar signifying a religious identity, the monk would only get a "hello, Father." If a monk wore his monastic robes, "he might as well be led down the street by people blowing trumpets." The attention he would receive could well require the monk to do ten times more talking, answering questions from curious people, than if he wore ordinary clerical clothing. Merton did not mention that his personal choice of clothing, impersonating a poor farmer, eliminated all clues to his religious vocation.

In the fall, Merton had visits from Cardenal and Hildegard Goss-Mayr. Father Chrysogonus Waddell had returned from his assignment in Rome. He and Father Flavian Burns were allowed to visit Merton. Cardenal had established an experimental foundation at Solentiname on a Nicaraguan island and asked Merton again to join him. Merton, still feeling lonely, agreed to try to get permission to be released from his vow to go, while remaining canonically on the books at Gethsemani.

Merton drafted letters to Pope Paul VI, John XXIII's successor, and to Archbishop Paul Philippe. After three years, Merton still had no approval, but continued to hope he would eventually be released to take on this new role while at the same time continuing a solitary life. If it were never approved, then he told himself it was not God's will for him and he could accept it.

In Washington, disturbing events continued to unfold, each seeming to outdo the last in its horror. In November 1965, Merton learned that a pacifist had immolated himself in front of the Pentagon building. Tom Cornell of the Fellowship was indicted by a Federal court for burning his draft card. Then Roger Laporte, on the staff of *The Catholic Worker*, died after setting fire to himself at the United Nations building in New York City. Consumed with sorrow and anger, Merton prayed for deliverance of his country from these problems and for guidance to know what role he should play.

Merton sent telegrams to Dorothy Day at *The Catholic Worker* and Jim Forest at the Catholic Peace Fellowship declining further sponsorship of the fellowship and the peace movement. Immediately Merton was severely criticized by the peace movement's writers for withdrawing his support, which prompted him to revise his position. He then told the Fellowship leaders they could continue to use his name as a sponsor.

John Heidbrink of the Fellowship of Reconciliation wrote Merton a letter accusing him of leading a life of ease and evasion at the hermitage "quilted in mist." He said Merton should lead those he had led into the cloister back out to the world. Merton's reaction was that the pacifists were expecting him to act like a Scoutmaster. Merton felt they were guilty of exactly the same trait they accused him of – self-complacency. Merton agreed with the movement's ideals, but not all of its particular implementations. He prayed for "a more real faith."

Merton decided to limit his support of the peace movement to prayers and fasting as an offering to God. He began putting material together for his book, *Conjectures of a Guilty Bystander*, which was published by Doubleday in 1968. Merton was an existentialist, but did not subscribe to the participative aspect of that philosophy. He preferred to work from the sidelines, lifting up the corners of the rug to expose the things that he believed needed cleaning up. He believed that someone else should do the active part of the job.

Meanwhile, Dan Berrigan was sent to Europe by his superiors. Merton believed that this might have occurred to spare him from an outcome that would be dangerous for him as well as the Church.

A few years earlier, Merton had written the lyrics for eight freedom songs for Robert L. Williams, a black singer, to set to music. It was later discovered that Alexander Peloquin, the composer, used Merton's songs in a symphony concert. Williams had gone to Ireland to appear in a show. When he returned, he discovered the purpose of the songs had been diverted. Merton was criticized by Williams for allowing his work that had been written in sympathy for blacks to be exploited in a commercial enterprise. Since Merton had not safeguarded their use, he came to regret his failure to track the project.

By the end of 1965, Merton had chronic dysentery. The use of the outside latrine was becoming a major problem for him. Dom James made no effort to provide habitable conditions for the hermitage. Merton wondered if this could have been a test of his determination to live away from the monastery, or possibly a punishment for trying to get transferred to another Order. Merton called his little wood outhouse "the jakes," a term he learned in England. It often had gnats that bothered him. Much worse, there was a black snake that often occupied it and worried Merton. He had to yell before he entered to chase it away. He usually addressed the snake with profanity, he admitted, but never thought of killing it. He called it "you bastard." Sometimes the young kingsnake positioned itself on top of the door to get to the mice that nested just under the roof.

Merton's medical condition was not convenient for others at the monastery either. Those who drove into Louisville soon tired of including him in their errands to take him for medical appointments and pick him up for his return to the monastery. One morning he was three minutes late getting to the gate, and the driver had left him. Merton said later that he mainly was disappointed to miss getting lunch in Louisville. He wasn't well enough to prepare proper meals. He had no stove, only a hot plate, and probably did not know how to cook. No one helped him to organize his menus or food selection. Naomi Burton sometimes mailed him packages of Rice-a-roni, one of his favorite instant dishes, or instant Lipton soup. Still, he preferred his solitude to the community meals he could have had.

Not everyone at that time held Merton in low esteem. In the December 1965-January 1966 edition of *The Critic* magazine, Merton's picture appeared on the cover in a composite of "the 15 most important Catholics in the U.S.A." Others in the group included Cardinal Cushing, Robert and Jacqueline Kennedy, Dorothy Day, Richard Daley, Sister Mary Luke, and William Buckley. Notably missing was Bishop Fulton Sheen, who was later elevated to Archbishop.

In January 1966, Dom James invited Bishop Sheen to give a retreat at Gethsemani. Sheen had spoken at the centennial dedication there sixteen years earlier. Now that he was a hermit, Merton was not expected to participate in the retreat, so he invited Sheen up to see the hermitage. It was Dom James' idea, but one he totally agreed with. Merton's respect for the Bishop had increased over the years, and he enjoyed seeing him. Over time they had developed similar sentiments about the Vietnam war, the problems of racism in the U.S., and had even formed a common opinion about the policies of Cardinal Spellman in New York.

The community in general was not impressed by the Abbot's choice of a speaker with such common appeal. Sheen's lifestyle was hardly consistent with the Trappist concept: he drove a new car, maintained an upper-class home in Washington, DC, and dined in good restaurants with celebrities who sought his counsel and with wealthy donors who contributed to his foreign mission program. First he had broadcast on some 300 NBC network stations with a popular weekly radio program, "The Catholic Hour," for ten years. Then he added the TV weekly program, "Life is Worth Living," beginning in 1956, that was carried by more than 100 stations and won an Emmy. He had a syndicated newspaper column and published over 60 books. He was even more prolific than Merton!

The monks probably reacted negatively to Sheen because they considered themselves at a spiritual level above that to which his talks and publications were pitched. Sheen was known for being theatrical, amusing and dramatic in his presentations. Celebrities attributed their conversion to Catholicism to his counsel, including Fritz Kreisler, the noted violinist, Louis Boudain, a Communist leader, as well as the writer Clare Boothe Luce. The monks were as withdrawn as Sheen was out front. The fact that he held doctorate degrees and served as a delegate to the Second Vatican Council would not be seen as credentials for a monastic retreat master.

In January 1966, Merton was given his own local publicity. The monastery gave the Louisville Courier-Journal newspaper its permission to publish a story on Merton. This corrected rumors that he had left the

monastery and also publicized the fact that he would no longer be making statements on public issues. Merton himself contributed material
for the story, which was published on January 23.

By mid-March, two unknown and unannounced visitors appeared
at the hermitage, having no difficulty in finding it on their own. He
thought it might be the result of an article about him in *Jubilee*, but it
could have been from one of the many papers that re-ran the Louisville
paper's article. Merton said it was a bad sign that they had found him so
easily, and he planned to do something about it soon. He was concerned
about strangers coming to see him and feared their intentions now that
his reputation had become controversial.

From 1966 to early 1968, Merton had a rather brief exchange of
correspondence with Rosemary Ruether, a young liberal theologian
and university professor in Washington, DC. Merton disagreed with
her questioning of the value of monasticism in the modern world. He
defended her criticism of his lifestyle, which she saw as irrelevant. In
spite of their philosophical differences, they had a mutual respect for
each other. Merton gave her some calligraphies he had placed with an
art dealer in Washington so that she could include them in an auction
she was to hold for charity. The auction never actually occurred, so after
Merton's death she had them sold and donated the proceeds to the Berrigan Defense Fund. Dan and Philip Berrigan were defending themselves
against the U. S. Government's attempt to indict them for conspiracy.
Knowing Merton's sympathy for the Berrigan brothers' work in civil
rights, she believed Merton would have agreed with her decision.

Merton had also been carrying on a correspondence over the past
several years with a Sufi scholar, Aziz Ch. Abdul, a Muslim who lived
in Karachi, Pakistan. Aziz initiated the correspondence through a
mutual friend, Louis Massignon, in 1960. Aziz had been impressed
with Merton's *Ascent to Truth* and wanted to learn more about Western
monasticism. In 1961 Merton had written to him about his belief that
the world needs the people of the Third World countries to offset the
power battle of the two great Western nations, the U.S. and Russia,
threatening to destroy each other with nuclear weapons.

Aziz asked Merton how he spent his time in the hermitage. In January
1966, Merton replied that his life consisted more of prayer and meditation than anything else and described his daily schedule. He said that
he went to bed at night at about 7:30 p.m. and rose about 2:30 a.m.
He had coffee or tea and fruit or honey for breakfast before sunrise,

then after house maintenance work, went down to the monastery to say Mass, have his main meal, and pick up his mail. He would return immediately to the hermitage, carrying his gallon jug refilled with water and his dilapidated briefcase with the day's packages and letters from the mail room. He would not speak with anybody except the Abbot or another superior, about once a week, and then only on business. His supper at the hermitage consisted of a sandwich, tea, or soup that he prepared himself. He said he chose these so there would not be many dishes to wash. Not having potable water at the hermitage, he carried water for dishes as well as for drinking. Merton admitted he was not much of a cook. Dom James wisely directed that he have a daily hot meal at the refectory to safeguard his health. He told Abdul that his prayer and meditation were much like his "fana," putting himself in the presence of God and offering praise arising out of the center of Nothing and Silence, recognizing himself as an obstacle. He said he appreciated the tradition of Sufism. He promised to unite himself with his friend during the month of Ramadan and remember him on the Night of Destiny.

Merton was wearing dermal gloves while he typed, and he was suffering from a nagging pain in his back. His right hand grew numb when he wrote more than a few lines. He discovered that he now had a small tumor in his stomach, and it seemed to be growing. At Merton's request, Father Eudes looked at it and told him he didn't think it could be a malignancy. Merton's anxiety about his deteriorating health could well have reminded him of his mother's terminal stomach cancer and caused him to fear a similar outcome.

In March Merton had X-rays taken at St. Joseph's Infirmary for his back pain. He had been given what he termed "a traction outfit" in the fall of 1965, which he used at the hermitage as he needed it. The problem was diagnosed as a herniated cervical disc. The indicated treatment was removal of the disc, which should be accomplished before the sensory symptoms and signs became more severe and longlasting, even permanent. A bone graft from his hip would be necessary to stabilize the cervical spine. Sitting for extended periods typically caused problems with this condition. Sometimes his hand lost feeling, or he would have pain in his shoulder and down his arm. The operation was scheduled for March 24, 1966.

Merton was frightened and had premonitions that he would not survive the surgery. He said he wondered if he was saying good-bye as

Bernard Fox, Dom James' brother, drove him to Louisville on the day before. On March 25, after a day's delay, Dr. Thomas M. Marshall, a neurosurgeon, performed the anterior cervical fusion to correct the cervical spondylosis, using a graft from his left ilium. In layman's language, there was a separation in his upper spinal column at the base of his neck caused by a deteriorated disc that was to be closed by a graft of cartilage taken from his hip. Spine damage of this type can result from trauma, infections, tumors, or arthritis. The matchstick-size pieces of bone grafts are placed along the sides of the vertebrae, like an interior brace to hold the reconstructed area together, and form a fusion knitting the vertebrae together in the healing process.

Merton's health problems were interfering with the work he felt driven to accomplish. He began to panic that his life was now threatened when he knew he had much more work to do.

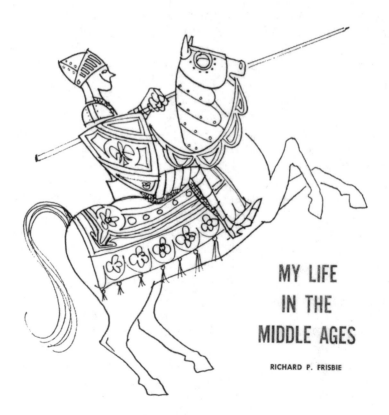

MY LIFE
IN THE
MIDDLE AGES

RICHARD P. FRISBIE

A number of periodicals in the 1960s published Merton's articles. Merton later incorporated some of his articles into larger works. The artwork in these articles is apparently Merton's. "Hagia Sophia," **Ramparts**, Vol. 1, No. 5, March 1963, p. 65. "Herakleitos the Obscure, **Jubilee**, Vol. 8,No. 5, September 1960, pp. 25-26. "Is the World a Problem?", **Commonweal**, Vol. LXXXIV, No. 11, June 3, 1966, cover page. "The English Mystics," **Jubilee**, Vol. 9 No. 5, September 1961, p. 37. "My Life in the Middle Ages," **U.S. Catholic**, Vol. XXXI, No. 3, July 1965, pp. 31-33. "Zen: Sense and Sensibility," **America**, Vol. 108, No. 21, May 25, 1963, p. 754.

Volume LXXXIV No. 11     June 3, 1966     50 cents

# IS THE WORLD
# A PROBLEM?

### *Ambiguities in the secular*

### *Thomas Merton*

HAGIA SOPHIA

*by*

*Thomas Merton*

# BOOK THREE

Book Three is an impressionistic version of Merton's diary, based on an in-depth study of all published material, using his own words and statements of fact to the maximum within an abridged format.

"Spiritual nakedness ... strips life down to the root where life and death are equal ... . The point where you become free not to kill, not to exploit, not to destroy, not to compete, because you are no longer afraid of death or the devil or poverty or failure. If you discover this nakedness, you'd better keep it private ... . Society continues to do you the service of keeping you in disguises, not for your comfort, but for its own ... .

The final metaphysical stripping goes too far, unless you happen to be in Auschwitz" (p. 5).

*Love and Living*

4. Drawing by Thomas Merton. Used with permission of the Merton Legacy Trust and the Thomas Merton Center at Bellarmine University.

# Chapter 26

Merton began to feel his age. He was no longer young, and he was not well.

He had been chopping a lot of wood lately—it was a cold spring—and his back wasn't up to it. Sitting for so many hours a day didn't help matters either, at his desk and in the chapel.

The doctors in Louisville said he had a deteriorated disc in his spinal column, and surgery would be required to replace it.

The night before the operation, two of the Brothers drove him into town to St. Joseph's Infirmary. There was a driving rain on the ride into Louisville. He surrendered himself reluctantly to the hospital staff in a state of major annoyance. He wondered if this might be the end of his life, and he wasn't nearly ready to go yet. At the least it would be a major loss of time, hindering him from getting more work out to his publishers. He tried to accept this as God's will for him.

> The surgery was long but went well, the Doctors tell me. When I woke up, a couple of friendly nurses who knew my identity seemed willing to assist me, although personally indifferent to my feelings. I was uncomfortable, in pain, and unhappy at the lack of privacy, even though I had a room to myself. I hated being on display when they were bathing, bandaging, and massaging my sore body. They put hot compresses to my left hip where the incision was made to remove the cartilage for the disc. It was a miserable experience. I tried repeatedly to persuade the attendant to postpone the compresses while I finished my meditation, but the nurses didn't fall for my ruse. The only consolation was my new Eckhart book.

On March 31, six days after the operation, a different nurse's assistant appeared and told me she had been assigned full time to care for my needs. She was young, friendly, and very pretty, with large gray eyes and fair skin. Her dark hair was obviously fairly long from the bulge in her cap.

She told me that she would like to talk about my writing. She had read *The Sign of Jonas* and liked most of it, she said. What did I think of the new Church liturgy? Had I ever seen *Mad Magazine* and did I like the "Peanuts" comic strip?

I thought, "Oh, no, what penance—trapped in this bed with a nurse who will tell me about my books and has no idea what she is talking about. She thinks my books and *Mad Magazine* are all more or less just something to read."

I thought she must be Irish, but then again, she looked like she might be a Jewish girl, too. Then I realized—she looked a lot like the girl I had dreamed of, Proverb, and the sketch I had made years ago at Bellarmine, with Christ unveiling her solemn, beautiful face. I didn't know if this was an incredible coincidence or if I was still affected by heavy sedation.

I knew it would be useless to try to tune her out and just enjoy her attentiveness. I dreaded the conversation that would be inevitable, about subjects she probably would ask me to explain in one or two statements. I didn't feel like talking to anyone. Well, at least I had brought some good books and my breviary of prayers to read, and I could always pretend to be too immersed in them to talk with her.

I was surprised she didn't say anything more about my writing that day. In fact, she was cheerful in helping me to deal with my painful body. She didn't comment on the sad state of my rough skin and middle-aged shape.

I asked her what her name was.

"Margie."

I thought to myself, what a simple unimaginative name.

"You don't have to call me Father. You can just make it "Tom." The name on my chart is Latin for my monastery name, which in English is Father Louis.

She smiled a knowing smile, like she could read me through my eyes.

The next few days passed easily. Margie was there from breakfast to mid-afternoon. She started each day bringing me the morning Louisville paper with the "Peanuts" strip to amuse me. For me this was such a unique event that I found it very flattering as well as enjoyable. Eventually she asked me about what I was working on before I came to the hospital.

I found myself freely beginning to tell her about my current project, about my concerns with the world situation, and even my frustrations about trying to write material that would really make a difference.

I couldn't believe I was telling her my inmost hopes and personal feelings without even knowing her. It was so easy. She really seemed interested in what I had to say. It was a real surprise.

Margie was a much more attractive person than I had first noticed. I asked her to tell me about herself, and I listened attentively as she opened up to me.

She was Catholic and had first thought of becoming a nun before she decided instead to be a nurse. She now considered nursing her vocation. She was so young--probably only about 20. I didn't ask because I didn't want to talk about the 30 or so year difference in our ages.

Palm Sunday weekend came. Margie did not appear. I went for a short walk in the hospital garden, since Margie had brought my ambulatory ability back in record time. There was a Lourdes grotto, and I told myself this would bring me back to a contemplative state of mind, but it didn't. I noted the nurses' dormitory was adjacent to the garden. I wondered which window was Margie's. I couldn't stop wondering what had happened to her. I was hoping she was in her room and would see me from her window and come out to the grotto. I had known her now for all of three days and worried about ever seeing her again. Maybe she had been reassigned. I didn't dare ask anyone, so returned to the refuge of my reading. Solitude for once held no appeal for me, and the days were long.

On Monday morning she reappeared at the foot of my bed. She had had a cold, she said. I wasn't sure that was really the whole story. She brought me the comics section from Sunday's paper, and we laughed together about the "Peanuts" strip. I was happier to see it than any of the literary gifts I had received from old friends.

The next day I almost bumped into her in the corridor outside my room. I was happy to be up and around now, but the down side was I knew I would be leaving St. Joseph's Infirmary soon. The head nurse, Margie's instructor, saw her speaking to me in the hall, and I soon overheard her scolding Margie.

"He's a monk, and he's supposed to be silent," she pontificated in a voice I feared others could overhear. The instructor told Margie that she noted she had spent extra time visiting my room, bringing me extra sandwiches and reading material that she knew I otherwise would never see. Margie was submissive and attributed it all to her inexperience. I was amused but also a bit sorry she had had to be subjected to all that.

I loaned her my manuscript of a Preface for the Japanese edition of *Thoughts in Solitude*. I asked her to read it in order to better understand what I meant by solitude and why I find it so appealing. She seemed genuinely interested in giving me her reaction.

Wednesday was Margie's day off. I found it almost impossible to concentrate on Eckhart or anything else. I spent the day reasoning with myself about the concept of love. That afternoon I went for another walk to the grotto, hoping to see Margie. She had told me she saw me from her dorm window the last time I was there, and hoped she would see me again so she could come out and we could spend some private time together. I wanted her to help me go across the street to the drug-store to buy some earplugs so I could sleep better. She didn't come, so I crossed the street alone.

On Wednesday night Margie didn't disappoint me. She had promised me a visit before she left for her Easter vacation. For the first time I saw her without the white uniform. She was wearing a bright red dress, her beautiful black hair falling to her shoulders. She was smiling, but it was not genuine. I asked her what was bothering her.

She said, "Nothing," but that was clearly a lie. I insisted on hearing about it.

"I just came to say good-bye. You'll be released while I'm gone. So you can go back to your monastery and finish your book," she added with some bravado.

"Will you write your address on my notebook here so I can send you more manuscripts to read?"

"Sure." She picked up my pen and notebook quickly without hesitation.

We were both silent for a minute.

"Will I see you again? Maybe I could come out to the monastery on a Sunday, like you said some people do."

"That would be impossible," I responded rapidly.

She reached into her large black shoulder bag and pulled out the manuscript I had loaned her. "I want to give you back your paper. I showed it to a girlfriend in the dorm to get more ideas for you."

She hesitated for a minute, then added, "I didn't really like it. Too much solitude in it! I guess it's not the way I see the idea of worship. I mean, why be alone? If you really like solitude so much, you'll probably never need friendship." She looked at me for a signal, but I couldn't react.

"Well, it's time to go. I'm flying out to Chicago to see my fiancé." She was clearly troubled. She put on her white raincoat, tied the sash tightly at her waist, and placed her purse strap on her shoulder.

She searched for a reaction. I couldn't speak.

"Good-bye, Tom."

"Take care, Margie." This was the first time I had called her by her first name.

I lay there helpless in the silence, and there was no peace. I could only concentrate on the sound of the hard rain against my hospital window. I worried about the plane taking off in such a downpour. I tried to listen for the sound, since the Louisville airport was not far from the hospital, but I could only imagine hearing it take off. Like trying to sleep, I just gave it up. I knew my feelings for Margie were serious. I held the notebook she had written her address on and studied her handwriting. It was so clear and simple, like a child's writing. I wondered what this would all mean in my life.

I was left alone for the next two days, but I could not enjoy the solitude. I had to start writing as soon as I collected my thoughts.

"Margie, this is just a note to say I really am not without need for friendship, although, of course, I do cherish solitude. If you still feel inclined to continue our friendship, you can write to me in privacy. Just mark the envelope, "Conscience Matter," and no one will open it before I get it." I sealed the note in an envelope and gave it to the nurse's aide who was assigned to replace Margie.

"Just a little thank-you note, since I didn't get a chance to thank her personally before she left," I told the substitute attendant as though it were true. She promised to deliver it for me the following week. I decided with amusement that this wasn't really a lie because I certainly had failed to say how much I appreciated the way she had cared for me.

Outgoing mail at the monastery was almost never screened anymore. With all the letters I was sending out every day, who would notice any one of them. Women and men both wrote to me about their problems or their writing and asked for my guidance. What a perfect cover-up!

If anyone found out, they would just be jealous like they are every time one of my books gets released and they have to hear me read it to them in the refectory. I don't care what they think. As they say, it's a conscience matter.

On Saturday, when the two Brothers arrived to drive me back to the monastery, Margie's head nurse wheeled me down to the hospital entrance. She had little to say on the chair ride, except to ask me if everything had been satisfactory on her floor. I wondered if she was being sarcastic. I knew she watched the student nurses like a hawk. She handed my books and suitcase to one of the Brothers abruptly, like a hot plate, I noticed.

On the long ride back to Gethsemani I thought of nothing but Margie, but tried to lecture myself to face reality and put the experience behind me. I spent Saturday night in the monastery's infirmary and tried to adjust to being back while I prayed the Easter liturgy.

The next day I went up to the hermitage for a visit, to try to regain my strength as well as my solitude, since I would still be confined to the infirmary for a while to finish my recovery. I was suffering intense sweating during the night and pain from the incision in my hip. For the remainder of the week I concerned myself with readjusting to my old daily schedule, telling myself I will have a new friend to correspond with occasionally and send manuscripts to for review. I'll send her *Disputed Questions* and *The New Man*, I noted in my work papers.

I had stacks of mail and other material waiting for me, but my activities no longer interested me. My entire thought process was absorbed in the moment, principally through some excruciating pain. Everything else was literally out of focus.

Ten days after I returned to the monastery, it was a perfect spring day, textbook, you might say. I noted with some irony that this was the day the church steeple was being permanently removed. It was sad seeing it dismantled, its lead plates covering the old lumber that had had its day. It was a symbol, though, that would now be gone and really represented for many of us the identity of the place. You could see it rising above the trees in the distance, and know you were almost at the monastery.

It was a beacon for me when I first arrived for the retreat. Still, the overall appearance of the abbey without it is much less forbidding. It takes on a strange charm unlike any other place.

I walked over to the post office to pick up my mail. There was a letter from Margie! Her careful penmanship gave me a lift that no other mail ever had. There were four pages, two with her drawings of Peanuts characters and two pages of reflections on the good times we had had together. It was so like her. She said she missed me, but said she accepted the fact that she would not see me again. The rest of her letter was a quote from *Jonas*. It gave me chills to read my own words given back to me in the context of a woman's feelings for me. She wrote of my own experience, trying to touch another with "the deep fire" in one's heart, only to discover the beauty of it could never belong to me.

Immediately I walked back to the hermitage and typed a note to her. I marked the envelope "Conscience Matter" and walked quickly back to the monastery to drop it in the outgoing box before the next mail pick-up.

Three days later, on Friday, April 22, I couldn't wait any longer for Margie's reply. I had to know whether she cared for me as she did in the hospital, now that she had gone to Chicago to see her fiancé. I wanted to hear the sound of her voice since I couldn't see her.

I could call her. The phones around the monastery were hooked up to a switchboard operated by the monks. But then I remembered: the phone in the cheese factory wasn't on the switchboard. There was a direct phone line into Louisville to handle monastery business. Perfect! I walked down to the farm, to the Steel Building, to the office with the phone, and called her. My hand was shaking as I dialed the number. I knew I was making decisions about my life but couldn't stop now to think about it.

She was not there. Of course, she was on her shift. Tomorrow I'll call earlier, and ask to see her when I come into town for my check-up. I put a call through to Jim Wygal and had better luck. Jim agreed to meet me at the doctor's office after my check-up and have lunch. I even persuaded him to drive me back to the monastery afterwards. He was very upset and depressed because he had had a fire at his house recently. He had lost almost everything. He was having a problem accepting this, just like anyone else would. Being a psychologist didn't seem to make it any easier. I guess he thought taking time out with me would be a diversion.

I spent the remainder of the day emotionally on hold, checking my mail, worrying that maybe her reply was intercepted by the Abbot or misplaced in the rest of the mail at the monastery, as sometimes happened.

On Saturday morning I remembered the Steel Building would be closed, so I wouldn't be able to use the phone. Then I checked in the cellarer's office since it was almost lunchtime. The cellarer had not left yet and asked me what I needed. I told him I was looking for a phone with a line to Louisville so I could call my doctor. He said his phone was direct, and it was no problem. As he reached the door, though, he said he had to lock me in his office while he was gone. I was taken aback, but was ready to pay the price for the use of a private phone. I called the dormitory number and waited expectantly. Again she was not there. I refused to be discouraged. Then I had her paged in the hospital cafeteria. Success! Hearing her speak to me was worth all my effort.

"I have to come into town on Tuesday for a check-up with the Doc. Do you think you could meet me? It's at his office—the Med Arts Building at 10:30."

She immediately agreed. I told her we'd go for lunch at Cunningham's Restaurant with my friend, Jim Wygal, for a chaperone. I said that I couldn't wait to see her again, but that I also wanted to say up front that I had to be true to my calling. I explained I wanted to keep our relationship on a spiritual level. She seemed to agree with everything I said.

What harm could it do to see Margie with this understanding? As soon as I had this thought I knew it was a rationalization. My physical self was making no headway in convincing my inner self of my true intentions.

I began to wonder what was happening to me. She was the most desirable woman I had ever seen. The conflict and anxiety of my feelings for Margie left me sleepless. After several nights, I took a sleeping pill and Brother Camillus, the infirmarian, gave me some old bourbon that had been in his closet since Dom Edmund was Abbot. I slept almost nine hours and awoke feeling positive about everything. The resonance between Margie and me is a sign of truth, and I will trust God to bring me through it all right.

The restaurant I selected was walking distance from the hospital, so Margie could get back for her next shift. I had been there several times before with Dr. Wygal. They had good food, but that wasn't the reason I chose it. To the rear there was a section of booths with high, solid wood panel dividers that afforded maximum privacy. In fact, you couldn't see over the tops from one booth to the next unless you were standing or walking down the aisle between the two rows. Behind the booths there was a pay phone on the wall and even a rear door that opened on the parking lot. It was ideal.

It was raining when the Brothers drove me into Louisville, and I hoped the weather would clear by lunchtime. I told the Brothers not to wait for me, because the doctor would drive me back. They were obviously happy to be relieved of any further demands on them from me.

The doctor said I was healing at a normal rate. I used the medical building's men's room to wash up and check on my appearance. Jim Wygal was waiting for me in the hallway when I came out. I told him about my check-up and then mentioned that Margie, my nurse, was joining them for lunch. Jim was speechless, which is pretty unusual for him. Then he began to get angry. Before he could say anything, I started down the hall to the entrance where I had arranged for Margie to meet us.

She was just coming around the corner. I felt awkward. I didn't dare shake her hand or make any other physical gesture. She smiled. I told her my check-up was routine and introduced her to Jim. He mumbled a greeting, then led us to his car. It was a new two-door black Chevy Impala. I sat up front with Jim, which was easier for me, and Margie climbed into the back. By this time the sun had come out and given us its blessing with a beautiful day.

Margie had seen Jim Wygal around the hospital and knew of his good reputation. He was a local man who had grown up in the medical community and enjoyed a sizeable practice, including nuns and priests who were having problems adjusting to religious life in the 60's. He was middle-aged, quick-witted, and handsome. He talked fast to keep me from getting the best of him, I thought. I liked him for his honesty, but frankly I became impatient with what I considered his narrow view of the universe. He could be brutally frank. He came across to me as a professional with a single point of view.

Since Jim and I had been to Cunningham's before, we walked directly to the booths in the back. Margie was taking a quick look at all the authentic equestrian décor from years of Kentucky Derby races, as we cut through the main dining room. It was certainly an improvement over the exterior of the place, with its obvious living quarters above the little restaurant. The sign was a bit dated, too, the long thin type with the name spelled out vertically, and no lights on it.

I chose the booth closest to the back door. Jim and I sat together on one side of the black naugahide booth. Margie sat across from me, with her usual big smile. I thought of the day in the hospital when I caught the fragrance of her perfume, now returned to my consciousness. I found myself comparing her face to the one I had sketched years ago in Olean and given to a nun at St. Bonaventure's. Margie had the high intelligent forehead, the wide, set-apart piercing eyes, the delicate facial structure pointing down to her little-girl chin. I had to get a photograph of her so I could compare each detail to insure I was not losing my mind.

Jim was edgy and preoccupied and made no effort to conceal his mood. He had seen Margie around the hospital, but had not met her. He acknowledged her presence with little animation.

"Jim, I hope you don't mind if we give you the check today—I didn't pick up any money before I came into town today."

"What's new, Tom? I knew to come prepared."

Margie giggled rather than display any embarrassment at this exchange.

Margie saw my nervousness and asked for more details about how my back and leg were healing. That being a familiar subject for us to discuss, I relaxed a bit. She suggested we play something on the jukebox. I told her to pick something and handed her some change out of my pocket.

I was pleased she selected a Joan Baez song, "Diamonds and Rust."

She smiled when she saw that I liked her choice. I wasn't nervous anymore.

"How do you know this song? They don't play popular music at the monastery, do they?"

"Jim plays it sometimes when we come here for lunch. Right, Jim?"

Jim nodded in agreement but was obviously distracted. He waited impatiently to leave the restaurant after our lunch. Then he drove Margie back to the hospital and headed for the highway to return me to Gethsemani.

Back at the monastery, in my hermitage, I threw myself on my cot and stared at the ceiling. But I didn't see it. I saw Margie's beautiful face framed by her soft black hair approaching her small shoulders, and those piercing gray eyes that looked right through me. I hadn't realized I was living in a black and white world until now, when it became a spectrum of color that was changing my life forever.

I began to feel lonely at the hermitage. Solitude was losing its appeal. I wondered if I had wanted to be a hermit only because I had not met Margie yet.

I went for a walk in the woods. It always helped me to feel better when I was upset. It was more beautiful than I had ever noticed. I was still experiencing numbness in my left leg from the incision in my hip. I was determined to rid myself of my body's problems. I'll write a poem for Margie.

We began a pattern of letters and calls, but it seemed we were both growing more miserable. Trying to carry on my full schedule of monastic duties and publishing activities was almost impossible. I no longer enjoyed answering letters from my old friends.

I wondered if my feelings were written all over me. I believed I was in love. This is what it had to be. This was no flirtation or even infatuation. This is what the love songs were all about, what all the writers in the world had been talking about when they described the love of two people. For me it was above and beyond all that. It was beautiful, not dirty, and beauty belongs to God, I told myself.

Soon the Abbot would be leaving for one of his long trips, and I would be more comfortable about getting mail out of here and using the telephone. Everybody takes it a little easier when Dom James is away. And there's less reporting on others without the Abbot around to tell.

Nine days after our lunch, I had a visit from Laughlin and a poet from Chile, Nicanor Parra, whose poetry I would be translating into English. I suggested we make a picnic at Bernheim Forest. It is a beautiful arboretum and research facility, with a nature center, hiking trails, and picnic tables overlooking small lakes. We enjoyed the drive over to Clermont, near Bardstown, and the picnic grounds. After our lunch, there was a shower so we returned to Laughlin's rented car. I asked him for some change to make a call at a pay phone. We drove through rural Kentucky until we finally found a phone. I called Margie, leaving Laughlin to wonder about her significance to me.

"Hi, are you free today?" It was a Thursday and Margie was off duty. I asked Laughlin to drive to St. Joseph's Infirmary to add a friend to our group. He had little choice since I had already committed us, and he was probably a bit curious, too. I walked around the hospital entrance and parking area for Lourdes Hall looking for Margie, hoping no one would recognize me from my recent stay there. As disreputable as I looked, it was not a problem. She had quickly dressed up for the occasion, I noticed, as she hurried over to join me near the dorm entrance. By then it was five o'clock.

I introduced Margie to Laughlin and Parra as a very special friend of mine, but not in any particular context. I hadn't prepared them for what kind of friend of mine we would be picking up. Laughlin probably figured Margie would either be a religious or literary associate, since all of my companions fitted into one of those two categories. Margie looked more like an overgrown child, so hadn't lived long enough yet to bear any similarity to my friends. Laughlin looked at Margie, then looked at me in amazement. Parra and I only knew each other through our respective writing, so he didn't show any reaction to Margie.

I suggested we all go to the airport for dinner at the Luau Room. It was considered a place with little appeal to locals, since it was furnished as a pseudo-tropical lounge, so I thought we would probably not be recognized there. My two visitors agreed it would be appropriate under the circumstances.

I was still dressed in my working overalls, and I hadn't shaved that day. Laughlin probably wondered if I would even be seated in such a nice restaurant. Naturally my two associates were correctly dressed in suits. It was Derby time, the week of the annual Kentucky Derby, and the restaurant was full of out of town visitors who had flown in, probably in private corporate planes, for the race. Laughlin reminded me that if we had been in Manhattan, our group would not have been admitted because of the way I looked. Happy for the occasion as well as a good dinner, I didn't even care if I wasn't presentable.

She was wearing a beautiful brown dress and looked feminine, with her hair free flowing, but not sexy. She looked too much like a little girl for that, and she was vivacious and displayed a quick wit. She charmed all of us in record time.

I had brought my camera and asked Margie if I could take a few pictures. She seemed really surprised, and I started preparations to shoot her close up before she could refuse. I couldn't wait to get these pictures and try to figure out who this girl really was and why she had dropped into my life.

When I got back to the hermitage, I composed a poem I called "Louisville Airport, May 5, 1966."

Laughlin was silent for the entire ride back to the monastery from Louisville, once we dropped Margie off, since Parra was with us. The next morning Laughlin came out to the hermitage alone to get an accounting of my behavior.

"Tom, what in Heaven's name are you doing with that nurse? Have you lost all your good sense? I can't believe what I see, and I certainly can't believe you would use me like that to escort you so you could see the girl.

"Jay, Margie's just a really sweet young girl and a great nurse who cared for me and helped me recover from a difficult surgery. I really feel affectionate toward her for all her kindness to me."

"Merton, I am not a fool. Tell it to the Marines."

"OK, Jay, my feelings are a little more than fatherly. But it's really a platonic relationship. She's a very nice girl, and I've grown attached to her. I'm keeping all the laws and proprieties as far as the strict obligations go. Anyway, the experience has opened up a whole new avenue of thought for me. I've been writing poetry again, and expressing feelings that are new to me. I want you to take a look at it."

"Well, OK, I'd like to read the poetry, but not if it means driving you over to see Margie again. That's too high a price, my friend."

"Actually, Jay, I was thinking of passing all the poems about Margie to you for safekeeping. If the management here ever gets wind of this, they're liable to use them to start a bonfire."

"Sure, Tom, that doesn't offend my conscience."

"How about we set up a code. We'll call it the 'Menendez file,' for your chef at the Alta ski lodge you like so much. I'll send along copies of each piece and mark it for the Menendez file. No publishing rights, now, for you. If you're lucky, that will probably come later. Maybe after I die, for example."

"Merton, you're the limit. I'll take the deal, but only if you promise me you won't disgrace yourself. I'm your friend, I know you, and, believe me, you don't need this girl. You're a monk (remember that?) and besides, one of my best writers. How am I gonna sell your books if you get involved with a girl?"

I hated what Laughlin was saying, but I had to admit that he was realistic. And he really was my friend. And he really wanted to sell books, I also reminded myself.

Two days later I was hosting a get-together I had previously arranged: a picnic with some "regulars" from Louisville, Jack Ford and his wife, Gladys, and Father John. Dom James had given me permission to have my friends out for the day. This was set up before I even dreamed of seeing Margie on Thursday when Laughlin came. So I decided to take advantage of this occasion too, to include her. I called her and luckily she was free to come. Or else she just cancelled everything else she had planned—she didn't say.

It was Derby Day, the biggest day of the year in Louisville, which the whole city celebrated on the first Saturday of May. For the first time, it would be a special day for me, too. I had never seen a Derby race in person or on television, but even at Gethsemani we felt the excitement of the event, called the Run for the Roses, at Churchill Downs, on that day. It's kind of like a hometown Fourth of July, with balloons and even fireworks after dark.

With my expert knowledge of the woods around the monastery, I knew instantly where we could have our picnic with no one wandering around, unless there was a fire out there. I could enjoy some good food, and we could follow the race on a portable radio I borrowed from the office.

Margie did not have a car, or even drive, just like me, so I asked Jack if he and his wife could pick her up at the hospital and bring her along. They also brought Father John and all the refreshments. All through the meal, I tried to sit there and pretend to be interested in my old friends, but could only wonder what I had now got myself into.

I didn't feel like we'd done anything wrong. We had a beautiful friendship going. We didn't know where it would lead us, but we could put this in the hands of God for now, I thought, until things looked clearer to us. Well, priests were leaving the Church all the time these days and getting married, and they didn't have to give up their faith. Some say it's only a matter of time till Rome allows priests to marry. The logic is, why wait for the inevitable approval? Renounce the vows, get on with your life, and it will all work out eventually with the Church. After all, haven't they relaxed everything else lately?

On the other hand, I knew that I was a man who had always wanted to live alone. I didn't know if I could live with anyone else all the time and be a decent companion.

I looked at myself. I wasn't wearing monastery robes anymore. I had jeans and a regular shirt on, and a cocky tilt to my belt. Did I really feel like a monk?

I asked the group to allow me to snap some unposed pictures. After a few shots, mostly of Margie, I began to feel the discomfort in the group.

Father John was clearly embarrassed. Luckily it was time for the Derby. Jack turned the volume up on the portable radio so we could hear the race. Then the group left with Margie in tow, and I managed to avoid any unwelcome comments.

What I did not avoid was the realistic questions that were flying through my consciousness.

# Chapter 27

On the small porch, I rocked back on my chair and stared across the fields. What was happening to me? Had God sent this woman to me—or Satan? No, she was too good. I would say prayers of thanksgiving to God for sending her into my life.

This was after all only a friendship, and I could control it. I can't be bothered with changes that may be coming from Vatican II to ease up on the celibacy rules. It won't apply to me. Celibacy is really just the absence of someone to come home to. I didn't really need to live with a woman. After all, I had managed without one all these years. But then that was before I met Margie. On the other hand, I sometimes found myself questioning the legitimacy of my feelings for her. My thinking was becoming circular. I was not consistent. I told myself that in solitude things get magnified beyond belief. And confused, too.

I needed to get back to work, and I was sure that all this would settle itself. I needed to get back to a regular prayer schedule, too. I was beginning to feel detached from God. I hoped it was only my intense preoccupation with this change in my life. When I thought of Margie, I wasn't so sure I could live without her. That night was the first of many with tears preceding sleep, agonizing over the feelings that had come into my life.

My love for Margie is not a distraction. It is part of my solitude now and surely a gift of God. I told myself that physical affection is only an expression of this marvelous gift of love for each other. In saying my Mass, I feel absolutely united to Margie in Christ. She is part of my emptiness and unknowing, and has now become the source of my strength to bear the pain of this life.

Before long, Margie and I planned to communicate by thinking of each other at the same time. We arranged this by letter and phone call, and also by knowing each other's schedule which was pretty consistent. We would agree to be quiet and think about our love for each other and try to share the love mentally as we would if we were together physically. It seemed to ease our loneliness. Sometimes I wrote poetry about our love at these special times. It was a small consolation for both of us.

A few days later, I received the pictures in the mail that I had taken of Margie. I could hardly wait to see them and try to figure out how

Margie compared to the picture I had drawn years before. I walked over to the window to get a stronger light on them. Yes, the forehead, the space between the eyes, soulful with a sort of shadow of grief underlining them, the chin, the free flowing dark hair. It was all there, like the line drawing had been made from the photograph. What did it mean? I had never encountered anything like this in anything I'd ever read, even in fiction. My drawing had been called "Christ Unveils the Meaning of the Old Testament." I would pray over this coincidence, if that's what it is, and ask God for understanding. I decided that for the time being I would not tell anyone about this. Maybe I never would. If I couldn't understand it, I couldn't explain it to anyone else anyway.

I called Margie to talk about our next meeting, and she suddenly interrupted our conversation to say she had another call and had to take it. I found myself feeling jealous. It was probably her fiancé whom she never talked about. I had hoped that she might be forgetting about him too. Two days later she explained it was her mother calling from Cincinnati. I felt foolish and wondered how my emotions had gotten so far out of my control. This relationship was rattling me and shaking my self-confidence.

It was now Ascension Thursday, and one month since I had received Margie's first letter. I decided to take a long walk around the monastery grounds to my favorite places for meditation.

The fire tower was important to me when it was first built. Now it was like a sentinel to me, keeping watch over my love as well as my safety. Fire would burn us, and all we hold dear. I prayed the fire of our love would not also destroy us.

I began to think I should take some action to distance myself from Margie's love. It was unsafe. I was 25 years a monk. I thought my jealousy over her long distance call from her mother might have been a pretext in my mind to find an excuse to loosen her hold on me. I had always terminated relationships with girls I dated before there was any development to this stage. I was now in deeper than I had ever allowed myself to get before. All the letters and poetry I had been sending her just fueled my emotions and made my situation more difficult for me. I determined I would pray for wisdom and guidance.

On May 26, we received a group from the Fellowship of Reconciliation who brought the Vietnamese Buddhist monk, Thich Nhat Hanh. The FOR was escorting him in a speaking tour around the U.S. on behalf of world peace. I discovered that Nhat Hanh and I had more in common than I realized from brief articles I had read about him. He and I were of similar background and shared an interest in the tradition of Camus' existentialist philosophy and understanding of the urgent need for settlement of the war. He was a soft-spoken monk who had difficulty speaking due to his fatigue, so I spoke to the group at the monastery on his behalf. We also made a tape for Dan Berrigan. Due to the rigors of their travels, the group decided to stay over the weekend, and I was happy for this extended experience. I wrote a letter in tribute to him for publication in the program for the upcoming Town Hall meeting in New York on June 9. I titled it, "Nhat Hanh Is My Brother" to document the spiritual bond that amazingly formed in our short meeting.

I had been losing so much spiritual energy recently, I was feeling depleted. I knew I had placed myself in an impossible conflict, but continued to rationalize that I was happy living like this. So long as we did not consummate our feelings for each other, I refused to believe our love was wrong. There was another level to our love, and I was determined I could maintain our feelings on a transcendent plane. Yet I knew the stakes couldn't be higher: our salvation was involved. I told myself I must seek a solution, not accepting perpetual improvisation.

I couldn't help but believe that some day there must be an end to our relationship, this obsession. I knew that there was no hope of a dispensation for me, and apostasy was impossible. We both wanted our love to go on in spite of all the obstacles, at least in our hearts. We doggedly hoped to be united at last forever in heaven.

Sunday morning at Mass I was almost in tears thinking of her. I prayed the Mass for our relationship and thanked God for it. The following night I had a frightening dream that reminded me of the cruelty I can impose on her by withdrawing my feelings after I have accepted her love. When I woke up, I begged God not to take away the gift of her love for me. Her sincerity moved me to tears when I thought of it. I have always feared receiving an enormous amount of love, but now I wanted to surrender to it and be healed of the fear of love I had carried for so many years.

Tuesday night I called Margie, and she told me about her long weekend. I couldn't get in the Steel Building, so went to the Gatehouse phone, which I knew would be very risky. There was no direct line, so I had to go through the switchboard, and the Brother on duty could cut in at any time to check on the call. I had just gotten back from a walk to the place where we had our picnic.

I thought I would crack up over this relationship. I feared what it meant to my life, but at the same time I felt that, handled properly, it could be a liberation from the burden of loneliness I had been carrying all my life. I hoped we could find a new higher consciousness. I wanted my love to be as honest and true as I knew it could be. I didn't want to "get off the bus" with this relationship as I had so many years ago with other girls. I searched the issue repeatedly in my mind, seeking a solution.

I knew the answer. And I didn't like the answer.

The occasion was Sunday, the feast of Corpus Christi, and a big hullabaloo every year at the monastery. The monks designed liturgical patterns with rose petals on the Church walkway at the entrance. Devotion hits a feverish pitch for most of the monks on this occasion.

I stood at the altar in a joint celebration of the Mass with the other professed monks. I suddenly saw myself among the others as a priest who has a woman. It was a disgusting feeling.

I prayed that in heaven we might be one, although it could not happen now. I could only love her as the beautiful person she is, and not physically. She would probably eventually marry someone else, I thought, because I knew that ending our relationship would be necessary.

I was always afraid of the anxiety that comes from loss. At the same time, I was afraid that love would change me completely. I had already begun to feel the changes. I had scruples about maintaining my old identity and living up to my vocation. I resented losing both. Now only a miracle would give me earthly love. I walked out to St. Edmund's field near the fire tower and had an afternoon of Zen emptiness. I told myself I lack nothing. Anyway, there is no such thing as "lack."

Walking back to the hermitage, I knew there could be no life for Margie and me together because I had already vowed to live as a monk for the rest of my life in solitude. I knew our love could only mean suffering for both of us. I would have to do something to alleviate our pain.

# Chapter 28

On Monday, June 13, Dom James returned from his extended trip. I went down to the Steel Building to call Margie that night. Brother Clement told me that the Brother on the switchboard had overheard my conversation with Margie and had told the Abbot. I wondered which call he had heard. I hoped it hadn't been the one about marriage.

I immediately went down to the gatehouse and called Margie. She was inconsolable, afraid she would never see me again.

The next day I waited to be summoned by Dom James to his office. The day passed without a word. I decided the only defense was an offense, so I went to see him instead.

He received me after only a few minutes' wait. That was a change. Usually the waiting time seemed to be consistent with the gravity of the matter to be discussed.

I told Dom James about Margie as though he probably hadn't heard, although I knew, of course, he had.

"Father Abbot, there's something I've got to tell you. I met a nurse when I was in the hospital, and I've been in touch with her since I've been back."

Dom James just looked at me. He did not register surprise or anger, which surprised me, but I knew what was coming.

"Sit down and listen to me. Everyone has temptations and everyone sins. There's nothing new about what you're going through. Monks sometimes think they fall in love with their nurse when they go to the hospital. That's because the young nurses aides are usually assigned to the routine, time-consuming patient care to free up the nurses to perform more technical duties. This results in our monks spending a lot of time while they're recuperating with young, often physically attractive young aides who have not yet learned to keep their emotional distance from the patients, especially the monks who come from a life of celibacy. When our men get back to the monastery, they get over it. That's because they don't stay in touch with the nurse. Now just forget about it and get on with your vocation. Just be sure you don't see her again. I'll write a letter for you to tell her of your decision, if you'd like. He had a thick letter on his desk that I could see was marked "conscience matter" and asked me if it was hers. He obviously enjoyed not giving it to me.

Dom James recommended I start sleeping in the infirmary, using the hermitage only during the day. He said the incident happened because of loneliness, which I needed to overcome, he believed, to solve my problem. I begged him to let me stay at the hermitage. I suggested I could come down to the retreat house for ecumenical work with people of other faiths. That would assuage the loneliness and solve my problem, I suggested. He agreed to let me stay at the hermitage on that basis.

There was nothing more to say. He seemed to be saying, shut the door to your feelings, and we won't have to talk about it anymore. Now get back to your place, and act like you're supposed to. That was his basic message.

I was now even more stunned than when I learned I had been found out. He asked me no questions, he gave me no sympathy, no advice about how to deal with the pain, the memories, and the new isolation I now faced. Just get on with it. Get on with what—the money-making books?

He gave me no absolution, no penance—nothing, leaving me alone in the abyss of my loneliness. Was that his punishment? He registered no emotion. He was completely detached. I wondered, does the man ever feel anything?

I did see Margie again, in spite of Father Abbot's words. After all, I told myself, it wasn't an order and wasn't given as penance in Confession. It was only his version of fatherly advice. So I was breaking no vow of obedience to see her again. I felt I had to close the door, as he said, but gently.

It was all too depressing. I walked back to the hermitage and put on a record of Joan Baez that I had borrowed recently from Father Chrysogonus. I also got a Dylan record from him. But I wanted to hear Baez sing "Silver Dagger" and think about Margie. Then Dylan's "Tombstone Blues" and "Mister Jones." I drank some iced Christian Brothers brandy out of an old marmalade jar and sat back and enjoyed the music and my memories.

I was getting uncomfortable now walking around the abbey. I felt separated from everyone else. The gatehouse Brothers seemed to be smiling whenever they saw me. I felt disconnected, as the song says, "like a rolling stone." Dom James' secretary looked away when he saw me, embarrassed. I will write a new book, in a new language. I know

I think with my hands. I can work through this. If I had access to a piano—but it's better to do the writing.

The day after my meeting with Dom James, Jim Wygal came out unexpectedly to the abbey. I imagined that Dom James had summoned him to be sure I didn't go off the deep end or do anything foolish—like quit! He was probably given a mandate to help me get through my obsession with Margie. We drove "off campus" to New Haven. I used the pay phone to call Margie. It was a Wednesday, so I called the hospital and had her paged. She had received the last letters I had sent before I saw her on Saturday. I told her it was useless to write to me now. She was on duty, so our call was too brief.

On the drive back to Gethsemani, Jim gave me his counsel, which I had not solicited.

"You better watch it, Tom. You're on a collision course."

"I know what you're saying. I'll take care. Don't worry about me. Haven't I survived every emotional crisis up to now?"

I resented Jim's advice but had to admit to myself that he was right. Still, I believed that a gradual wind-down of this affair made more sense than cutting it off abruptly.

The next day, Dom James told me I was forbidden to contact Margie by phone or letter. I knew this would be difficult, if not impossible, to obey. At the same time it felt liberating. My phone calls this week were painful, and I could not sleep much all week.

I went out and looked at the stars. It helps to speak to God like this. I knew I had to get back to the center and my real self and to find God's peace in this.

The following day, the Hammers came out to see me. We enjoyed a picnic lunch together at the same place where I had hosted the Derby Day get-together. I showed them the poems I had been writing for Margie, and they were as enthusiastic as I was about publishing them privately on their press. I said I had to discuss it with Laughlin, because he had all of them in his files.

A few days later, on Friday night, I had a strange dream. I was talking to another nurse who happened to be ill and her mother, and I knew that I would begin to love this nurse when I went to see her in the hospital. I woke up feeling guilty that the dream was not about Margie. I fell asleep again and dreamed of roses in a tangle of dark briars. One bright pink rose caught my attention, and it became luminous. I noted the beautiful soft texture of its petals, and suddenly they all disappeared and my own mother's face was there behind them. I had never dreamed of my mother before, that I remembered. I wondered what it meant.

The next morning I went for X-rays again, now three months after my surgery. Margie had known before about this appointment because I had mentioned it in a recent phone conversation. I hoped she would meet me there without my need to violate the prohibition against contacting her.

During the past week I had been writing the story of our relationship that I named "Midsummer Diary." I took it with me to the Doctor's office to give her if she should come. In it I described the beauty I saw in our relationship which was growing until it was cut off by the ban on our communication. I said we were really both waifs, that we had wanted to make one reality out of two voids. I said it is not the Church that separated us. The Church was blamed by some for burning Joan of Arc at the stake, too. Our paths in life were obviously not the same in the Will of God. Our love was a profound event in my life. I had found something, someone, I had always been looking for, and believe I will always feel it was too deep and too real to ever be changed essentially.

The Doctor gave me a good report on the X-ray, and I left his office. Margie was not there. I took the elevator down, and as the door opened, she approached to get on the elevator to meet me. We rode up together to the fourth floor. On the fourth floor there was a bench at the end of the hall near a window, and I led her to it so we could sit together.

I gave her the "Midsummer Diary" to take with her to read. She was obviously touched. I tried to tell her that if only we could be patient and stubborn in our desire to be together, maybe the magic would work forever, until we meet in Heaven. Then no magic would be needed.

Then I said a too-abrupt good-bye so that I could keep my lunch date with Wygal and get a ride back to the monastery.

I was so depressed after seeing Margie that Jim didn't find it necessary to lecture me about managing my relationship with Margie. I knew and admitted to him that I didn't need this kind of activity in my life, for my emotional health or spiritual wellbeing. I told him I was going to wind it down.

That night I couldn't sleep no matter what I tried. I paced up and down the porch of the hermitage while I thought of Margie reading my "Midsummer Diary." I contemplated the hopelessness of any future with her except for occasional meetings like this last one. Margie had such a beautiful soul--it was wrong to keep her entangled in such a miserable relationship.

I determined to end this agony for both of us. After many pages of attempts, I finally finished a letter to her a few days later that I thought would be my last letter to her. I didn't mention any future get- togethers. Certainly this would ease the situation, and I could just avoid setting up any more meetings as circumstances offered them. I hoped my letter was not too sentimental. I was determined to stop walking around the hermitage singing "Silver Dagger" anymore, from Joan Baez' record, although I knew I would be dying the death of a hundred daggers, as the saying goes.

A few days later I had a visit from Ping Ferry. I had called him and asked him to come—ASAP. We enjoyed a long ride together in his rental car. We picked up some hamburgers in Bardstown and stopped at a tobacco farm to have our lunch, while we discussed the peace movement. I told him about Margie, and he was fully sympathetic. Apparently the number of priests leaving to marry had now reached the point where a lot of liberal Catholics were accepting it without question. Ping said I could have a job at the Center in Santa Barbara if Margie and I wanted to come out there together. I found myself telling him I couldn't break my vows or live with a woman. It wouldn't work for me.

I was still humming "Silver Dagger," but I refused to risk losing the hermitage and my solitary life. I had to preserve this, because it was the most valuable possession I had. I prayed to God that He would not take it away from me. I had taken a risk, but I would not jeopardize it again.

On the following Saturday, I listened to some records: Bob Dylan's "Highway 61" and Baez' "Silver Dagger" which I used to confuse with "East Virginia." I played my bongo drums to accompany some of the records—a nice gift from some friends. They put me closer in touch with the music and I felt a little more human, too, I suppose.

Then I walked down to see the new hermitage being built for Father Flavian. He had decided to move to a hermitage, too. I had chosen him recently for my confessor. I noted his place would be smaller than mine, but would be much more modern. It even had an inside john!

Three weeks passed slowly as I tried hard to get interested in my reading and adjust to not hearing from Margie. Then Jim Wygal came out to pick up some books he had loaned me. I wondered if he was getting paid to check on me. We walked in the woods together around the hermitage, and naturally talked about Margie. He said she was too immature to be capable of loving me. I thought he was being unfair in his criticism.

He suggested we stop over at Loretto and say hello to Sister Luke and the other nuns there. I said, why not. Sister Luke was another good friend of mine who shared reading material and ideas, and was probably as lonely as I was. When we arrived, Sister Luke wasn't even there, but we sat around for a while with other nuns, some of them probably Jim's patients, and talked mostly about Zen. I enjoyed hearing one of the nuns play the piano for us—some soothing cerebral classical pieces.

It was unbearably hot walking back to the hermitage after he dropped me off. In my haste to get back and out of sight, I turned my ankle on the path. It hurt all night, but I tried to ignore it. The next day I realized I couldn't put my weight on it. It was a bad sprain. I called Dr. Mitchell for an appointment. I went right in to see him.

The sprain was simple, but the pain during the slow recovery would be persistent and I knew would keep my attention focused on my emotional distress.

If I left the monastery and tried to establish myself independently, I couldn't manage to support myself or anyone else. No one would buy the books of a man who had bragged about the religious life and then walked out and left it for the love of a woman. Well, they'd probably buy one more book—the one that would tell them why I did it, but that would be the last one I'd ever sell. But that was not the determining factor for my decision. God would not take "no" for an answer about my vocation. Nevertheless, I dreaded meeting Margie face to face and saying good-bye. I knew she would look back just like John Paul had done when he left for the war.

On the return ride back to Gethsemani after seeing Dr. Mitchell, I told myself I was convinced of two things: that I was doing the right thing and that it was the most painful experience of my life.

Lying around the hermitage, I had plenty of time to think about Margie and me. She was unique in my life because she recognized in me a gentleness and tenderness that no one in my life before ever believed I had. How could I turn my back on the gift of a lifetime? I had to, because I believed that God wills it for me to live in solitude to pay for my offenses and to do the work He planned for me. After all, the real purpose of life must be our union with the saving Will of God. I must trust in Him. I also couldn't stop believing I must be faithful to some other inscrutable call from God that I did not understand.

I found myself in need of writing another analysis of our love and where it now stands. I wanted to think through this by writing it, and at the same time have something I could send to Margie. It took hours of painful work, probably the most distressing experience in my writing life. I wrote it straight through, without changing anything. When I finished, I titled it "Retrospect." I would trust that God would enlighten Margie to understand how I see our need for each other within the context of responsibility.

There is a relationship of mysticism to sex—a continuum of emotionality with imagination. As a child I had my imaginary playmate, just as I now feel that God is a companion. He is more of a reality in my life than that playmate and his dog were. Much of daily life is really illusion. I am convinced that the so-called need for sex is a myth. The sexual freedom concept is an empty box—it's death. Flower children and a lot of other people have been sold a lie. The only important task for all of us is to identify what is reality and what is imaginary.

Almost two weeks later I began to have the same pain in my arm that I experienced before the surgery to replace the disc. I guessed that the procedure probably set up the next disc for the same repair job. I called Dr. Mitchell's office for an appointment. I went to see Dom James to ask permission to make the call to Dr. Mitchell. He was so angry with me he could barely discuss my medical problems and related logistics to get back and forth. I figured afterwards that he must have received the letter Ping Ferry said he would write, asking him to send me out to California for two or three months for my health. That would have done it. Dom James told me he wanted what was best for my mental health, but I didn't react to his remarks even though I didn't believe he was sincere. There was no reason to get worked up anymore about him; I believed that he'd never change.

Two days later, Dom James offered to give me back my old assignment as Master of Novices or a new one as Scripture professor, whatever would get me out of the hermitage and under closer supervision. I felt that Dom James would let me stay at the hermitage, at least for the time being. I believed that he knew instinctively that I didn't do anything wrong.

I went to Dr. Mitchell as I had planned for the inevitable cortisone shot for my bursitis. I arranged for lunch and a ride home afterwards with Jim. Compared to our recent get-togethers, it was dull. Even he was losing interest in my problems. Before I met up with Jim, I posted a letter to Margie so it wouldn't go through the monastery censorship process. I told her in effect this had to be good-bye. I attached a copy of my "Retrospect" to give her my detailed analysis of our situation. We had planned one last picnic in the park, now that I was able to walk, for August 12, the day before her graduation and move back to Cincinnati. I told her in my letter that I had to call it off because it was too dangerous.

Once I had dropped the letter in the box I regretted it. I went to the nearest pay phone to call her, but she was on extra duty somewhere. I went then to my appointment with the Doctor. He said there was nothing he could do about the numbness in my leg still lingering since the surgery. As he examined me, I was almost in tears thinking of Margie and my missed opportunity to see or even to talk with her for the last time.

On the ride back to the monastery, I was overcome with anxiety that silently cried out to her in the depths of my being. I knew she could feel it, because I could sense her reaction to it, and the mutual agony was almost unbearable. It did not stop until I set foot on the monastery grounds. I was frightened. Wygal had his car radio set to WKLO, and Bob Dylan's "I Want You" was played. I couldn't get it out of my head. When I got back to the hermitage, I knew I couldn't sleep with the combination of the rain and the frogs croaking. My love for Margie was like a fatal disease. I wrote another poem I later called "Cancer Blues," sort of in the Dylan style, which obviously fascinated me.

On the path not far from the hermitage, I saw a copperhead snake. I took a stick and hit it repeatedly, until finally I killed it. I thought how it could have gotten to me while I was working or sleeping. I wondered if I was safe anymore here for more reasons than one.

The next day, Father Eudes summoned me to discuss my recent behavior. Dom James had informed Father Eudes of my activities, which I did not appreciate, even though he *was* a psychiatrist. We discussed the change in my behavior from religious correctness to my current alienation from the group. I had been naïve and imprudent, thinking that no one would know or care about my attitude. I was surprised to learn from him that some of the younger monks were concerned about it. I knew I had decided firmly to stay in the life of solitude, but I really needed to go through that experience to find my true intentions. I had no trouble admitting I was wrong, but not so much because of the lack of external correctness as the disturbance to my internal unity.

I now felt like I was broken in pieces, after finding wholeness for the first time in my life within my relationship with Margie. I would have to create a new wholeness in myself, because it wasn't there in the first place. My religious fervor was not from wholeness. It was a pseudo-wholeness based on my lack of knowledge of myself. I promised Father Eudes not to project any self-hate on the community or give a bad example to the others. I said I could best do this work on myself from the hermitage. Close involvement with the group would not help me. He accepted my understanding of my problems and my commitment.

A few days later Dom James called me in to talk about a lot of petty details and mainly get under my skin, it seemed to me. He gave me a short-wave radio for the hermitage so that I could call the gatehouse in an emergency. It was a joke to me, because I knew the monks at the gatehouse never answered it. He absolutely gloated over my lovesickness, which I tried unsuccessfully to conceal from him. He laughed at my predicament, and said he was thinking of writing a book on how to get hermits into heaven.

"I strongly suggest you go back and read your pamphlet on monastic courtesy. Some of that direction could apply to you right now."

"Sure," I said. "You mean like don't act superior to other monks?"

"No," he responded. He walked over to his desk and picked up a copy of the little mimeographed pamphlet I had written fifteen years before. He began reading, "Courtesy in Relations with Superiors ... many faults can be committed in our dealings with them: Being too blunt in stating one's views. Trying to force one's opinions on a superior. Demanding to know the reason for this or that decision."

"That's enough," I interrupted.

He began to lose his control, for a change. "You better watch it, Father, or I'll restrict your correspondence to four letters a year out of this place, the way it was in the old days."

Now Dom James laid down new rules for me, or rather revoked privileges I had enjoyed. No more meeting Jim Wygal in town, less visits with Dan Walsh, and no more visits at the Hammers' home, seeing them only in restaurants. No more hospitalization at St. Joe's, so I would have to change doctors and go to Lexington if I needed more surgery. It was my turn to be shocked. Now I knew why they called this place Gethsemani—it's an agony in the garden, all right.

My arm was hurting unbearably now, so that I could hardly type one letter. Still, I knew I had to resume my former activities and concentrate on my work.

On August 13, Margie graduated. It rained, and I thought of how I had missed her. I wanted to die and prayed we could soon be united in Heaven.

# Chapter 29

Now that Margie had moved away, I asked Dom James to allow me to make a profession as a hermit. I felt I wanted a deeper consecration to God. I wanted to stabilize my status at the hermitage so long as my health allowed. The Abbot agreed, and I assured him I would cause no more tension from my misdeeds. He had not lost his asset.

I could now see that Dom James was more right than even *he* realized. I decided to make a sort of retreat of my own to prepare for my upcoming profession in recognition of the mistakes I had made. I would maintain a fidelity to my love for Margie, because my love for her was pure and in God's love. My life had a fullness now even without her that I didn't have before. There would be no other lover for me.

I had discovered that with a serious love there is much suffering involved. It is worse than enduring a loved one's death, since the decision is taken out of your hands and there's no will involved in putting it to rest. For all, though, there must be a will to go forward, alone. On August 18, I wrote to Jay Laughlin to tell him there was nothing going on anymore with Margie and me. I asked him to notify Margie if I should die or suddenly be transported to the moon or something, because no one here at the monastery would notify her. I did not feel sure that my death would be reported in the newspapers.

It was September now. I sat on my porch at the hermitage and watched a pair of robins sitting on the power line to the house. Down at the monastery, five monks were leaving for Chile to take over the Las Condes foundation. My only part was to join in the celebration of the Solemn Mass for the occasion. I felt so disconnected. I was amazed to think that there was a day when being left out of this would have made me almost hysterical.

Ed Rice sent me some Dylan records to help me write a piece on him for *Jubilee*. I particularly liked his "Gates of Eden." I sang Dylan and Baez songs to myself, but was not yet ready to compose anything that would remind me of Margie.

The next day I was back in Louisville again seeing Dr. Mitchell for X-rays. The disc was fine and no further surgery would be required, thank God! Afterwards I took the bus over to the University of Louisville library where Carolyn Hammer worked as one of the librarians. Wygal was out of town, and I wasn't supposed to be socializing with him anymore anyway. I had lunch alone in the University cafeteria, and listened to the Beatles on the juke box. I enjoyed their music. I took the bus to Bardstown. The Brothers would be driving over to take me back to the monastery.

On September 25, I had a rainy trip into Louisville to see Dr. Mitchell again. My elbow was hurting badly, and I got another painful cortisone shot. Afterward I went over to the University library. When I got out to Bardstown, it was still raining. I was in pain and depressed.

Walking back to the hermitage on a Sunday, I found a jacket of a monk's work outfit in the grass near the main road. I learned later that Brother Ralph had disappeared on Friday and had hitched a ride into Bardstown with an employee of the monastery who didn't recognize him. There was always a deep, wrenching loss felt when someone left without saying good-bye to anyone. It made me start to question my own state of mind, whether or not I was a good monk—maybe not honest enough. And it brought back again the awful emptiness that I experienced when Ruth died without an opportunity to say good-bye to her for the rest of my life.

A few weeks later, I learned that Brother Paul, one of the most elderly in our community, had died. I went down to the monastery for the funeral. To my amazement, Brother Ralph was standing next to the Abbot and Brother Paul's body. I discovered later that Dom James required him to return in order to leave legally. He had gone to Florida and would now be with us until the paperwork was processed to free him from his vows. The Abbot did not have to do that. He must be setting an example for others—like me, for example. He probably enjoyed watching Brother Ralph squirm as they dropped Brother Paul into the ground.

Dom James loves to conceal his true motives for his decisions. It is his insincerity that turns off the young monks. No wonder they leave. Those who stay eventually become resentful or rebellious individualists like me, staying to themselves and salvaging what they can of themselves. Some of the monks are now changing their names to those of other saints who are more familiar to them. Although they had no choice in the initial selection, I don't see how a name change would improve their state of mind here. Fortunately for me, my work saves me.

Dom James is a providential affliction. He has good desires and a potential warmth and concern for his monks, but underneath I think he harbors a contempt for any kind of love, and in general for the personhood of his monks. Even though he is wrong about my motives, I must accept his judgment without evasion or retaliation. It is my vow. Sometimes I wonder, though, if I have given away too much of my freedom to Dom James, to the point that I cannot fulfill God's Will for me. Surely His Will is not merely for me to obey Dom James, no matter what trivialities he comes up with for me. The thought haunts me when I can't sleep at night.

I know now why this place is called Gethsemani. Matthew's gospel gives us Jesus' words in the garden before his return to the Father through death in this life: "Father, if it is possible, let this cup pass from me; yet not as I will, but as Thou willest."

I dream of Margie frequently, but usually I see a woman who is not Margie, but seems to represent her. Then when I wake up, the archetypal Margie and the reality merge together. Earlier I had dreamed that I was sending a child to the hospital to tell Margie I loved her, and I was frustrated that the child would not be able to convey my feelings. This time the dream was more vivid and memorable. She is swimming alone in one of the abbey's lakes. I was afraid to join her because of the consequences. Then she is wading and looks so sad and alone that I go over to her, wearing my monastery robes. There is no one else in view until I get closer to her and find one of the monks sitting in my way. I cannot reach her. I then wake up distressed.

In October I saw Father Stephen, one of our more elderly monks, fall suddenly. Luckily, there was a small group nearby. We carried him inside the monastery post office and knelt beside him as he quietly died. We prayed the psalms over his body. Then several monks carried him to the provisional chapel on the third floor, being used while the church was being renovated. I volunteered to keep the traditional vigil overnight. The next day I was there for his burial in the monastery cemetery behind the church.

We sang the Gregorian chant for the dead. We used the fourth tone, which is always used in the burial rites. It reminded me of all the other funerals I had attended at the monastery, probably because there were two deaths shortly after I joined, and the mournful tone stuck in my memory.

Through all my years at Gethsemani, I had seen the old monks die, one by one, usually quietly in their sleep. Their death was a joy for them, going to their eternal reward, and being relieved of their assorted maladies as well as the confinement they had signed on for. Death was what they expected and even looked forward to. This was the first time I actually saw a monk die, and all the while I was thinking of the shortness of life. All the emotions we feel as human beings as so important suddenly evaporate. My love for Margie suddenly felt hollow.

The monastery maintained only one coffin. It was a wood box painted black that was kept in the laundry drying room. It was used from day to day to hang small articles of clothing to dry, such as handkerchiefs. It had long handles and an open top. The deceased monk was carried in it to the cemetery in procession and removed at the gravesite.

We buried Father Stephen, like all the other old monks, his face covered with a small cloth. His body was dropped gently into the dirt cavity prepared for him the previous evening, the dirt thrown directly on him in his thick white choir robe, and returned to the earth.

It seems so cruel to bury a person without a container of some sort. Yet it is so natural. Really, coffins only allow us to be an ostrich about it, helping us to avoid seeing the harsh reality of death. It is difficult for many of the young monks to get through these funerals. They suddenly become aware that the only thing they have to look forward to at this monastery is their own death. That's why I volunteer to give the first remarks in Chapter after a monk dies. I like to set the tone to help the younger ones see the deceased monk for his value to the group, now that he is gone from us—to see that his life really did matter to someone.

For years now, whenever I walked past the drying room, I would consciously look at the bier to remind myself of the shortness of my life. I also walked around the cemetery periodically and looked at the graves to remember the good monks buried there, those I had known and the majority who preceded me at the monastery. For me, this funeral was different. I could see myself following in Father Stephen's footsteps. I hoped I could bear the judgment of God when my time would come.

The following day, John Griffin brought my old friend, Jacques Maritain, and his young French assistant, Babeth Manual, for a visit. Babeth's father was an admirer of Maritain and had offered to share their apartment in Paris with him during his declining years. Now in his eighties, Maritain wanted to make one final visit to the U.S. and brought Babeth along to assist him.

It was an event I had been looking forward to for a long time. They arrived by car through the fields at the hermitage, since there was no road. It was a perfect fall day, with the foliage at its golden height. I invited Penn Jones to join us. Later, Father J. Stanley Murphy, Dan Walsh, and Jack Ford came over. I had only met Maritain once, and I was immediately attracted to him as a fellow convert to Catholicism. I had never had an opportunity to talk to him about his important writings on philosophy, although we had corresponded over the years. It was obvious that Maritain was now in poor health. I read some of my poems to the group, including my latest effort, "Edifying Cables," as we sat around my fireplace. Maritain liked my counter-culture approach. I also read some of Bob Dylan's lyrics and played a record of Dylan singing the same songs. The group was less than impressed with Dylan's work, but they did not dim my enthusiasm.

I spoke to Maritain about the world situation, including the war, the problem of drugs, and the Church. Maritain's penetrating blue eyes came alive as we saw a wild deer pass my front window. The years seemed to leave his face as we discussed his opinions about everything we could think of. His sense of humor was in evidence, too, as he mentioned some detective stories he had recently enjoyed reading. Babette said later that to her I was a *force de nature*, a real compliment I could appreciate, that I appeared to her as a person of real strength. When I exchanged ideas with Maritain, he often closed his eyes as he thought intently about a point he was making. Later Maritain gave a talk down at the monastery for the community. It was obvious that he had lost some of his ability to speak about his work, but I hung on to every word he said, knowing I would never see him again.

I offered to say Mass for the group, and Maritain asked me to say the old Latin Mass. I was happy to oblige. I couldn't record my feelings about this event in my journal because they went too deep. In fact, I could never record what it was like to perform the consecration of bread and wine into the body and blood of Jesus Christ Himself.

With Griffin's excellent photographs of this occasion, I put together a six-page article for *Jubilee* (the January 1968 issue) of my favorite quotes from Maritain's works. I wanted to share the experience with those who appreciated Maritain's contribution to Catholic philosophy but did not have the opportunity to meet him.

Penn Jones brought me a copy of the book he had written on the assassination of John F. Kennedy. I read it the following day, another rainy one. He quite convincingly pointed out defects in the Warren Commission Report of the Government's investigation. It led me to believe that some very powerful people might have been behind the murder. It was a thought I didn't want to pursue, because it was too painful.

The next day I had to go to the proctologist. Father Raymond shared the ride, but was going to see a different doctor. I could not help but envy him. He had all the visitors he wanted, and received a lot of mail from his readers. I assumed it wasn't censored like mine. There were no restrictions on him—"that beast." That was our term at Oakham for guys like him who didn't even try to get along with the rest of the group. I guess you might say we had a natural dislike for each other that would override the love of writing that we shared. He told me he had problems getting his work approved by the censors too. I was surprised. How could they quarrel with the platitudes he put out? I could hardly even get through his latest pontifical effort, *The Silent Spire Speaks*. I guess my open-minded approach is as extreme as his closed-mind opinion on just about any subject. I see our spiritual life as an interminable journey, and Raymond sees himself as already home, I think.

The following day, I had a surprise visit from Dan Berrigan. He brought a new English Mass that we celebrated together. I found it quite moving and simple. I don't know if it was legal or not, but I liked it as much as Dan did. We also celebrated the regular Mass together. This was a contrast to my visit with Maritain, who wanted to hear the traditional Latin Mass. We all appreciated the beauty of the old Mass, although I feel it is austere and intense. Berrigan updated me on current events in the peace movement and cheered me up considerably. He's a real friend.

I resumed writing poetry again, in my new brash style. I called it "Edifying Cables" for the time being. I liked it and hoped it continued to look good to me. I was seeing my past work with greater clarity now. Some readers rejected my new work because what I was writing was not as "spiritual" or "unworldly" as the early work. Others rejected all my earlier writing for being too "monastic." I read some of "Cables" to Maritain when he was here, and he liked it immensely. He said that the best way of approaching philosophical and theological problems now that there was so much chaos might well be through creative writing and literary criticism. I tried now to find a new voice and hopefully silence both groups of critics. I want to stop this preoccupation with a *persona*. I've learned that trying to construct a professional self is dangerous and a complete waste of time. I would stay in touch with the woods, the birds, the sun melting the snow, and the moon and stars at night, to keep me in touch with what is real and authentic.

Laughlin arranged for some of my drawings to be exhibited at the Paraclete Book Center in New York. He selected the Poor People's Corporation to be the beneficiary because they were organizing a co-operative in Mississippi and it seemed to be a worthy cause. I agreed to send out invitations to some of my correspondents who might want to attend.

I unexpectedly received a letter from Aunt Gwyn after all these years. She sent some old letters she had received from Owen. I submitted one of them to the Catholic Art Association that I called "Sincerity in Art and Life," that was published in the spring of 1967. I was proud of Owen's expression of his spiritual approach to his work as a dedicated artist. I wished that I could have known what happened to Father's paintings, if they survived the war.

My bursitis continued to give me problems. I couldn't enjoy my fireplace now because I couldn't chop wood. I wouldn't ask any of the others to chop it for me. I now had a gas heater, which was very efficient. I was warmer, but missed the open fire's coziness.

The following week I was admitted to St. Anthony's Hospital, another hospital in Louisville, for X-rays of my stomach. I was glad to have a sunny private room.

I had just about finished "Edifying Cables" but found it unsatisfying. I wanted to think of it as merely an exercise in writing, because it didn't ring true for me. It had a glib, worldly spirit that really isn't me. I decided to let it go to publication anyway. I felt a lot better about my foreword to Nhat Hanh's new book, *Vietnam: Lotus in a Sea of Fire* that I was honored to write for him. It was published by Hill and Wang. I hoped I helped him in breaking down the comic-strip mythology about Asia that seemed so prevalent in the U.S.

On the weekend before Halloween, I had a special guest—Sidi Abde-salam, an Islamic mystic from Algeria. He came with Bernard Phillips and another Algerian and his wife, who translated for Sidi because he only speaks Arabic. He told me I had arrived, that I was close now to mystical union, and that the slightest thing, so to speak, could push me over the edge. He said I was in a prison and I was supposed to go out among small groups. He believes that dreams are important and give us messages. He said Dom James would not be Abbot by next year. I found it all quite hard to believe, and yet I found myself convinced that this man had been given information for me and that I should pay attention to what he said. Speaking with Sidi, I could feel the presence of God in our friendship. As we all sat around, it felt like an experience of Sufism, as I imagined it would be. As I thought about all the things Sidi told me, I got the sense that he was a messenger from God. He told me that he had the same sensation when he spoke to me.

On Sunday when I said Mass, I felt the closeness to God that Sidi had told me about. At the end of the Gospel, I had the sense of a blinding light, a helplessness, but with overwhelming joy about the goodness of God and my own nothingness. It frightened me.

It was time to get back to work. I was beginning again to see the reality of my purpose in life. I knew my escape from the unreality of the world, filled with such violence, hatred, and insanity, was only for the purpose of calling attention to it. In this time, I believe the very existence of life is threatened, but I know that the forces of evil will not prevail. Before I could accomplish anything, though, I had to stop all this self-analysis. I had a fatal versatility in examining every issue from every possible viewpoint and expressing this in the analytical eighteenth century English style of Swift and others of his day.

As the leaves died and fell, my spirits were in the same free-fall. I felt now that Margie was permanently out of my life since I started the break up. I hoped that I hadn't deceived myself that our love was given to us by God. I still loved her deeply but admitted to myself that I made a mistake in letting it go so far. I now felt freer to get back to my vocation and not seek another substitute for my solitude and loneliness. Fortunately, God's grace had protected me from making a worse error. I was silly to think I could escape the vocation of this life.

On All Saints' Day, the first of November, I went down in the rain to celebrate Mass together with the others. I returned to my hermitage with eggs in my pocket for a great breakfast. Then I walked to the Lake Knob after the skies cleared. For the past seven months, I realized I had been like a drunk driver going through red lights. A purification was needed and some repentance before I would be ready for the mystical union Sidi spoke to me about.

In spite of the frustration, I am grateful for the world of reality that is our real world. It is a world of love in which we have chosen to be essential to each other's meaning. Only God can reconcile it.

I knew it would be wrong to leave Gethsemani in order to marry Margie. I knew that neither of us could stand the pressure of what would transpire if we were to take that step. Besides the damage to both of us, there would be a disastrous effect on this community and on the hermit experiment I finally got approved. No, going away with Margie was tempting, but impossible.

In mid-November a strange event occurred. A priest came to see me for counsel and asked me to go for a drive with him. As we drove down the highway, he told me he had left his diocese and got married, and that his wife was pregnant. He was extremely nervous and chain smoked, and he made me very nervous the way he drove the car. He wanted my advice about setting up an order of married priests. Well, he persuaded me to write a letter for him supporting his project, and I hoped that wherever he took it, I wouldn't get into trouble. I refused to worry about that, because the whole business was really tragic. The experience really confirmed my resolve not to take any action to leave the priesthood to marry Margie. I wondered if it was a sign.

A week later, another unusual event occurred. One of the monks, taking his turn delivering a sermon at Mass, began to speak irrationally. He spoke emotionally against the Abbot, but in such a fashion that it was plain that he was having a nervous breakdown. Some of the brothers escorted him off the altar and took him to the hospital for treatment. Again I meditated on the meaning of this and previous events.

Walking around without paying attention, I ran into a large bush and scratched my eye on a branch. I called Mrs. Tommie O'Callahan to ask for a ride back to the monastery. She invited me to join her family for lunch. Her children were wonderful company and a great pleasure for me. I accepted every invitation she and her husband offered for repeat visits to their home. The kids called me "Uncle Tom," which I really appreciated. Obviously they didn't know the literary reference to that name.

A few days later, one of the Brothers approached me and asked for my advice about leaving the monastery. He felt the changes being made by Dom James were peripheral and not addressing basic changes that the Brother had expected would be made after Vatican II. I could only be a listener for this man—the decision was entirely his, and I offered no solution.

Solitude for extended periods of time can result in a dislike for other human contact. It causes a person to seek further solitude, even though it is lonely and sometimes depressing. Of course there are normal problems of personalities grating on one another which become magnified in a closed environment. With so much change going on in the world, it is much more difficult to maintain a traditional monastic lifestyle that seems relevant to reality. This Brother is unfortunately not the only one who is having second thoughts about staying here. Some of the men want to leave now because they don't trust Dom James and have lost respect for his authority. It's the same now in society. It's a disillusion with authority, and it has now entered our walls. Dom James is really a tragic figure. He's been trying to relax the rules of the Order expecting the young men to relate better to the life here, but his way of proceeding just turns them off.

Dom James just returned from Chile and was bragging about the important people he met there. The rumor around the abbey was that the Abbot General would not make visitations here because he knew that Dom James didn't want him here. He always sent Dom Columban, who just went through the formalities of a review. Dom James has apparently acquired so much prestige, even those in Rome don't say "boo" to him. He was exhibiting the same self-satisfied attitude you see from Wall Street and from Washington that had us in the Vietnam impasse. I feared the Government's actions would eventually lead to a war with China.

Now our Archbishop wanted to ordain Dan Walsh, which even amazed Dan, since he had not had a conventional program of training for the priesthood. Dom James, of course, was negative and suspicious of what such an action would mean in the Church. Dan had been living here for about ten years, and teaching as well at Loretto College in Nerinx and at Bellarmine. He had helped me, too, reading the original Greek texts of Aristotle and other texts I could not understand. His credentials were solid at Columbia, before he ever relocated down here. He just hadn't followed the traditional path through the seminary, so naturally Dom James couldn't adjust to the inconsistency. He just had no imagination. No wonder he was a tax auditor before he entered the monastery!

As the year 1966 was almost over, I was invited over to Thompson Willett's house to discuss the manuscript collection at Bellarmine College. Thompson was one of the local donors in Louisville, so it seemed a legitimate reason for me to leave the monastery grounds. I accepted a ride with Jim Wygal, which gave me some pangs of conscience. I enjoyed the comforts of the old Southern home. Willett's children were captivating, but I had to control myself when he spoke of his son serving in Vietnam and his hope that it was a holy war as Cardinal Spellman had called it. I believe this war to be a crime perpetrated for the benefit of special interests.

A week later, on December 8, I had a wonderful visit with Joan Baez. Her friend, Ira Sandperl, had tried before to get Dom James' approval for her to visit me and was refused. Our mutual friend, Ping Ferry, phoned Dom James and persuaded him to say yes. Good old Ping! I had sent Joan a book and a note recently, and she wanted to talk to me about taking a more active role in the peace movement. Joan was surprised that my first priority, before we got down to a serious discussion, was a fast food restaurant. She was amazed when I ordered two cheeseburgers, a chocolate milkshake, and a large order of fries—not the monastic preconception she had of a guru in the woods. Ira brought beer, and we went for a walk out in the open fields. Joan loved running up and down the hills, her black sailor pants flying, as well as her long black hair. She pleaded with me to leave Gethsemani and come with them to give talks to the young people she sang for. She said they needed my message. I tried to explain my solitude, but she didn't see its value compared to the social needs she knew so much about from her tours. I walked back to the gatehouse with them and introduced them to Dom James.

Since it was almost Christmas, she brought me her new long-play record, "Noel." I played one side on my little phonograph while we talked. Father Chrysogonus dropped by and was absolutely entranced to meet Joan. We talked of Bob Dylan and the non-violent institute she established. She does not use or condone drugs as many celebrities do. She is really like a saint in the peace movement, a totally authentic, totally human person. I went to the Louisville airport with them to see them off. My friend, Jack Ford, came over to drive me back to Gethsemani. We stopped off at his house on the way to Gethsemani, and I came down out of the clouds after my wonderful day with Joan. We were lucky to catch a rerun of "The Glass Menagerie" on TV, which I thoroughly enjoyed. I told myself I didn't feel guilty about any of it. It was Christmas time, and Dom James had no comment the following day.

Then I had a visit from Amiya Chakravarty, the Indian poet and philosopher, on his holiday break from Smith College. I was eager to speak with him, especially about his impressions of Gandhi, whom he had participated with in peace demonstrations. We spoke about New Directions and some ideas for projects of mutual interest, including a paper on Marcel and Buddhism that I agreed to write. It was first published by Howard University, and later included as "Nirvana" in *Zen and the Birds of Appetite*, which I dedicated to Chakravarty.

I decided I'd go to Confession to prepare for Christmas. I chose to go to Father Matthew. Whether or not it was our common Celtic ancestry or some empathy I noted in his mischievous eyes, I knew instinctively that he would be a compassionate listener. We found an empty office and closed the door. As he sat on the chair pulled out from behind the desk, I knelt on the floor alongside him and told him about the recent events that made me feel guilty. I emphasized my dissatisfaction with my lack of growth in the spiritual life and basically blamed this on my feelings about Dom James rather than on my love for Margie.

I know I am not pure either, but at least I don't inflict my problems on other people. I am living according to my own conscience, and not anyone else's. I now really believe that falling in love with Margie was not a cause but an effect of roots that were dormant at the time I entered the monastery. I know now from my sessions with Wygal that I had not dealt adequately with some issues before I came here and repressed a lot of feelings I didn't want to face at the time. Father Matthew was a good listener and always had positive ideas for dealing with problems. No wonder I chose him for a confessor.

It is time now for the revolving door of visitors to close unless I can find a way to be productive in my writing as an outcome from these visits.

> Dear God, I empty myself – of physical love
> Of myself, of my beloved Margie.
> I give it to you.
> Return to my emptiness
> And fill me with your mercy.

Now at almost the end of the year, I had to have one final encounter with Dom James, this time over my gift subscriptions to *Poetry* magazine from Jay Laughlin and to the *NY Review* from Jim Holloway. I had asked Dom James in advance if I would be permitted to receive these two publications, and he did not qualify his approval. Now he said his secretaries must have lost them. I received the first issue of both magazines, so I didn't wonder what happened. My dealings with the Abbot were now only on the "yassah white boss" level. He treated me like an inferior slave laborer on a plantation. To top it off, he asked me how my spiritual life was getting along. I couldn't believe he even cared. More young monks were talking of leaving, and one of the Brothers told me it was directly because of their dislike of Dom James. He was said to be keeping files on the monks' correspondence. Jim Wygal says it is pathological. I believe it.

My last act of the year, December 31, was a trip to Louisville to see the doctor again about my bursitis and get another shot. I also saw another doctor about my ears. I rode in with George, one of our workers, in the truck. I walked over to Cunningham's for a sandwich and beer and thought about everything. I had to play "Together Again" on the juke box to fill the void of the moment. Then I rode back to Gethsemani with another empty feeling.

A week later I was surprised by a visit from Doris Dana, the literary executor of Gabriela Mistral. She stopped on her way to see John Griffin in Texas. We drove around in her car and got some carryout beer, which we drank out in the woods outside the monastery grounds. She told me about Ishi, an Indian with a story that so fascinated me that she promised to send me a book about him. He was the last of the Yahi Indians, victims of genocide, nothing for an American to be proud of. When I received the book a couple of weeks later, I was fascinated by the heartrending story. I was taken with the fact that he liked the song, "The Road to Mandalay." That song used to break my heart when I was a boy. Stories of lost love because couples were of different ancestry always moved me. I wondered why it had to be like that. I wrote an article on Ishi that was published in *The Catholic Worker* to call attention to this discrimination that had been so swept under the rug.

In mid-January, I had a visit from Jim Holloway and Will Campbell, both active in the civil rights movement. Then we drove into Bardstown to the Willett home.

Before I got too melancholy, I had a visit from three local men, Jonathan Williams, Guy Davenport, and Gene Meatyard. We talked about publishing and photography. Jonathan Williams is a local poet and publisher. Guy Davenport is a critic, teacher, and translator, as well as a writer and artist. I was particularly impressed with Gene Meatyard and his visionary photographs. He took some pictures of me, and I was really pleased when he sent them a few weeks later. They almost look out of focus, but give a strange, other-worldly effect which I liked because they are unique and imaginative.

All these years I have tried to accept the policy of no friendships, but it is impossible. When I am discouraged within our group from making friends, I find them outside the monastery in the local area, and, by correspondence, around the world. I believe friendship is an expression of the love of God, and it is unnatural to forbid it, so long as it is a healthy relationship.

Finally the Abbot's own Council put pressure on him to stop censoring all our mail. He was even removing money and clippings from the letters. Now that I was receiving my magazines, I could hardly bear to read them. The war was more inhuman and irrational than ever.

On my 52$^{nd}$ birthday, I received an invitation to come to France for the presentation of the Legion of Honor to Dom Columban at Melleray. Since he was the Father Immediate of Gethsemani, it would be expected I would attend because I was involved in writing the French documentation for the award. I could not imagine that Dom James would have the nerve to decline this, but that is exactly what he did. First, he wrote me a note offering me his "humble advice." Then he added it must be a temptation of the devil, and I dare not make such a dreadful request. I knew that Dom James realized the significance of the award, the highest honor awarded by France to its most valued citizens. He knew I would love to see France again after so many years. I believed the Abbot was really sick. I tore up his notes and threw them in the fireplace. I wished later that I had saved them to show Jim Wygal for his professional evaluation.

A week later I went to see Dr. Mitchell again. He said I must have surgery for the bursitis. Fortunately, Dom James did not enforce his order for me to change doctors and go to the free hospital in Lexington.

Tommie O'Callaghan was generous to invite me over after my appointment. She is a handsome woman, with beautiful dark hair and strong womanly features that inspire confidence. Tommie is one of those special women who can successfully juggle homemaking and raising a house full of children while still maintaining her marvelous unique spirit and grounding in her love for God. Her generosity is exhibited in her elastic schedule that she can always expand to meet the demands that come her way. God and man alike love a cheerful giver.

I am so grateful to Dan Walsh for introducing her to me. Besides all the rides she gives me without sufficient notice, she brings me up to date on the issues that concern Catholics today—the Pill, and Catholic schools. I have to be moderately informed, though I am not a journalist.

The monastery started to build other hermitages, and my favorite spots were being covered up by them. Soon we would have a *laura*, a whole cluster of hermitages, at the rate we were going. Brother Giles put in bronze statues and dogwoods on the edge of St. Malachy's field, not far from St. Edmond's field I so loved. It's a sort of artificial place of meditation. The natural beauty there is too subtle, I guess.

I wondered if it was time for me to move on. My hermitage would soon be one of several, and I would not be surprised if the others who move out here might not want to socialize when they find out how lonely this life is away from the group. This was not the deep reality I came out here to live. I need the reality of my purpose for living, away from the unreality of a sick world that threatens our very existence. Up to now my books had been my earthly companions and comforting ones. I didn't plan to trade them for the brethren I left behind at the abbey.

I had an unexpected visit from Sy Freedgood, and he found me depressed. He thought I should get out more and meet people, and maybe he's right. It would do no good to ask Dom James for permission. He would probably think I wanted to go out to meet another girl. What I would really like to do is go visit Sidi Abdesalam in Algeria or the Zen place in Japan. I must be dreaming. It was St. Patrick's Day, so we drove over to Lexington.

Rosemary Ruether, the liberal Catholic theologian, wrote to me quite realistically about the state of the Church in America today. I was troubled, though, about her outrageous conclusions. For example, she said that monastic life is unchristian, that it began as an institutionalized radical elite. I believe that she is accurate, though, in saying that the problem lies in the disparity between the original message of Jesus and its subversion in the institutional Church. I see hope through reform, but I'm not sure she is hopeful.

I was beginning to realize that monasticism that is limited to the medieval Western tradition could not survive in the modern world. We have embalmed Christianity, not renewed it. I'm not sure how much of St. Benedict's Rule can survive in practice. Maybe monasticism needs to be started in a different way, in new small monasteries. It seems to me we need to open up a path to old ways that have been forgotten over the centuries. I will give this much thought and prayer. The monastery is becoming largely a holy sham. Yet it is more authentic than the sham of the world outside.

The monastery procedures, called usages, are sometimes like the rules followed by the Pharisees whom Jesus condemned in his teaching. Man must have a direct relationship with God in concrete reality, in a way that is truly natural, so that it then becomes supernatural.

I am seeking the reality of the purpose of life and an escape from the unreality of the world. Today this world is filled with violence, hatred, and an insane and cunning fury that seems to threaten our very existence.

I've always thought that my path lay beyond both Communism and Capitalism. I find, though, that I can get into trouble if I am not allied with the principles of Capitalism, whether in or outside the monastery. I may be wrong in many ways, but at least I'm living the hermit life trying to cope with my wrongness here. The world of the senses is the world of Muzak, and I cannot abide its phoniness. The devil takes on interesting, up-to-date secular shapes these days, but in reality he is the malicious manipulator and hostile scorekeeper that some would lead us to believe that God is.

I meditate again on Matthew's description of Jesus' agony in the garden of Gethsemani. "Could you not, then, watch one hour with me? Watch and pray, that you may not enter into temptation. The spirit indeed is willing, but the flesh is weak." I will not allow my eyes to get heavy and fall asleep in my watch.

# Chapter 30

The most important man in the world to me in March of 1967 was PeeWee McGruder, our contractor. His well diggers finally found water when they drilled through the limestone under my hermitage. My ailing body cried out in thanks, that soon I would no longer have to carry those heavy gallon jugs of water up to the hermitage.

I finished my article on Ishi before I went to the hospital for another bursitis operation. I also reviewed the typed manuscript of articles to be called *Faith and Violence* that got released after the surgery.

The stay at St. Joe's was five days, since the operation ended up being routine. I called Margie and learned she might come to see me, but later found she couldn't make it because she had to work. Our phone calls from the hospital were warm and affectionate, but I was sure now that our love affair was really all over. There was no point in trying to keep it alive.

I returned to the hermitage after one night at the monastery infirmary. I tried to type. With so many good monks gone now, I could not find a typist to help me. Brother Martin had been in charge of getting things typed and mimeographed for me. He left me a note in the infirmary refectory saying my work now was upsetting and beyond his limit. He was offended by the poem of Rafael Alberti, "Roman Nocturnes," that I had translated. He had probably mistakenly thought it was profane since he didn't understand my vocabulary. There was no point in trying to explain anything to Brother Martin or his crew—they didn't have the literary foundation to understand the poetry I was working on. They wouldn't believe me anyway, with all the rumors that had probably been circulating around the monastery about me.

Two weeks later I went back to Dr. Mitchell's office to have the stitches removed. Afterwards I went over to the O'Callaghans' home and met Marie Charron, whom Tommie recruited to type for me.

Donald Allchin came to see me just after Easter. We went in to Louisville together, he to the Baptist Seminary, me to the Doctor again. I had not been able to use my arm much. He said the surgery was not successful, so I would have to go back to hot water bottles. Worse than that, I would not be able to type much at all. I wondered if it was providential.

I went to the Old House Restaurant for lunch alone, and then made a visit across the street to the Cathedral for the first time in a long time. Afterwards I went to a newsstand and bought some paperback science fiction books, simply because I hadn't done that in twenty-five years.

Naomi Burton and Jay Laughlin suggested I make a will to protect my writing. They offered to help with the details. To do the legal work for me, I asked John Slate to come down from New York to handle it, to make sure nothing got in the hands of people who didn't represent my point of view. I was relieved he agreed to come down to do it. It had been thirty years. It didn't take me long to realize he was still the great sport I knew at Columbia. The guy who could converse in dog barks had now mastered legalese.

The literary estate documents would insure that Gethsemani received all the proceeds of my work in the future. Slate and I went together to Bellarmine to make arrangements for turning over my material for the Merton Room. We gave two of the staff a ride to the airport, and I suggested we all have dinner at the Luau Room. I watched the planes again, as I had with Margie and with Wygal, from the window. Talking about my estate, it made me wonder how soon the day would come when I would be an estate instead of a man. It was a creepy feeling, since we usually think of our present as ongoing and our current problems and emotions as of paramount importance. We all know we should remind ourselves we won't be here forever, but we seldom do unless it is directly in our faces.

Driving back to Gethsemani, Slate drove almost 100 mph on the Turnpike, really frightening me. He drank too much at the airport. He was matching me drink for drink, but he wasn't supposed to drink because of his heart condition. I couldn't slow him down. Later I wrote to Bob Lax in Greece about my concern for Slate.

When Slate and I were at Bellarmine, I was practically accosted by some of the faculty and students for my autograph. I was surprised, not understanding the value of my signature on a book to anyone. It was my first experience since we had the centennial event in June of 1949, when I was the new author. I have never resolved my conflict with wanting recognition but feeling guilty about it.

I received my copy of *Mystics and Zen Masters*, which was for the most part a compilation of a lot of recent magazine articles, with some improvements I had added. To my horror, there was a photograph of me on the back cover. I never gave Farrar, Straus and Giroux that privilege. I believed that now everywhere I go, more people would recognize me and either want to make contact or make judgments about what I might be doing. I'll bet they cleared it with Dom James. I thought it was probably his latest strategy for further isolating me, knowing I would flee from public recognition of this type.

I simply do not belong to the age of traveling by jet to conferences and making appearances. That's good for people who are acclimatized to that kind of activity. I belong in these woods, watching the jets go over my trees. I feel uneasy that I do not belong when I'm in the spotlight. Yet I have a compelling desire to be somebody, not needing it or wanting it, yet continually going after it. Not that I should stop writing or publishing, but I should not allow myself to be flattered or used. When a picture appears like this, I'm ashamed of myself. If I were serious about wanting to be unknown, I would not accept what eventually shames me. The truth is I want to be known, loved, and admired, but not in a cheap or silly way.

In April the redbuds and dogwoods were in full bloom. One warm, sunny day I returned to the Derby Day picnic site. To my surprise, I felt the old freedom, the peace of being without care for the first time since I had met Margie. The hidden pond with the pines around it and the little open patch of dry shale looked the same, but I couldn't believe how different my feelings were now. I was no longer a one-dimensional man, but in developing this fullness I risked losing the essence I had been created to develop. I know now only the grace of God saved me from a terrible mistake. It was good that the Abbot stopped me, but it should have been done differently.

I now had a sense of stability and substantiality, of not being deceived by emotions that had caused me to lie to myself. The silence of my life sustained me and empowered me. It was undoubtedly necessary for me to go through this experience to learn a truth that would have been otherwise inaccessible to me.

I took off my shirt and let the warm sun shine on my back where there were now scars from two operations. I looked up at the pine tops and the sunny clouds and thanked God for all His gifts to me. Then I saw Father Raymond drive by the lake with a carload of visiting nuns. I reflected that he definitely exists on a different plane. I told myself I must control my sarcasm when I encounter him in Chapter meetings.

Naomi Burton came to visit again, and offered her usual mothering care. She brought me some Rice-a-roni and Lipton soup to help me with my dietary restrictions. We enjoyed a picnic with some of my local friends and took pictures. I photographed a large hook suspended from a construction crane. I later titled the picture "the only known photograph of God." She suggested I write something on Sufism, but it is not a priority for me. Anyway, I believed she was just trying to get me interested in publishing again. I reassured her that I had not abandoned my work. I had a tape recorder now to dictate my work and thereby save my arms. She drove me to an appointment I had with Dr. Lucas in Louisville before she left.

On April 22, it was one year since the steeple was taken down from the church. I said a Mass for Margie that she would be happy. I tried to persuade myself that I wasn't sad. Still, I continued to worry a little about her. Nevertheless, it was liberation day for me, because I made up my mind that it was over between us.

My affair with Margie will be a permanent part of my life story, though. I will provide that my journal be kept under wraps for twenty-five years after my death. Then my readers can know about my love for Margie because it is part of me, my limitations, my need for love, my loneliness, my inner division in which solitude is at once a problem and a solution for me.

I made another trip to Louisville, this time to see Dr.Roser for an audiogram of my colon. I also saw Dr. Smith, an allergist, about a sinus infection. His office was in St. Matthews in East Louisville, so I could not combine the visit with any other stops like the University library on the other side of town. Now the doctor said I had to avoid all foods with milk in them, and no beer. I went to a nearby deli for some Kosher food before I went back to the hermitage to enjoy it.

I finished "Day of a Stranger" for the *Hudson Review*. In writing this piece, I thought of my imprisonment here by Dom James.

I have continually been invited to attend events with my way paid, and he will not allow me to accept. I do prefer solitude, but I want it to be authentic, not an imposed sentence. Dom James has his own CIA of faithful followers to keep him informed of what everyone is doing. Their distorted idea of monastic obedience alienates them from those of us who are happy doing what we know we need to do in spite of the Abbot.

I found a dead mouse on my doorstep on the afternoon of May 5 when I returned from the monastery. What does it mean? One of the priests received a postcard from Dom James from his meeting at Citeaux, tore it up in a neat pile of pieces, and left it in the room where work clothes are kept, and disappeared. I guess he is tired of Dom James' phony gestures of affection for the community. He always sends a lot of postcards when he travels.

Dan Berrigan came down again from New York, and we discussed the war and what our roles should or should not be to help bring it to an end. Dan wanted to offer himself as a "hostage for peace." I feared for his personal safety if he proceeded with this. He went with me to my allergist, Dr. Smith. Then the doctor drove us to the airport so I could see Dan off for his return to Cornell where he was teaching. He was wearing a black beret and turtleneck windbreaker, like the French worker-priests.

Dr. Smith drove me back to Gethsemani. To relax and meditate on the matters that Dan and I had discussed, I watched the birds on my porch and wrote in my journal. I loved the towhee sparrows, black and white, just like Trappists, and with red eyes! If I were a bird I would want to look like that. The little brown patches on their sides really set off their beauty.

On May 11, I wrote a piece on Malcolm X and his assassination. I wondered if he would have been so enshrined if he had lived longer. The same question occurred to me about John F. Kennedy, if he had lived to carry on the Vietnam war. Maybe they were both saved by death before they could be corrupted in a new way.

I signed off on the Prologue for "Edifying Cables" to send off to Laughlin.

My bitterness extended even to the point that I tell the reader to "go write your own prologue." I would see if New Directions would publish that!

I personally feel a deep need for conversion and penance and getting back on the right path. I need to pray for forgiveness for the way I trifled with life and grace. I have a real sense of being flawed and having a need for immense help and pardon to recover some capacity to love God. I feel Mary is near me and shows me mercy. I feel there is a decay in everything in this society, including the Church and the monastery. God's beautiful world is being sullied. We are rotting in our own garbage, and yet have so much potential! I must try to bring life back into society, along with the others who see this. I can be of maximum use to the world by keeping my distance and my freedom.

I have been giving Dan Walsh some guidance on liturgical procedures to help prepare for his ordination, since he had never attended a seminary. In only two months, Archbishop Floersh considered him ready. On May 14, Pentecost Sunday, Dan was ordained a priest. I rode to St. Thomas' Seminary in the car with Dom James and his brother, Bernard Fox. Dan asked me to concelebrate with the Archbishop, and I was happy to accept. Dan was a little nervous. I knew how he felt from my own ordination. It was such a huge step because it was absolutely irreversible under most circumstances. After Dan's ceremony, I got a ride with a bunch of ex-monks to the O'Callaghans' home for the reception. I talked too much, I thought afterwards, but we all had a great time.

The next day I concelebrated with Dan at his church and then saw the new Archbishop, McDonough. He encouraged my writing and even said he thought I ought to go to Morocco to see people like Sidi Abdesalam. He told me the Apostolic Delegate was also in favor of my work and wanted to come down to talk with me. He is one of the new cardinals. I was optimistic that something might be cooking for me in the church's political circles.

I have been reading about quantum physics. It dazzles and baffles me. I wish I had a better grounding in science. This confirms what Herakleitos was reaching for by intuition. I yearn to better understand what is happening in matter, and what energy is really all about. There is certainly a connection in my mind with the world around me—people, nature, and objects. It's no wonder we are all connected by free-flowing atoms. The stars, too, are part of me. Even in thought, I can see the continuum from down-to-earth reality to asceticism—from the extraterrestrial to the goodness that is God in infinity.

My next writing was a booklet on Camus'"Plague" for Seabury Press. I dedicated it to Dan Berrigan, who likes Camus' work as much as I do. Camus is really impressive. He wrote about a dead rat, and I wondered at the coincidence of finding one on my doorstep recently.

In June I was concerned that we might be entering World War III with the Arabs and Israelis fighting. I thought I might go up in smoke with the gold of Fort Knox and all the fissionable material stored there. In a straight line, the hermitage was only 15 or 20 miles away. I told myself that we all have to face death alone anyway. I felt like it was 1939 again and that we were poised on the verge of another world holocaust.

The Order continued to grant lenience to following the traditional ways of the monastery. Diet was relaxed, and private rooms were allowed. There was less work, less prayer, and more of nothing. The only purpose seemed to be to keep people comfortable so they wouldn't run away, content to live an easy and pointless life. Well, I believed that more monks than ever would leave, and there would be fewer vocations than under the original rules. Only the mail censorship would continue with the same intensity. Naturally, Dom James would not cut himself off from such a rich treat to his paranoia.

I went to Louisville and finally got an allergy shot that was effective. I wouldn't be expecting to see Dr. Smith or Dr. Mitchell much anymore. I thought I could get by with traction and some bufferin.

My health was better when I was seeing Margie, but I didn't want to live anywhere else but my hermitage. I didn't really want to see her and dredge up all those memories of our feelings of last year. I had gotten away completely from self-disciplines like fasting. The solitude of the woods was the only thing in my life that saved me from a stupid mistake.

I live in an apparent contradiction, as an absurd kind of hermit, living as a writer, yet not knowing if I want to write anymore, or what I want to write, a seemingly typical monk when I am now questioning the present interpretation of the monastic life. " ... what I really have to do is the same thing I have always had to do: to find my own way, without a map, taking neither this nor that except in so far as I have to, and working it out as I go along" (Journal, June 23, 1966).

In late June I went to Lexington to see Victor Hammer. I got a ride with the Meatyards, Gene and Madie, who are two of my favorite people. Gene is a marvelous photographic artist. Victor was too weak to say much, and I saw him drifting away, just as I remembered watching Father slowly pass on. Victor and Carolyn gave me his two latest *New Yorker* magazines—passing the torch, so to speak. Carolyn knew that the literary life she enjoyed with him was now over. I too would miss him. Whether we were having a serious discussion or just talking, we could always enjoy a good bottle of wine together and some Spanish brandy on top of it. I never felt distracted or restless after their visits, as I did with so many others. It was as if we belonged together.

Within weeks, Victor died. We had a hard rain for days, to the point of flooding up to the porches of houses in the area. I said a Mass for him and wondered if the last sacraments had been given to him. He had said he didn't want them because they did not conform to his particular kind of faith. I would not violate his wishes and impose the sacraments on him, but I didn't know if a priest at the hospital might have given them to him anyway. Carolyn was not Catholic, but respected the Church and wanted to give him the benefit of his faith. He just did not believe in the sacraments and saw them as the Church's intrusion on his relationship with God. I would leave him in God's hands, knowing it was not my concern.

My new cedar bookcases arrived for the hermitage, along with the kitchen sink and a cabinet. The water was hooked up, now six months since the well-rigger arrived. Still I had to use the outhouse since the bathroom had not been completed. It was obviously not a priority for the monastery management to get me going out here any sooner, but that was past history now. Anyway, the lack of comforts resembled much that I had experienced in my childhood in France and England. I cleaned the hermitage and admired my accomplishment. I had curtains and Venetian blinds now on the windows and supplies to make myself more independent. I was at peace! I put up a tall cross of two large cedar tree trunks in front of the place to show it is a house of God. I placed an old wagon wheel at its base. It seemed to represent finding union with God through the cross of Christ.

The Buddhist nun, Nhat Chi, immolated herself in May, in protest of the Vietnam war. I didn't learn of it until July when I read Victor's *New Yorker* magazine. I was horrified that the war had come to this. I received a request to participate in a seven-day fast for world peace. I had never gone without food for even half that time. I planned to begin slowly and do what I could.

It was almost seven years since I got the hermitage, and soon the anniversary of the feast of Our Lady of Mount Carmel in July, that I had dedicated to her honor. I finally got Dom James' approval to order an altar, and rushed to get it in time to say Mass in the hermitage on her feast. It was a sweet-smelling cedar. I barely made the date. I placed my icons on it and worshiped the Lord with thanksgiving for this long-awaited gift. I then prepared a hot meal for myself, and I walked out to the Grove I loved to visit. Now it had the Jon Daniels life-size bronzes of the Lord's agony in the Gethsemani garden. It was not the same as before, but a lovely place for meditation nevertheless.

Ed Rice wrote that he couldn't keep *Jubilee* going any longer on his own funds. For a while he thought he could sell it to Herder & Herder, even though it was deeply in debt, but he had to go ahead and shut it down. It was the death of the greatest Catholic magazine I'd ever seen. It was a heartbreak because Lax and I were in on its birth when we were all young and optimistic about a healthy market for a thinking Catholic's publication. I believed that some of my own negative writing was at least partly the cause of its failure. Rice was too loyal a friend to me not to print the stuff I sent him. This was the result, and I had to live with it.

I felt I should be grateful that I had no problem finding publishers. I got *Faith and Violence* published in paperback by Notre Dame Press. This was only thanks to Naomi, who got past the legal restrictions of my contract with Farrar, Straus, & Giroux. I dedicated it jointly to Dan's brother, Phil Berrigan, and to Jim Forest. Both had sacrificed so much of themselves to oppose violence in this country, I felt it was a mandate. On the other hand, a lot of others probably wouldn't have wanted it dedicated to them. It was not a popular message for readers, but I wrote what others would not say.

I included my essays on the God is dead philosophy. I had to catch up with Father Raymond. He had given it his usual cursory treatment in *The Silent Spire Speaks*, that came out in 1966. He said he could see a difference in mental attitude between graduates of Catholic universities compared with those from schools like Columbia and some other secular institutions. I wondered why he specified Columbia. Then there was the comment that some "'peaceniks' are powerful talkers," obviously believing that wars solve problems. I most agreed with his point that the "rumble" of the heavy gunfire from nearby Fort Knox was really unsettling.

I felt detached from the publishing process now as well as the monastery, like I was not in the same reality anymore. I knew I belonged in the woods, these woods or some other woods somewhere. I didn't feel like I belonged to this community anymore. To see many of them made me feel guilty that they were enduring Dom James' wacky and pathetic ways because they were following my example in the monastic life. So I was part of their madness. It was too difficult to observe. For example, Brother Odilo, with a long red beard, was now building himself a hermitage out of wood and plastic. It looked to me like a squatter's place. This, I believed, was at least partly my fault.

Saying Mass in the hermitage was a moving experience I hadn't adequately anticipated. It was incredible to be alone with the Lord. If I couldn't have the mystical Chant to accompany the Mass anymore with the modernization of the liturgy, at least I had the solitude to say the Mass at my own pace. I was so pleased I finally asked Dom James for permission again, when I heard that he had given Father Flavian permission when his first year would be completed in his hermitage. It amazed me that the Abbot would not explain what changed his mind.

In July I heard about the travels of my friend, Dom Leclercq, who had just returned from an extended visit around Asia to monasteries and holy sites. I envied him the experience. Sometimes I felt an oppressive sense of my own immobility. While all the while everyone I knew was flying overhead to every part of the world, I sat there losing touch with reality, with the knowledge of the state of the world, and wondered how I could write for people effectively.

Expressing my restlessness to Dom Leclercq, I must have introduced the idea that he might get approval for me to join him in a monastic meeting where we could mutually benefit in furthering our interests in advancing the eremitical life in the universal Church. He suggested a meeting of Eastern and Western monks that he was planning to be held in Bangkok later in the following year. He expressed the thought that I had been "cut off long enough" from being able to speak personally with a group of this type. I responded to him that I would be eager to do it if it were possible, which I certainly doubted.

Father Hilarion told me he had now received permission to become a hermit, and I knew he was just doing it to get away from Dom James and his program. He said that Brother Jude was leaving the monastery for the same reason. Father Hilarion would have a trailer. Meanwhile, Dom James told everyone he would rather be a hermit than an abbot, but must do his duty to run the monastery.

In August I went to see Dr. Mitchell about a bad knee, which hurt so much I could not kneel. He said it must have been an old soccer injury, but he didn't ask me if I ever played soccer. I didn't—it was rugby.

Bellarmine College and Sister Therese Lentfoehr each have much of my writing. At least that will last. I received a silver key to the Merton Room at Bellarmine, where I never go but where strangers go to get to know me. The Merton Room is my escape from Gethsemani, a protest against the destruction of everything I have put my heart into here. That is more a reality than I feel that I now am. I read some of my poems for "Edifying Cables" into the tape recorder and they sounded good, at least to me. There is still something I have not said to the world, and maybe I have to say it by not saying, in an emptiness that can only be stated in what is called anti-poetry. I want to express my deep concern for society and its struggle with today's social problems. Maybe *Geography of Lograire* will be my final liberation from all diaries. It could be my one remaining task.

In late August we had our first Visitation from Dom Ignace Gillet, the successor to Dom Gabriel. Early in his visit, his interpreter, Father Nicholas, a Canadian who spoke French, had a heart attack and died on the spot. His body was returned to his own monastery in Georgia. I was drafted to be one of the substitutes since Dom Ignace did not speak English. One of my assignments was his talk on his trip to Japan. Afterwards I went back to the hermitage and some bourbon. As a bonus, the following night I translated his talk on Hong Kong, with slides, no less.

The summer of 1967 brought a strange and new sensation: the censors would not read my material. Father Paul Bourne, my chief censor, returned my latest manuscript to me. He said the whole requirement for censorship was now suspended and may be repealed. I couldn't believe it was a permanent arrangement, so I continued mailing all my articles to Father Paul, who returned each one. I felt like a prisoner being suddenly released.

I started doing some fasting then, trying to get myself back into a frame of mind I liked better than the depressed one I had been in since I let Margie leave my life. There was a summer storm and lightning hit the utility pole next to the hermitage. I read by my old kerosene lamp until it was over. It was frightening—kind of like the wrath of God.

The monastery church was finally finished, and I was happy to see it was still recognizable as the Church of Gethsemani. Father Timothy objected to air conditioning the new church, and Dom James relegated him to two more years of study in Rome to study moral theology. Actually, this was a gift since Father Timothy probably preferred the liturgical level of Vatican life. He was unaccustomed to air conditioning anyway, from his previous years in Europe.

I was happy I did not have to express my reaction to the new sacristy. The new altar was black stone, with two heavy black posts supporting it. I thought it would make a perfect Aztec altar for the sacrifice of the heart or for some Druidical immolations. It was definitely for the real thing! The new throne for the Abbot was narrow, rigid, and fierce. A judge could pass sentence from it, with fists on the two arms, and be ready to spring up and grab the knife and rush at the victim. It was definitely all Dom James. It echoed the abbots before him and made me shiver.

Sometimes I wonder if I might someday have the urge to leave here in a hurry. I should arrange my affairs more efficiently in case I have that feeling. I wonder if I will someday be confined to the infirmary as a semi-idiot in hopeless arrogance. It is very quiet here at the monastery now that the building is completed. I fast in silence. I feel like Pasternak in his dacha.

In August a request came from Pope Paul VI that I write something special for him—a message of contemplatives to the world. Fighting an attack of flu, I wrote it quickly, between Linden tea and periods of sleep. I was told the Pope spoke of me and sent a cordial message. I felt much better. The writing for him came to me readily.

I then decided to try to publish my old *Journal of My Escape from the Nazis*, which still read well to me. It was unfinished business, in my head. I would take care to disguise references to certain matters to avoid offending Iris Bennett, Dr. Bennett's widow. She had wanted to sue me when she read *The Seven Storey Mountain*. She thought I was critical of my guardian, which only led me to conclude that she was a prize neurotic. I always thought of this early work as one of my best books. It came from my center, where I really experienced myself and my life, a very vital and crucial moment of breakthrough in my existence. Father Paul, my former censor, returned the manuscript to me unread, saying he was not even allowed to read novels, let alone censor them.

Ed Rice wrote to me that Ad Reinhardt had died. At least he got a good obit in the *NY Times*, and some other papers, but his name was misspelled. What a paradox—to be remembered but not exactly. I looked at the painting I had received from Ad for the hermitage, a subtle presentation of black crosses he called "Black on Black." I had to look at it for an extended time to give my eyes time to adjust to the blackness so I could see the subtle geometry. Ad said he sought to portray a reductionist kind of perfection in neutrality. It fit the way I felt.

Actually I had always preferred black and white to color in my drawings. Japanese prints, sumie, are more expressive because the black and white make the whole view one. In that unity it becomes more than the sum of its parts.

I thought about the old days at Columbia when all of our gang were taken with Bramachari and the attractiveness of ancient Eastern philosophy. From Ad's obituary I saw that he had remained a thinker, as well as an outspoken activist in politics. One of the art critics, Harold Rosenberg, called Reinhardt "the black monk of the anti-abstract expressionist crusade" in 1963. Ad's work was called a paradox of material objects denying their physicality, aggressive in their reticence, about death and commemoration. Reinhardt had once said art must be pure and empty. I could see that Ad and I were one in our maturity of thought. I too was beginning to experiment with a radical form of expression.

First, I wrote to Lax on September 5, 1967, in our typical macaronic style: " ... Ad is well out of sight in his blacks. It is likely too true the bad fortunes and the sorrows. Gypsy Rose Lee look in her crystal ball and see no more jokes and no more funnies it is not any more like thirty seven college chums. I must therefore cease and sit in the sorrows ... ."

I wrote to Dan Berrigan on September 16 about Ad's death. I doubted that any of our Columbia group would outlast sixty. I felt pretty moth-eaten myself.

In September, John Slate died from a heart attack. That was no surprise, after I had seen the shape he was in. As if that weren't enough, I received a letter from Lax that Benji Marcus had died in Olean.

It was time for me to face my own end more realistically. Slate and I hadn't finished my will before he died, so I had to proceed with someone else. I thought of Julian Cornell, Ezra Pound's lawyer, but decided it made more sense to work with John Ford here. I felt compelled to proceed quickly. The trustees were all busy with their own divergent interests, and I knew I represented only one segment of their lives. I also knew that my recent socially-oriented work had been eclipsed by the solid rejection of the Church and the indifference or inaction of many of my readers. I had a growing instinct that there was no more in my script to act out. I felt like a character in a drama who had been written out of the next scene. I called Jay Laughlin for advice. Before I knew it, I learned that Sy Freedgood was in the hospital with an inflamed heart. I wondered if I could live much longer than my friends. Maybe another four or five years at the most, I think, of my sheer silliness.

Near the end of September, I visited Dr. Mitchell again, this time for a back X-ray and my knee. Afterwards it was lunch again at Cunningham's with Jim Wygal, like old times. At first we were both depressed, but gradually felt better. Then we went over to Pat Welsh's house. She worked at Bellarmine, and we had a good conversation about the library and some drinks. It was a relief to be around people living in the future rather than in the past. I returned to the hermitage like a prisoner to his cell. As I walked across the field, I heard a saxophone—what a sad song coming across the hill. Another monk was trying to find himself.

Soon after this outing, I got a ride with Carolyn Hammer to John Jacob Niles' farm for lunch. John brought in a singer and pianist to perform some songs he had written, using my poetry as the lyrics. I was really moved by them. He made me value my own work more, adding his beautiful music. Carolyn did not agree with my reaction, since his music has almost an other-worldly, atonal sound. I liked John Niles and believed that he captured something of the spirit of my words. It was an oasis of an experience for me in the natural death of the fall season.

Later that evening, I had a special experience.

*A storm comes up, with hard rain blown by an early fall wind. I decide to build a fire with the few pieces of wood I have left to cheer myself up and add some light to the single kerosene lamp I had. My door slams from the draft before I can think to close it. Then I hear a pounding. It must be something caught in the wind. But it persists. It couldn't be a visitor, but I should check to see if someone is stranded out here with me. I open the door, pulling against the wind blowing it out of my hand.*

*Ðom James!" I could not believe the sight. He huddled against the wind and rain, stooped and completely soaked.*

*"May I come in?" I was incredulous.*

*"Of course, Reverend Father." The next few minutes were consumed with our mutual attempts to get him drier and minimally comfortable. It was his first time at the hermitage since I moved in.*

*"Well, how about some dry clothes, then I'll show you around."*

*"No, I'd rather stay put here by your fire and I'll be fine in a few minutes."*

*I motioned for him to take my rocking chair. He sat forward, nervously, with his hands capped on his knees. I decided to just stand by the fireplace since I was not anymore at ease than he was.*

*"Did you get caught in the storm while out walking, Father? I didn't know you walked in this area." I couldn't contain my curiosity at how he landed at my door like a stray pet.*

*"No, Father Louis. May I call you Tom? That's how I always think of you."*

*"'Course, Father, whatever you'd like." I was flabbergasted at his remark. I wondered if he was somehow trying to disarm me, and why.*

"Tom, I came here tonight to speak with you. Privately. I didn't let the rain stop me. You see, I have decided I want to resign as Abbot. I want your opinion. Do you think I would be shirking my duty?"

"Dom James, is this your Confession? Are you here to receive absolution for this?"

"No, Tom. This is not a Confession. But you are my confessor, and for fifteen years you have heard me recite my faults under the seal of the confessional. This time I'm speaking to you as your Abbot, and, I hope, as your old friend, asking you for your opinion, since you know me so well. You also know what it's like living in solitude. Do you think I could do it? Do you think it would be right for me to step down and give up my management of this place? I really value your ideas. You have experience here. What would I be getting myself into?"

"Dom James, I am so flattered at your trust in my advice, but surely you know what you want. It's really between you and God as to how you live out your religious vocation. You've served all these years, and you deserve to proceed as you see fit." I was shocked at the entire encounter and hedged my comments, not sure what he might be leading up to.

"Tom, I can't go on." He fell silent. We both stared into the fire in the open fireplace.

"I don't believe you should take any precipitous action, Father, just in case you've had a bad time of it recently or are not feeling well." I was groping for the motivation that might be behind this.

"No, Tom. There's nothing in particular going on now. It's just that I see the monastery losing good men, not attracting the boys who have come to see us, and in general I feel like I'm making management mistakes, more every day. You don't know this, but I have been asking my superiors for several years to give me permission to step down. I've been turned down every time, until now. I'm burned out, Tom. But I'm not a shirker."

I couldn't believe what I was hearing. In nineteen years I had never heard this man speak candidly about himself.

"Tom, I have been moved when I've thought about you, and how you put your life and your career in my hands, in obedience. I know it came hard for you many times, and I just want you to know I respect you for living up to your vow of obedience, accepting your vow of poverty, and remaining loyal to Gethsemani rather than wandering off to some other part of the world. I knew you could walk away, as so many others have done. And I'm sure you've had plenty of days when it was tempting. You are the one man here I most admire. You've never let me down in coming for our weekly visits. I *have really depended on them, although I doubt you know that. If I step down and move into a hermitage, we won't have that relationship anymore. Of course I would still want you to be my confessor, but I would not be guiding your spiritual or material path. I would pass you to another. I need your permission to break our bond, and I hope you will give it to me."*

*I thought of all the years of Mondays when I had heard his Confession, and sometimes he had heard mine. We had blessed each other and conveyed the Lord's forgiveness for our petty failings. I began to get choked up and couldn't believe that welling up inside me I actually had feelings for this poor, old man huddled before me in the firelight.*

*"Dom James," I hurriedly replied, "you must be in touch with God's Will for you. Do what you believe is right for you. Thanks for your tribute, but it is definitely undeserving. I appreciate it, even so. I believe you will like it out here in the woods. Sometimes you will have the thought that the community has disowned you or ostracized you. It can be torture at times. Whenever you feel alone, you can rejoin the group down at the Abbey, and the feeling will pass. Before you know it, you won't particularly want to very often."*

*"Thank you, Tom. Please don't think of me anymore as your 'public enemy number one.' I've always wanted what would be best for you, and followed the guidance of the Holy Spirit in advising you with your problems. And in the future, please call me James, will you?"*

*I saw that he was exhausted from this entire episode, so I turned my attention to his coat, drying near the fire.*

*"It's beginning to dry out, Father. Do you think you should get back so you can get out of all those wet clothes?"*

*"Yes, you're right, Tom. I need to go." He stood up and reached for his coat. "I enjoyed our talk and feel more confident now, that I am on the right track."*

*I handed him the umbrella I had for emergencies. As I helped him into the wet coat, I gave his shoulders a slight squeeze. He turned and looked into my eyes. His eyes shone through his glasses, filled with gratitude for my gesture. He patted me on the hand, too emotional to say more.*

*"See you tomorrow at Mass, Dom James. And I won't say anything to anyone about our conversation."*

*I watched him hurry down the path back to the monastery. I could not even manage to analyze the event. I went into my chapel and knelt down. I asked God to help that man.*

*A lump in my throat came from nowhere. Was this the death of a relationship with this man, or was it a new life for both of us in our future dealings with each other?*

When the sun broke through my window in the morning, I realized this encounter must have been a very realistic dream or something that I experienced in my subconscious, because I was not too surprised at the next development.

At Mass, Dom James arose at the time of the homily.

"Today I have an announcement that I make with both joy and regret. I will retire on October 2, and become a hermit at Gethsemani for the remainder of my life."

Soon I found myself musing over all the possible choices for his replacement. Who would it be? Father Flavian, who had recently been my confessor, would be the most likely of those here now. But he was a hermit, too, and probably wouldn't want it. Would the others vote for him? I prayed to God they would.

Suppose the group tried to draft me. I must do what I could to see that the best man took over Gethsemani, someone who would allow the hermits to stay and give us all the peace we seek here.

# BOOK FOUR

"*Every one of us is shadowed by an illusory person: a false self. This is 'the man that I want myself to be but who cannot exist, because God does not know anything about him. And to be unknown of God is altogether too much privacy.' "My false and private self is the one who" wants to exist outside the reach of God's will and God's love." But there is no substance under the things with which I am clothed. I am hollow, and my structure of pleasures and ambitions has no foundation. I am objectified in them. But they are all destined by their very contingency to be destroyed. And when they "are gone there will be nothing left of me but my own nakedness and emptiness and hollowness, to tell me that I am my own mistake … . If I find Him I will find myself and if I find my true self I will find Him*" (pp. 34-36).

*New Seeds of Contemplation*

Merton's denim clothing and boots on exhibit at the Thomas Merton Center, Bellarmine University, Louisville, KY. Photographed by the author in 1998.

*Photograph of Thomas Merton and Sister Therese Lentfoehr. November 5, 1967.*
*Used with permission of the Merton Legacy Trust and the*
*Thomas Merton Center at Bellarmine University.*

# Chapter 31

Merton had a dream about going on a journey somewhere with Dom James, but he had trouble finding clothes to travel in. Surely now his journey through life would begin to be different without Dom James calling all the shots about where and when he would do almost everything.

In late October, Dr. Rosemary Haughton, a noted female theologian, came to meet Merton. Then there was a visit from Doris Dana, her second trip there. They drove together over to Lexington to see Carolyn Hammer, who joined them for a visit to the Niles' farm. Niles had finished writing music for three of Merton's poems, and Merton wanted to hear it. It pleased him a great deal—music was always moving to him and he thought it enhanced poetry.

Merton began to send out his writing again, and in a remarkable variety : "Two Leggings," his review of a book by the same name about Native Americans, the preface to the Japanese translation of *The New Man*, and "The Street is for Celebration," to be a preface for a book of photographs of Spanish Harlem by Monsignor Fox.

On November 5, Merton met Sister Therese in person for the first time after twenty years of correspondence. At this time, Sister Therese was teaching at Marquette and Georgetown universities. She had been invited to speak at Bellarmine College during Town-and-Gown-Week on the subject of Merton's poetry. When Merton heard about this, he asked Mrs. Tommie O'Callaghan to drive Sister Therese out to Gethsemani for a picnic lunch. The three celebrated the occasion, with lunch supplied by Tommie, as was her custom in assisting Merton to host occasions like this. She also snapped pictures of the group, which they all appreciated. Merton gave Sister Therese more of his papers for her collection and inscribed one of his books to her. His exuberance at their long-awaited meeting and her natural reticence left them both a little bewildered, according to reports, since their friendship had always been on a literary basis. Nevertheless, their correspondence continued without change, to their mutual enjoyment.

He was getting involved in the creation of a new form of expression that mirrored Ad Reinhardt's artistic minimalist style. He called it the "West" section of *The Geography of Lograire*. Ping Ferry was having it transcribed for him out in Santa Barbara from the audio tapes he was recording. Merton showed Sister Therese his *Lograire* work, and she was enthusiastic, giving him the reassurance he needed to proceed with a major work that seemed a radical departure from spiritual work. She knew, though, that it was the culmination of his years of study and thought.

One day Merton walked out by St. Bernard's lake and saw the loblolly pines he and the novices had planted ten or fifteen years earlier. Some were now twenty feet high. The fire tower shone in the afternoon sun just as it had ten years before. He walked over to see the Jonathan Daniel sculptures again.

This was one of the good days when meditation brought him closer to God.

Jim Wygal had recently tried to encourage him to accept an abbatial election, should he be chosen to head up the monastery. Merton thought that was as stupid an idea as his earlier advice to write a story for a movie or something that would make a big splash and get him back in the center of attention. Merton considered this to be "childish." He did not want to be a "personage" at this stage of his life. He just wanted to thank God for his faith and his many gifts. Merton was glad for Jim's day-to-day friendship, if not for all of his suggestions. He had for the most part resisted making friends with his companions at the monastery over the years. So many of the monks had left sick and confused, Merton hesitated to try to form a friendship with most of them. Although the Abbot had always seemed such a threat, Merton realized paradoxically that it was Dom James who had kept him on his toes. It was a continual challenge just trying to stay ahead of him in his attempts at control over Merton's life.

By the end of November, Merton had closed another chapter of his life, the one about his dental problems. He went to Lexington to the Dental School of the University of Kentucky, to get five teeth capped. They had so badly decayed that he was having trouble eating. He had two and a half hours on the imitation leather divan of the dentist, Dr. Loughlin. Dom James meanwhile was upstairs in the medical center for surgery. Dom James did not divulge the reason for his operation, so it was assumed that it wasn't serious. His resignation as Abbot had now been accepted in Rome, so it was official. There would be new leadership soon.

One day while Dom James was hospitalized, a group of monks decided to ride in the monastery Jeep up to see the progress on the Abbot's new hermitage. They invited Merton to join them. Merton was curious to see it, too, especially since he had found the location and recommended it to the Abbot because of the unusually beautiful view. Brother Clement, a former architect under Frank Lloyd Wright, had designed it for him. It was even going to be air-conditioned. Merton was amazed to find that the beautiful little house would be built on a high ridge overlooking the valley. It would be like a hawk's nest, Merton thought. Six months earlier, Merton had been hiking in the area and found the site and told the Abbot about it. Merton admired him for acting on the information, but wasn't surprised that Dom James had not told him he had chosen the site Merton had recommended.

Merton was scandalized by the quality of Dom James' new home. Whoever heard of a monk walking away from every sensory pleasure in the world, secluding himself in the middle of nowhere, and then air conditioning the place. Merton probably reacted like this because all his life he had lived in places where air conditioning did not exist. In Europe the climate didn't really require it, and until a few years ago, no one in the history of the world had air conditioning or thought it to be necessary. Certainly not the Desert Fathers—or Saint Bernard, he thought.

Merton went over to see Father Hilarion in his trailer. The contrast was stark. The trailer was dull looking, very small, but clean. The site was sunny but chosen without much thought. Father Hilarion had been eager to relieve the tension he was suffering at the monastery, so made a fast move. He said he was happy with it, so Merton thought it probably did not much matter.

Meanwhile, John Ford proceeded to draw up the legal documents to complete the establishment of the Merton Trust. At Merton's request, Tommie O'Callaghan agreed to be one of the trustees. Merton thought this would give the Board a balance and objectivity not necessarily possible in an all-clerical group. He really liked Tommie and her family and trusted her judgment in protecting his work.

On his way back from Louisville, he stopped in Bardstown to call Margie. It was about time for her birthday. She was so happy to hear from him after the past few months that she cried. She again advised him to "reach out for happiness" and leave the monastery, but he knew it was not what he wanted and didn't make sense for either of them.

She told him she was planning to move to Miami. He knew there was nothing more to say to her. He wouldn't have her phone number there, so wouldn't be tempted to call her. Two days before Christmas, he received a Christmas card, mailed from her parents' home. He didn't know what that meant in terms of her plan to move to Miami, but he decided not to respond. After all, the intensity of their communion was now gone. He knew he would never marry anyone at this stage of his life, now approaching his fifty-third birthday. Yet he wondered if maybe he had really missed the point of life after all. The Christmas card would be the last correspondence from Margie and their last communication.

In December Merton began *Monks Pond*, to be four offset collections of poetry and prose of an *avant garde* nature, featuring new and unknown writers. Merton served as editor, and mailed out the publication without cost, distributing the four issues in 1968. He was excited about this new project, and looked forward to assisting undiscovered writers in getting published, even if it was only mimeographed and privately distributed.

Merton closed out the year hosting a retreat at the hermitage for fifteen contemplative nuns, including Carmelite prioresses, some Poor Clares, two Passionists, and two nuns from Loretto. He busied himself around the hermitage to prepare for these special visitors, women at that, so he thought that he had better clean the place thoroughly. He said Mass for them at the hermitage, and the group responded to his presentation enthusiastically. They wound up their session singing together, "We Shall Overcome" with a great deal of gusto. Merton enlisted his farming neighbors, the Gannons, to bring over a tray of doughnuts to serve the nuns. The whole event was a success and gave him a feeling of exhilaration.

In January the new Abbot was scheduled to be elected. Merton confided to his diary that the only other candidates he could in conscience vote for were Fathers Callistus now in Chile; Eudes, the psychiatrist; Timothy, now in Rome; and Hilarion, the hermit. He believed, though, that Father Flavian Burns was the only candidate of his choice who had any chance whatever of being elected by the group, even though he had recently been living as a hermit.

On Christmas Day of 1967, Merton invited the other hermits, except Dom James, to his place for a glass of wine. He wanted to discuss the upcoming election of a new Abbot. With Merton guiding this meeting, the group persuaded Father Flavian to give up his hermitage, if elected, to accept the role of Abbot. Merton argued that Father Flavian had only become a hermit in the first place because Dom James had selected him to head up a new foundation, and he would not accept Dom James' supervision in this capacity. Reluctantly, Father Flavian agreed to be a candidate. He was young and inexperienced, but well liked by the other monks. There were other serious contenders, but he was elected early in the balloting on January 13, 1968. Also very significantly, the monks voted that the new Abbot would not serve a life term. With a temporary term, no Abbot would have a free hand to impose his will on the group for the rest of his life.

Merton had insured there would be no chance of his consideration for the job. First he announced at one of his conferences that he would not accept the position if elected. Then he posted a notice on the community bulletin board that he had taken a private vow never to serve as an Abbot. He added gratuitously that he was not willing to spend the rest of his life "arguing about trifles with 125 slightly confused and anxiety-ridden monks," being beyond his "mental, moral and physical capabilities." The Prior sent Merton a note saying that the monks considered his remarks to be insulting. Finally, Merton passed a remark around the monastery that it would be embarrassing for the monastery if a child of the Abbot "turned up at the gate house." He chose to feed whatever rumors had circulated about his affair to avoid being tapped for the abbatial position, even at the cost of debasing himself.

In January, Dom Colomban Bissey from Melleray and Father Charles Dumont from Chimary came to supervise the election. They had dinner privately with Dom James and included Merton on the pretext that he could translate their French as help was needed. The visitors told Merton that Dom Jean Leclercq had told them about a meeting in Bangkok that he thought Merton might want to attend. It was being held to discuss monastic-ecumenical matters from an international perspective. The purpose of the Bangkok meeting was to explore monasticism in the Far East to take advantage of the wisdom of their non-Christian monastic traditions so that there could be a revitalization of Western monasticism. The meeting would be held in December 1968, so Merton knew it would be up to the new Abbot, whoever he might be, to decide whether he could go. It would also depend on whether there was any expansion of the war in Southeast Asia by that time. Merton realized that this was the meeting that Dom Leclercq had written him about a few months ago, and obviously he was to be included, provided he could get approval from his new Abbot. Merton decided not to translate this part of the conversation for Dom James, who seemed to have no inkling of the invitation that had been extended. The French visitors did not call attention to the fact that Merton did not translate this news to Dom James. They knew it would not be a matter for Dom James to decide. The Abbot was apparently never the wiser.

When Father Flavian was elected to be the new Abbot, Merton experienced real joy concerning the management of the monastery. To be free of his suffocating relationship with Dom James and to know the hermitage would remain, and in fact be valued, was the answer to his prayers. Merton knelt at the feet of his new Abbot and gave his profession of obedience, putting his future in Dom Flavian's hands without any hesitation.

The monastery celebrated a new Mass with beautiful music composed by Father Chrysogonus. It was a farewell tribute to Dom James, who thought he had sacrificed himself by presenting a dramatic "presence" to influence the group, and expected them to make an equal sacrifice of their wills to conform to his direction. Now it was finished. His isolation from the group became obvious.

Merton took an active part in celebrating this Mass with the community. It was a victory for Merton to have survived all the hurts and disappointments of the past. He felt that now they could build a cohesive unit at Gethsemani as a monastery instead of a corporation. Merton resumed his place on the Council to assist Father Flavian in getting his program underway. Father Flavian selected Father Eudes to be Novice Master, Father Matthews as Master of Juniors, and Father Timothy, Prefect of Studies.

Dom James continued to occupy his office for some weeks for no apparent reason. Dom Flavian, coming from his hermitage, had no office, so had to operate out of a room in the guesthouse until Dom James finally vacated the office. No one was surprised.

It was a new year on the calendar as well as for the monks. 1968 was the year of the monkey in the Chinese calendar, Merton reflected. He could not help believing there could be some truth in these ancient systems of prognostication. They inevitably seem to contain some degree of accuracy in predictions, or at least enough to have them survive through the ages. Merton wondered what this year of the monkey might bring. He had just been looking over his earlier essays on Zen that had been published in various scholarly journals. He put together a manuscript called *Zen and the Birds of Appetite*, which was published by New Directions in 1968.

He was not born in the year of the monkey, although he thought he could have been. According to the tradition, he would be fun loving, creative, renowned, emotional, unreasonable, always right or believing he was, and having some hard-to-control appetites. Merton had a premonition that the year 1968 would bring trouble when the monkey would lead the dance. He was not wrong. On January 24, he recorded in his journal that he saw the old moon at dawn "hung in the South with Antares (of Scorpius) almost caught in the crescent, as if the moon were holding up Scorpius in a balancing act. A forbidding sign."

In late January, Merton received the news that Sy Freedgood had died. The Brothers on phone duty had taken a long distance call for Merton, and they walked up to the hermitage to tell him. Merton called Sy's wife, Anne, only to discover their house in Bridgehampton, NY, had burned to the ground as well. Sy, heavily sedated due to his bursitis, could not get out of the house. The events were surreal. His wife said he had been having a hard time recently doing his job at *Fortune* magazine. Merton wired the news to Lax.

Merton's melancholy returned. On his 53rd birthday, January 31, he was listening to the guns at Fort Knox firing heavy artillery. All the windows of the hermitage were rattling. Soon after, Brother Alban stopped by to return a book he had borrowed. Merton asked him to stay for a glass of wine. In the ensuing conversation, Brother Alban told Merton that he didn't think he really acted like a hermit. Once having said it, Brother Alban was appalled at his own brashness, then was surprised when Merton agreed with him. He said that he needed a lot of time to himself, and this life provided it. Later Merton learned that the Viet Cong had launched their Tet Offensive on his birthday. They had even invaded the U.S. Embassy in Saigon.

Merton soon had to return to Louisville to see his proctologist. He was also having occasional chest pains. His doctor found his heart was in good condition, and he was embarrassed that he had raised the issue. He decided to go shopping afterwards to cheer himself up. He bought the new Dylan record, "John Wesley Hardin," and John Coltrane's "Ascension," which he described as "shattering—fantastic and prophetic." Then he decided to use the outing to visit a couple of good friends--Tommie O'Callaghan, who had been ill, and then Dan Walsh at Lenahan Hall.

Merton decided to pursue the publishing of his *Journal of my Escape from the Nazis*. He retitled it, *My Argument with the Gestapo, A Macaronic Journal*, and added an introduction that he thought was necessary to put it into context. He submitted it to Doubleday, but their editors were not clear about what Merton was trying to do in releasing this early material now. Laughlin published it in 1969 with Merton's explanatory Preface and an introductory note by Naomi Burton. The term macaronic means a mixture of languages. Merton uses Latin words mixed with French, German, and some of his own creation, to convey his message that world peace is crucial to insure the dignity of man. As Naomi Burton's "Note" states, Merton had come full circle since his early years in Europe witnessing the effects of the Nazis.

Merton continued his interest in stargazing, particularly on cold, clear nights. Sometimes he felt he was becoming closer to the concern of earlier peoples. Skywatching meant their very survival. Knowing when to plant crops to avoid a killing frost made the difference in their food supply. He prided himself on now being able to tell where constellations would be in the daylight hours when they would not be visible. In February, Merton knew the sun was rising in Aquarius. He recorded in his journal that the beautiful invisible swan in the blue sky was spreading its wide wings over him. This is considered by astrologers to be indicative of a high energy period for one born under the zodiac sign of Aquarius, as Merton was.

Merton had always been fascinated with astrology. He couldn't resist reading his horoscope when he picked up an occasional newspaper. He knew that much of astrology was superstition, but his past experiences with the unknown had left him with a residue of openness to synchronicity. Merton did not exclude any source of information out of hand unless it didn't make sense to him.

He had seen that in some of the medieval monastic documents, the monk-scribes carefully delineated the astrological signs of the calendar. He didn't see this mystical sort of science as antithetical to his Catholicism. Water was among the first symbols of man's expression and one of the primary elements (earth, air, fire, and water). According to the ancient Chinese Lun yu, or *Analects* of Confucius, water is the symbol of humility, yet a lifeline to survival. According to Sydney Omarr, a recognized astrologer, persons born under the sign of Aquarius, the Water Bearer, are said to be linked to the positive and negative charges of electrical energy and intuitively tuned to higher forces via this electrical force.

Water is said to symbolize the power of inactivity such as in solitude. It is malleable and soft, yet powerful enough to erode stone. Water had always figured larger than life to Merton, from his multiple trans-Atlantic crossings to his preoccupation with rain at significant times in his life. At Gethsemani he was a water carrier: as a firefighter, watering the seedlings and flowers he planted, and then carrying water to the hermitage. And it would become significant that water conducts electricity.

Jay Laughlin came down to meet with John Ford and Merton to finalize the documents that would establish the Trust. Tommie O'Callaghan and Father John Loftus joined them for lunch. Merton thought he would like to go to Cunningham's for old time's sake. When he looked in, he found changes had been made in the restaurant, so steered the group to the Old House, his other favorite restaurant.

The group later went out to hear some live jazz in the local clubs. There was a new place on Washington Street, and with a large group Merton thought it would be OK for him to go. Merton was thrilled to hear live music for the first time in decades. The group all had a great time. His friends got him back to the monastery about 2 a.m. A week later, Tommie O'Callaghan and some of her relatives came out to take him downtown again to Washington Street to hear the jazz and talk to the musicians. Again he returned to the hermitage late. After this second event, Merton told his journal that this was no life for him, even if he learned to drive a car to get back and forth.

Merton was thankful that the new Abbot authorized an expansion of his hermitage. A 14 X 20 foot wing would be built for a chapel and a small bathroom. Merton looked forward to getting away from the outdoor "jakes." He said he always left the outhouse door open when he used it, to protect himself from any unwelcome wildlife or other intruders, including spiders, but sometimes he just enjoyed watching the birds and even occasionally wild ducks from this vantage point. The work proceeded slowly due to a late spring snow. It was so heavy that two large loblolly pines snapped under the weight of the snow in a repeat sequence that Merton found more than unnerving.

Merton was working on his material for *Faith and Violence*, which would be published by the University of Notre Dame Press later in 1968. Merton believed his mission was to express his opinions through publishing. For him, joining in marches or making public appearances would not be of any value. It was not what he was called to do, he was convinced.

In March, a controversial local issue came to his attention, and he decided to get involved. Joseph Mulloy, a local college student who had had a troubled past, was trying to avoid the draft. Merton wrote to the draft board in defense of Mulloy being exempted from the Vietnam war and expressing his own disagreement with the morality of the war itself. Merton was publicly criticized in the Catholic diocesan paper for his involvement in this case and for expressing his opinions about the war. For the next five weeks, the paper published letters from readers who disapproved of Merton's comments.

One day Merton went over to the monastery to change clothes to go to a doctor's appointment. He encountered Father Raymond, who had seen the negative material in the diocesan papers. He scolded Merton for getting involved in the student's case. This led to a heated discussion about the war and the build-up of nuclear weapons. Father Raymond angrily threatened that he would begin to write material against Merton and "cut (him) to pieces." Merton responded that that would only make Raymond look cheap. Father Raymond said he would be a hero if he published against Merton. Merton responded that Raymond had a right to express his opinion, and this infuriated Raymond, who said, in his rapid-fire fashion, it was not a matter of opinion but of truth. He told Merton he could prove he was an atheist. Merton was disgusted at the remark. He knew Raymond had always thought of him as an "arrant heretic."

He decided to ignore Father Raymond because Merton thought that Raymond probably believed himself to be infallible. Merton later concluded that Father Raymond was frustrated because the Bruce Publishing Company had refused his latest manuscript. Merton thought that Raymond's recent book, *Forty Years Behind the Wall*, was poorly written, although he had to acknowledge that Raymond did have seventeen published books at his last count. He had heard that the monastery was printing the next one privately, under the name Culligan. Raymond's explanation for his turn-down was that it was "a liberal plot" to suppress the "truth" from the public. Merton wondered if his own writing was any less ridiculous.

Father Raymond may have just seen Merton's new book, *Cables to the Ace or Familiar Liturgies of Misunderstanding*, just released in March by New Directions. It was the work he had titled "Edifying Cables."

Certainly it would scandalize Father Raymond. None of the 88 sections would please him, especially Number 64: "Note to subversives: Uncle has two extreme right hands and means business!"

Others, both in and out of the monastery, criticized Merton's pacifist stand, and were obviously voicing the frustrations and tensions of the times, including an incident involving burning his books. Merton believed there was a "growing barbarism" in the country that was becoming intolerable. He found himself losing touch with his group of local friends, including Carolyn Hammer, as Merton became more intolerant of the entire political situation.

He was corresponding with John and June Yungblut, Quakers who lived in Georgia, about the peace movement. They were friends of Martin Luther King, Jr., and had met Merton in a visit to Bardstown in 1967. They told Merton that King might be able to visit Gethsemani to pray with him for the civil rights movement. Many of King's fellow leaders were becoming frustrated at the slow pace of King's non-violent tactics in effecting changes for minorities in the south. Merton had respect for King's approach to the civil rights issue. He did not believe King was a fanatic, and told his journal that King was "perhaps one of the few really great Christians in America."

Like Merton, King was strongly influenced by Gandhi and his linkage of religion and politics, applying the principle of a love ethic to change public opinion. Although Gandhi and King were two of the greatest political figures of the 20th century, neither of them ever held public office. They saw the means they employed as the end intended for their work, as Marianne Williamson once observed.

Merton agreed to give a private retreat for King at his hermitage without involving the rest of the monastery. June Yungblut wrote in March that Coretta King had Merton's schedule and would pin Martin down to confirm the date he would come to see Merton.

In November 1967, June Yungblut had recommended that Merton participate with a team of Quakers from Philadelphia who wanted to go to Southeast Asia as an unofficial peace team. They planned to meet with representatives of the National Liberation Front (NLF), the Viet Cong, to develop some concrete proposals for ending the war to submit to the U.S. Government for agreement. Merton was excited about this opportunity to do something that might expedite the end of the war, but he knew that if the plan materialized, he would probably not be allowed to participate.

Merton had passed the invitation on to Dom James for his decision. He had assumed it would be turned down as everything else usually was, even though the monastery was in a transitional stage with Dom James' retirement and the new Abbot not yet elected. Several months later, June Yungblut wrote to Merton that the North Vietnamese National Liberation Front had refused to enter into any negotiations. Now he knew it would not be possible to combine any peace initiative with his tentative trip to Asia.

Merton wondered if maybe he should publicly renounce his American citizenship as a form of protest of the American government's policies. He was willing to sacrifice anything to advance the cause of peace. He could imagine how the FBI would like to hear about that, assuming they must undoubtedly have a file on him. (Actually, it has been learned that both the CIA and FBI maintained files on Merton. The FBI tracked the anti-war movement, including the Catholic Peace Fellowship and Joseph Mulloy, the draft resister. See Robert Grip, "The Merton Files: Washington Watches the Monk," *The Merton Seasonal of Bellarmine College*, Vol. 11, No. 1, Winter 1986, pp. 5-7.) Merton thought that he could always move to Chile or some other Latin country and join another monastic group, but he worried that his digestive tract could not handle the diet.

On March 9, Merton wrote to Dom Jean Leclercq that he now believed the U.S. was under the "judgment of God" for its aggressive war policies and wondered if he should continue to live in this country. Typical of his thinking, he added that maybe he should continue his allegiance because he was a sinner and likewise probably deserved to be with his fellow citizens under God's judgment and accept the punishment this mandated. Merton soon learned that the Bangkok meeting was still planned, in spite of the war. On March 16, an invitation arrived at Gethsemani for the new Abbot and Merton to attend. The conference was sponsored by an international Benedictine organization, *Aide a l'Implantation Monastique* (AIM), whose headquarters was in Paris. Dom Flavian passed the invitation to Merton without a decision.

Soon other invitations came in, and Dom Flavian referred them regularly to Merton for his own reaction. Merton could hardly believe this complete reversal of Dom James' policy. Merton found himself declining them himself on the basis of his renewed sense of monastic dedication. Without Dom James to "run interference," Merton had to reinforce his own identity as a hermit and contemplative. Otherwise he could see himself becoming a public figure on the lecture circuit, making the rounds of "significant" occasions.

On March 21, Dom James delivered his final sermon and gave the monks his Abbatial Blessing at a farewell Mass. Archbishop McDonough from Louisville attended, and after the service, Merton asked for the Archbishop's assistance in backing off of invitations without offending Church hierarchy. The Archbishop referred Merton back to his new Abbot, and added that he did not see a problem with Merton travelling two or three times in a given year. Merton asked the Archbishop for his advice about attending the Bangkok meeting, inasmuch as Dom Flavian had already indicated he was undecided about Merton's acceptance of the invitation. Merton wanted to go, but wanted to insure that he had adequate approval to make such an extensive trip. The Archbishop had no objection and encouraged Merton to attend selected meetings.

Soon after Merton first knew of this event, he wrote to Dom Willibrord Van Dijh for support. He had assumed the position of Abbot at Rawa Seneng in Indonesia in 1966 after serving as Abbot of the Trappist Abbey of Tilburg in the Netherlands for the past twenty years. He had originally founded the monastery at Rawa Seneng in 1945 before moving to Tilburg. In 1964 Merton had thought that Dom Willibrord might be the next Abbot General, and would hopefully support Merton's efforts to write on peace. Instead, Dom Ignace Gillet was elected. Merton asked Dom Willibrord to intercede for him to Father Flavian. He characterized Father Flavian as young and inexperienced and therefore somewhat hesitant to OK his appearance at the AIM meeting without "some strong letters" "urging my presence." Merton wanted to visit Dom Willibrord and his monastery to broaden his perspective on the problems of monasticism, to get insight that he believed he could not obtain "in this very prosperous community."

In March Merton wrote to Dom Jean Leclercq at Clervaux in Luxembourg, asking him for support as well. He said that Father Flavian had advised him that he would probably consent to Merton's appearance if Abbots Floris (in Vannes, France) and Leclercq wrote to him strongly urging it. Father Flavian finally did give his consent, whether by influence of Church hierarchy or Merton's relentless intercession.

Merton asked the Archbishop for permission to reserve the Blessed Sacrament in the hermitage chapel when it was complete. He was overjoyed to receive this privilege. At last his dream would come true, to have the Divine Presence with him on his altar at all times.

The timing of this consolation could not have been better. Merton began to fear opening his mail. He was receiving critical and even threatening letters now that there was no censorship from Dom James and his staff to protect him from mail that would be frightening or upsetting. He didn't really know whether the mail had become more negative, or whether the screen that Dom James had provided had really been a gift to him for which he would have been very grateful.

One day he received a package, which could always be suspect in such unsettling times. He was very happy when he carefully unwrapped it to find it contained a new camera from John Howard Griffin. Merton termed it his "Zen camera." It was a Canon FX with two lenses. Merton was touched, because he had had an accident with the monastery's Rolleiflex camera when he fell one day out in the woods taking pictures. Griffin, being sensitive to Merton's vow of poverty, told him it wasn't a gift but a permanent loan. Merton's thank-you letter promised that it would go straight back to Griffin "if anything happens to me."

Merton was becoming fearful for good reason. Some people were becoming unstable living in a time with so much social upheaval. The changes in the Church, the civil disorder, and a major war combined to push some emotionally fragile people over the edge. As a result, Merton sometimes had uninvited guests at the hermitage. The previous October, a man who called himself Ken Hill managed to get to the hermitage unannounced by finding the back road and figuring out the combination padlock on the highway gate. He told Merton that he was a private investigator and asked him a number of questions. Afterwards Merton regretted being agreeable to answer the man's questions and wished he had thought to get the man's car license number to report the incident.

In January an ex-nun had come to the monastery gatehouse talking incoherently about wanting a spiritual marriage. Another woman came a few weeks later saying she was the woman in the Biblical Book of Revelation. Merton tried to talk to her, to dissuade her from her desire to see the Abbot. He also received strange, unsettling mail from people with problems. A telegram from an unknown woman said she wanted to arrange a meeting with him "where we were before." He also received a Chinese scroll written in blood.

Merton began to fear intruders in the hermitage when he was out walking. He adopted the habit of approaching the house cautiously to check for signs of anyone there before reentering. Once he returned to see a group of priests he was not expecting, waiting for him on his porch. He stayed in the brush until they tired of waiting for him and left. One warm spring day he was outside the hermitage reading in his shorts when a group approached unexpectedly to see him. Merton was no more surprised than his visitors to catch him in this embarrassing situation. Fortunately, they departed quickly.

Merton felt that the close proximity of casual guests was damaging his image as a serious spiritual writer. He had tried so hard to maintain his detachment. Part of the problem came from his own naivete in telling some of his close friends about the back way to the hermitage to avoid the gatehouse. The word spread, and his privacy was consequently jeopardized. Merton concluded that real solitude was no longer possible there, at least for him. He was too near the road. He thought he would prefer to give his efforts to "the most abandoned and remote," people "from whom there is also so much to learn."

On the other hand, some of Merton's guests were more than welcome. He noticed that there began to be fewer of them who were fellow Cistercians or even fellow clergymen. In March, Barbara Ann Braveman came from Washington University in St. Louis, Missouri, with some students to interview Merton. Barbara asked Merton to come to St. Louis to be the school's poet. Obviously he could not accept, so instead they asked to interview him for their literary magazine. Merton took them to Thompson Willett's home for a lively discussion of current events, and then to Colonel Hawk's Restaurant in Bardstown. Hawk Rogers, or Colonel Hawk, the black owner, was a friend of Merton's and welcomed the group. Merton got a bottle of bourbon and admitted to his journal that they all drank too much. The Willett family's maid, Beatrice, was married to Colonel Hawk's son. The next morning, Merton said Mass at their home for the entire group. Merton reflected later that he had not had permission to say this Mass outside the monastery, but thought it was good that he had done it anyway.

On April 4, Merton had a visit from Donald Allchin and a seminary friend of his to discuss progress in the ecumenical movement. At Merton's suggestion, they drove through the area with Merton as town guide. They visited Shakertown, then stopped at a Lum's Restaurant in Lexington en route back to Gethsemani. They watched a TV as they had supper, and saw Martin Luther King, Jr., in a public appearance in Memphis. June Yungblut had written to Merton that she feared the young black militants might create violence there during King's visit. She said it was planned for King to settle on the dates of his visit to Gethsemani after this trip to Memphis, although she thought it would have been better to go first for the retreat, since King was going directly into a hot situation in Memphis without adequate preparation. After their meal, Merton and his companions played the car radio on the drive back to the monastery. A news bulletin interrupted the program to announce that King had been shot and killed. The group was stunned.

Merton suggested they stop in Bardstown at Colonel Hawk's Restaurant. When Merton and his friends arrived, Colonel Hawk threw his arms around Merton and hugged him. Merton showed his support for the group at the restaurant, who were brokenhearted at the news. Returning to the hermitage, he wrote a letter of sympathy to Coretta King. Then he cried. He probably thought about the assassination of Gandhi twenty years earlier. He knew the effects would extend long into the future.

Merton received June Yungblut's letter of March 12 before King's assassination on April 4. Merton was so taken with the prophetic nature of her letter that he copied the pertinent parts in his journal to preserve it.

Merton told himself it was a brute of a year. He wondered what more dire events could follow. The next news he heard was that blacks were rioting in fifteen U.S. cities. Soon the riots would begin in Louisville.

Merton was not feeling well and wondered if the chest pains and fatigue were significant. He had hurt his back again, but decided to postpone seeing a doctor until later in the year.

In April Merton had a visit from Alex Peloquin, who came down from Boston. At the O'Callaghans' home, he played the accompaniment he had composed for Merton's "Four Freedom Songs." The songs were good and tough, and Merton regretted that they would not be played at the Liturgical Conference where Martin Luther King, Jr. would have been present.

Then Merton received a letter from Cardenal asking him again to come to Solentiname to join him on this island in the tropical lake in Central America. Merton again thought he would like to go there, at least temporarily, but then reasoned that he was "getting old, might have a hard time adjusting to a tropical climate, diet, etc." It was the end of that dream, too.

On April 25, Merton received a newspaper in the mail from New Zealand reporting that his Aunt Kit had died. She had drowned in a

ferryboat accident in a storm between the two islands of New Zealand
two weeks earlier. Like John Paul, she died in a lifeboat. He was numb at
the thought of another family loss. Just reading a newspaper account of
his aunt's death was too impersonal. He walked down into the bottoms
to be sure that he was alone to mourn. Then he said a special Mass for
her in his chapel. He had hoped to stop in New Zealand to see her after
his meeting in Bangkok. The thought of the socks that she had knit for
him broke him up. With each family death, Merton suffered another
disconnect from his past.

The Vietnam war and civil unrest were continuing unabated. The
farmers in areas around the monastery had always kept their monastic
neighbors informed of radio news bulletins. The monks would not rely
on Dom James to tell them what was going on. In May a serious riot
broke out in Louisville, and the neighboring farmers were hesitant to
talk to anyone. A curfew was imposed in Louisville to keep order. This
was more typical of the times than an isolated event. Across the country
there were riots and burnings, particularly in the urban areas. Lyndon
Johnson announced in early April that he would not be a candidate
for reelecton to the Presidency. Robert Kennedy entered the race and
began winning Presidential primaries. Merton was hopeful for an end
to what seemed to be a civil war in slow motion.

Merton and Dom Flavian agreed it was a good time for Merton to
get away from the hermitage and travel a bit. He could now respond
to requests from remote groups of the Order who had been asking to
see him.

Merton left quickly and quietly for the West Coast with few people
aware of his departure. Two days before he left, on Derby Day, May
4, he hosted a picnic for some local friends on the monastery grounds
out by the old silver spire from the Church. It would be a two-week
trip to California, and New Mexico. First he gave a conference for the
Trappestine nuns at Our Lady of the Redwoods, Whitehorn, California.
Merton had a lot of respect for the superior, Mother Myriam Dardenne,
whom he had met once at a retreat at Gethsemani. Her Belgian and
American nuns were easy for Merton to relate to. He spoke with the
nuns in the afternoon, and spent the mornings exploring the area. He
also went into a nearby town and bought himself a pair of Levi jeans.

Dom Flavian had asked Merton to look for a site that could possibly be acquired for a hermitage or other small facility in an isolated
area near the California coast. Merton enlisted Ping Ferry, a long-time

Californian, to help him find potential sites. Ping provided Merton with useful background information about the area. Merton found some scenic places but was unsure about them being suitable because of nearby development or traffic. He loved the area, though, and thought it would be worthwhile for Dom Flavian to take a closer look.

Merton then heard that Phil and Dan Berrigan had been arrested for pouring blood on U.S. Government draft files in Baltimore. Dan had sent Merton a copy of a preface to his new book, with the news that he was going to stage this event, and asked him to wish him luck. At the end of the week, Merton was driven from the conference to San Francisco. He hoped for lighter days.

Lawrence Ferlinghetti met him. They went over to the City Lights Bookstore on Columbus Avenue that Ferlinghetti operated as an outlet to his publishing, under the name of City Lights Books. Merton was always excited to read the books he sent—books that would never find their way to the monastery or even to many conventional bookstores. He was content to sleep on a mattress on the floor of a two-room apartment above the editorial office overnight. He liked San Francisco, commenting it was as pretty as Havana but with less noise, except for the sound of cars driving uphill everywhere. Ferlinghetti was as interested as Merton in Asian beliefs. He had just published *The Secret Oral Teachings in Tibetan Buddhist Sects* written by David-Neel and Yongden, with a Foreword by Alan Watts. Merton and Ferlinghetti went for a walk that night and stopped at the Malvina Coffee Shop. Merton admired some pretty girls who walked by, which was no surprise to Ferlinghetti. With a common background in Greenwich Village years before, it was probably a reminiscence for both of them.

The following day Merton flew from San Francisco via Las Vegas to Albuquerque, to visit an experimental foundation, called Christ in the Desert. He was driven to the monastery, thirteen miles away, on a dirt road. Only three men comprised the community, but their welcome was a warm one. They drove Merton around the area and gave him handmade Navajo rugs to take back for his chapel at the hermitage.

The New Mexico scenery made him homesick for Gethsemani. He met Don Devereux and his wife, who were friends of Ping Ferry, and they talked about Native American dances. The Indians' drums fascinated Merton. They obviously had the power to affect a person's psyche to the point of providing transcendent experiences through a kind of self-hypnosis.

To the Indians, drumbeats were considered the universal primal language, the heartbeat of Mother Earth. They give closeness and integrity to natural roots that have not been lost by Native Americans, even if lost in cities. Merton agreed that in drumming one could get in touch with a primal self that is suppressed by industrial culture. The Indians believed that one's spirit becomes the rhythm rather than creating it in the drumbeat. For them, drumming was a means of spiritual transformation.

Merton was happy for the opportunity to meet Peter Nabokov, whose book, *Two Leggings*, he had reviewed. The entire trip was a great adventure that included exploring the Chama Canyon, swimming in the cold natural water, and visiting Ghost Ranch. Merton loved seeing different wildlife, especially the birds, but he was careful to avoid the rattlesnakes.

Merton could see why the area had so influenced others who wrote of their experiences in New Mexico. Jung said he discovered God through a Pueblo Indian's eyes. D. H. Lawrence had a ranch there, and it was a popular vacation spot for New York writers. Ansel Adams photographed the area, which was no surprise, given the convergence of desert mountains, purple skies, and wild flowers in abundance.

When he flew back into Louisville, Frank and Tommie O'Callaghan met his plane and had him over to their home to spend the night before they drove him back to Gethsemani. Once he was back at the hermitage, he found himself longing for the places he had just left. He pored over the project to edit his notes for eventual publication. His photographs and notebook of impressions were later published as *Woods, Shore, Desert* by the Museum of New Mexico Press in Santa Fe in 1982.

Significant mail was waiting for Merton when he returned. He got more news of the Berrigans. Philip Berrigan had been sentenced to serve six years in Federal prison for desecrating draft records. Dan ended up serving 18 months. Merton was astonished that the Government would punish two priests so severely. He wondered to himself if this could also happen to him. Although they had gone out of their way to challenge the law, nevertheless Merton concluded he was living in a totalitarian society in which his freedom had become "pure illusion." He told himself he might someday find himself in a position where he would also feel compelled to express himself for moral reasons without regard to the consequences. Father John Eudes Bamberger called for the community to pray for the Berrigan brothers in a Chapter meeting.

Merton was visibly moved almost to tears. He soon learned that John Yungblut was also in jail on behalf of peace initiatives.

In June, Merton received a letter from Aunt Ka about Aunt Kit's accidental death. "No faked death for Aunt Kit—the real thing," Merton told his journal. "When it is naked and terrible we remember what death really is." He appreciated Aunt Ka writing to him. Merton's life had now seemed to become a relentless series of endings.

On June 5, Robert Kennedy was assassinated, like his brother, and like King. Merton was struck by the fact that all three leaders had been the victims of a single gunman. Merton sent a telegram of condolence to Ethel Kennedy, Robert's widow, and said a Mass for him at the hermitage chapel. Dom James decided to go to New York to attend the funeral, although he had only begun his hermit lifestyle eight months earlier, a fact that Merton noted, considering the former Abbot's policy on travel when he was denying others' requests. Merton wondered where Father Dan Walsh might be, since he hadn't heard from him. As a friend of the Kennedy family, Dan's superiors probably considered him to be in jeopardy in the immediate aftermath of the tragedy and thought he should be sequestered. Merton agreed with that idea.

The summer of 1968 was a sequence of frightening news. Overseas there were riots in Paris of workers protesting their wages, a people's revolt against the government in Mexico City, Soviet troops in tanks invading Prague, and the murder of participants at the Olympic Games. Within the U.S., there was the poor people's march in Washington, DC, following the riots after the King assassination, the assassination of Robert Kennedy, riots at the Democratic National Convention in Chicago protesting the Vietnam war, as well as problems in Miami at the Republican National Convention. A crisis mentality seemed to prevail everywhere. It was said that America was closer to anarchy than ever before. The country seemed to be falling apart. Gethsemani was a haven.

Merton prophesied to his journal: "there will be more murders. They will become more and more part of political life. The definitive way of making one's point." Now wire taps, bugging equipment, armored cars, and gassing of protesters were used by the Government. Merton told his journal, the U.S. is already in a "police state in many respects." Merton felt he no longer needed to write. He decided he would only respond to requests for prefaces and articles he was really interested in. He talked with Father Flavian about his need for solitude, and the

Abbot suggested he go to Asia and see some Buddhist centers. He was thrilled at the idea.

He was beginning to feel inadequate as a writer and described his current opinion of his work as "provisional, inconclusive, half-baked" and "extremely dissatisfying," and "trivial." "I hardly have the heart to continue with it—certainly not with the old stuff. But is the new any better?"

In June Father Flavian received a request from the Trappist monastery in Indonesia for Merton to give a retreat at Rawa Seneng in conjunction with his trip to the Bangkok meeting. Merton wanted to go. It would extend his stay in Asia. He was eager to see the effect of the Anti-Communist Christians in successfully putting down the attempted Communist overthrow of the government in late 1965 that was said to have cost the country a million lives. He thought it might be a good idea to visit other Cistercian monasteries in the East—Japan and Lantao, near Hong Kong, as well. He was hoping only to do what God asked of him, "whatever it may be," he recorded in his journal. In July Merton confirmed his plans to meet Father Frans Harjawiyata in Bangkok and go with him to Rawa Seneng. Father Frans was a Cistercian and native-born Indonesian. He planned to conduct a retreat at Rawa Seneng before travelling on to New Zealand to see his father's relatives. Merton said this retreat would satisfy the legality for extending his trip.

Now that the hermitage was completed, Merton felt he must leave. What a paradox—an apparent contradiction. The bathroom was finished, so he did not have to visit the "jakes" anymore and worry about whether the snake would be there too. And the brown spider he recently had to kill there worried him, a sign that more would come. He had decorated the hermitage as he wanted it, with his icons on the altar, the rugs from New Mexico on the chapel floor, and on the walls some of his favorite photographs, Ad Reinhardt's painting of the black crosses, and Suzuki's scroll near—but not too near—the fireplace. He was beginning to be physically stronger now, too, so could do some gardening. He had crocuses planted on his walkway.

Dom Flavian had an intercom phone installed between the hermitage and the monastery, and the security was somewhat comforting. Ultimately it would be no solution during an emergency. Merton's visitors, including the unwelcome ones, always ignored Merton's "No Trespassing" sign and the heavy gate made of iron bars when they came to the hermitage on the back road.

Merton approached Dom Flavian again about going to the meeting in Bangkok. He offered some tentative itineraries based on recent invitations and Merton's special interests from California to Asia. Dom Flavian obviously agreed with Merton that there was no longer any real solitude at Gethsemani and thought they had gone as far as they could go to establish hermitages for those who wanted to lead a fully contemplative life. Now retreatants were showing up on Merton's porch, just wanting to "see" him, like an exhibit, or like an animal in a zoo. Merton commented in his journal that he wanted "to find a really quiet, isolated place—where no one knows I am (I want to disappear)." Again, a few days later, he said he wanted to find somewhere to disappear to.

Then in June, Bob Lax came to visit. Merton was more than happy to see him. Lax and Merton had continued their life-long correspondence in spite of the geographical limitations. Most of their letters were in Joyce-speak, a cryptic language involving misuse of grammar and spelling that would only be fully understood by the two. Their letters followed a pattern of irreverent commentary regardless of subject, including their own and the other's behavior. They made many references to their school days and mutual friends. They swapped manuscripts of works in progress, including Lax's vertical poems. Merton and Lax both assumed that their mail was subject to censorship, Merton from the monastery, and Lax from the government in power in Greece at that time. Their use of cryptic language may have been at least partly due to their desire to conceal their ideas from unwanted readers.

When Lax stopped at Gethsemani, he had just left the university where he was teaching in South Dakota. It had folded due to lack of students, probably because of the Army draft. He was en route back to Greece to live on the secluded island of Kalymnos. Merton told him he worried that Lax would be unhappy living in a place rumored to be a police state and sustained by the CIA. Lax was well informed, he said, and could not be deterred. He had moved to Greece in 1964 and lived there for three years before he accepted the position in South Dakota. After Kalymnos, he lived for a time on Lipsos, and finally on the island of Patmos. While Lax was there, Merton hosted another of his special picnics, which included the O'Callaghans and Ron and Sally Seitz. He was happy to discuss his own international travel plans with Lax to get his ideas.

In readiness for his trip, Merton made an appointment to check in with his doctor in Louisville, but instead cancelled the appointment to

spend the time in town at the University library and at an airline office
to get information on visas and shots for the Far East. Father John Eudes
also advised him about the shots and medicines he should carry to the
Far East for contingencies. This was only the beginning of Merton's trips
into Louisville to prepare for his trip. He went repeatedly to the Health
Building for shots and to the library for books on Asia. His excitement
grew as he modified his itinerary. His sore arm was tolerable because it
was part of his preparation. He told his journal that he may never come
back, "not that I expect anything to go wrong—though it might."

The hot summer weather again took its toll on Merton, particularly
when he tried to sleep. He had always had an insomnia problem to some
extent, but now it was worse. Heat was always a problem, too. Andy
Boone's dogs were barking incessantly now on the adjoining property
and keeping him awake. Boone was a poor black farmer who kept a
number of dogs for his protection as well as to chase the foxes and deer
away from his livestock.

Merton was concerned that the dogs would kill or frighten away too
many of the wild animals in the area that he enjoyed watching on his
walks around the hermitage. He would not miss those howling dogs
when he left. The summer also brought an unusual amount of rain, and
consequently, heavy foliage. Merton felt uneasy if he could not see the
surrounding area from his windows. He feared he could not see anyone
who might be approaching.

One stormy night, lightning struck and blew out the bulb in his desk
lamp. It was frightening to be alone at times like this.

In mid-July, Wygal came out to see Merton to introduce his girl
friend. It was a surprise. Just last March Wygal had had a heart attack
and Merton had visited him in Baptist Hospital. Merton was happy
to see he had recovered and was getting on with his life. The three
spent the afternoon driving around in Wygal's car and stopping for a
couple of beers. They decided to go out to the Tobacco Barn to finish
their drinks and ran into Father Raymond with two friends, having a
beer, too. They all talked together about the Vietnam war, but Merton
avoided making any controversial statements that might resurrect the
angry exchange of last March.

The following day Merton went to St. Matthews to see his allergist
and get inoculations for the trip. He stopped at the Canary Cottage
and watched TV over the bar. He found himself disgusted with how
uninteresting the people on TV were. Then he went over to Tommie

O'Callaghan's home and got a ride back to the hermitage. He enjoyed his own scrambled eggs, rye bread, and cold beer, along with the current *New Yorker* magazine.

At the end of July, Father Raymond had surgery for what might possibly be cancer. Merton went to the hospital to visit him and heard his good news that the growth was not malignant. Father Raymond told Merton how happy he was that the Pope had just issued an encyclical against birth control. He prophesied that there would be a schism in the Church because of it. Merton found himself mildly amused at Raymond's consistently hard and fast judgments.

Merton decided to take part of his journal and edit it for publication. He selected the years 1964 and 1965 up to September. After extensive deletions, he typed it and sent it off to Naomi Burton Stone for her reaction. She was still employed part time at Doubleday, but had their permission to work on the side with Merton. He asked her to hold this manuscript for publication in 1971, because he wanted to release his earlier work, *My Argument with the Gestapo*, for purposes of the material being consecutive. After that, Merton planned to release a book of monastic essays, which actually were published by Doubleday in 1971, as *Contemplation in a World of Action*. The journal was to follow that project. Since it covered recent events, Merton thought a little passage of time might be in order before its release to give it a more positive reception. He asked that it be titled, *A Vow of Conversation*, and it was so published by Farrar, Straus, Giroux in 1988.

By August Merton had three of his four *Monks Pond* issues published, with the help of Phil Stark, a Jesuit scholastic at Gethsemani, who offered to assist him. The monastery had purchased an offset press for business use, and Merton used it for his publications. If he had not been leaving soon for Asia, Merton thought he might have put together more than four issues.

Merton also used the monastery's press to print changes in the liturgical texts for the monks to use to comply with the changes in the prayers to the vernacular.

In August, Merton saw a newspaper that now came to the monastery. There was an article about Dan Berrigan's latest activities in support of disarmament. Merton recorded in his journal that Father Berrigan had asked him to come up to New York in the fall for his trial, but he definitely did not want to do anything "that savors of a public 'appearance' ... especially in America."

Merton also read a newspaper article posted at the refectory about the Carthusians now located in Vermont. Merton discovered from the article that the Order had never introduced reforms. Hanging on to their customs seemed to him now to be "a bit ridiculous ... .How glad I am I never joined them ... .Yet the road I am on is the right one for me and I hope I stay on it wisely—or that my luck holds."

Merton began sorting his books and papers. He decided to destroy Margie's letters to him that he had so carefully assembled and preserved. Without a second thought, he set fire to them, along with some other papers, using some pine branches out in the sun. He knew Jay Laughlin would still have the poems he had written for her. He wanted them preserved for the future as part of his body of work. Merton believed burning papers was a serious and important way of putting something behind him. He had done it once when he burned the letters from Diane, the young girl in England he had had a summer romance with, and again at St. Bonaventure's when he burned some of his early manuscripts that he had not been able to get published.

Merton continued to prepare for the trip. Dom Jean Leclercq visited Gethsemani so that Merton's talk at the AIM meeting in Bangkok could be finalized. Father John Eudes advised Merton to get in touch with a friend of his in Washington, DC, a Dr. Nicco Camara Peron, a psychologist, who could provide him with useful information. Merton did not explain in his journal why he should go to see him in person.

Merton made a one-day trip to Washington in late August. Lionel Landry, a representative of an organization known as the Asia Society, recommended that Merton meet the Indonesian Ambassador before his trip to that country. Ron Seitz, a poet and teacher at Bellarmine College, drove Merton to the airport. Dr. Peron, Father John Eudes' friend, met his plane on Friday night in Washington. Merton spent the night Japanese-style at Dr. Peron's downtown apartment. They had dinner at a neighborhood restaurant and rathskeller, "Old Europe." They discussed the fact that a large number of the doctor's patients were from the religious community and were having psychological problems adjusting to the recent changes in the Church and their communities. Merton probably told the doctor about his recent experiences at the monastery with visitors who were not well balanced and novices who could not adjust.

Early the next morning Merton walked alone down Massachusetts Avenue in the Rock Creek Park area to find a church. He said Mass at a large old church he did not identify, with only one other person there because of the early hour.

Later on Saturday morning, Merton went to the Indonesian Embassy to meet the new Ambassador, Dr. Giacomo Soedjatmoko. He also met the Ambassador's wife and children. The Embassy, located in downtown Washington near Dupont Circle, is an imposing four-story structure covering most of a city block. The architecture is nineteenth century European, with balconies and large double windows that resemble a country home of some level of royalty or the privileged class. Merton arrived at the side entrance under a long canopy. The front entrance is recessed from the street with a grand walkway to the door, flanked by stone urns on either side. After decades of deprivation at the monastery, this was out of the realm of even Merton's imagination.

Merton and the Ambassador and his family had lunch in the embassy's dining room, followed by a meeting of the two men. The Ambassador gave him some addresses of interesting people in Java to contact. Merton commented that they "had a great deal to say" and that he could communicate fully and freely with the Ambassador on a deep level without double-talk. Merton said that the Ambassador was "a person I have been waiting to meet for a lifetime," "companions on the same strange way, whatever it may be." Merton was excited about the possibilities he could look forward to, "much of which will not get on paper." The Ambassador later said that he felt he had really gotten to know Merton in this meeting. He loaned Merton a book on Indonesian Mysticism. Merton referred to the Indonesian Trappists he planned to visit at Rawa Seneng as some "who may or may not understand," and the Javanese mystics he described as some more, some less esoteric."

In response to a question about the use of drugs, Merton told the Ambassador that he felt no need for LSD or similar drugs because a cup of coffee was sufficient to turn him on in the morning for his meditation.

He and the Ambassador may well have discussed the recent so-called "miracles of healing" and "visions" being reported from the Indonesian islands by missionaries of several Christian denominations. It was said that within two and a half years, 200,000 new converts were experiencing 30,000 miracles of healing.

Merton did not explain in his journal why he was in contact with only one of the embassies of the countries he would visit. Merton alluded to his plan to visit Indonesia as feeling he was "summoned to meet Asia on the *deepest* level—and it may mean a hard business of breaking through a lamentable crust of ruins, decadence and misery." Merton said he was at the Indonesian Embassy for five hours.

Merton was driven directly to Washington National Airport from the Embassy in the Ambassador's chauffeur-driven black Cadillac for an evening return flight to Louisville. He felt like a celebrity. He had never been in a limousine before. He had only seen them in New York and never imagined that he would ever ride in one.

He decided not to change out of the clerical black suit and Roman collar for the flight back. He said later it kept him from meditation, though, because his seatmate was a young female passenger who engaged him in conversation. He felt he could not refuse. Merton bought her a couple of drinks to be sociable, and reported in his journal he later regretted the loss of time for solitude.

Ron and Sally Seitz met the plane. Then Father John Loftus joined them for dinner at the Embassy Club in Louisville. Merton spent the night at the Franciscan Friary. Still excited from the events of the day, Merton couldn't think about sleeping. He ended the evening by watching a late-night rebroadcast of a professional football game and thoroughly enjoyed it. He commented in his journal that football has "a religious seriousness" that U.S. religion "can never achieve."

Merton was in Washington just as a national Liturgical Conference there had ended. The Ebenezer Baptist Choir had performed Merton's "Freedom Songs" at the meeting. Both Alexander Peloquin, the composer of the music, and June Yungblat reported back to Merton that it was a success. He regretted that he could not have heard it.

The Trappist monastery at Vina was electing a new Abbot, and Dom Flavian went to preside over the election as well as look at the sites Merton had recommended for a cluster of hermitages on the West Coast. He found Bear Harbor to be full of snakes and could not believe Merton had found the place appealing. Needle Rock he found to be equally unrealistic. It would require purchasing a whole ranch to provide the necessary privacy because of the hippies passing through the area.

Merton then received an invitation from the Archbishop of Anchorage to give a retreat to the contemplative nuns in his diocese. Dom Flavian approved the idea, with the possibility of Merton finding a place for a hermitage there that would be more suitable than the California area. Merton thought it might best be scheduled in September at the front end of his trip to Asia. Merton was excited at the possibility of exploring a whole new area, and overjoyed to have an Abbot with such a positive attitude toward change.

On the other hand, Merton began to feel uneasy with his new Abbot's focus on other locations. He wondered if this meant that Father Flavian was thinking about Merton moving to another location, and maybe not even returning to Gethsemani after the trip. It dazed him to think of never returning to Gethsemani. He was such a bad driver. How could he manage in Alaska if he ended up there?

Father Flavian had told Merton to arrange his things so that others could use the hermitage in his absence. Merton had occupied it for three years now, and it had really become his home, the only one he had ever really had. He did not know how he could pack only 44 pounds, the weight allowance, when he had so much of his life to leave behind. According to his friend, Jim Forest, he mailed packages of books ahead to one of his stopping points, addressing them to a fictional Rabbi Vandata.

Brother Patrick Hart, previously Dom James' secretary for some ten years, had just returned from a two-year assignment in Rome. He brought Merton a special gift from Pope Paul VI himself, a beautiful bronze cross along with a personal message of good wishes. Dom James assigned Brother Patrick Hart to assist Merton as his secretary until his departure in getting his papers in order and to occupy the hermitage in his absence, assisting in handling Merton's correspondence. Merton was gratified to receive the memento from the Pope, although he never spoke of it. He was relieved to have Brother Patrick help him to tie up the loose ends now. He was so preoccupied with the adventure before him and distracted by all the miscellaneous administrative require-ments to prepare for his departure, he really needed an assistant. The numerous inoculations had drained his energies, and he found himself involved in more last-minute commitments than he had the time or energy for. He worked to complete *Lograire* before his departure, the only unfinished work.

Merton's trip to Asia was supposed to be kept confidential, like the trip to the West Coast. Naively, Merton told several of his friends of his plans, asking each of them to keep his secret. Naturally, the news became so widespread that eventually Dorothy Day announced it at the annual PAX conference in Tivoli, New York.

Ed Rice was one of Merton's friends notified about the trip. He had work to do in Louisville anyway, so came down to visit in early Sep-tember. Rice had traveled before in the Far East and could give Merton a great deal of useful information, and they could talk over old times. He gave Merton advice about how to handle his money since his funds would be severely limited, given the itinerary and the budget that was imposed by the Abbot. Laughlin helped Merton to get an American Express credit card to cover expenses along the way. The cash given him would only be a start to cover his extensive travel. He must have thought of Bramachari's trip from India to the U.S. and hoped for a smoother outcome.

It was now two weeks until Merton's departure. Frank O'Callaghan, Tommie's husband, offered to take him shopping for luggage and clothes. Merton bought a drip-dry suit that did not fit him properly simply because he liked it and it would be practical. To keep his luggage weight down, he left his Cistercian habit at the monastery. Later he found it was expected that he would be wearing monastic clothing, so the monastery mailed it to him.

Merton confided to his journal that he was nervous and insecure about making the trip. He wondered if he would die or be shot somewhere along the way. He wanted to see Dr. Mitchell one more time for an X-ray of his back and to check on whether he now possibly had bursitis in his jaw. Preparing for the trip, he started wearing his old yellow shoes, but they gave him blisters. Also he was experiencing a lot of discomfort from his allergy. Nevertheless he was impatient to leave.

Now it seemed as though his hermitage was on a rifle range. He worried he might be shot before he could leave. It couldn't be kids because in Kentucky they couldn't afford so much ammunition. It was "an eerie business!" Andrew Boone told Merton it was mainly hunters shooting the doves. He packed his eight relics of saints that had been given to him, telling himself they would be safer with him than left behind, but really just wanting them for a feeling of security. He put his tickets and passport in his leather wallet that Dr. Bennett, his guardian, had given him for his eighteenth birthday. Other things he distributed to different friends for safekeeping until his return. He entrusted his *Mad* magazine collection to one of the O'Callaghan girls, with the caution to take good care of them because he wanted them back.

The last morning at the hermitage, Merton said Mass. Brothers Maurice Flood and Patrick Hart, and Phil Stark came up from the monastery to attend. After breakfast with the group, Merton mailed the manuscript for *Geography of Lograire* to Jay Laughlin.

Most of the monks did not know Merton was leaving for this trip, or that he may not necessarily return. Merton was determined to remain a monk of Gethsemani, even if not necessarily physically present there.

He went in to say good-bye to Dom Flavian, who advised him not to allow himself to be televised or interviewed by the press. Merton jokingly promised Dom Flavian that he would behave himself. Merton wrote in a letter to Laughlin on September 9, "my new Abbot just keeps saying he trusts me, and shakes when he says it." Merton knew his departure was to be kept confidential for his own security, but at the same time he was disappointed that there was no send-off from the group. He really felt the community had abandoned him. He thought of the men he had known in the past 27 years who had left without saying good-bye, and he never dreamed he would some day experience the emptiness of their feeling.

Merton went down to the office to pick up the money for the trip from the assistant bookkeeper, a young novice. Merton told him that he was sorry he would not be there for his ordination, which was yet two years away. The novice was surprised that Merton knew when his ordination would be, and that Merton expected to be away for such a long time. He was gratified that Merton had the confidence in him to believe that he would continue his training to the point of ordination into the priesthood.

Merton asked for a jacket that he could take on the trip. The novice selected a rather old and worn one, with laundry mark #127 on it, thinking it would be comfortable. Later he wished he had given him a new one.

Merton had Ron Seitz drive him around town for new shoes, more allergy medicine, and travelers' cheques. They stopped at the Seitz home to say good-bye to the family. Then they drove over to the O'Callaghans' house. He would really miss all of their seven children as well as Tommie's peanut butter and jelly sandwiches. Merton took a shower and rested. Tommie told Merton to take care of himself, and after a good-natured exchange, she cried. Then they drove over to Bellarmine. Merton wanted to see Father Dan Walsh again. Later there was a farewell dinner at the Pine Room on River Road. It made him uncomfortable to see the sadness of his friends and thought it was a little like attending his own funeral. He spent the night before his departure at St. Bonaventure's Friary at Bellarmine.

The following morning, on September 11, he left Louisville. In his heart Merton experienced the brutal severing of his roots, just as he had so many times before. This time the roots he had put down were mature. Almost exactly half of his life had now been spent at Gethsemani. They were his best twenty-seven years on earth.

Merton looked back on his life and thought of all the conflict and dissatisfaction he had experienced over the years—his disappointment in his superiors, his inability to persuade others to follow his lead, his discouragement with physical incapacity. But, he reflected, what joy—the emptiness that brought the peace and love of God into his heart!

*I had no words or clever remarks to express that. Maybe every person has to get that directly from the Creator, certainly not from a popular writer's latest release. Indeed, it is "the peace that surpasses all understanding," as the Bible says. I guess I didn't have to come to a monastery to receive the gift of faith, but could I have held on to it if I hadn't come—and stayed? No human love could ever substitute for the fullness of God's love that I have received. I surrender my will to my God to keep me in the palm of His hands.*

*Embassy of the Republic of Indonesia, 2020 Massachusetts Avenue NW, Washington, DC. A 4-story mansion of more than 50 rooms, with a center courtyard covered by a stained glass ceiling, it is considered a historic landmark. Built in 1903 in the Beaux Arts style by Mr. Thomas F. Walsh, a gold miner, and his wife, owner of the Hope Diamond at that time, it was used by the White House for foreign royal visitors. Dr. Soedjatmoko had been serving as Indonesia's Ambassador to the US for only 3 months at the time of Merton's visit.*

# BOOK FIVE

Book Five serves to capture the tone of Merton's diary of his trip to Asia. It paraphrases Merton's commentary and describes his most significant experiences.

Mere passivity won't do at this point. But activism won't do either. A time of wordless deepening, to grasp the inner reality of my nothingness in Him who is ... . My prayer is peace and struggle in silence, to be aware and true, beyond myself. To go outside the door of myself, not because I will it but because I am called and must respond." (p. 224)

*Dancing in the Water of Life,*

# Chapter 32

I flew out of Louisville to Chicago, changing at O'Hara for a flight to Albuquerque. This time I wore no religious clothing. The first stop was the monastery, Christ in the Desert. I wanted to visit the Jicarilla Apache reservation to see their celebration of the Feast of the Tabernacles, with their marvelous dances, and to hear the drumbeats that led them into mystical states. They let me stay with them for the entire two-day event. I also wanted to meet Georgia O'Keeffe. I had missed her on my last visit. Her simple adobe house and patio on Ghost Ranch provide an incredible view of the mountains and the mesa of Pedernal. The site she chose was a statement that she quietly does everything right. She had met my parents, I thought, back in Greenwich Village when I was a child, when they went into the city to see other artists. I wanted to try to make that connection. I also love the way her paintings portray the existential beauty in nature.

Then I flew back to Chicago in the rain and gave a one-day conference there to a group of Poor Clares. They appreciated my visit. The following day I flew to Anchorage. Then to Eagle River, where I conducted a conference for the sisters at the Convent of the Precious Blood. They made me feel comfortable. There is a marvelous view of Mount McKinley from the convent, but I stayed in a trailer. It was the first time I tried it, and I had to admit it was comfortable, although artificial as a residence. I found these contemplative nuns were experiencing the same anxieties as those in urban locations. I realized that the effect of changes in society and the church were really pervasive, but I could not solve them. Archbishop Ryan in Anchorage arranged a small plane to take me around the area to look for sites for another hermitage. I saw property at Yakutat, a small village of Tlingit Indians, and also land around Eyak Lake. I appreciated the tour. These places would undoubtedly bring solitude, but I could not identify with them.

I caught up on my correspondence, happy to use the diocesan electric typewriter. I wrote to Naomi about my concerns and my enthusiasm. I had not told her in advance about the trip. I asked for her prayers, telling her this trip was necessary both for me and for the Asian part of the Church, which is yet to experience the same crisis the Western Church is now in.

I received a letter from Phil Berrigan, in Allentown, Pennsylvania, prison, that was forwarded from Gethsemani. He said he didn't mind being incarcerated for his pacifist activities. He had seen the article I had in *Ave Maria* magazine on draft card burning and non-violence and appreciated my support of his position. He asked me to be a witness at his upcoming trial in Catonsville, Maryland, in October. I replied that I would be in India then raising money to pay for my Asian trip.

I conducted a two-day retreat at the Archbishop's place in Anchorage on September 25 and 26. Then I was flown in a small two-engine plane over mountains and volcanoes to Dillingham, a nerve-racking experience for me. I gave a day of recollection for some 50 priests, most of them from remote missile sites. I was fortunate to miss a minor earthquake that occurred shortly after I left. This trip rekindled my devotion and prayer for my own safety, which seemed very much an issue at this time.

On October 2, I flew to San Francisco, over six forest fires and another volcano. I was relieved that this terrifying trip was finished. Modern civilization held a new appeal. A young correspondent, Suzanne Butorovich, met me and took me to her home for dinner with her family. Suzanne had written me several disarming letters that amused me and gave me a special insight into the point of view of college students who were not affected by the hippies of their generation. She was as charming as I had believed her to be from her clever letters. I stayed at the International Inn that night.

The next day I flew into Santa Barbara to see Ping Ferry, Vice President of the Center for the Study of Democratic Institutions, and to speak to the students there, including some French Marxist students. They saw themselves as a sort of monk coping with the hardships of contemporary struggles confronting them. I agreed with them. I also met Irvin F. Laucks of the Laucks Foundation, and several others, including Maw Karam, who had typed my manuscript of *Lograire* from the tapes I had sent to Ping.

We had a party at the Madonna Inn near San Luis Obispo, a wacky Disneyland-type motel. I sent Dom Flavian a picture postcard showing one of the luxurious hotel rooms, with the reassurance that I had not stayed there. I didn't tell him about the men's restroom, equipped with an electric eye that set off a waterfall in the urinal.

The following day there was a party at Yen Ching's restaurant in San Francisco, where I met Paul Jacobs and Czeslaw Milosz and their wives.

It was a thrill to meet Milosz in person and to speak with him at length. The dinner was great, too.

The next stop was the Redwoods again, and Mother Myriam's nuns for a three-day conference. I was disappointed to find bulldozers now at Bear Harbor, which radically changed the appearance of the place in the five months since I was last there. I borrowed her typewriter to write to Dom Flavian. I was inconclusive about any particular sites that I had found, but added that in the future Kentucky would probably be only a mailing address for me. I enjoyed photographing the surroundings at Needle Rock, figuring I probably wouldn't be returning there again. I loved watching the sea lions and the crashing surf at the foot of the cliff.

I drove back to San Francisco on October 13 with Portia Webster and Sister Marie, IHM, who were both postulants at the Redwoods. We stopped for drinks in Sausalito and visited a bookstore. I checked in at the Clift Hotel. Unfortunately my room was noisy from street sounds. I heard Ella Fitzgerald on the hotel's radio. The next day I went to get my Indonesian visa, and that evening I had dinner with Portia Webster on Fisherman's Wharf. The next morning I was at the airport ready to board my flight to Asia. I was surprised and dismayed that I had to pay an excess baggage fee because of all the books I had picked up. Once on the plane, I immediately started a new journal, to be like *Woods, Shore, Desert*. This one will be my "Asian Notes." My journal on the Alaska part of the trip I will keep separate.

I have wanted to see Asia since my Columbia days, when I met Bramachari. It feels like I'm going home to a place I have never been before. The journey is of course primarily an interior one. It's a matter of growth, of deepening, and of surrender to God's creative action in my heart. Of course I am curious, as I have always been. I have to investigate everything. That's how I found God, the Catholic Church, the Trappists, the priesthood, and even the love of a woman—for a while. What am I looking for now? I only know that I am not satisfied—the engine is still running. When the search is finished, I will be at the top of the mountain.

I landed in Honolulu, then flew to Tokyo on October 16, and changed planes for Bangkok. The stewardess began making routine announcements in Chinese, not English anymore. It sounded like the language of Heaven to me. I checked into the Oriental Hotel for two days to recover from the time change and to get organized. I enjoyed having my meals on the hotel's terrace by the river.

First I went to the home of Phra Khantipalo, an English Buddhist monk and author of two Buddhist texts. Through him I then met the abbot, Venerable Chao Khun Sasana Sobhana. The Buddhist abbot told me that one must ascend all the steps on the way to knowledge, but then when there are no more steps, one must make the leap, and this leap gives the knowledge of freedom. As we spoke, a young boy served us tea on his knees. I also visited several Buddhist monasteries. I was able to say Mass at a Catholic cathedral there.

Then I moved on to Calcutta on October 18th. The poverty was overwhelming and depressing—the children hung on to my taxi for coins until they had to let go for safety. I attended a four-day conference at the Birla Academy in South Calcutta for representatives of ten world religions. It was organized under the founder of the Temple of Understanding, Judith Hollister, an American who started the international organization to increase understanding among religious people of the world. I spoke on the importance of keeping tradition while trying to appeal to the modern world. My main point was that the key is communion—we are all one, whether we realize it or not. There is a unity that does not have to be discovered because it is already there, beyond speech and beyond concept.

I was particularly happy to meet Amiya Chakravarty in person, after our correspondence. I also met Swami Lokesvarananda, a Ramakrishna monk, whom I liked very much. A Tibetan lama, Chogyam Trungpa Rimpoche, who is a poet and has a Tibetan monastery in Scotland, invited me to visit him there. He also recommended I go to Bhutan, which I would certainly love to do. I stayed at the Grand Oberoi Hotel during the meeting, which gave me the impression it was crumbling, like the culture there. Chakravarty and a friend of his took me by car to the home of Jamini Roy, an elderly painter of religious subjects. His work was unutterably beautiful. I would have bought a dozen of his canvasses if I had had the money. I said Mass on October 26 at Calcutta's Loreto House for an order of Irish nuns. They graciously thanked me for visiting them.

I received a telegram from Tenzin Geshe, secretary of the Dalai Lama, saying I had an interview scheduled at Dharamsala for the first week of November. On October 28, I was off to New Delhi. I was met by Harold Talbott, an American living there, who was a friend and student of Dom Aelred Graham. When we saw each other, we realized we had met years before at Gethsemani. He was now a sophisticated young man, tall, slim, and erect, well dressed in a Western suit, with large horn-rimmed glasses. He could have passed for a young diplomat. Harold was studying under the Dalai Lama, so I arranged to stay with him in the simple bungalow provided him near the Dalai Lama's quarters. Harold accompanied me around New Delhi to the extent I needed him. I had my own hotel room at The Grand Hotel Oberoi Karma, a vast improvement over the hotel in Calcutta. Here I had the experience of being greeted by cows on the front doorstep and receiving endless salaams from the staff, even by the elevator operator. I settled down on the balcony outside my room, writing in my journal and sending cards to friends, making daily meditations, and reading all the new material I had acquired. I was in good company—five green parrots perched there, with eight more flying around overhead and making a racket.

In New Delhi I had lunch with Anthony Quainton and his wife from the American Embassy, who gave me much welcomed advice about seeing Indian officials. Then I went to tea with Dr. Syed Vahiduddin, one of the other speakers at the conference of the Temple of Understanding in Calcutta. On the street I saw a man with a bag of cobras, accompanied by a man with some kind of a horn-shaped musical instrument. They offered to make the snakes dance for me, in the dust of the street. I tried to conceal my horror. I felt like the prototype classical hero traveling in an imaginary land, with each successive experience more challenging to my imagination than the one before.

Harold took me to a place where Tibetan refugees live in a combination school and monastery. It was enlightening to meet some of the monks there. One of the monks said he thought that Westerners need to understand meditation better. Boys in their culture begin to meditate at fifteen or sixteen years of age. Dr. Lokesh Chandra offered me a mandala, one of his reprints. I chose one rather quickly that seemed to me to be quite lively. I planned to study the drawings more closely after I returned to my hotel room. When I looked at it later, I discovered to my amazement that it was full of scenes of copulation, which I hadn't even noticed. Don't ask me how I'm supposed to meditate with that!

On my last night in Delhi, I was invited to have dinner at the Canadian Embassy with Commissioner and Mrs. James George. Also included were Harold, as well as Gene Smith, an American I had been corresponding with, who is considered to be one of the leading

Tibetanists among Western scholars. I had already been entertained at
the French Embassy by Madame Daridan. The French food and wine
were for me an echo of a long distant past. I asked the Commissioner
about Shaivism, to better understand the Hindu beliefs. From what I
knew of it, it did not appeal to me, at least at this point. I preferred to
analyze the philosophy of Eastern religions.

On October 31, Harold and I took the train to Pathankot, in a
sleeper car. It reminded me of my overnight train ride from New York
to Louisville many years ago. And it was really no more comfortable, but
I was tired so even the sound of the clicking rails didn't keep me awake.
Then we went by jeep to Dharamsala, which is approximately 265 miles
northwest of New Delhi and located on a mountainside. Even though
it was raining when we arrived, we saw Tibetan monks praying with
their rosaries in hand on a nearby path. I was surprised at how primitive
Harold's cottage was—not like my hermitage. In my exploration of the
area, I discovered that there were Tibetans living all over the mountain
in huts or tents. Prayer flags of red, yellow, and white solid color cloth
waved in the breeze from the small tree branches. There were rock
mandalas all along the walkways. Harold said they were proclaiming
"Hail to the jewel in the lotus" carved into the rock in Tibetan.

It was not always quiet and peaceful, though. I discovered there was
daily gunfire from the Indian Army at a small-arms range not far away.
It reminded me of Gethsemani and the gunfire from Fort Knox. Could
I ever escape this reminder of violence? And here there was an added
feature to the unrest—earth tremors. That was a new one for me.

Nevertheless, I was not thinking about a quick return to Gethsemani.
I wrote to Dom Flavian and asked his opinion about extending my trip
to include visits to Switzerland, Scotland, England, and Wales to see
some of my correspondents, with a final destination of either Kentucky
or Alaska. I would eagerly await his reply, and wondered how long it
would take in reaching me.

Walking down the path on the mountain, I was surprised to meet
a man wearing European clothing. He told me he was Sonam Kazi, a
teacher of Tantric Buddhism with an extensive education under several
Nyingmapa Buddhist masters in Tibet. We walked together down
to the Tourist Hotel and enjoyed tea and a good talk. We were both
probably equally happy to meet another English-speaking person there.
He encouraged me to find a Tibetan guru and try their techniques of
meditation and contemplation. I thought, why not? I felt very much

at home with the Tibetans, who are not as bizarre as they seemed sometimes in books.

Sonam Kazi taught me some practical things about Tibetan Buddhism. A new concept for me was the Tibetan view of taking vows. He said the highest vow is that in which there is nothing promised because there is no longer anything to be accomplished. He said there is no need to use vows as a path to spiritual communion. That idea was so novel I dared not draw any conclusions about my reaction until I gave it a lot more thought.

I also learned that in the Tibetan language, the word Trappist, for them, "Trapa," meant "monk" or "schoolman." That served me in good stead, but being known as a writer did not sit so well. There was a prevailing distrust that visitors who were writers might go back to the world and publish something inaccurate or harmful to their situation. With the Communist Chinese take-over of Tibet and their flight to Dharamsala, India, in 1959, they had reason to fear anything that could upset the delicate balance of the environment in which they now lived. They had no hope that any of their visitors could do much to help them, so they screened them carefully and watched their words even more carefully, especially in speaking to writers. The Beatle, George Harrison, had preceded me to India the previous year, and they were not looking for any more Western tourists or seekers, famous or not, invading their world and publicizing their activities.

Harold and I went to look for Khamtul Rinpoche, who was said to be setting up a new monastery and lay colony. We met him by chance on the road to a tea plantation near Palampur. I was told I could learn something significant from Rinpoche. Luckily, we had Sonam Kazi with us to translate. Rinpoche, a Tibetan, advised me not to rely on book knowledge to learn about meditation. He said I needed a guru to assist me in direct experience. He asked me if I had come there to write "a strange book." He recommended I try to meet Gyalwa Karmapa, a guru who had a monastery in Sikkim.

We planned to climb the mountainous road to the top to see the Dalai Lama at his residence, but he sent his jeep to drive us up for each of our visits. I was surprised to see a family of gray apes with black faces swinging on the branches of the trees nearby. They are called Hanumans, and were almost as large as us. They seemed to be quite agile and smart. They didn't frighten anyone, so I assumed they were no more dangerous than my squirrels at the hermitage. Actually, being

in the Himalayas to visit the Dalai Lama was surreal in itself. To see
these creatures climbing around us in this exotic setting made it seem
a bit like a trip to another dimension of reality.

Harold and I first visited a small monastic community of lamas under
the Dalai Lama's private chaplain, the Khempo of Namgyal Tra-Tsang.
The chaplain received us in his room. He was studying the Tibetan block-
print texts of their doctrine. I found him to be an articulate, scholarly
man. He advised me to read the "Prajnaparamita" on suffering. He said
that when "all the hairs of the body stood on end," one was ready for
meditation. He said he would not speak directly of symbols, such as
mandalas, because they were too sacred to speak openly about them. I
found his ideas interesting and stimulating, to put it mildly.

At the gate of the Dalai Lama's place, an Indian official examined our
passports before letting us pass in. There were several Tibetan monks
standing around outside the residence. First we were escorted into a
sitting room, then invited into the Dalai Lama's study.

His birth name was Gejong Tenzin Gyatsho. He was a young man
of 33, born twenty years after me, and unusually mature, I thought, for
his age. The anxiety he suffered in being exiled from Tibet in 1959 and
fearing for his very life had had its effect. He had only agreed to meet
with me one time, but we got on so well together that he suggested three
meetings. I was frankly delighted to meet this master of Buddhism in
person. I had never visited the Pope in Rome or even the Abbot General at Citeaux. This opportunity would rank in close proximity to the
significance of those events, had they ever occurred.

Our first meeting was on November 4 in his study. His young interpreter helped in translating the difficult abstract concepts we discussed.
His quarters were simple but elegant, reflecting the charm of the holy
man himself. His saffron and maroon robe was beautiful in its simplicity. The fragrance of the incense added to the atmosphere. On the wall
were Tibetan wall hangings obviously of a religious nature, and on small
shelves there were Tibetan block print texts in narrow oblong sheets
wrapped in yellow and orange cloth, books, and rows of small brass
bowls of what appeared to be water. Everything was carefully arranged
and obviously had a religious significance, as though it were a shrine,
which in a sense it actually was.

The Dalai Lama approached me with a marked composure. He was
somewhat taller than I imagined him to be. His face radiated a certain
compassion and at the same time he looked at me in a light-hearted,

optimistic way. He spoke softly with a perspective that could come only from living on another plane from the down-to-earth reality most of us experience every day. I couldn't wait to see how our conversation would go and what I would take away from our meeting.

The Dalai Lama gave me names of others that he recommended I contact for more information about Eastern religions. He made no mention of politics. We spoke only of religion and philosophy and, in particular, meditation. He told me he had heard quite a bit about me, which put me at ease. I told him of my personal interest in Tibetan mysticism, and his reply was frank and too confidential for me to record.

That night the electricity in Harold's cottage went out for a while for reasons unknown, because the weather was very clear. I went outside to look at the stars. I saw the same constellations I saw in Gethsemani. It made me homesick. Then I realized that this mountain with the Dalai Lama at the top was itself a mandala, and he was a fully awake, nondusty, nonwhispering Buddha. Then there was a mild earthquake, followed by crying birds and many dogs barking. Then quiet again. It was getting easier to pray all the time there, with the realistic reminders of my mortality.

Two days later, on November 6, the Dalai Lama and I got into more of a discussion of consciousness and methods of concentration, a subject of utmost interest to me. He showed me the Tibetan sitting position for meditation, which he said was essential. It requires the right hand, signifying discipline, to be above the left, for wisdom. This is the reverse hand position of Zen. He emphasized the need to renounce and detach from "unworldly" things in the pursuit of an interior life.

The following day, I visited with Chobgye Thicchen Rinpoche, a poet and mystic who is considered quite advanced in Tantrism. He claimed he could sever his soul from his body and could teach others to do it as well. I didn't feel ready to try this, but we exchanged poems that we had composed for each other. Maybe I thought his claim might well be possible, and I wasn't ready to risk getting my soul back to my body if he should sever it.

In our third meeting, November 8, the Dalai Lama asked me a number of questions about monasticism in the West, particularly the part that vows play in our spiritual journey. I spoke to him about the paper I planned to read in Bangkok about Marxism and monasticism. I wanted to know what he thought about the Marxist concept of alienation as compared to the Buddhist desire to deny an ego-centered existence.

The Dalai Lama thought a bridge between our religious cultures could be built, but not with Western churches operating in a structure that involves power and worldly possessions.

At the end of our last meeting, we went outside and posed in front of his home for pictures. The flowering vines overhanging the roof gave the place a warmth that added to our cordial meeting. We left with mutual feelings for each other as friends with a definite spiritual bond between us. He called me a "Catholic geshe," or "learned lama," which was the highest possible praise, Harold told me later.

Harold and I returned to his hut further down the mountain to meditate on all that had just taken place. After a long interlude, I told Harold that in my spiritual life I had found it possible to overcome both grief and guilt for past mistakes and to move on with my life in communion with God. I told him about the life I had led at Cambridge and the burden I had carried about it. All my life I had tried to atone for this mistake and pray for forgiveness. This was the first time I had told anyone the entire story. It was an unburdening I badly needed. Harold didn't say anything, and I didn't want him to.

Harold and I then took the evening train back to New Delhi for the weekend. I checked in at the Imperial Hotel. The first thing I did was take a bath, have some hot tea, and read the newspaper. Nixon had just been elected—how depressing. We went to the 18th century observatory, Jantar Mantar, and I took a lot of pictures. Then we had dinner at the Oberoi Intercontinental, very American in style and a poor choice after my recent experiences. The American Muzak on the PA system almost ruined my dinner.

I wrote to Dom Flavian on November 9 that I should probably not return to the hermitage at Gethsemani, but just come back to plan any future steps. I felt I ought to be elsewhere, maybe Alaska, but always as a member of the monastic family there. I said we should both be praying to know God's will for my future.

The next day we drove out into the country with the Lhalungpas to see the Cambodian monk at the Ashoka Vihara. It was really an experience to see the old mosque, sit on the floor, and talk to the elderly monk there. On Sunday morning we drove out to a Moslem College with Lobsang Lhalungpa and Deki. It was an impressive place, except for the snake charmers outside when we arrived. I was happy that they had left by the time we were ready to depart. Then I said Mass at Holy Family Hospital in the room of James George, the Canadian High

Commissioner. He was just recovering from minor surgery there. He and his family attended the Mass next to his hospital bed. I also had the Lhalungpas, Kunga, the companion of Trungpa Rinpoche, and Harold there. After Mass the George family invited us for lunch at their home with Trungpa Rinpoche. After lunch I borrowed Commissioner George's typewriter to write a letter to Dom Flavian. I again asked his permission to extend my trip through Europe, in case he hadn't received my earlier letter.

On November 12, we returned to Calcutta. Mrs. George drove us to the Palam airport. Before I left, I mailed off rolls of film to John Howard Griffin for processing. I sent Brother Patrick a newsletter I had written about my visit with the Dalai Lama for him to mimeograph and distribute. It was a relief to have him at the hermitage keeping my mail sorted, sending me what seemed to be really important, and maintaining my connection with my correspondents. The people I was writing to were those I was reaching out to on an immediate basis.

With my books and articles, I have been seeking a broader group of readers I'll never meet, but I want to love them and bring them closer to the Almighty. This is what keeps me alive, I believe; otherwise I am not a whole person. I cannot have a partner to reach out to, so this is my family.

Calcutta was a bigger shock to me than on my first visit. Now that my vision had adjusted to the overall scene, I saw in greater detail the poverty, hunger, disease, and crime that was intensified by the overpopulation. On the outskirts of the city there were cows and slate-blue buffaloes, many more than in Delhi. Closer into town we saw rickshaws, pulled by skinny men in bare feet, shabby buildings, and tattered posters that reflected a sordid and miserable culture. Rather than a judgment of these people, it was more like they were a judgment on the rest of the world. I tried to find the Ashram of Bramachari, my old friend from Columbia days, but with no success. I was told that his group had moved, but no one knew where they had gone. That was a major disappointment for me.

We took a plane from Calcutta to Bagdogra, over the mountains and the Ganges. I saw Kanchenjunga for the first time from the air, the most fascinating mountain in Asia. Then we drove on a primitive road up a steep incline, where there had recently been some seventy landslides, to Darjeeling, a four-hour trip with the delays. I stayed at the Windamere Hotel. The lights went out in the middle of dinner due to an electrical problem. From the hotel, I could see the occupying Chinese troops in the hillside guarding the city. I had developed a cold in Calcutta, and it got progressively worse. Medicine was expensive, so I relied on my old standby, brewed tea. I also got some beer. At dawn I went out to see Kanchenjunga by first light. It was spectacular, blue gray without the sun on it yet. I climbed up the hill from the hotel to the temple where there were many prayer flags and containers of incense. Then later I returned and photographed the mountain in full daylight, hoping to capture my mood there.

Next to the hotel was Loreto College, a Government school run by Catholic nuns. I walked over and introduced myself, and said Mass for the sisters and some of their students at the convent. Afterwards we visited the Tibetan Refugee Center, where I met some monks and a nun with her head shaved. They all worked in a local carpet factory. I bought a shaggy wool coat to wear because it was cold even in the hotel. Then I went by jeep to St. Joseph's School in North Point, run by the Jesuits. I found a place near the hotel on the side of Observatory Hill to say Lauds. Tibetans passed me on the road, chanting or using prayer wheels, completely disregarding my presence. It was fascinating to witness the integration of religious activity into daily life of even the most destitute. I felt like I was in a time tunnel, that Western monasticism was a mere reflection of the existential reality of what I was now seeing in its primitive origin. Some of our practices at Gethsemani seemed an inadequate progression from the ancient religious life that gave birth to our way of life. It was a subject to give further thought to and deeper meditation.

I had heard about the Mim Tea Estate before I came to India as a suitable place for a semi-retreat. On November 15, I went to check it out. I found a quiet guesthouse where I could return in a few days to get away from the commercial city hotel atmosphere. I was given the manager's bungalow for the night. I began to photograph Kanchenjunga, but there was a cloud continuously hanging over the peak that I thought would devalue my shot. I nursed my cold, slept a lot, and even dreamed of this mountain. I began to think it was symbolic of the fact that whatever I had come to Asia to find seemed to be hidden from view. Yet I knew it was there. The following night, it occurred to me that there was another side to this mountain, and every other mountain, that the viewer did not see. That was the side that wasn't on the postcards, and that was the only side worth seeing. Finally the clouds cleared and I saw it. Knowing about the unknown part of the mountain now allowed me to see it more realistically. I was content with this paradox.

On November 16, Harold and I, along with Jimpa Rimpoche, Father Sherburne, and a Tibetan guide went to look for Chatral Rimpoche. He had a hermitage above Ghoom. When we arrived, he wasn't there, but we found him visiting at a nunnery near Bagdogra. I enjoyed speaking with him. He looked like an old peasant, with an overgrown beard, and he wore a Bhutanese jacket, thongs, and a red wool cap. He looked like a picture out of a *National Geographic* magazine. He spoke clearly and was quite communicative, through his interpreter, Jimpa.

We spoke for about two hours. He told me he had been meditating for thirty years and still had not reached his goal of perfect emptiness, which he said involves compassion for all creatures to the point of "direct realization." We both believed we were on the edge of great realization and knew we had to keep trying to get lost in it. We agreed that it was a grace for us to meet each other, since we were convinced that spiritually we had so much in common in our quest. He called me "rangjung Sangay," which means something like a "natural Buddha." We agreed to try to reach complete Buddhahood in this life, not waiting for a next life to achieve this. If I had had to select a Tibetan guru to help me spiritually, I would certainly have chosen Chatral. I wasn't sure I needed a guru to pursue my spiritual growth, though I didn't tell him so.

Then we drove down to the Sakyapa monastery on the hillside near Ghoom. We met the "rinpoche," the master there, a friend of Jimpa's. I asked him about the use of psychedelic drugs, and he said he had never even heard of them. He was surprised to hear that people in the West even tried to practice meditation. He told me he thought the West had great potential for creation, but also for destruction. We returned to the hotel at Darjeeling, and I went to bed with a sore throat, aggravated by the coal smoke and the chilly temperatures, both inside and outside. The Jesuits gave me some medicine. I had purchased some cold remedies and brandy, but did not open them.

On November 17, I concelebrated Mass with Father Curmi at St. Joseph's College in two languages, his native Nepali and my English said under my breath. Some of the parishioners played drums and small bell-like cymbals. It was certainly unique in my experience, and I found it quite moving. After Mass I enjoyed breakfast with the Jesuits at the College. The librarian, a Belgian priest, told me he had twenty-two of my books in his school library. He embarrassed me, but I was nevertheless gratified to know that my ideas had spread to this extent. I assured my hosts that the American Church was not exactly as they found it described in *Time* magazine.

Later that day I returned by Land Rover to the Mim Tea Estate to check in for my small retreat. I was alone, since Harold decided to remain at the Windamere Hotel. Martin Hall, the manager, and his wife were solicitous of my sore throat. I had lunch in their dining room, but I had them bring me soup at night instead of the evening meal. I unpacked my books with anticipation. I had been experiencing more mindlessness than mindfulness recently. I couldn't believe I had now been in Asia for a month.

The Halls gave me two candles and a matchbox in case the lights went out. I could also build a fire in the bungalow's fireplace. It reminded me of the hermitage, and my hours in front of the fireplace drinking hot tea. I realized I really loved Gethsemani. I knew, though, that it would now be more realistic for me to stay connected there legally and actually live in seclusion either in Alaska or somewhere in the area around the Redwoods in California. Asia, especially Darjeeling, seemed to be a quaint but fraudulent relic of something that was incredible for me. I was discovering I didn't really need to have seen it. This was a comforting realization. If I found this experience to have been unnecessary, then it was not a waste of time to have come here.

Like Dorothy and her trip to Oz, I had found no Wizard. And there's no place like home.

The 28,000 foot living postcard of Kanchenjunga was outside my window, usually clouded over. That night I had a strange dream about the mountain. I heard in my mind what seemed like a voice saying, "There is another side to the mountain." In the dream I thought I was seeing it from the Tibetan side, and everything was turned around. When I awoke, I no longer felt negative about this mountain as a tourist attraction.

On November 21, I said Mass again at the Loreto Convent, and gave a short sermon in spite of my hoarseness. I had tried double whiskies the night before as well as the Jesuits' remedies, but nothing seemed to have an effect. My intense interest in Buddhism seemed to disturb the nuns. One old sister commented that this trip might be "the mountain of myrrh" for me. The bishop, Eric Benjamin, who was Nepalese, asked me to return the following week. Father Curmi then accompanied me to the home of Dr. Pemba. I was happy to see a physician since my cold was not getting any better.

From the road leaving this area, I saw the Natu-la-Pass in the distance. It was a sunny day, and women were washing their hair and drying it in the sun. Some of them were delousing their children, I was told. I heard that in Calcutta there had been a Marxist riot led by Maoist students, and they had set fire to some buses. They burned a paper likeness of Robert McNamara, the U.S. Secretary of Defense, in effigy. Obviously this was in protest of the U.S. involvement in the Vietnam war. The news was chilling. I became aware of the significance of the topic assigned to me for the Bangkok conference—Marxism and monasticism.

On November 23 we visited Kalu Rinpoche at his hermitage at Sonada. He was a small man, and very quiet. He fingered his beads as he spoke to me. Many of the Buddhists I was seeing carried their mala, made of 108 strung beads wound around their wrists several times like a bracelet. It made me comfortable with my rosary. Rinpoche was running a three-year retreat for sixteen hermits. Each hermit would see only his guru during the entire three years. The purpose was to seek eternal salvation for all sentient beings, not just themselves. I was really impressed by their compassion and unselfishness. Kalu Rinpoche gave me three pictures of his deities, each in outline in black and white, that he had personally colored. I was touched at his faith as well as his generosity.

The next day we left the area, which seemed to me very desirable in spite of the continuous firing of automatic rifles in the nearby valley. Returning to Darjeeling, Harold and I parted after a short visit in my hotel room. I was too ill to go out. He kindly paid my bill at the Windamere Hotel before he left. I said good-bye, regretting to lose his company. In addition to the severe cold, I was having headaches. I wondered how I could proceed on to Kurseong to give a short retreat that had been scheduled for the Jesuit scholastics.

Somehow I managed to get through my visit to Kurseong. The scholasticate was housed in a big, cold Belgian-type structure that seemed to me to symbolize the Jesuits' traditional point of view. We were high on a mountain, overlooking the Ganges plain. The Jesuits seemed to like my talk, with a few exceptions. Many weren't too sure about my point that it might be possible for Indians to contribute to a renewal of the Catholic theology of prayer. Father Cherian Curiyikad, an Indian and their scripture scholar, appreciated my remarks.

I spent the night in his cell, reading some of his books that I was not familiar with. One of the books contained a Preface by Pierre Emmanuel, a French hermit in India. He said a religious vocation is a mysterious form of death when one consecrates it to such a height of sacrifice that it ruptures from the apparent order of being. This then becomes a development in the person that is not visible to others in the efficacy or development of the vocation. At the end of my visit, I concelebrated Mass in English in their renovated chapel. I was amazed to see the word "Om" inscribed on their lectern where I gave my sermon.

I went by taxi to the airport in Bagdogra for my flight to Calcutta. The ride was an experience in itself. The driver turned off his motor for most of the trip down the mountain, obviously to save gas. It was of some comfort that I was one of several passengers in the cab. Finally, we could go no farther, and we had to walk some 50 to 100 yards to the terminal. It was a relief to be back on level ground.

In Calcutta I spent the night at the apartment of Bob Boylan. He was a Cultural Affairs Officer with the U.S. Information Service. I had met him on my first visit to Calcutta, and he allowed me to give his address for mail to be sent to me. I was happy to see the mound of mail he had received for me. I learned that Dom Leclercq had arrived in Delhi, en route to the Bangkok conference. John Griffin had sent me contact prints of some of my pictures. The one with the Dalai Lama was particularly nice. Dom Flavian wrote that I should come home if I got sick. It was written before he received my request to extend my trip through Europe. That must have surprised him. He probably discovered that he didn't know me as well as he thought he did when it comes to my insatiable love for travel. Dan Walsh sent a big check for my travel expenses—joy! I'm told the article I wrote for Time-Life Books on the Bible is going to be published, and, even better, that Doubleday is proceeding to publish *My Argument with the Gestapo*.

The following day, November 26, I flew into Madras, an Indian city that is a much more leisurely place than Calcutta or Delhi. Dr. Raghavan from the local university drove me around, and we had tea. He is considered one of the foremost Sanskritists in the world. I was concerned to hear that there was cholera now in North Madras. We visited a number of South Indian Hindu shrines and temples, as well as the Catholic cathedral at San Thome. The next morning I said Mass at St. Thomas Mount in a small church that overlooked an army camp and the airport. It reminded me of a hermitage, with its old folk art décor. I found it quite moving. I stopped in at the orphanage next door, run by Franciscan nuns, and signed the guest book. I left quickly before they saw my signature and recognized me.

I was given a Catholic driver for the trip to Mahabalipuram. It was a charming place, with shrines built into an ancient rock formation, fishing villages, and a peaceful view of the Bay of Bengal. Then I visited the National Gallery and Government Museum, where I was fascinated with the musical instruments displayed, especially the temple drums. I was particularly curious about an arrangement of eighteen porcelain cups to be filled to various levels with water for different sounds, to be played with a small stick of bamboo. I would have loved to try them out!

On November 29 I flew out of Madras to Columbo, Ceylon (later called Sri Lanka), landing over a harbor of lighted ships. I checked in at the Galle Face Hotel and went to their Mascarella Room. I ordered a local rum drink. They had a live band that played American music of the thirties. That brought back some memories. I could hear it almost as well in my room, which turned out to be directly over the bar, but I was so tired I slept right through the music. The next day I walked around and visited an old Anglican Church and other old English buildings. There was a Post Office strike going on there, and I saw armed guards everywhere in the streets. I went over to the Taprobane Hotel in the evening for dinner. They had an accordionist playing Irish songs, and a view of the harbor, but the food was inferior to that at my own hotel. Looking at the night sky, I saw how different the star formations looked from this part of the world. The following morning I contacted Victor Stier, the local director of the U.S. Information Service, and he invited me to lunch at his home. Ping Ferry had given me a letter of introduction to him. Also Bob Boylan had thought it a good idea for me to meet his Ceylon counterpart.

On November 30 I went by train to Kandy. I checked into a nearby hotel overlooking an English-style village church. There were coconut palms in front of it. I had a letter waiting for me inviting me to see the German hermit, Nyanaponika Thera. There was a jungle on the edge of town where there were several somewhat attractive caves housing some Buddhist monks. He was one of this group. Originally he was a German Jew, but was later known for his writing and editorial work for a Buddhist publishing outfit. He had traveled to Europe recently to handle some of his business, so wasn't really that cut off from modern society like others I had been meeting.

I saw a little temple, Gangaramaya, on the edge of the jungle, where a great Buddha is carved out of a huge rock coming right out of the earth. There was a small temple built around it. Then I visited Bishop Nanayakkara in the cathedral. He drove me up to the top of the hill for a view of Kandy. I spoke to him about my idea of Buddhist-Christian dialogue and of a meditation monastery that would be open to Buddhism. We also talked about the Church today. He seemed to agree with me about the problems that Christians are facing worldwide. It was an interesting problem to explore how one might establish an interfaith program there.

The following day I visited the monastery of the Sylvestrines with the bishop. It was a very attractive large Romanesque German-style church. I was invited to give a talk to the seminarians. Bishop Regno, now retired and rather deaf, told me he had read *Seven Storey Mountain*. He thought I must have been one of the first hippies. I tried to explain to him that hippies smoked pot, not cigarettes, and did not drink whiskey, but he didn't seem to understand me.

The bishop took me out to see Ibbagamuwa, a village where there is an Anglican ashram on a coconut estate. The chapel was actually an open chicken house with a concrete floor. I thought it was a good example of what a monastic experiment in Asia should look like. The postulants had left, but they were expecting at least one in the near future. For the time being, there were lay volunteers helping the Anglican priest, Brother Johan Devananda.

In a village on the way back, I saw a temple standing next to a movie house, and a couple of elephants working with logs along the road. A steel frame in the shape of a Buddha figure looked like it would be a statue when the concrete was poured. Then I went to the Kandy museum, past the Temple of the Tooth. It contained mostly folk art, with the exception of the lacquers and ivories. I participated in a Mass that evening and gave the homily.

On December 2, I made a long trip by car to Dambulla and Polonnaruwa. The bishop was kind to furnish a car for me. He asked about the possibility of establishing a small foundation or hermitage in Dambulla connected to Gethsemani. I wondered if I should return to see more of the area after my trip to Indonesia. Dambulla was known as an important archeological site. There is a huge black rock there with five ancient cave-temples inside with beautiful carvings. At Dambulla I went into the caves with a guide. We carried two small candles. I went in barefoot, the dirt floor damp under my feet. There was a large gold Buddha and a line of stone and sandalwood Buddhas guarding the frescoes on the roof and walls of the caves. The artwork took my breath away.

Polonnaruwa was the royal residence for a sequence of Sinhalese kings in the eighth to twelfth centuries. What I saw was an ancient ruin of what was once a beautiful city. I traveled to Polonnaruwa with the vicar general of the Kandy diocese, a Celonese Sylvestrine with a Dutch name. He preferred to lag behind at both sites. At Polonnaruwa he sat under a tree reading his guidebook, probably wishing to shy away from the paganism as well as the possibility of natives trying to sell us something worthless.

I found Polonnaruwa to be largely neglected. It was on a dirt road, under some trees, with few people around. The mountains in the distance reminded me of Yucatan. The path goes down to Gal Vihara, a wide hollow surrounded by trees. There is a low rock containing a cave, and next to it a large Buddha seated on the left, a reclining Buddha on the right, and Ananda, the Buddha's attendant and favorite disciple.

I removed my shoes and climbed in the tall wet grass and sand to see them more closely. The silent, smiling faces were extraordinary and spoke to my heart. As I later described them in my journal, they were "filled with every possibility, questioning nothing, knowing everything, rejecting nothing." The clarity of the figures, the shape and line carved into the rock in the landscape was more spectacular than I even imagined. On the other side of the hollow, I could walk around and see different aspects of the figures from the sweep of bare rock that sloped away from them.

The experience jerked me out of the mental state I had been in. I gained an inner clearness and clarity that told me "there is no puzzle, no problem, and really no 'mystery' ... .everything is emptiness and ... compassion ... .I know and have seen what I was obscurely looking for." I was now "beyond the shadow and the disguise."

It was like a Zen garden for me. Although the figures were motionless, I felt the movement in their bodily form that was for me like a holy vision. I did not care to see the rest of the ruins, even the palace complex, after this experience. We drove back then to Kandy. When I spoke about this to Walpola Rahula at the Buddhist University, he said they were not carved by "ordinary men."

On December 4, I flew to Singapore and was met by Lee Beng Tjie, a professor at the local university, and his wife. They drove me to my hotel,

The Raffles, and then out to Mount Faber. There we had a great view of the harbor and the lights of the city. I said Mass at his apartment in the dining room. Then we all went to a restaurant in Chinatown. They picked me up again for dinner that night and we went up Beach Road to a restaurant where we cooked our own meal by dipping meats in boiling water. I felt I had more to learn about enjoying this type of meal.

On December 6, I left Singapore armed with a fresh supply of film. It was pleasant seeing the clean, modern Western architecture after my visits to cities with so much decay. In the suburbs it looked a bit like California. The next stop was Bangkok and the conference. I was not looking forward to it. After that, Indonesia, and a whole new experience. Based on my experience so far, I would not try to predict where that would take me or what to plan on. The journey had only begun.

# Chapter 33

I flew back to Bangkok, over Malaysia, for the meeting. I ended up in first class because Japan Air Lines offered unlimited baggage allowance with the upgrade, so it was cheaper than paying excess baggage in economy. On the flight, I enjoyed two Bloody Marys and much food as well as good conversation with a diplomatic courier for the U.S. State Department.

Bangkok, known as the City of Angels, looked much better to me than on my first visit. I checked into the Oriental Hotel again, which was my first hotel of the trip, and this time I really appreciated the accommodations compared to those I had had in the month and a half since I was last there. My hotel room was a split-level structure overlooking the river, with an open veranda. I immediately started identifying clothing and books that I would leave behind to avoid the extra charges on my next flight.

I reserved a flight for December 15 to Djakarta. I took nine rolls of film to a local shop to be developed and sent some contact prints I had previously taken to John Griffin to make some enlargements.

Then I went to the Temple of the Emerald Buddha. Though actually a single piece of jasper, the green Buddha was a moving experience for me, enshrined high up in a lighted niche. I thought the guardian deities were grotesque rather than frightening, as they are supposed to be, to protect the Buddha, considered the most sacred image in the kingdom. The buildings and sculptures were precious and bizarre, but not really beautiful, in my opinion. The frescoes reminded me of a comic strip with their monkey god, Hanuman, and villains of the temple whom he finally slays. I started thinking about old cartoons in *New Yorker* magazines of years ago that were probably influenced by some of these ancient creatures.

On December 7, a Dutch abbot staying with an attaché of the Dutch Legation came to the hotel to meet me. He wanted me to participate in a TV interview, but I thought it inappropriate for me. I turned down his invitation as courteously as I could. The next day I went to the French Foreign Missions office and was happy to see Dom Leclercq and others who had just arrived for the conference. This mission group had notified me that I had received mail there, but it turned out to be only one letter from one of the novices at the Redwoods, forwarded from Calcutta. I figured that some of my mail must have gotten lost. That night I walked around the city and into Chinatown. I ended up going to a kind of fair, where there were people of all ages who seemed to be having a great time. It seemed to have something to do with their King, who had just had his birthday. Then I went to a Hungarian restaurant for dinner, which wasn't very good. Afterwards I saw an Italian movie, a quasi-documentary about Milan that I enjoyed. The day was an eclectic combination of activities that managed to divert me from my thoughts about the upcoming meeting.

The next day, the feast of the Immaculate Conception, and a Sunday, I went to St. Louis Church and said Mass. It was a nice feeling to be in a church of my namesake in religion. Then I had lunch at the Apostolic Delegation. In the afternoon I went out to Samut Praharn, the Red Cross facility where we were staying for our meeting, a drive of 30 kilometers out of Bangkok. It is an extensive property with flowering trees, an ornamental lake, and several swimming ponds, not what we would have pictured for a charitable organization overseas.

There was a conference hall in the Sawang Kaniwat Park, a small hotel, a large guesthouse, and a number of four-room cottages. I was assigned to Cottage Number 2 in a white frame fourplex structure on the edge of a canal. My unit was on the lower right side. It was surrounded with thick flowering shrubs under the windows. My room was next to Father Celestine Say, a Benedictine prior from Manila, who had the left side. Each unit consisted of a bedroom with a small bathroom in the rear. Between our rooms there was a small receiving hall. The walls were actually high partitions that you could look above from across the room. Upstairs were John Moffitt, poetry editor of *America* magazine and an expert on Hinduism, and Father Francois de Grunne from Belgium, who served as an auditor. There was only one key for the four of us to share, so we decided to designate a place where we would keep it so that all of us could come or go as we pleased and still keep the place locked.

I was in no mood for this conference. I still had not fully recovered from my cold, and I felt distant. I saw old friends and some of the people I had been corresponding with that I had been looking forward to meeting in person for the first time. Even the fellowship with my friends held less interest for me than ever before. There were some 65 abbots and prioresses from all over the world there, along with Buddhists and others who were interested in ecumenicism and the future of monasticism. I had thought I would be stimulated by exchanges with this group, including an update on Church politics, but I was tired of being around people, and I was bored with small talk. I just wasn't interested in anything that anyone had to say. My thoughts were still immersed on a plane that did not provide a path to this reality. I had had a transcendent experience at Polonnaruwa. Everything I saw now seemed irrelevant and uninteresting.

I moved into my assigned quarters. I reviewed the material for my presentation, scheduled for the second day of the meeting. I wished I could speak to the group about what I had learned in Asia, things that are eternally important. That would not be tolerated, and I knew it. The program was set. Then I thought I could add some extemporaneous remarks to it so long as it was within the context of the assigned subject.

On Sunday evening, December 8, there was a reception and sign-up sheets for the attendees to choose the breakout sessions they would prefer. The sheet for my group-discussion meeting contained many names beyond the prescribed limit of ten. I was then pretty sure that I was considered the most popular speaker in the group, based on the sign-up sheets, which was embarrassing. I went outside for some air and quiet. Using the excuse that it was too warm for me in the reception room. I noticed the sky was clear, and I could identify the star formations. Before I knew it, I was joined by some of the group who asked me what I was looking at. I was happy to talk about the stars and explain how one could identify north by their position. I much preferred to talk about the stars than monastic politics, since I knew I'd be wise to remain silent about my recent experiences.

Dom Rembert Weakland, Primate of the Benedictine Order, conducted the meeting. He was a progressive American himself and a recognized leader. Each morning consisted of two two-hour talks, followed by Mass and lunch. A break in the afternoons from 2:00 to 4:30 would be followed by group discussions. In the evenings there would be informal discussions and cultural events.

Sister Bernadette, a delegate from France, asked to borrow my camera because she had only brought film with her. I responded that I had a camera but no film, so offered to take pictures of the group for her. She persuaded me to pose for a picture after my talk, along with a small group of delegates.

The morning sessions provided for official translators, but the afternoon get-togethers were translated by volunteers, willing or unwilling. I was drafted the afternoon of December 9 to help translate, and it was even televised. There were Dutch and Italian TV crews there. That evening, there was a discussion of the issue of marriage in the priesthood. I had lent my name earlier as an advisor of the National Association for Pastoral Renewal, an organization that advocated approval of marriage for priests. I had never published anything on the subject, but had written a number of letters about my opinion. I took a basically liberal view that it should not matter, but said that personally I did not think it was appropriate for me to marry. There was a polite silence from my friends, and I was happy when the session ended.

That night some animals, probably wild cats, decided to visit the roof of our bungalow. None of us got much sleep from their cries. I thought the incident was funny, and my bungalow companions said the next morning that they had heard me laughing. It reminded me of the incident years earlier at Oakham, when the headmaster's cat used to keep me awake, and I got into trouble one time trying to silence him. I had even written a short story about the incident. The next morning, Tuesday, December 10, I went for a swim to revive me for my upcoming presentation, but soon I felt the loss of sleep along with the dread of the public attention to come.

I was the second speaker of the morning, following Father Jacques Amyot, a professor at the local Jesuit university. My presentation was late, starting at about 10:45. Both TV crews turned on their cameras for my talk. Seated behind the large Red Cross rostrum, I made the final decision not to restrict my presentation to my prepared paper. Since it was to be televised, I rationalized that I would be less nervous if I added some extemporaneous remarks. I kept my glasses on, though, so that I could refer to my prepared text to some extent.

I gave the sort of lecture I liked to do—a little bit edgy and provocative to keep the audience attentive to what I was saying and to stimulate their thought. I wanted to talk about what I had learned on this trip to Asia about monasticism and its current problems, while at the same time staying within the assigned subject, "Marxism and Monastic Perspectives."

I offered the concept I picked up in California from some French revolutionary student leaders who said they believed they were also monks. They were critical of the contemporary world and its social structures. I compared this to the Marxist philosophy of rejecting social structures and forcibly changing them. Then I repeated the idea I had heard from a Marxist professor I had met in Singapore, who said he thought that Marxism was not essentially antireligious and would disappear when man matures. I made the point that both Buddhist and Christian monasticism begin from within, in man's consciousness. Buddhists call it *avidya*, or ignorance, and Christians call it original sin.

I pointed out that the Christian monk seeks full realization, passing through a sort of convalescence to begin a process of education as a "new man." Communism, likewise, moves one from materialism to a redistribution of goods according to man's needs. I then made the provocative point that this is precisely what a monastic community seeks to do, and it is only in this kind of group that it can be successfully accomplished. I quoted Herbert Marcuse, who said that the U.S. and the Soviet Union are equally totalitarian in one way or another, although the U.S. version is benevolent and Russia's is tougher. The point is that significant choices are no longer possible today in society in either culture. The choices are only alternatives within the structure already in place, which have no real meaning. Then I referred to Erich Fromm's idea that modern society is alienated, and that is the very state that Christianity is against.

My next point was that today in the monastic life there are many men and women who live alienated lives because the structure of their group doesn't allow them to fulfill their potentialities. They have willingly surrendered some things they should not have surrendered, and this makes for an enormous problem in religious communities. I said we could join the Marxists in admitting that something should be done about it.

Then I told the group about some of my experiences in traveling around Asia. I explained the Dalai Lama's reaction to the Communist take-over of Tibet and of how some of the richer Tibetan monasteries had failed to meet the challenge of Communism by refusing to give land to their people who needed it for survival. I reported the Dalai Lama's interest in the reason why Christian monks take vows. My reaction was that St. Bernard's vow of conversion of manners actually required the monk to seek a total inner transformation, and it was in fact a commitment to becoming a completely new man.

I told the story of Chogyam Trungpa Rimpoche, the Tibetan lama I had met who escaped Tibet to save his life and ended up hiding in a peasant's house. When he sent a message to another abbot friend of his about what they should do in the face of the Communist take-over, the abbot sent back the message, "From now on, Brother, everybody stands on his own feet." I told the conference group they should remember this advice in their own future decisions. It may have sounded ominous, but I said it was the one thing I believed they should remember from my talk.

I told them that monks could no longer rely on being supported by artificial structures, but should maintain an inner strength in case something happened to the institutional protection they now enjoyed. I quoted the Zen question, "Where do you go from the top of a thirty-foot pole?" Cassian's concept of purity of heart is what we should be tending toward to support us. I spoke of the original purity of both Christian and Buddhist teachings as the place where we could mutually go beyond the division of our two philosophies.

I could feel the silence in the room. Nevertheless, I proceeded with my remarks.

The Buddhist begging bowl represents the ultimate theological root of the belief not only in begging as a right, but in openness to the idea that all gifts are an expression of the interdependence of all beings. I pointed out that compassion is central to Mahayana Buddhism. We are all immersed in illusion together, but we have to remember that the illusion is also a reality, and nirvana is present within it. I told them that I believe Christianity is very close to this view of reality. Behind both philosophies we can reach the freedom of the inner secret of the ground of our ordinary experience. It is attainable in the Buddhist tradition through the formation achieved with spiritual masters.

As Christians, we can accomplish renewal by being open to the ideas of Buddhism, Hinduism, and other great Asian traditions, to go deeper into the potentiality of our own traditions. The Asian groups have been working at it and have gone much deeper into it than Christians. Both can seek to arrive at a transcendent liberty that is beyond cultural differences and externals. I concluded by saying that this is the kind of monasticism that cannot be extinguished by any force because it represents a charism given to man by God Himself.

As a final remark, I said I would now disappear from view, suggesting we all have a Coke or something, and thanked them for listening. Disappearing was one of my favorite concepts, and I believe we can all do this mentally as well as physically, although I didn't explain to the group what I meant by my remark—better to leave it to them to discern.

The applause was measured, and I was unsure of my effect on the group. The cameras were turned off and the group adjourned for the lunch break. I felt distant and distracted, and it wasn't because of the television cameras. I thought that it might be because the question and answer period for all of the talks was scheduled separately for the evening session of the same day, so there was no interaction with them that might have clarified anything. I avoided engaging anyone in conversation, and hurried through the meal. At about 1:30 I went to my quarters to rest during the remainder of the break. I put off everyone who tried to engage me in conversation by saying that we would be covering it in the question and answer session later.

It was hot, and I was tired. I decided to take a shower before I laid down for a short nap. When I came out of the bath, I was not completely dry, so I tracked water across the bare terrazzo floor. The large standing fan was blowing too hard for me to sleep under it. Something in my head said "turn it off." Suddenly I felt the agonizing charge of electricity flash through my arm up to my heart. I screamed. The impact threw me down to the floor, and the fan fell on my chest, still running. I fell into unconsciousness.

My heart was stilled by 220 volts of alternating electrical current. I had become the ground.

"'Union with God!' So mysterious that in the end man would perhaps do anything to evade it, once he realizes it means the end of his own Ego-self-realization, once for all. Am I ready? Of course not. Yet the course of my life is set in this direction" (p. 322).

*Dancing in the Water of Life*

# Epilogue

It was an accidental death.

The direct cause was the defective electric fan. There may or may not have been other causes.

Some of the surviving information is contradictory. There may or may not have been an autopsy. There was an investigation, but it was cursory. The scene of the accident was altered before any authorities arrived.

There are spoken and unspoken theories, other than a simple accident:

He could have been struck by an intruder. There was a cut bleeding on the back of his head. The fan could have been set on him after his fall to resemble an accident. His hands were by his sides when he was found.

The fan could have been deliberately damaged while he was out, or a defective fan could have been substituted, in order to set up the accident. Merton had no problem with his fan for the first two days of his stay.

An attendant entered the room daily to provide maid service.

A member of the group could have been outraged by Merton's ideology and decided precipitously to silence him. Such a person could have resented the liberal views he expressed about Marxism, about the celibacy of priests, or about monastic life being more successful in carrying out Communist principles of common ownership than the Communists themselves.

In Thailand the police at that time had a reputation for being inefficient in solving crimes. Before 1977, the U.S. CIA was known to fund religious organizations abroad for its own purposes. Some missionaries worked for the CIA, either on a single assignment or as agents performing clandestine work. The possible connection of Merton with any Government activity is only speculative. Merton's visit to the Indonesian Embassy in Washington and his remark in his journal that he expected to have "a whole new experience" in Indonesia are puzzling. Merton had been interested in playing an active role in ending the Vietnam war. One theory is that he was assassinated by the CIA.

There is no evidence to support any of these theories, but they persist.

An even more important question is whether Merton died in the good graces of his God. Views on this subject run the gamut of opinion. Some believe him to be a saint, and others view him as a misguided seeker. Many see his moral struggles as typical of all men.

About an hour before he died, Merton walked back to the cottage with Father de Grunne, each going to his own room. Just before 3:00, Father de Grunne, whose room was upstairs, heard a cry and the sound of something falling below him. He went downstairs and knocked on Merton's door, but there was no response. Father Celestine Say, who occupied the room next to Merton's, said he heard nothing when he returned. The fourth occupant, John Moffitt, had gone out, so wasn't there.

Then Father Celestine began to notice an unpleasant odor, but couldn't identify it. Father de Grunne was pacing the floor upstairs, and Father Celestine was unable to fall asleep as a result. An hour after the sound of the cry, about 4:00, Father de Grunne went downstairs again to check on Merton and get the door key. After no response, he checked and found the door locked from the inside.

He looked through the long glass louver window in the door. He saw Merton lying in an odd position on the floor with the five-foot standing fan lying diagonally across the top of Merton's chest. Father Celestine then joined Father de Grunne. They called out to Merton without result.

Father de Grunne ran for help. He first saw Abbot Odo Haas of Waekwan, and Archabbot Egbert Donovan, who were returning to the cottage area from a swim. The four men tried to break through the glass panel of the door to open it. Then they realized that the panel was on hinges, and could be opened rather easily to reach inside to unbolt the door.

The fan was still running on top of his chest. Abbot Haas reached to remove the fan, but an electrical shock jerked him sideways. He was held by force to the fan until Father Celestine pulled the cord from the socket, which was under the head of the bed across the room. It was determined that Abbot Haas was not also electrocuted because he was wearing shoes.

They noticed that Merton's hands were at his sides, with a long, raw burn mark on his right side almost to the groin. His hands showed no burns. His face was discolored, a deep bluish-red, and contorted; Sister Bernadette Smeyers described it as "partly burnt." His mouth was half open. There were bluish-red spots on his lower arms and hands. His hands and feet were contorted, a sign that he had suffered before he died.

The priests gave Merton absolution. Abbot Haas went to get the Abbot Primate, Dom Weakland, who gave Merton the sacrament of Extreme Unction, the Church's sacrament for the dying.

Sister M. Edeltrud Weist, a Benedictine prioress from Taegu, South Korea, and a physician, examined the body and pronounced Merton dead by electric shock to the face. Father Celestine then took several photographs of his body.

Dr. Luksana Narkvachara, a Thai physician, was summoned and examined the body. He determined that the cause of death was heart failure induced by electric shock, probably causing Merton to faint and collide with the fan. He conjectured that Merton's head had hit the floor when he fainted which caused a cut on the back of his head. Then the Bangkok police arrived and conducted their investigation.

He was laid out on his bed in the small pavilion and the door was opened to allow the delegates to pay their last respects. A vigil began as the group spontaneously recited the psalms and the rosary.

The six Trappist delegates to the conference received permission to prepare the body for the funeral. Five of the six were Abbots of Asian and Australian monasteries, and one was a prioress from Japan. They washed and dressed the body in the Order's robe and scapular, placing the hood over Merton's head. They moved his body to the chapel at the conference center. Beginning at about 6:00 PM, they kept vigil beside the body, reciting the rosary and then the Psalter. They reported later that Merton's "face was set in a great and deep peace, and it was obvious that he had found Him Whom he had searched for so diligently." All of the delegates to the conference came to pay their respects and participate in reciting the psalms.

At 10:00 the following morning, there was a Requiem Mass concelebrated by all the priests at the conference, with Dom Weakland as principal celebrant and Archbishop Jadot, the apostolic delegate in Thailand at the time, in attendance. In monastic tradition, the vestments worn were all white, which signified that death was a happy occasion, in the belief that their brother had truly gone home to God.

U. S. Army officials then arrived and took Merton's body at about 1:30 PM to their hospital in Bangkok. A representative of the American Consulate came to claim Merton's possessions and arrange for the transfer of his body back to the U.S. The Primate, Dom Weakland, and Dom Joachim handled this procedure. The eight relics Merton had brought with him from Gethsemani were returned with his body. A list was prepared of the items being returned. It included his glasses, Timex watch, prayer book, broken rosary, and wood icon of the Virgin and Child. Griffin's camera was also sent back, but was not listed. There was no mention of his leather wallet, cash, airline tickets, passport, or books and papers.

Merton's three companions at the bungalow relocated to other quarters. The cottage was cleaned and the fan was disposed of, without further investigation. The flowers in front of the bungalow were dug up and removed, apparently in accordance with local custom.

The Primate attempted to notify the Abbot at Gethsemani of the occurrence, but apparently did not get through initially. The monastery first received word from a telegram sent by Mr. Hobart Luppi, Director of Special Consular Services, of the Bangkok office of the U.S. State Department. Sent that night after Merton's death but crossing the International Date Line, it arrived about fourteen hours after his death at 10:00 am on December 10 at the monastery. It was followed by a telephone call from the American Embassy in Bangkok.

After dinner at noon, Dom Flavian rang the bell to indicate he had an announcement to make. The monks seated in the refectory waited expectantly. Father Louis had died in Bangkok, an accidental death, and no other details were yet available, he added. He immediately followed his announcement with the closing prayers after the meal. The group filed out of the dining room and resumed their daily schedule of activities. Father Matthew Kelty later remarked that he knew then that it would never be the same at Gethsemani.

Almost a week later, Merton's body was flown by U.S. Air Force jet originating in Vietnam to Oakland, California. Some believe the U.S. Government performed an autopsy in Thailand before shipment. Others claim this did not occur because a body that had been autopsied must be buried in Thailand by local law. Also, it would have been impossible to obtain written approval from Dom Flavian in the limited time available after the death before deterioration set in. Merton's body was wrapped in an army blanket and placed in a gray military casket.

From Oakland, the body was transferred to a commercial plane to Louisville. Dom Flavian and several other monks accompanying him, along with a local undertaker, met the plane. The casket was opened at a funeral home in New Haven, KY, to perform the legal requirement for identification of the body. Some of the monks could not recognize Merton because of the swelling. Fortunately, Father John Eudes was present to make the positive identification, possibly from an examination of the teeth. Father John Eudes had been out of town and had returned immediately for the funeral when he got the news, and is said to have almost suffered a serious accident himself, driving in the winter weather. The casket was sealed and not opened again after this identification.

The monastery was in silent mourning along with shock at this unexpected event. Merton's body arrived at Gethsemani on the afternoon of December 17. The shiny gray coffin was brought into the monastery, a unique sight since coffins were not used. One of the monks commented that it reminded him of a beached whale. It was not possible to perform a Cistercian burial, with the body going directly into the ground in a white cloth, because of the condition of his body. Only Merton and his first Abbot, Dom Frederic, would lie in the monastery cemetery in a coffin, since both of their deaths had occurred away from the monastery.

Many of Merton's friends, primarily in the local area, attended the final rites, held immediately after the coffin arrived. Others paid their respects later when they could travel to Louisville.

The community chanted the funeral liturgy in the church. Father Chrysogonus composed special music for the Mass and burial service. At the funeral Dom Flavian said that Merton spoke to him about the possibility of his death before he left for the trip to Asia, first in a joking fashion, then seriously. Merton had confided that he was ready for death and thought it would be fitting to die among the Asian monks who were symbols for him of "man's ancient and perennial desire for the deep things of God." Father Dan Walsh summed up Merton's greatness: " ... a deep and abiding sense" of " ... the Christ who is in us when we love and serve one another in true brotherhood—when we realize that we are not our brother's keeper but our brother's brother." Father Walsh quoted Merton's remarks in their last conversation before Merton left for Asia: "Of course I will come back but only if God wills it, and if He doesn't, what better place and time to leave this world."

Rain, turning to a light snow, fell during the ceremony, which was held at dusk. It was reported that Dom Flavian asked Father Raymond to begin the ritual of placing the dirt on the top of the coffin in recognition of their close relationship. At the request of Father Chrysogonus, the burial service ended with the reading of Merton's final passage in *The*

*Seven Storey Mountain*. It was a prophecy of how his life would end, and it was stunning in its parallel to the reality of the event. He had now joined "the Christ of the burnt men." It was exactly 27 years since he had entered Gethsemani. He had left New York on December 10, 1941, within weeks of his 27th birthday when he arrived.

Later a white metal cross, identical to all of the other monks' markers, was placed on his grave, near a red cedar tree. His Cistercian name, Fr. Louis Merton, was inscribed on the cross, along with the date of his death.

The word spread quickly of Merton's unusual, tragic death. His death was reported on the front page of *The New York Times*. Dom James Fox telephoned Naomi Burton Stone. She said she cried when she was shopping and saw a package of Rice-a-Roni, because she had sent it to Merton when he was cooking his own meals. Margie learned of his death from a newspaper. Harold Jenkins heard the news on television. Jinny Burton saw it reported in a news magazine. Gladys Marcus phoned Robert Lax in the Greek islands to tell him. Ed Rice received a telephone call from a friend when he had just returned home after he had been in a car accident that almost killed him. He returned to his abandoned car and waited in the cold night air for the wrecker while he contemplated the news.

Dan Berrigan got the news at Cornell, where he had been released on bond awaiting a retrial. In 1970, he dedicated his book, *No Bars to Manhood*, jointly to Merton, calling him his brother, and to his father, who had died in 1969. He credited Merton with writing the notes on Camus that he had included in the book.

Merton was always intrigued with the possible meanings of his dreams. He had had a dream in August of 1961 that he was in a city overlooking a large bay, an arm of the harbor, after he had been lost. He then realized that he had far to go but would no longer be lost because the two arms of the harbor would help him to find his way. He included this incident in his *Conjectures of a Guilty Bystander*. The monastery returned the camera to John Griffin that he had loaned to Merton, which had been shipped back with his body. To his delight, Griffin found exposed film still in the camera. He developed it with a great deal of anticipation. He was amazed to find a picture taken from the Oriental Hotel in Bangkok that exactly pictured the scene of the harbor Merton had described from his dream. He knew that Merton must have taken this picture because it represented the dream that gave him the feeling that he might die soon and that he would accept God's will "and His mystery." Griffin also contacted the film store in Bangkok and obtained the film that Merton had left there to be developed.

Another dream occurred in 1958, according to one of Merton's fellow monks. Merton had dreamed that he was electrocuted and that a number of monks and nuns were standing over him as he lay on the floor, including the Primate of the Benedictines. This monk said he had a similar dream the same night. When he told Merton about it, they were both surprised at the synchronicity in their dreams.

Merton's death occurred on Dom James Fox's birthday. Two of the monks drove up to Dom James' hermitage to inform him of the accident. He reminisced that Merton's perseverance in the Order for 27 years was a miracle in itself. Although he had worked to help Merton in living his vocation, he did not credit himself with Merton's success as a monk or as a published author. He and Merton actually helped each other, he believed. Dom James also reflected on the Biblical passage that Merton had chosen for his ordination ceremony: "He walked with God, and was seen no more because God took him" (Genesis V, 24). Dom James moved into the Abbey's infirmary after he was attacked and robbed at his hermitage a few years later. When Dom James died on Good Friday in 1987, he was buried next to Merton.

When Father Raymond heard the news, he said, with tears in his eyes, that Merton was "a damn good monk."

Dan Walsh cried out, "It's like I've been split down the middle. Like someone took half of me away. He was part of me ... .I don't think I can ever be the same again."

Ed Rice told Jim Knight, shortly before Rice died in 2001, that he was "not comfortable with the plastic saint image of Merton ... He was Merton, and he has his influence as Merton," "a world figure," "an individual in the grand scheme ... , of the universal holy man with an appeal to everybody."

Karl Barth, the Swiss theologian, and Merton died on the same day. Barth has been considered the greatest theologian of the twentieth century, known for his outspoken resistance to Hitler's aggression and his prodigious literary output, including a 12-volume work, *Christian Dogmatics*. A common interest of Barth and Merton was their love of Mozart's music. Merton wrote: "Fear not, Karl Barth! Trust in the divine mercy. Your books and mine matter less than we might think. Though you have grown up to be a theologian, Christ remains a child within you. There is in us a Mozart who will be our salvation." Barth's obituary likewise appeared on the front page of *The New York Times* with Merton's. Later a joint ecumenical memorial service for Merton and Barth was held in St. Agnes Church in downtown Louisville. The music of Mozart was played, including Merton's favorite Sonata No. 8 in D Major, Andante movement.

Dorothy Day eulogized Merton in *The Catholic Worker*. She stated that there was no truth to the rumors that Merton had left his monastery or his Order when he traveled to Asia.

Merton had premonitions of a premature death that he mentioned in California and at Gethsemani, as well as in his writings. Whether this was based on fact, intuition, or a vivid imagination is unknown. In Merton's early monastic life, he said in his journal, Nov. 9, 1948, that he used to think it would be a good thing to die young and quickly, but then decided a long life with much labor and suffering would be preferable. "If God wills you to die suddenly, there is a greater grace for you than any other death, because it is the one He has chosen, by His love, with all the circumstances of our life and His glory in view."

The Dalai Lama visited Gethsemani on April 25, 1994, to pay his respects at Merton's grave. Accompanied by Abbot Timothy Kelly and Brother Patrick Hart, the Dalai Lama prayed in lotus position at the foot of the grave. He draped a white silk scarf on the cross bearing Merton's name at the gravesite.

Some wondered how Merton could be interested in going to the Far East to meet with Buddhists, since they did not believe in the tenets of the Church that Merton so loved. How could he be so fascinated by "unbelievers," yet not attempt to convert them. What could their belief systems possibly offer to one who had the richness of the Catholic faith. Merton did not speak about this subject in a way that others could understand. The ineffable is in fact just that.

Merton and his namesake, St. Louis, followed a similar life pattern. Father Louis died at age 53, St. Louis at 56. Father Louis died while traveling to find something intangible. St. Louis was killed while on a Crusade near Carthage in 1270, looking for Christ's tomb.

In 1961, Merton recorded in his journal that he expected an early death. Reading the life of Father Joseph Metzger, who was executed by the Nazis for his peace efforts, Merton said that he "may end up that way" and felt unworthy of such a death. At the end of 1961, he stated he didn't believe he had much time left. In October 1962, he told his journal that his body wanted to slow down but not die yet. He said it was time to give as a writer what he had to others "because the night will come and my work will come to an end." On Christmas Eve, 1962, he prophesied that he would die "probably within a few years, say five or ten—if not much sooner." In November 1967, he said, "I have no guarantee of living many more years. Perhaps five, perhaps ten."

Merton's trust provided for the disposition of his tangible assets, but his readers received some much more valuable intangibles. He gave his privacy, revealing his most personal thoughts and actions. He gave his humanness, in full detail, in some 10,000 letters collected, 70 working notebooks from his reading, 29 years of personal journals, 15 volumes of magazine articles, hundreds of essays, 600 audiotaped conferences to novices, hundreds of poems, and his books translated into 28 languages during his life. His will provided that this material be maintained by the Merton Center at Bellarmine College. And, in the collected books, photographs, and art, he gave his thoughts and ideas, his dreams, his hopes, and his love.

It is said that Merton died a Zen death. Jung said that Zen had therapeutic possibilities. Merton agreed that the student of Zen has to stand on his own two feet, not depending on external props. There is a universal Zen principle that different doctrines all come from the same source and reach for the same truth. The wine that all drink is the same wine, but tastes different for each.

Jesus' prayer "that all may be one as I in thee, and thee in Me" was Merton's charter. He could see it was possible for all humanity to form a unity in this world of "all in one": East and West, Christian and Buddhist, Hindu, Sufi, Jew, and Moslem. He addressed the commonness of religious traditions, the shared experiences, rather than the differences in rituals or practice. He would not refute the teachings of other traditions, but rather affirm the truth that he found in them while adding the fullness of Catholic beliefs. He believed it was his vocation to lead the world into his dream of one mystical body and make it the existential reality he envisioned.

John Wu wrote in *The Golden Age of Zen*, in 1966: "Humanity is one, and it is moving beyond East and West. It is only by moving beyond that the East and the West will be vitally synthesized." Once attained, this vital synthesis will spread to the whole world, he predicted.

Merton continues this mission of universal unification through his writings and his example. He has not really disappeared.

Like a shooting star
He crosses the heavens of our lives.
Too soon he passes
But the searing power of the light shines on.

# Bibliography

Abbott, Walter M., S.J., General Editor. *The Documents of Vatican II*. New York: The America Press, 1966.

Anderholm, Judith. "Thomas Merton and Aldous Huxley, The Springboard of *Ends and Means*." *The Merton Seasonal* 16:2 (Spring 1991): 8-10.

Andrews, Edward Deming, and Faith Andrews. *Religion in Wood: A Book of Shaker Furniture*. Bloomington and London: Indiana University Press, 1966.

Aprile, Dianne. *The Abbey of Gethsemani: Place of Peace and Paradox*. Louisville: Trout Lily Press, 1998.

Bailey, Blake. *The 60s*. New York: Mallard Press, 1992.

Baker, Rob and Gray Henry, eds. *Merton & Sufism, The Untold Story*. Louisville: Fons Vitae, 1999.

Bamberger, John Eudes, O.C.S.O., "The Cistercian." *In Memory of Thomas Merton*. Continuum 7:2 (Summer 1969): 227-241.

————. "Merton's Vocation as Monastic and Writer," an interview conducted by Victor A. Kramer, ed. by Dewey Weiss Kramer, *The Merton Annual*, 4, (1991): 21-38. New York: AMS Press, Inc., 1992.

Barakat, Robert. *Cistercian Sign Language*. Cistercian Study Series No. 11. Kalamazoo: Cistercian Publications, Inc., 1975.

Barrett, William, ed. *Zen Buddhism: Selected Writings of D. T. Suzuki*. New York: Doubleday, 1996.

Belloc, Hilaire. *The Cruise of the "Nona."* London: Constable & Company Ltd., 1955.

Berrigan, Daniel, S. J. *The Dark Night of Resistance*. New York: Doubleday and Company, 1972.

————. *No Bars to Manhood*. Garden City, NY: Doubleday and Company, 1970.

Berrigan, Philip, S.S.J. *No More Strangers*. Introduction by Thomas Merton. New York: The Macmillan Company, 1965.

Bianco, Frank. *Voices of Silence, Lives of the Trappists Today*. New York: Doubleday, 1991.

Biddle, Arthur W. *When Prophecy Still Had a Voice, the Letters of Thomas Merton and Robert Lax*. Lexington: The University Press of Kentucky, 2001.

Birchfield, James D., ed. *A Thomas Merton Symposium*. Kentucky Review, VII: 2 (Summer 1987). Lexington: University of Kentucky Libraries, 1987.

Bochen, Christine M., ed. *The Courage for Truth: The Letters of Thomas Merton to Writers*. New York: Farrar, Straus & Giroux, 1993.

————, ed. *Learning to Love, The Journals of Thomas Merton*, Volume Six. San Francisco: HarperSanFrancisco, 1997.

Burden, Shirley C. *The Many Faces of Mary, Photographs and Reminiscenses.* New York: Aperture Foundation, Inc., 1989.

Cardenal, Ernesto. *Abide in Love.* Foreword by Thomas Merton. Maryknoll, NY: Orbis Books, 1995.

Casey, William VanEtten, S. J., and Nobile, Philip, eds. *The Berrigans.* New York: Avon Books, 1971.

Callard, D.A. "Father of the Man: An Investigation into the Roots of Thomas Merton." *The Merton Seasonal of Bellarmine College* 11:3 (Summer 1986): 5-8.

Chautard, Dom Jean-Baptiste, *The Soul of the Apostolate*, translated by A Monk of Our Lady of Gethsemani. Trappist, KY: The Abbey of Gethsemani, Inc., 1946.

Cistercian Order. *The Spirit of Simplicity*, translation and commentary by A Cistercian Monk of Our Lady of Gethsemani. Trappist, KY: The Abbey of Gethsemani, 1948.

Cook, Bruce, "Dorothy Day and the Catholic Worker." *U. S. Catholic*, XXXI:11 (March 1966): 6-13.

————. "The Real Dorothy Day," *U. S. Catholic*, XXXI:12 (April 1966): 25-31.

Cooper, David D., ed. *Thomas Merton and James Laughlin, Selected Letters.* New York and London: W.W. Norton and Company, 1997.

Cunningham, Lawrence S., ed. *A Search for Solitude.* Journals of Thomas Merton 3. San Francisco: HarperCollins Publishers, Inc., 1996.

Daggy, Robert E., ed. *Dancing in the Water of Life.* Journals of Thomas Merton 5. San Francisco: HarperCollins Publishers, Inc., 1997.

————. "Discoveries and Rediscoveries Twenty-five Years After Thomas Merton's Death." *The Merton Seasonal* 19:1 (Winter 1994): 2-3.

————. "'A Great Soul': Owen Merton, May 14, 1887 – January 18, 1931." *The Merton Seasonal of Bellarmine College* 11:3 (Summer 1988): 2-5.

————. "Merton and Initiation: Being 'Educated' and Educating." *The Merton Seasonal* 16: 1 (Winter 1991): 2-5.

————. "In Pursuit of Thomas Merton." *The Merton Seasonal of Bellarmine College* 13:3 (Summer 1988): 2-5.

———. "Question and Revelation: Thomas Merton's Recovery of the Ground of Birth." Transcript of a speech to the Thomas Merton Society of Great Britain and Ireland, Southampton, UK, May 1996.

———, ed. *The Road to Joy: Letters to New and Old Friends.* New York: Farrar, Straus & Giroux, 1989.

————, ed. *"Honorable Reader": Reflections on my Work*, Thomas Merton. New York: The Crossword Publishing Company, 1989.

————·"Sister Therese Lentfoehr, S.D.S.: Custodian of 'Grace's House' and
  Other Mertoniana." *The Merton Seasonal of Bellarmine College* 6:3 (Au-
  tumn 1981): 2-11.
————·"Thomas Merton: Connecting East and West More Than Twenty-
  five Years After His Death." *The Merton Seasonal* 19:2 (Spring 1994):
  2-3.
————·"Thomas Merton: The Desert Call." *The Merton Seasonal* 18:2
  (Spring 1993): 8-15.
————·"Thomas Merton and the Quiz Show Scandal: American Loss of
  Innocence." *The Merton Seasonal* 20:2 *(Spring 1995): 4-11.*
————, ed. *Thomas Merton in Alaska: The Alaskan Conferences, Journals
  and Letters.* New York: New Directions, 1989.
Dalai Lama, His Holiness. *A Policy of Kindness.* Sidney Piburn, ed. Ithaca,
  NY: Snow Lion Publications, 1990.
————· *Spiritual Advice for Buddhists and Christians.* Donald W. Mitchell,
  ed. New York: Continuum Publishing Company, 1998.
David-Neel, Alexandra and Yongden, Lama. *The Secret Oral Teachings in Ti-
  betan Buddhist Sects.* San Francisco: City Lights Books, 1967.
Day, Dorothy. *The Long Loneliness.* An Autobiography. Introduction by
  Daniel Berrigan. San Francisco: Harper & Row, Publishers, 1981.
————·"Thomas Merton, Trappist, 1915-1968," *The Catholic Worker,*
  XXXIV:16 (December 1968) 1 and 6.
Delp, Father Alfred. *The Prison Meditations of Father Alfred Delp.* Introduc-
  tion by Thomas Merton. New York: Herder and Herder, 1963.
Del Prete, Thomas."Merton at Bonaventure: Some Student Recollections."
  *The Merton Seasonal* 20:3 (Summer 1995): 10-12.
Desmons, Gilles and Lefebure, Christophe. *Mysteres et Beaute des Abbayes
  Cisterciennes.* Toulouse, France: Editions Privat, 1996.
Distefano, Anthony."Dan Walsh's Influence on the Spirituality of Thomas
  Merton." *The Merton Seasonal of Bellarmine College* 5:2 (Late Summer
  1980): 4-13.
Downey, Michael. *Trappist, Living in the Land of Desire.* Mahwah, NJ: Pau-
  list Press, 1997.
Dylan, Bob. *Tarantula.* New York: The Macmillan Company, 1971.
Engelberg, Joseph."Two Monks." *The Merton Seasonal of Bellarmine College*
  14:2 (Spring 1989): 10-13.
Faggen, Robert, ed. *Striving Towards Being, The Letters of Thomas Merton
  and Czeslaw Milosz.* New York: Farrar, Straus & Giroux, 1997.
Feiss, Hugh, O.S.B. *Essential Monastic Wisdom.* San Francisco: HarperCol-
  lins, 1999.
Ferry, W.H., ed. *Letters from Tom.* Scarsdale: Fort Hill Press, 1983.
Finley, Mitch."Barry Ulanov:'I Remember Tom with Great Fondness.'" *The
  Merton Seasonal* 19:3 (Summer 1994): 5-6.

Ford, Michael. *Wounded Prophet: A Portrait of Henri J. M. Nouwen.* New York: Doubleday, 1999.

Forest, Jim. *Living With Wisdom.* Maryknoll, NY: Orbis Books, 1991.

————. "Various Identities, Review of *The Seven Mountains of Thomas Merton.*" *The Merton Seasonal of Bellarmine College* 10:1 (Winter 1985): 16-18.

France, Peter. *Hermits, The Insights of Solitude.* London: Pimlico, 1997.

Francois, Father, of Saint Mary, O.C.D. *The Simple Steps to God,* Introduction by Thomas Merton. Wilkes-Barre, PA, Dimension Books, 1943.

Fry, Timothy, O.S.B., ed. *The Rule of Saint Benedict.* New York: Random House, Inc., 1998.

Furlong, Monica. *Merton: A Biography.* San Francisco: Harper & Row, 1980 and revised, London: SPCK, 1995.

Gelernter, David. *1939, The Lost World of the Fair.* New York: Free Press, 1995.

Gitlin, Todd. *The Sixties: Years of Hope, Days of Rage.* New York: Bantam Doubleday Dell Publishing Group, Inc., 1989.

Griffin, John Howard. *Follow the Ecstasy.* Fort Worth, TX: Latitudes Press, 1983. Revised, ed. by Robert Bonazzi. Maryknoll, NY: Orbis Books, 1993.

Grip, Robert. "The Merton Files: Washington Watches the Monk." *The Merton Seasonal of Bellarmine College* 11:1 (Winter 1986): 5-7.

————. "Pop's Office: A Reminiscence, Interview with Helen Kelly Phares." *The Merton Seasonal* 16:1 (Winter 1991): 6-1.

Gutman, Roy, David Ruff, and Anna Cataldi, et al. *Crimes of War: What the Public Should Know.* New York: W. W. Norton & Company, 1999.

Halpert, Stephen and Murray, Tom. *Witness of the Berrigans.* Garden City, NY: Doubleday & Company, 1972.

Hanson, Eric O. *The Catholic Church in World Politics.* Princeton, NJ: Princeton University Press, 1987.

Harford, James. "Ed Rice: A Remembrance." *The Merton Seasonal* 26:4 (Winter 2001): 9-13.

Hart, Patrick, O.C.S.O. "The Center Dialogue, Review of *Thomas Merton, Preview of the Asian Journey.*" *The Merton Seasonal* 15:3 (Summer 1990): 23-24.

————. "The Dalai Lama Descends on Gethsemani: In Memory of Thomas Merton." *The Merton Seasonal* 19:2 (Spring 1994): 7-9.

————, ed. "My Visits to the Secular Bookhouse." *The Merton Seasonal* 22:2 (Summer 1997):3-4.

————, ed. *The Other Side of the Mountain.* Journals of Thomas Merton 7. San Francisco: Harper Collins Publishers, 1998.

————, ed. *Run to the Mountain.* Journals of Thomas Merton 1. San Francisco: HarperCollins Publishers, Inc., 1995.

————, ed. *The School of Charity, Letters of Thomas Merton*. New York: Farrar Straus Giroux, 1990.

————, ed. *Survival or Prophecy? The Letters of Thomas Merton and Jean Leclercq*. New York: Farrar Straus and Giroux, 2002.

————, ed. *Thomas Merton, Monk: A Monastic Tribute*. Garden City, NY: Doubleday & Company, 1976.

Hempstead, Sheila M. "Some of the Treasures of a Sunday Afternoon." *The Merton Seasonal* 19:1 (Winter 1994): 4-6.

Hempstead-Milton, Sheila M. "Merton's Search for Paradise and his Integration of Ruth Merton, Sophia and Mary." *The Merton Seasonal* 21:1 (Spring 1996): 9-14.

Hollenback, Jess Byron. *Mysticism, Experience, Response, and Empowerment*. University Park, PA: The Pennsylvania State University Press, 1996.

*International Herald Tribune*. "1949: The Cost of War." September 11-12, 1999.

Kaiser, Charles. *1968 in America*. New York: Weidenfeld & Nicolson, 1988.

Kelly, Marcia and Jack. "Conversation with Robert Lax." *The Merton Seasonal* 16:3 (Summer 1991): 4-9.

Kelty, Matthew, O.C.S.O. "Merton: Monitoring Self." *The Merton Seasonal of Bellarmine College* 10:3 (Summer 1985): 12-13.

————. "Touched by Fire," an unpublished homily, Louisville Cathedral, December 10, 1998.

Keys, Donald, ed. *God and the H-Bomb*. New York: Macfadden-Bartell Corporation, 1962.

Kilcourse, George. *Ace of Freedoms: Thomas Merton's Christ*. Notre Dame, IN: University of Notre Dame Press, 1993.

King, John E. "A Small Disagreement with Fr. Basil Pennington … What is Thomas Merton's First Book?" *The Merton Seasonal* 21:4 (Winter 1996): 7-11.

King, Thomas M. "Berrigan: Artist and Activist, Review of Ross Labrie, *The Writings of Daniel Berrigan*." *The Merton Seasonal of Bellarmine College* 15:2 (Spring 1990): 20-22.

Knight, Jim. "The Merton I Knew." *The Merton Seasonal* 27:3 (Fall 2002): 11-20.

Koch, Bill. "The Love Poems of Thomas Merton: On Being a Hermit in Love." *The Merton Seasonal* 17:1 (Winter 1992): 16-19.

Koch, Kurt, Th.D. *The Revival in Indonesia*. Grand Rapids: Kregel Publications, 1971

Kramer, Victor A. "Looking Back to Merton, Memories and Impressions, An Interview with Matthew Kelty, O.C.S.O." edited by Dewey Weiss Kramer, a tape recorded at the Abbey of Gethsemani, October 26, 1982.

————. *Thomas Merton*. Boston: Twayne Publishers, 1984.

————, ed.. *Turning Toward the World*. Journals of Thomas Merton 4. San Francisco: HarperCollins Publishers, Inc., 1996.

Lawler, Justus George. *In Memory of Thomas Merton.* Continuum 7:2 (Summer 1969): New York: Herder and Herder, 1969.

Lawlor, Patrick T., ed. *Thomas Merton, The Poet and the Contemplative Life.* New York: Columbia University Libraries, 1990.

Lentfoehr, M. Therese, S.D.S., "The Spiritual Writer," *In Memory of Thomas Merton.* Continuum 7:2 (Summer 1969): 242-254.

Leroux-Dhuys, Jean-Francois and Gaud, Henri. *Cistercian Abbeys, History and Architecture.* Koln, Germany: Konemann, 1998.

Luce, Clare Boothe, ed. *Saints for Now.* New York: Sheed & Ward, 1952.

Lundin, Roger and Noll, Mark A., eds. *Voices from the Heart.* Grand Rapids, MI: William B. Eerdmans Publishing Company, 1987.

Malet, Dom Andre, O.C.R., *An Artist Soul, Roger Durey,* trans. Mother Mary St. Thomas (of Tyburn) O.S.B. Trappist, KY: Abbey of Our Lady of Gethsemani, 1947.

Marie de la Croix, O.C.S.O., Mere. "The Last Days of Thomas Merton." *The Merton Seasonal* 28:4 (Winter 2003): 9-13.

Maritain, Jacques, "Action is an Epiphany of Being," A Maritain Catena Aurea compiled by Thomas Merton, *Jubilee* 15:7 (January 1968): 14-19.

———· *The Peasant of the Garonne.* Trans. by Michael Cuddihy and Elizabeth Hughes. New York: The Macmillan Company, 1969.

McEwen, John, trans. *Fenelon Letters,* Introduction by Thomas Merton. London: Harvill Press, 1964.

McHargue, Tim, MSC. "A Pilgrimage in Bangkok." *Merton Seasonal* 21:4 (Winter 1996): 3-6.

Meatyard, Ralph Eugene. *Father Louie, Photographs of Thomas Merton.* New York: Timken Publishers Inc., 1991.

Merton, John J. and Andrew Winser. "Two Letters about Thomas Merton." *The Merton Seasonal* 16:1 (Winter 1991): 11-12.

Merton, Thomas. *The Ascent to Truth.* New York: Harcourt, Brace & Company, 1951.

———· *The Asian Journal of Thomas Merton,* ed. Naomi Burton Stone, Brother Patrick Hart, and James Laughlin. Consulting editor: Amiya Chakravarty. New York: New Directions Publishing Corporation, 1973.

———· "The Black Sheep," Foreword by Paul Pearson, pp. 13-32. *The Merton Annual* 11, George A. Kilcourse, Jr., ed. Sheffield, England: Sheffield Academic Press Limited, 1998.

———· and Robert Lax. *A Catch of Anti-Letters.* Kansas City: Sheed Andrews and McMeel, Inc., 1978.

———· *The Collected Poems of Thomas Merton.* New York: New Directions Publishing Corporation, 1977.

———· *Conjectures of a Guilty Bystander.* Garden City, NY: Doubleday & Company, Inc., 1966.

———· "The Contemplative Life, Its Meaning and Necessity," *The Dublin Review* 446 (Winter 1949): 26-35.

———— *Elected Silence*. Dublin: Clonmore & Reynolds, 1949.

———— *Exile Ends in Glory*. Milwaukee: The Bruce Publishing Company, 1948.

———— *Faith and Violence*. Notre Dame, IN: University of Notre Dame Press, 1968.

———— "Five Limericks for Father Raymond Languishing in St. Joseph's Infirmary." *The Merton Seasonal* 23: 2 (Summer 1998):11-12.

———— ed. *Gandhi on Non-Violence*. New York: New Directions Publishing Corporation, 1965.

———— and Burden, Shirley. *God Is My Life. The Story of Our Lady of Gethsemani*. New York: Reynal & Company, 1960.

———— *Gethsemani: A Life of Praise*. Trappist, KY: Abbey of Our Lady of Gethsemani, 1966.

———— and Griffin, John Howard Griffin. *A Hidden Wholeness*. Boston: Houghton Mifflin Company, 1970.

———— *Ishi Means Man*. Greensboro, NC: Unicorn Press, Inc., 1976.

———— (pseud. Richard P. Frisbie), Letter to the Editor, "You May Be Right," concerning his article, "The Loyalty Oath of Henry VIII," previously published in June 1964. *U. S. Catholic*, XXX: 6 (October 1964): 58.

———— (pseud. Richard P. Frisbie), "Mother Was a Coat Hanger," *U. S. Catholic* XXXI:8 (December 1965) 63-66.

———— (pseud. Richard P. Frisbie), "My Life in the Middle Ages," *U. S. Catholic*, Vol. XXXI, No. 3, July 1965, pp. 31-33.

———— and John Jacob Niles. *The Niles-Merton Songs, Opus 171 and 172*. Champaign, IL: Mark Foster Music Company, 1981.

———— *New Seeds of Contemplation*. New York: New Dimensions Publishing Corporation, 1961.

———— *Original Child Bomb*. Santa Barbara, CA: Unicorn Press, (no date).

———— *The Seven Storey Mountain*. New York: Harcourt, Brace and Company, 1948.

———— *The Sign of Jonas*. New York: Harcourt, Brace Jovanovich, 1979.

———— *Silence in Heaven: A Book of Monastic Life*. New York: Studio Publications, Inc. and Thomas Y. Crowell, 1956.

———— *A Thomas Merton Reader*. Revised Edition. Thomas P. McDonnell, ed. Garden City, NY: Doubleday & Company, Inc., 1974.

———— (pseud. Richard P. Frisbie), "The Voice of the Turtleneck," *U. S. Catholic* XXX:11 (March 1965): 47-52.

———— *What Are These Wounds?* Milwaukee: The Bruce Publishing Company, 1950.

Miller, William D. *A Harsh and Dreadful Love. Dorothy Day and the Catholic Worker Movement*. New York: Liveright, 1973.

Mitchell, Donald W. and Wiseman, James. *The Gethsemani Encounter*. New York: Continuum Publishing Company, 1998.

Molnar, Thomas. *The Church, Pilgrim of Centuries*. Grand Rapids, MI: William B. Eerdmans Publishing Company, 1990.

Montaldo, Jonathan, "Damaged Goods: A Monk's Public 'Inner Work,'" *The Merton Seasonal* 28:1 (Spring 2003): 18-23.

———, ed. *Entering the Silence*. Journals of Thomas Merton 2. San Francisco: Harper Collins Publishers, Inc., 1996.

———, "'Going Home to Where I Have Never Been': Thomas Merton's Flight Toward Joy," *The Merton Seasonal* 28:3 (Fall 2003): 3-11.

Morris, Jan. *Manhattan '45*. New York: Oxford University Press, 1987.

Mott, Michael. *The Seven Mountains of Thomas Merton*. New York: Harcourt Brace & Company, 1993.

Nouwen, Henri J. M. *Pray to Live. Thomas Merton: Contemplative Critic*. Trans. by David Schlaver, C.S.C. Notre Dame, IN: Fides Publishers, Inc., 1972.

O'Connell, Patrick F., ed. *The Vision of Thomas Merton*. Notre Dame, IN: Ave Maria Press, Inc., 2003.

Omarr, Sydney. *Aquarius*. New York: Penguin Books USA Inc., 1997.

Panichas, George A., ed. *Mansions of the Spirit*, Introductory Essay by Thomas Merton. New York: Hawthorn Books, Inc., 1967.

Patnaik, Deba, ed. *A Merton Concelebration*. Notre Dame, IN: Ave Maria Press, 1981.

Pearson, Paul M. "'Life in the Damned Thing': The Letters of Thomas Merton to Reginald Marsh," *The Merton Seasonal* 29:3 (Fall 2004): 3-7.

———, ed, *Thomas Merton, Seeking Paradise: The Spirit of the Shakers*. Maryknoll, NY: Orbis Books, 2003.

Pennington, M. Basil, O.C.S.O., ed. *The Cistercian Spirit, A Symposium in Memory of Thomas Merton*. Cistercian Studies Series 3. Washington, DC: Cistercian Publications, 1973.

———, "Merton's Bell Rings Out in Thailand," *The Merton Seasonal* 15:3 (Summer 1990): 13-14.

——— *Thomas Merton, Brother Monk: The Quest for True Freedom*. San Francisco: Harper & Row, 1987.

———, ed. *Toward an Integrated Humanity: Thomas Merton's Journey*. Cistercian Studies Series 103. Kalamazoo, MI: Cistercian Publications, 1988.

——— *Thomas Merton, My Brother*. Hyde Park, NY: New City Press, 1996.

——— *Vatican II, We've Only Just Begun*. New York: Crossroad Publishing Company, 1994.

Quigley, Margaret and Garvey, Michael. *The Dorothy Day Book*. Springfield, IL: Templegate Publishers, 1982.

Raymond, M., O.C.S.O. *Burnt Out Incense*. New York: P. J. Kenedy & Sons, 1949.

————· *God Goes to Murderer's Row*. Milwaukee: The Bruce Publishing Company, 1951.

————· *The Man Who Got Even With God*. Milwaukee: The Bruce Publishing Company, 1941.

————· *The Silent Spire Speaks*. Milwaukee: The Bruce Publishing Company, 1966.

————· *Three Religious Rebels*. New York: P. J. Kenedy & Sons, 1944.

Remele, Kurt, "'Das ist Mein personliches Gefuhl,' A Conversation with Brother Patrick Hart," *The Merton Seasonal of Bellarmine College* 12:4 (Autumn 1987): 16-18.

Rice, Edward. *The Man in the Sycamore Tree*. Garden City, NY: Doubleday & Company, Inc.,1970.

————., "Trivia Game, Review of *The Seven Mountains of Thomas Merton*," *The Merton Seasonal of Bellarmine College* 10:1 (Winter 1985): 8-10.

Richardson, Jane Marie, S.L., "Sturdy Shelter, The Road to Joy: A Review Symposium," *The Merton Seasonal of Bellarmine College* 14:4 (Autumn 1989): 12-15.

Rosen, Sheila, "Hunting the Unicorn: Thomas Merton's New York," *The Merton Seasonal* 29:1 (Spring 2004): 3-6.

Ryan, Gregory J., "Death of a 'Mertoniac': An Appreciation of W. H. Ferry," *The Merton Seasonal* 20:4 (Autumn 1995): 17-23.

Rynne, Xavier. *Letters from Vatican City. Vatican Council II (First Session): Background and Debates*. New York: Farrar, Straus & Company, 1963.

Scovel, Carl, "Mozart, Merton, and Karl Barth," *The Merton Seasonal* 16:4 (Autumn 1991): 5-8.

Seitz, Ron. *Song for Nobody*. Liguori, MO, Triumph Books, 1993.

Shannon, William H., "The Farmer from Nelson County," *The Merton Seasonal of Bellarmine College* 14:3 (Summer 1989): 3-7.

————, ed. *The Hidden Ground of Love: The Letters of Thomas Merton on Religious Experience and Social Concerns*. New York: Farrar, Straus & Giroux, 1985.

————· *Silent Lamp, The Thomas Merton Story*. New York: Crossroad Publishing Company, 1993.

————· *Something of a Rebel, Thomas Merton, His Life and Works*. Cincinnati, OH: St. Anthony Messenger Press, 1997.

————· *Thomas Merton's Dark Path*. New York: Farrar Straus Giroux, 1981.

————, ed. *Witness to Freedom, The Letters of Thomas Merton in Times of Crisis*, New York: Farrar Straus Giroux, 1994.

Shepherd, Robert Marshall, "A Book Worth Knowing, A Review of Ron Seitz, *Song for Nobody*: A Memory Vision of Thomas Merton," *The Merton Seasonal* 18:3-4 (Summer-Autumn 1993): 30-32.

Skillin, Edward S. *The Commonweal Reader*. New York: Harper & Brothers Publishers, 1949.

Smeyers, Bernadette M., Sister,"Thomas Merton and Bangkok," *The Merton Seasonal* 18:3-4 (Summer-Autumn 1993): 16-17.

Spencer, Thomas T., "'Tom's Guardian Angels': Merton's Franciscan Mentors," *The Merton Seasonal* 26:2 (Summer 2001): 17-22.

Staggs, John. "Reinventing the Wheel: Thomas Merton and the Christ of the Cross." *The Merton Seasonal* 27:1 (Spring 2002): 17-19.

Stone, Naomi Burton and Hart, Brother Patrick. *Thomas Merton, Love and Living.* New York: Harcourt Brace Jovanovich, Publishers, 1985.

Storr, Anthony *Solitude, A Return to the Self.* New York: Ballantine Books, 1988.

Suzuki, Daisetz Teitaro. *The Essence of Buddhism.* London: The Buddhist Society, 1957.

Swanberg, W. A. *Luce and His Empire.* New York: Charles Scribner's Sons, 1972.

Talbot, Michael. *Mysticism and the New Physics.* London: Penguin Group, 1993.

Tardiff, Mary, OP, ed. *At Home in the World. The Letters of Thomas Merton & Rosemary Radford Ruether.* Maryknoll, NY: Orbis Books, 1995.

Thich Nhat Hanh. *Being Peace.* Berkeley, CA: Parallax Press, 1987.

_____. "The Buddhists," *Jubilee* 14:4 (August 1966): 7-13.

Thomas Merton Society of Great Britain and Ireland, transcript. "Remembering Merton: A Round Table Discussion Between a Few of Merton's Friends–Tommie O'Callaghan, Donald Allchin, Jim Forest and John Wu, Jr.," chaired by David Scott. 1996.

Thompson, E. P. and Smith, Dan, ed. *Protest and Survive.* New York: Monthly Review Press, 1981.

Thurman, Robert A. F. *Inside Tibetan Buddhism: Rituals and Symbols Revealed.* San Francisco: Collins Publishers San Francisco, 1995.

Thurston, Bonnie B., "The Tobin Tapes," *The Merton Seasonal* 16:3 (Summer 1991): 23-24.

Twomey, Gerald, ed. *Thomas Merton: Prophet in the Belly of a Paradox.* New York: Paulist Press, 1978.

Van Doren, Mark. *The Autobiography of Mark Van Doren.* New York: Harcourt Brace and Company, 1958.

Waldron, Robert, "A Novel Twist on Merton's Death," *The Merton Seasonal* 29:2 (Summer 2004): 42-43.

Weis, Monica, SSJ., "Rambling with the Early Merton," *The Merton Seasonal* 28:2 (Summer 2003): 3-6.

Wells, Joel, Editor, "The 15 Most Important Catholics in the U.S.A." cover, *The Critic* XXIV: 3, Dec. 1965-Jan. 1966.

Wilkes, Paul. *Beyond the Walls: Monastic Wisdom for Everyday Life.* New York: Random House, Inc., 1999.

_____, ed. *Merton: By Those Who Knew Him Best.* San Francisco: Harper & Row, Publishers, 1984.

Witcover, Jules. *The Year The Dream Died, Revisiting 1968 in America*. New York: Warner Books, Inc., 1997.

Wu, John C. H. *The Golden Age of Zen*, Revised edition. Taipei, Taiwan, Republic of China, United Publishing Center, 1975.

Yungblut, John R. *Discovering God Within*. Rockport, MA: Element, Inc., 1991.

VIDEO TAPES:

*Merton, A Film Biography*, Produced by Paul Wilkes/Audrey L. Glynn. New York: First Run Features, 1984.

*Life at Gethsemani, The Tradition Continues*. Trappist, KY: Gethsemani Abbey, 1995.

*A Taste of Gethsemani, Trappist Monks Remember Merton*. Louisville, KY: The Thomas Merton Center Foundation, 1997.

*Women Who Knew Merton*. Louisville, KY: The Thomas Merton Center Foundation, 1998.

*Jacques Maritain's Farewell to America: A Visit with Elizabeth Fourest*. Tyra Arraj. Chiloquin, OR: Inner Growth Videos, 1996.

AUDIO TAPES:

Day, Dorothy. *On Prayer*. Lecture at Marquette University, 1971, to the Ohio Catholic Education Association. Kansas City, MO: The National Catholic Reporter Publishing Company, Credence Cassettes, AA2249.

Merton, Thomas. *Loving Criticism*. Comments on Abelard. Kansas City, MO: The National Catholic Reporter Publishing Company, Credence Cassettes, AA2621.

Merton, Thomas. *Love is Enough*. Comments on John Paul Merton. Kansas City, MO: The National Catholic Reporter Publishing Company, Credence Cassettes, AA2907.

# Index

## Z